THE SACRED BOOKS OF THE EAST

F. MAX MULLER (ED.)

LIST OF THE 50 VOLUMES

1. Upanishads.
2. Sacred Laws of Aryas.
3. Texts of Confucianism.
4. Zend-Avesta.
5. Pahlavi Texts.
6. Qur'an.
7. Institutes of Vishnu.
8. Bhagavadgita, & c.
9. Qur'an.
10. (i) Dhammapada.
10. (ii) Sutta-Nipata.
11. Buddhist Suttas.
12. Satapatha-Brahmana.
13. Vinaya Texts.
14. Sacred Laws of Aryas.
15. Upanishads.
16. Texts of Confucianism.
17. Vinaya Texts.
18. Pahlavi Texts.
19. Fo-sho-hing-tsanking.
20. Vinaya Texts.
21. Saddharma Pundarika.
22. Gaina-Sutras.
23. Zend-Avesta.
24. Pahlavi Texts.
25. Laws of Manu.
26. Satapatha-Brahmana.
27. Texts of Confucianism (Li Ki).
28. Texts of Confucianism (Li Ki).
29. Grihya-Sutras.
30 Grihya-Sutras.
31. Zend-Avesta.
32. Vedic Hymns.
33. Minor Law-Books.
34. Vedanta-Sutras.
35. Milinda.
36. Milinda.
37. Pahlavi Texts.
38. Vedanta-Sutras.
39. Texts of Taoism
40. Texts of Taoism
41. Satapatha-Brahmana
42. Atharva-veda.
43. Satapatha-Brahmana.
44. Satapatha-Brahmana.
45. Gaina-Sutras.
46. Vedic Hymns.
47. Pahlavi Texts.
48. Vedanta-Sutras.
49. (i) Buddhakarita.
49. (ii) Mahayana Texts.
50. A General Index

The Sacred Books of the East, Vol. 8

THE BHAGAVADGITA
WITH
THE SANATSUGATIYA
AND
THE ANUGITA

Edited by

F. MAX MULLER

Translated by the Late

KASHINATH TRIMBAK TELANG, M.A.

GYAN

Published by

GYAN

Gyan Publishing House
5, Ansari Road
Daryaganj, New Delhi-110002
Phone: 011-47034999, 9811692060
E-mail: books@gyanbooks.com

Distribution Network
gyanbooks.com
India, USA, Canada, UK, Australia, France

ISBN : 978-81-212-2937-1 (Set)
ISBN : 978-81-212-2880-0 (PB)
First Published, 1882

2nd Impression 2021

Printed at: Gyan Press, Delhi.

The Sacred Books of the East, Vol. 8

The Bhagavadgita with the Sanatsugatiya and the Anugita
Edited by: F. Max Muller, Translated by the Late: Kashinath Trimbak Telang

THE

SACRED BOOKS OF THE EAST

TRANSLATED

BY VARIOUS ORIENTAL SCHOLARS

AND EDITED BY

F. MAX MÜLLER

VOL. VIII

SECOND EDITION

Oxford

AT THE CLARENDON PRESS

1898

THE BHAGAVADGÎTÂ

WITH

THE SANATSUGÂTÎYA

AND

THE ANUGÎTÂ

TRANSLATED BY THE LATE

KÂSHINÂTH TRIMBAK TELANG, M.A.

SECOND EDITION, REVISED

Oxford

AT THE CLARENDON PRESS

1898

CONTENTS.

BHAGAVADGÎTÂ.

INTRODUCTION

TO

BHAGAVADGÎTÂ.

It has become quite a literary commonplace, that—to borrow the words of Professor Max Müller in one of his recent lectures—history, in the ordinary sense of the word, is almost unknown in Indian literature [1]. And it is certainly a remarkable irony of fate, that we should be obliged to make this remark on the very threshold of an introduction to the Bhagavadgîtâ; for according to the eminent French philosopher, Cousin [2], this great deficiency in Sanskrit literature is due, in no inconsiderable measure, to the doctrines propounded in the Bhagavadgîtâ itself. But however that may be, this much is certain, that the student of the Bhagavadgîtâ must, for the present, go without that reliable historical information touching the author of the work, the time at which it was composed, and even the place it occupies in literature, which one naturally desires, when entering upon the study of any work. More especially in an attempt like the present, intended as it mainly is for students of the history of religion, I should have been better pleased, if I could, in this Introduction, have concentrated to a focus, as it were, only those well ascertained historical results, on which there is something like a consensus of opinion among persons qualified to judge. But there is no exaggeration in saying, that it is almost impossible to lay down even a single proposition respecting any important

---

[1] Hibbert Lectures, p. 131.

[2] Lectures on the History of Modern Philosophy (translated by O. W. Wight), vol. i, pp. 49, 50. At p. 433 seq. of the second volume, M. Cousin gives a general view of the doctrine of the Gîtâ. See also Mr. Maurice's and Ritter's Histories of Philosophy.

matter connected with the Bhagavadgîtâ, about which any such consensus can be said to exist. The conclusions arrived at in this Introduction must, therefore, be distinctly understood to embody individual opinions only, and must be taken accordingly for what they are worth.

The full name of the work is Bhagavadgîtâ. In common parlance, we often abbreviate the name into Gîtâ, and in Sanskrit literature the name occurs in both forms. In the works of *S*ankarâ*k*ârya, quotations from the Gîtâ are introduced, sometimes with the words 'In the Gîtâ,' or 'In the Bhagavadgîtâ,' and sometimes with words which may be rendered 'In the Gîtâs,' the plural form being used[1]. In the colophons to the MSS. of the work, the form current, apparently throughout India, is, 'In the Upanishads sung (Gîtâs) by the Deity.' *S*ankarâ*k*ârya, indeed, sometimes calls it the Î*s*vara Gîtâ[2], which, I believe, is the specific title of a different work altogether. The signification, however, of the two names is identical, namely, the song sung by the Deity, or, as Wilkins translates it, the Divine Lay.

This Divine Lay forms part of the Bhîshma Parvan of the Mahâbhârata—one of the two well-known national epics of India. The Gîtâ gives its name to a subdivision of the Bhîshma Parvan, which is called the Bhagavadgîtâ Parvan, and which includes, in addition to the eighteen chapters of which the Gîtâ consists, twelve other chapters. Upon this the question has naturally arisen, Is the Gîtâ a genuine portion of the Mahâbhârata, or is it a later addition? The question is one of considerable difficulty. But I cannot help saying, that the manner in which it has been generally dealt with is not altogether satisfactory to my mind. Before going any further into that question, however, it is desirable to state some of the facts on which the decision must be based. It appears, then, that the royal family of Hastinâpura was divided into two branches: the one called the Kauravas, and the other the Pâ*nd*avas. The

[1] Ex gr. *S*ârîraka Bhâshya, vol. ii, p. 840. It is also often cited as a Smr*i*ti, ibid. vol. i. p. 152.

[2] See inter alia *S*ârîraka Bhâshya, vol. i, p. 455, vol. ii, p. 687, and Colebrooke's Essays, vol. i, p. 355 (Madras); Lassen's edition of the Gîtâ, XXXV.

former wished to keep the latter out of the share of the kingdom claimed by them; and so, after many attempts at an amicable arrangement had proved fruitless, it was determined to decide the differences between the two parties by the arbitrament of arms. Each party accordingly collected its adherents, and the hostile armies met on the 'holy field of Kurukshetra,' mentioned in the opening lines of our poem. At this juncture, K*r*ish*n*a Dvaipâyana, alias Vyâsa, a relative of both parties and endowed with more than human powers, presents himself before Dh*r*itarâsh*t*ra, the father of the Kauravas, who is stated to be altogether blind. Vyâsa asks Dh*r*itarâsh*t*ra whether it is his wish to look with his own eyes on the course of the battle; and on Dh*r*itarâsh*t*ra's expressing his reluctance, Vyâsa deputes one Sañ*g*aya to relate to Dh*r*itarâsh*t*ra all the events of the battle, giving to Sañ*g*aya, by means of his own superhuman powers, all necessary aids for performing the duty. Then the battle begins, and after a ten days' struggle, the first great general of the Kauravas, namely Bhîshma, falls[1]. At this point Sañ*g*aya comes up to Dh*r*itarâsh*t*ra, and announces to him the sad result, which is of course a great blow to his party. Dh*r*itarâsh*t*ra then makes numerous enquiries of Sañ*g*aya regarding the course of the conflict, all of which Sañ*g*aya duly answers. And among his earliest answers is the account of the conversation between K*r*ish*n*a and Ar*g*una at the commencement of the battle, which constitutes the Bhagavadgîtâ. After relating to Dh*r*itarâsh*t*ra that 'wonderful and holy dialogue,' and after giving an account of what occurred in the intervals of the conversation, Sañ*g*aya proceeds to narrate the actual events of the battle.

With this rough outline of the framework of the story before us, we are now in a position to consider the opposing arguments on the point above noted. Mr. Talboys Wheeler writes on that point as follows[2]: 'But there remains one

[1] The whole story is given in brief by the late Professor Goldstücker in the Westminster Review, April 1868, p. 392 seq. See now his Literary Remains, II, 124 seq.

[2] History of India, vol. i, p. 293.

other anomalous characteristic of the history of the great war, as it is recorded in the Mahâbhârata, which cannot be passed over in silence; and that is the extraordinary abruptness and infelicity with which Brahmanical discourses, such as essays on law, on morals, sermons on divine things, and even instruction in the so-called sciences are recklessly grafted upon the main narrative. . . . K*ri*sh*n*a and Ar*g*una on the morning of the first day of the war, when both armies are drawn out in battle-array, and hostilities are about to begin, enter into a long and philosophical dialogue respecting the various forms of devotion which lead to the emancipation of the soul; and it cannot be denied that, however incongruous and irrelevant such a dialogue must appear on the eve of battle, the discourse of K*ri*sh*n*a, whilst acting as the charioteer of Ar*g*una, contains the essence of the most spiritual phases of Brahmanical teaching, and is expressed in language of such depth and sublimity, that it has become deservedly known as the Bhagavad-gîtâ or Divine Song. . . . Indeed no effort has been spared by the Brahmanical compilers to convert the history of the great war into a vehicle for Brahmanical teaching; and so skilfully are many of these interpolations interwoven with the story, that it is frequently impossible to narrate the one, without referring to the other, however irrelevant the matter may be to the main subject in hand.' It appears to me, I own, very difficult to accept that as a satisfactory argument, amounting, as it does, to no more than this—that 'interpolations,' which must needs be referred to in narrating the main story even to make it intelligible, are nevertheless to be regarded 'as evidently the product of a Brahmanical age[1],' and presumably also a later age, because, forsooth, they are irrelevant and incongruous according to the 'tastes and ideas[1]'—not of the time, be it remembered, when the 'main story' is supposed to have been written, but—of this enlightened nineteenth century. The support, too, which may be sup-

[1] History of India, vol. i, p. 288; and compare generally upon this point the remarks in Gladstone's Homer, especially vol. i, p. 70 seq.

posed to be derived by this argument from the allegation that there has been an attempt to Brahmanize, so to say, the history of the great war, appears to me to be extremely weak, so far as the Gîtâ is concerned. But that is a point which will have to be considered more at large in the sequel[1].

While, however, I am not prepared to admit the cogency of Mr. Wheeler's arguments, I am not, on the other hand, to be understood as holding that the Gîtâ must be accepted as a genuine part of the original Mahâbhârata. I own that my feeling on the subject is something akin to that of the great historian of Greece regarding the Homeric question, a feeling of painful diffidence regarding the soundness of any conclusion whatever. While it is impossible not to feel serious doubts about the critical condition of the Mahâbhârata generally; while, indeed, we may be almost certain that the work has been tampered with from time to time[2]; it is difficult to come to a satisfactory conclusion regarding any particular given section of it. And it must be remembered, also, that the alternatives for us to choose from in these cases are not only these two, that the section in question may be a genuine part of the work, or that it may be a later interpolation: but also this, as suggested recently, though not for the first time, by Mr. Freeman[3] with reference to the Homeric question, that the section may have been in existence at the date of the original epos, and may have been worked by the author of the epos into his own production. For that absence of dread, 'either of the law or sentiment of copyright,' which Mr. Freeman relies upon with regard to a primitive Greek poet, was by no means confined to the Greek people, but may be traced amongst us also. The commentator Madhusûdana Sarasvatî likens the Gîtâ to those dialogues which occur in sundry Vedic works, particularly the Upanishads[4]. Possibly—I will not use a stronger word—possibly the Gîtâ

[1] Infra, p. 21 seq.

[2] Compare the late Professor Goldstücker's remarks in the Westminster Review for April 1868, p. 389. [3] Contemporary Review February 1879.

[4] Madhusûdana mentions the dialogue between *Ganaka* and Yâgñavalkya as a specific parallel.

may have existed as such a dialogue before the Mahâbhârata, and may have been appropriated by the author of the Mahâbhârata to his own purposes [1]. But yet, upon the whole, having regard to the fact that those ideas of unity on which Mr. Wheeler and others set so much store are scarcely appropriate to our old literature; to the fact that the Gitâ fits pretty well into the setting given to it in the Bhishma Parvan; to the fact that the feeling of Arguna, which gives occasion to it, is not at all inconsistent, but is most consonant, with poetical justice; to the fact that there is not in the Gitâ, in my judgment, any trace of a sectarian or 'Brahmanizing' spirit [2], such as Mr. Wheeler and also the late Professor Goldstücker [3] hold to have animated the arrangers of the Mahâbhârata; having regard, I say, to all these facts, I am prepared to adhere, I will not say without diffidence, to the theory of the genuineness of the Bhagavadgitâ as a portion of the original Mahâbhârata.

The next point to consider is as to the authorship of the Gîtâ. The popular notion on this subject is pretty well known. The whole of the Mahâbhârata is, by our traditions, attributed to Vyâsa, whom we have already noticed as a relative of the Kauravas and Pâ*nd*avas; and therefore the Bhagavadgitâ, also, is naturally affiliated to the same author. The earliest written testimony to this authorship, that I can trace, is to be found in *S*aṅkarâ*k*ârya's commentary on the Gitâ [4] itself and on the B*ri*hadâra*n*yakopanishad [5]. To a certain extent, the mention of Vyâsa in the body of the Gitâ would, from a historic standpoint, seem to militate against this tradition. But I have not seen in any of the commentaries to which I have had access, any consideration of this point, as there is of the mention in some

---

[1] See to this effect M. Fauriel, quoted in Grote's Greece, II, 195 (Cabinet ed.).

[2] Compare also Weber's History of Indian Literature (English translation), p. 187. The instruction, however, as to 'the reverence due to the priesthood' from 'the military caste,' which is there spoken of, appears to me to be entirely absent from the Gîtâ; see p. 21 seq. infra.

[3] Westminster Review, April 1868, p. 388 seq.; and Remains, I, 104, 105.

[4] P. 6 (Calcutta ed., Samvat, 1927).

[5] P. 841 (Bibl. Indic. ed.); also *S*vetâsvatara, p. 278.

Smṛitis and Sûtras of the names of those to whom those Smṛitis and Sûtras are respectively ascribed[1].

We must now leave these preliminary questions, unluckily in a state far from satisfactory, and proceed to that most important topic—the date when the Gitâ was composed, and the position it occupies in Sanskrit literature. We have here to consider the external evidence bearing on these points, which is tantalizingly meagre; and the internal evidence, which is, perhaps, somewhat more full. And taking first the internal evidence, the various items falling under that head may be marshalled into four groups. Firstly, we have to consider the general character of the Gitâ with reference to its mode of handling its subject. Secondly, there is the character of its style and language. Thirdly, we have to consider the nature of the versification of the Gitâ. And fourthly and lastly, we must take note of sundry points of detail, such as the attitude of the Gitâ towards the Vedas and towards caste, its allusions to other systems of speculation, and other matters of the like nature. On each of these groups, in the order here stated, we now proceed to make a few observations.

And first about the manner in which the Gitâ deals with its subject. It appears to me, that the work bears on the face of it very plain marks indicating that it belongs to an age prior to the system-making age of Sanskrit philosophy. In 1875, I wrote as follows upon this point: 'My view is, that in the Gitâ and the Upanishads, the philosophical part has not been consistently and fully worked out. We have there the results of free thought, exercised on different subjects of great moment, unfettered by the exigencies of any foregone conclusions, or of any fully developed theory. It is afterwards, it is at a later stage of philosophical progress, that system-making arises. In that stage some thinkers interpret whole works by the light of some particular doctrines or expressions. And the result is the development of a whole multitude of philosophical sects, following the lead of those thinkers, and all professing to

[1] See, as to this, Colebrooke's Essays, vol. i, p. 328 (Madras).

draw their doctrine from the Gîtâ or the Upanishads, yet each differing remarkably from the other[1].' Since this was written, Professor Max Müller's Hibbert Lectures have been published. And I am happy to find, that as regards the Upanishads, his view coincides exactly with that which I have expressed in the words now quoted. Professor Max Müller says: 'There is not what may be called a philosophical system in these Upanishads. They are in the true sense of the word guesses at truth, frequently contradicting each other, yet all tending in one direction[2].' Further corroboration for the same view is also forthcoming. Professor Fitz-Edward Hall, in a passage which I had not noticed before, says[3]: 'In the Upanishads, the Bhagavadgîtâ, and other ancient Hindu books, we encounter, in combination, the doctrines which, after having been subjected to modifications that rendered them as wholes irreconcileable, were distinguished, at an uncertain period, into what have for many ages been styled the Sâṅkhya and the Vedânta.' We have thus very weighty authority for adhering to the view already expressed on this important topic. But as Professor Weber appears to have expressed an opinion[4] intended perhaps to throw some doubt on the correctness of that view, it is desirable to go a little more into detail to fortify it by actual reference to the contents of the Gîtâ, the more especially as we can thus elucidate the true character of that work. Before doing so, however, it may be pointed out, that the proposition we have laid down is one, the test of which lies more in a comprehensive review of the whole of the Gîtâ, than in the investigation of small details on which there is necessarily much room for difference of opinion.

And first, let us compare that indisputably systematized work, the current Yoga-sûtras[5], with the Bhagavadgîtâ on

[1] See the Introductory Essay to my Bhagavadgîtâ, translated into English blank verse, p. lxvii. See also Goldstucker's Remains, I, 48, 77; II, 10.

[2] P. 317; cf. also p. 338.

[3] Preface to Sâṅkhya Sâra, p. 7 (Bibl. Indic. ed.)

[4] History of Indian Literature, p. 28.

[5] Are we to infer from the circumstance mentioned in Weber's History of

one or two topics, where they both travel over common ground. In the Gîtâ, chapter VI, stanzas 33, 34 (p. 71), we have Arguna putting what is, in substance, a question to Krishna, as to how the mind, which is admittedly 'fickle, boisterous, strong, and obstinate,' is to be brought under control—such control having been declared by Krishna to be necessary for attaining devotion (yoga)? Krishna answers by saying that the mind may be restrained by 'practice (abhyâsa) and indifference to worldly objects (vairâgya).' He then goes on to say, that devotion cannot be attained without self-restraint, but that one who has self-restraint, and works to achieve devotion, may succeed in acquiring it. Here the subject drops. There is no further explanation of 'practice' or 'indifference to worldly objects,' no exposition of the mode in which they work, and so forth. Contrast now the Yoga-sûtras. The topic is there discussed at the very outset of the work. As usual the author begins with 'Now therefore the Yoga is to be taught.' He then explains Yoga by the well-known definition 'Yoga is the restraint of the movements of the mind.' And then after pointing out what the movements of the mind are, he proceeds: 'Their restraint is by means of practice and indifference to worldly objects[1],'—the very terms, be it remarked in passing, which are used in the Bhagavadgîtâ. But having come thus far, the author of the Sûtras does not drop the subject as the author of the Gîtâ does. He goes on in this wise: 'Practice is the effort for keeping it steady.' 'And that becomes firmly grounded when resorted to for a long time, without interruption, and with correct conduct.' So far we have a discussion of the first requisite specified, namely, practice. Patañgali then goes on to his second requisite for mental restraint. 'Indifference to worldly objects is the consciousness of having subdued desires &c. (Vasîkâra sañgñâ) which belongs to one having no longing for objects visible and those which

Indian Literature (p. 223, note 235), that the author of these Sûtras was older than Buddha?

[1] Sûtra 12, Abhyâsa-vairâgyâbhyâm tannirodhah.

are heard of' (from *S*âstras &c., such as heaven and so forth). He next proceeds to distinguish another and higher species of 'indifference,' and then he goes on to point out the results of that self-restraint which is to be acquired in the mode he has expounded. That is one instance. Now take another. In chapter VI, stanza 10 and following stanzas, the Gitâ sets forth elaborately the mode of practically achieving the mental abstraction called Yoga. It need not be reproduced here. The reader can readily find out how sundry directions are there given for the purpose specified, but without any attempt at systematizing. Contrast the Yoga-sûtras. In the Sâdhanapâda, the section treating of the acquisition of Yoga, Patañ*g*ali states in the twenty-ninth aphorism the well-known eight elements of Yoga. Then he subdivides these elements, and expatiates on each of them distinctly, defining them, indicating the mode of acquiring them, and hinting at the results which flow from them. 'That inordinate love of subdivision,' which Dr. F. E. Hall [1] has somewhere attributed to the Hindus, appears plainly in these aphorisms, while there is not a trace of it in the corresponding passage in the Bhagavadgitâ. In my opinion, therefore, these comparisons strongly corroborate the proposition we have laid down regarding the unsystematic, or rather non-systematic, character of the work. In the one we have definition, classification, division, and subdivision. In the other we have a set of practical directions, without any attempt to arrange them in any very scientific order. In the one you have a set of technical terms with specific significations. In the other no such precision is yet manifest. In one word, you have in the Gitâ the germs, and noteworthy germs too, of a system [2], and you have most of the raw material of a system, but you have no system ready-made.

Let us look at the matter now from a slightly different point of view. There are sundry words used in the Bhaga-

[1] In the Preface to his Sâṅkhya Sâra, I think.

[2] This is all that we can infer from the few cases of division and classification which we do meet with in the Gitâ. A subject like that treated of in this work could not well be discussed without some classifications &c.

vadgitâ, the significations of which are not quite identical throughout the work. Take, for instance, the word 'yoga,' which we have rendered 'devotion.' At Gîtâ, chapter II, stanza 48 (p. 49), a definition is given of that word. In chapter VI, the signification it bears is entirely different. And again in chapter IX, stanza 5, there is still another sense in which the word is used[1]. The word 'Brahman' too occurs in widely varying significations. And one of its meanings, indeed, is quite singular, namely, 'Nature' (see chapter XIV, stanza 3). Similar observations, to a greater or less extent, apply to the words Buddhi, Âtman, and Svabhâva[2]. Now these are words which stand for ideas not unimportant in the philosophy of the Bhagavadgîtâ. And the absence of scientific precision about their use appears to me to be some indication of that non-systematic character of which we have already spoken.

There is one other line of argument, which leads, I think, to the same conclusion. There are several passages in the Gîtâ which it is not very easy to reconcile with one another; and no attempt is made to harmonise them. Thus, for example, in stanza 16 of chapter VII, K*ri*sh*n*a divides his devotees into four classes, one of which consists of 'men of knowledge,' whom, K*ri*sh*n*a says, he considers 'as his own self.' It would probably be difficult to imagine any expression which could indicate higher esteem. Yet in stanza 46 of chapter VI, we have it laid down, that the devotee is superior not only to the mere performer of penances, but even to the men of knowledge. The commentators betray their gnostic bias by interpreting 'men of knowledge' in this latter passage to mean those who have acquired erudition in the *S*âstras and their significations. This is not an interpretation to be necessarily rejected. But there is in it a certain twisting of words, which, under the circumstances here, I am not inclined to accept. And on the other hand, it must not be forgotten, that the implication fairly derivable

[1] In chapter X the word occurs in two different senses in the same stanza (st. 7).

[2] Compare the various passages, references to which are collected in the Sanskrit Index at the end of this volume.

from chapter IV, stanza 38 (pp. 62, 63), would seem to be rather that knowledge is superior to devotion—is the higher stage to be reached by means of devotion as the stepping-stone. In another passage again at Gîtâ, chapter XII, stanza 12, concentration is preferred to knowledge, which also seems to me to be irreconcileable with chapter VII, stanza 16. Take still another instance. At Gîtâ, chapter V, stanza 15, it is said, that 'the Lord receives the sin or merit of none.' Yet at chapter V, stanza 29, and again at chapter IX, stanza 24, K*ri*sh*n*a calls himself 'the Lord and enjoyer' of all sacrifices and penances. How, it may well be asked, can the Supreme Being 'enjoy' that which he does not even 'receive?' Once more, at chapter X, stanza 29, K*ri*sh*n*a declares that 'none is hateful to me, none dear.' And yet the remarkable verses at the close of chapter XII seem to stand in point-blank contradiction to that declaration. There through a most elaborate series of stanzas, the burden of K*ri*sh*n*a's eloquent sermon is 'such a one is dear to me.' And again in those fine verses, where K*ri*sh*n*a winds up his Divine Lay, he similarly tells Ar*g*una, that he, Ar*g*una, is 'dear' to K*ri*sh*n*a. And K*ri*sh*n*a also speaks of that devotee as 'dear' to him, who may publish the mystery of the Gîtâ among those who reverence the Supreme Being[1]. And yet again, how are we to reconcile the same passage about none being 'hateful or dear' to K*ri*sh*n*a, with his own words at chapter XVI, stanza 18 and following stanzas? The language used in describing the 'demoniac' people there mentioned is not remarkable for sweetness towards them, while K*ri*sh*n*a says positively, 'I hurl down such people into demoniac wombs, whereby they go down into misery and the vilest condition.' These persons are scarcely characterised with accuracy 'as neither hateful nor dear' to K*ri*sh*n*a. It seems to me, that all these are real inconsistencies in the Gîtâ, not such, perhaps, as might not be explained away, but such, I think, as indicate a mind making guesses at truth, as Professor Max

[1] And see, too, chapter VII, stanza 17, where the man of knowledge is declared to be 'dear' to K*ri*sh*n*a.

Muller puts it, rather than a mind elaborating a complete and organised system of philosophy. There is not even a trace of consciousness on the part of the author that these inconsistencies exist. And the contexts of the various passages indicate, in my judgment, that a half-truth is struck out here, and another half-truth there, with special reference to the special subject then under discussion; but no attempt is made to organise the various half-truths, which are apparently incompatible, into a symmetrical whole, where the apparent inconsistencies might possibly vanish altogether in the higher synthesis. And having regard to these various points, and to the further point, that the sequence of ideas throughout the verses of the Gîtâ is not always easily followed, we are, I think, safe in adhering to the opinion expressed above, that the Gîtâ is a non-systematic work, and in that respect belongs to the same class as the older Upanishads.

We next come to the consideration of the style and language of the Bhagavadgîtâ. And that, I think, furnishes a strong argument for the proposition, that it belongs to an age considerably prior to the epoch of the artificial department of Sanskrit literature—the epoch, namely, of the dramas and poems. In its general character, the style impresses me as quite archaic in its simplicity. Compounds, properly so called, are not numerous; such as there are, are not long ones, and very rarely, if ever, present any puzzle in analysing. The contrast there presented with what is called the classical literature, as represented by Bâna or Da*nd*in, or even Kâlidâsa, is not a little striking. In Kâlidâsa, doubtless, the love for compounds is pretty well subdued, though I think his works have a perceptibly larger proportion of them than the Gîtâ. But after Kâlidâsa the love for compounds goes through a remarkable development, till in later writings it may be said almost to have gone mad. Even in Bâna and Da*nd*in, Subandhu and Bhavabhûti, the plethora of compounds is often wearisome. And the same remark applies to many of the copperplate and other inscriptions which have been recently deciphered, and some of which date from the early centuries of the Christian era. Take again the exuberance of figures and tropes which is so marked in the classical style. There is little or nothing of that in the Gîtâ, where you have a plain and direct style of natural simplicity, and yet a style not by any means devoid of æsthetic merit like the style of the Sûtra literature. There is also an almost complete absence of involved syntactical constructions; no attempt to secure that jingle of like sounds, which seems to have proved a temptation too strong even for Kâlidâsa's muse entirely to resist. But on the contrary, we have those repetitions of words and phrases, which are characteristic, and not only in Sanskrit, of the style of an archaic period[1]. Adverting specially to the language as distinguished from the style of the Gîtâ, we find such words as Anta, Bhâshâ, Brahman, some of which are collected in the Sanskrit Index in this volume, which have gone out of use in the classical literature in the significations they respectively bear in the Gîtâ. The word 'ha,' which occurs once, is worthy of special note. It is the equivalent of 'gha,' which occurs in the Vedic Sa*m*hitâs. In the form 'ha' it occurs in the Brâhma*n*as. But it never occurs, I think, in what is properly called the classical literature. It is, indeed, found in the Purâ*n*as. But that is a class of works which occupies a very unique position. There is a good deal in the Purâ*n*as that, I think, must be admitted to be very ancient[2]; while undoubtedly also there is a great deal in them that is very modern. It is, therefore, impossible to treat the use of 'ha' in that class of works as negativing an inference of the antiquity of any book where the word occurs; while its use in Vedic works and its total absence from modern works indicate such

[1] Compare Muir, Sanskrit Texts, vol. i, p. 5. See, too, Goldstücker's Remains, I, 177.

[2] This opinion, which I had expressed as long ago as 1874 in the Introduction to my edition of Bhart*ri*hari's *S*atakas, is, I find, also held by Dr. Buhler; see his Introduction to Âpastamba in this series, p. xx seq., note. Purâ*n*as are mentioned in the Sutta Nipâta (p. 115), as to the date of which, see inter alia Swamy's Introduction, p. xvii.

antiquity pretty strongly. We may, therefore, embody the result of this part of the discussion in the proposition, that the Gîtâ is removed by a considerable linguistic and chronological distance from classical Sanskrit literature. And so far as it goes, this proposition agrees with the result of our investigation of the first branch of internal evidence.

The next branch of that evidence brings us to the character of the versification of the Gîtâ. Here, again, a survey of Sanskrit verse generally, and the verse of the Gîtâ in particular, leads us to a conclusion regarding the position of the Gîtâ in Sanskrit literature, which is in strict accord with the conclusions we have already drawn. In the verse of the Vedic Sa*m*hitâs, there is almost nothing like a rigidly fixed scheme of versification, no particular collocation of long and short syllables is absolutely necessary. If we attempt to chant them in the mode in which classical Sanskrit verse is chanted, we invariably come across lines where the chanting cannot be smooth. If we come next to the versification of the Upanishads, we observe some progress made towards such fixity of scheme as we have alluded to above. Though there are still numerous lines, which cannot be smoothly chanted, there are, on the other hand, a not altogether inconsiderable number which can be smoothly chanted. In the Bhagavadgîtâ a still further advance, though a slight one, may, I think, be marked. A visibly larger proportion of the stanzas in the Gîtâ conform to the metrical schemes as laid down by the writers on prosody, though there are still sundry verses which do not so conform, and cannot, accordingly, be chanted in the regular way. Lastly, we come to the Kâvyas and Nâ*t*akas—the classical literature. And here in practice we find everywhere a most inflexible rigidity of scheme, while the theory is laid down in a rule which says, that 'even mâsha may be changed to masha, but a break of metre should be avoided.' This survey of Sanskrit verse may, I think, be fairly treated as showing, that adhesion to the metrical schemes is one test of the chronological position of a work—the later the work, the more undeviating is such adhesion. I need not stay here to point out, how this view receives corroboration from the rules given on this subject in the standard work of Piṅgala on the *Kh*andas *S*âstra. I will only conclude this point by saying, that the argument from the versification of the Gitâ, so far as it goes, indicates its position as being prior to the classical literature, and nearly contemporaneous with the Upanishad literature.

We now proceed to investigate the last group of facts falling under the head of internal evidence, as mentioned above. And first as regards the attitude of the Gitâ towards the Vedas. If we examine all the passages in the Gitâ, in which reference is made to the Vedas, the aggregate result appears to be, that the author of the Gitâ does not throw the Vedas entirely overboard. He feels and expresses reverence for them, only that reverence is of a somewhat special character. He says in effect, that the precepts of the Vedas are suitable to a certain class of people, of a certain intellectual and spiritual status, so to say. So far their authority is unimpeached. But if the unwise sticklers for the authority of the Vedas claim anything more for them than this, then the author of the Gitâ holds them to be wrong. He contends, on the contrary, that acting upon the ordinances of the Vedas is an obstacle to the attainment of the summum bonum[1]. Compare this with the doctrine of the Upanishads. The coincidence appears to me to be most noteworthy. In one of his recent lectures, Professor Max Müller uses the following eloquent language regarding the Upanishads[2]: 'Lastly come the Upanishads; and what is their object? To show the utter uselessness, nay, the mischievousness of all ritual performances (compare our Gitâ, pp. 47, 48, 84[3]); to condemn every sacrificial act which has for its motive a desire or hope of reward (comp. Gitâ, p. 119[4]); to deny, if not the existence, at least the exceptional and exalted character

[1] Compare the passages collected under the word Vedas in our Index.

[2] Hibbert Lectures, p. 340 seq.

[3] II, 42-45; IX, 20, 21.

[4] XVII, 12.

of the Devas (comp. Gîtâ, pp. 76–84[1]); and to teach that there is no hope of salvation and deliverance except by the individual self recognising the true and universal self, and finding rest there, where alone rest can be found[2]' (comp. our Gîtâ Translation, pp. 78–83).

The passages to which I have given references in brackets will show, that Professor Max Müller's words might all be used with strict accuracy regarding the essential teaching of the Bhagavadgîtâ. We have here, therefore, another strong circumstance in favour of grouping the Gîtâ with the Upanishads. One more point is worthy of note. Wherever the Gîtâ refers to the Vedas in the somewhat disparaging manner I have noted, no distinction is taken between the portion which relates to the ritual and the portion which relates to that higher science, viz. the science of the soul, which Sanatkumâra speaks of in his famous dialogue with Nârada[3]. At Gîtâ, chapter II, stanza 45, Arguna is told that the Vedas relate only to the effects of the three qualities, which effects Arguna is instructed to overcome. At Gîtâ, chapter VI, stanza 44, Arguna is told that he who has acquired some little devotion, and then exerts himself for further progress, rises above the Divine word—the Vedas. And there are also one or two other passages of the like nature. They all treat the Vedas as concerned with ritual alone. They make no reference to any portion of the Vedas dealing with the higher knowledge. If the word Vedânta, at Gîtâ, chapter XV, stanza 15 (p. 113), signifies, as it seems to signify, this latter portion of the Vedas, then that is the only allusion to it. But, from all the passages in the Gîtâ which refer to the Vedas, I am inclined to draw the inference, that the Upanishads of the Vedas were composed at a time not far removed from the time of the composition of the Gîtâ, and that at that period the Upanishads had not yet risen to the position of

[1] VII, 21–23; IX, 23–24.
[2] VIII, 14–16; IX, 29–33.
[3] See Khândogya-upanishad, p. 473, or rather I ought to have referred to the Mundaka-upanishad, where the superiority and inferiority is more distinctly stated in words, pp. 266, 267.

high importance which they afterwards commanded. In the passage referred to at chapter XV, the word Vedântas probably signifies the Âra*n*yakas, which may be regarded as marking the beginning of the epoch, which the composition of the Upanishads brought to its close. And it is to the close of this epoch, that I would assign the birth of the Gîtâ, which is probably one of the youngest members of the group to which it belongs.

It appears to me, that this conclusion is corroborated by the fact that a few stanzas in the Gîtâ are identical with some stanzas in some of the Upanishads. With regard to the epic age of Greece, Mr. E. A. Freeman has said that, in carrying ourselves back to that age, 'we must cast aside all the notions with which we are familiar in our own age about property legal or moral in literary compositions. It is plain that there were phrases, epithets, whole lines, which were the common property of the whole epic school of poetry[1].' It appears to me that we must accept this proposition as equally applicable to the early days of Sanskrit literature, having regard to the common passages which we meet with in sundry of the Vedic works, and also sometimes, I believe, in the different Purâ*n*as. If this view is correct, then the fact that the Gîtâ contains some stanzas in the very words which we meet with in some of the Upanishads, indicates, to my mind, that the conclusion already drawn from other data about the position of the Gîtâ with regard to the Upanishads, is not by any means unwarranted, but one to which the facts before us rather seem to point.

And here we may proceed to draw attention to another fact connected with the relation of the Gîtâ to the Vedas. In stanza 17 of the ninth chapter of the Gîtâ, only *Rik*, Sâman, and Ya*g*us are mentioned. The Atharva-veda is not referred to at all. This omission does certainly seem a very noteworthy one. For it is in a passage where the Supreme Being is identifying himself with everything, and where, therefore, the fourth Veda might fairly be expected

[1] Contemporary Review, February 1879.

to be mentioned. I may add that in commenting on *S*añkarâ*k*ârya's remarks on this passage, Ânandagiri (and Madhusûdana Sarasvatî also) seems evidently to have been conscious of the possible force of this omission of the Atharva-veda. He accordingly says that by force of the word 'and' in the verse in question, the Atharvâṅgirasas, or Atharva-veda, must also be included. Are we at liberty to infer from this, that the Atharva-veda did not exist in the days when the Gîtâ was composed? The explanation ordinarily given for the omission of that Veda, where such omission occurs, namely, that it is not of any use in ordinary sacrificial matters, is one which can scarcely have any force in the present instance; though it is adequate, perhaps, to explain the words 'those who know the three branches of knowledge,' which occur only a few lines after the verse now under consideration. The commentators render no further help than has been already stated. Upon the whole, however, while I am not yet quite prepared to say, that the priority of the Gîtâ, even to the recognition of the Atharva-veda as a real Veda, may be fairly inferred from the passage in question, I think that the passage is noteworthy as pointing in that direction. But further data in explanation of the omission referred to must be awaited.

If the conclusions here indicated about the relative positions of the Gîtâ and certain Vedic works are correct, we can fairly take the second century B.C. as a terminus before which the Gîtâ must have been composed. For the Upanishads are mentioned in the Mahâbhâshya of Pata*ñg*ali, which we are probably safe in assigning to the middle of that century. The epoch of the older Upanishads, therefore, to which reference has been so frequently made here, may well be placed at some period prior to the beginning of the second century B.C. The Atharva-veda is likewise mentioned by Pata*ñg*ali[1], and as 'ninefold,' too, be it remembered; so that if we are entitled to draw the conclusion which has been mentioned above from chapter IX, stanza 17, we come to the same period for the date of the Gîtâ.

[1] See also Sutta Nipâta, p. 115.

Another point to note in this connexion is the reference to the Sâma-veda as the best of the Vedas (see p. 88). That is a fact which seems to be capable of yielding some chronological information. For the estimation in which that Veda has been held appears to have varied at different times. Thus, in the Aitareya-brâhma*n*a [1], the glory of the Sâman is declared to be higher than that of the *Rik*. In the *Kh*ândogya-upanishad [2] the Sâman is said to be the essence of the *Rik*, which *S*aṅkara interprets by saying that the Sâman is more weighty. In the Pra*s*na-upanishad [3], too, the implication of the passage V, 5 (in which the Sâman is stated as the guide to the Brahmaloka, while the Ya*g*us is said to guide to the lunar world, and the *Rik* to the human world) is to the same effect. And we may also mention as on the same side the N*ri*si*m*ha Tâpinî-upanishad and the Vedic passage cited in the commentary of *S*aṅkara on the closing sentence of the first kha*n*d*a of that Upanishad [4]. On the other side, we have the statement in Manu that the sound of the Sâma-veda is unholy; and the consequent direction that where the sound of it is heard, the *Rik* and Ya*g*us should not be recited [5]. We have also the passages from some of the Purâ*n*as noted by Dr. Muir in his excellent work, Original Sanskrit Texts, which point in the same direction [6]. And we have further the direction in the Âpastamba Dharma-sûtra, that the Sâman hymns should not be recited where the other Vedas are being recited [7], as well as the grouping of the sound of the Sâman with various classes of objectionable and unholy noises, such as those of dogs and asses. It is pretty evident that the view of Âpastamba is based on the same theory as that of Manu. Now in looking at the two classes of authorities thus marshalled, it is plain that the Gîtâ ranges itself with those which are unquestionably the more ancient.

[1] Haug's edition, p. 68.

[2] Bibl. Ind. ed., p. 12.

[3] Bibl. Ind. ed., p. 221 seq.

[4] Bibl. Ind. ed., p. 11.

[5] Chapter IV, stanzas 123, 124.

[6] Vol. iii (2nd ed.), p. 11 seq. Cf. Goldstücker's Remains, I, 4, 28, 266; II, 67.

[7] Âpastamba (Bühler's ed.), I, 3, 17, 18 (pp. 38, 39 in this series); see further on this point Mr. Burnell's Devatâdhyâya-brâhma*n*a, Introd., pp. viii, ix, and notes.

And among the less ancient works, prior to which we may place the Gîtâ on account of the facts now under consideration, are Manu and Âpastamba. Now Manu's date is not ascertained, though, I believe, he is now generally considered to belong to about the second or third century B.C.[1] But Dr. Bühler, in the Preface to his Âpastamba in the present series, has adduced good reasons for holding that Âpastamba is prior to the third century B.C.[2], and we therefore obtain that as a point of time prior to which the Gîtâ must have been composed.

The next important item of internal evidence which we have to note, is the view taken of caste in the Bhagavadgîtâ. Here, again, a comparison of the doctrine of the Gîtâ with the conception of caste in Manu and Âpastamba is interesting and instructive. The view of Manu has been already contrasted by me with the Gîtâ in another place[3]. I do not propose to dwell on that point here, as the date of Manu is far from being satisfactorily ascertained. I prefer now to take up Âpastamba only, whose date, as just now stated, is fairly well fixed by Dr. Bühler. The division of castes, then, is twice referred to in the Bhagavadgîtâ. In the first passage (p. 59) it is stated that the division rests on differences of qualities and duties; in the second (pp. 126, 127) the various duties are distinctly stated according to the differences of qualities. Now in the first place, noting as we pass along, that there is nothing in the Gîtâ to indicate whether caste was hereditary, according to its view, whereas Âpastamba distinctly states it to be such, let us compare the second passage of the Gîtâ with the Sûtras of Âpastamba bearing on the point. The view enunciated in the Gîtâ appears to me plainly to belong to an earlier age—to an age of considerably less advancement in social and religious development. In the Gîtâ, for instance, the duties of a Brâhma*n*a are said to be tranquillity, self-restraint, and

[1] Professor Tiele (History of Ancient Religions, p. 127) considers the 'main features' of Manu to be 'pre-Buddhistic.'

[2] P. xxxv.

[3] See the Introductory Essay to my Bhagavadgîtâ in English verse, published in 1875, p. cxxi.

so forth. In Âpastamba, they are the famous six duties, namely, study, imparting instruction, sacrificing, officiating at others' sacrifices, making gifts, and receiving gifts; and three others, namely, inheritance, occupancy, and gleaning ears of corn, which, it may be remarked en passant, are not stated in Manu. The former seem to my mind to point to the age when the qualities which in early times gave the Brâhma*n*as their pre-eminence in Hindu society were still a living reality[1]. It will be noted, too, that there is nothing in that list of duties which has any necessary or natural connexion with any privilege as belonging to the caste. The Law lays down these duties, in the true sense of the word. In Âpastamba, on the contrary, we see an advance towards the later view on both points. You have no reference to moral and religious qualities now. You have to do with ceremonies and acts. You have under the head 'duties' not mere obligations, but rights. For the duty of receiving gifts is a right, and so is the duty of teaching others and officiating at others' sacrifices; as we know not merely from the subsequent course of events, but also from a comparison of the duties of Brâhma*n*as on the one hand, and Kshatriyas, Vai*s*yas, and *S*ûdras on the other, as laid down by Manu and Âpastamba themselves. Âpastamba's rules, therefore, appear to belong to the time when the Brâhma*n*as had long been an established power, and were assuming to themselves those valuable privileges which they have always claimed in later times. The rules of the Gitâ, on the other hand, point to a time considerably prior to this—to a time when the Brâhma*n*as were by their moral and intellectual qualities laying the foundation of that pre-eminence in Hindu society which afterwards enabled them to lord it over all castes. These observations mutatis mutandis apply to the rules regarding the other castes also. Here again, while the Gitâ still insists on the inner qualities, which properly constitute the military profession, for instance, the rules of Âpastamba indicate the powerful

[1] The remarks in the text will show how little there is in the Gîtâ of that 'Brahmanizing' which has been shortly noticed on a previous page.

influence of the Brâhma*n*as [1]. For, as stated before, officiating at others' sacrifices, instructing others, and receiving presents, are here expressly prohibited to Kshatriyas as also to Vaisyas. The result of that is, that the Brâhma*n*as become indispensable to the Kshatriyas and Vaisyas, for upon both the duty of study, of offering sacrifices, and making gifts and presents is inculcated. In his outline of the History of Ancient Religions, Professor Tiele, speaking of the 'increasing influence of the Brâhmans,' writes as follows: 'Subject at first to the princes and nobles, and dependent on them, they began by insinuating themselves into their favour, and representing it as a religious duty to show protection and liberality towards them. Meanwhile they endeavoured to make themselves indispensable to them, gradually acquired the sole right to conduct public worship, and made themselves masters of instruction [2].' And after pointing out the high position thus achieved by the Brâhmans, and the low position of the *K*â*nd*âlas and others of the inferior castes, he adds: 'Such a position could not long be endured; and this serves to explain not only the rise of Buddhism, but also its rapid diffusion, and the radical revolution which it brought about [3].' To proceed, however, with our comparison of the Gîtâ and Âpastamba. The superiority distinctly claimed by the latter for the Brâhma*n*a is not quite clearly brought out in the Gîtâ. 'Holy Brâhma*n*as and devoted royal saints' are bracketed together at p. 86; while the Kshatriyas are declared to have been the channel of communication between the Deity and mankind as regards the great doctrine of devotion propounded by the Bhagavadgîtâ. That indicates a position for the Kshatriyas much more like what the Upanishads disclose [4], than even that which

---

[1] As to the Kshatriyas the contrast with Manu's rules is even stronger than with Âpastamba's. See our Introduction to the Gîtâ in English verse, p. cxiii.

[2] P. 120.

[3] Pp. 129, 130.

[4] See p. 58 infra; and compare with this Weber's remarks on one of the classes into which he divides the whole body of Upanishads, History of Indian Literature, p. 165. See also Muir, Sanskrit Texts, vol. i, p. 508; Max Muller, Upanishads, vol. i, p. lxxv.

Âpastamba assigns to them. The fact is further noteworthy, that in the Gîtâ each caste has its own entirely distinct set of duties. There is no overlapping, so to say. And that is a circumstance indicating a very early stage in the development of the institution[1]. Besides, as already indicated, the duties laid down by Âpastamba and Manu as common to Kshatriyas and Vaisyas are the very duties which make those castes dependent to a very great extent on the Brâhmanas. Lastly, it is not altogether unworthy of note, that in the elaborate specification of the best of every species which we find in chapter X, the Brâhmana is not mentioned as the best of the castes, there is nothing to indicate the notion contained in the well-known later verse, 'The Brâhmana is the head of the castes.' On the contrary, the ruler of men is specified as the highest among men[2], indicating, perhaps, a state of society such as that described at the beginning of the extract from Professor Tiele's work quoted above.

We come now to another point. What is the position of the Gîtâ in regard to the great reform of Sâkya Muni? The question is one of much interest, having regard particularly to the remarkable coincidences between Buddhistic doctrines and the doctrines of the Gîtâ to which we have drawn attention in the foot-notes to our translation. But the materials for deciding the question are unhappily not forthcoming. Professor Wilson, indeed, thought that there was an allusion to Buddhism in the Gîtâ[3]. But his idea was based on a confusion between the Buddhists and the Kârvâkas or materialists[4]. Failing that allusion, we have nothing very tangible but the unsatisfactory 'negative argument' based on mere non-mention of Buddhism in the Gîtâ. That argument is not quite satisfactory to my own mind, although, as I have elsewhere pointed out[5], some of

---

[1] Cf. Sutta Nipâta, p. 32; and also Mr. Davids' note on that passage in his Buddhism, p. 131.

[2] P. 89 infra.

[3] Essays on Sanskrit Literature, vol. iii, p. 150.

[4] See our remarks on this point in the Introductory Essay to our Gîtâ in verse, p. ii seq.

[5] Introduction to Gîtâ in English verse, p. v seq.

the ground occupied by the Gîtâ is common to it with Buddhism, and although various previous thinkers are alluded to directly or indirectly in the Gîtâ. There is, however, one view of the facts of this question, which appears to me to corroborate the conclusion deducible by means of the negative argument here referred to. The main points on which Buddha's protest against Brahmanism rests, seem to be the true authority of the Vedas and the true view of the differences of caste. On most points of doctrinal speculation, Buddhism is still but one aspect of the older Brahmanism[1]. The various coincidences to which we have drawn attention show that, if there is need to show it. Well now, on both these points, the Gîtâ, while it does not go the whole length which Buddha goes, itself embodies a protest against the views current about the time of its composition. The Gîtâ does not, like Buddhism, absolutely reject the Vedas, but it shelves them. The Gîtâ does not totally root out caste. It places caste on a less untenable basis. One of two hypotheses therefore presents itself as a rational theory of these facts. Either the Gîtâ and Buddhism were alike the outward manifestation of one and the same spiritual upheaval which shook to its centre the current religion, the Gîtâ being the earlier and less thorough-going form of it; or Buddhism having already begun to tell on Brahmanism, the Gîtâ was an attempt to bolster it up, so to say, at its least weak points, the weaker ones being altogether abandoned. I do not accept the latter alternative, because I cannot see any indication in the Gîtâ of an attempt to compromise with a powerful attack on the old Hindu system; while the fact that, though strictly orthodox, the author of the Gîtâ still undermines the authority, as unwisely venerated, of the Vedic revelation; and the further fact, that in doing this, he is doing what others also had done before him or about his time; go, in my opinion, a considerable way towards

[1] Cf. Max Müller's Hibbert Lectures, p. 137; Weber's Indian Literature, pp. 288, 289; and Mr. Rhys Davids' excellent little volume on Buddhism, p. 151; and see also p. 83 of Mr. Davids' book.

fortifying the results of the negative argument already set forth. To me Buddhism is perfectly intelligible as one outcome of that play of thought on high spiritual topics, which in its other, and as we may say, less thorough-going manifestations, we see in the Upanishads and the Gitá [1]. But assume that Buddhism was a protest against Brahmanism prior to its purification and elevation by the theosophy of the Upanishads, and those remarkable productions of ancient Indian thought become difficult to account for. Let us compare our small modern events with those grand old occurrences. Suppose our ancestors to have been attached to the ceremonial law of the Vedas, as we are now attached to a lifeless ritualism, the Upanishads and the Gitâ might be, in a way, comparable to movements like that of the late Raja Rammohun Roy. Standing, as far as possible, on the antique ways, they attempt, as Raja Rammohun attempted in these latter days, to bring into prominence and to elaborate the higher and nobler aspects of the old beliefs. Buddhism would be comparable to the further departure from old traditions which was led by Babu Keshub Chander Sen. The points of dissent in the olden times were pretty nearly the same as the points of dissent now. The ultimate motive power also was in both cases identical—a sense of dissatisfaction in its integrity with what had come down from old times encrusted with the corruptions of years. In this view the old system, the philosophy of the Upanishads and the Gitâ, and the philosophy of Buddha, constitute a regular intelligible progression. But suppose the turn events took was different, as is supposed by the alternative theory indicated above. Suppose Babu Keshub's movement was chronologically prior, and had begun to tell on orthodox society. Is it likely, that then one of the orthodox party

[1] Cf. Weber's History of Indian Literature, p. 285. In Mr. Davids' Buddhism, p. 94, we have a noteworthy extract from a standard Buddhistic work, touching the existence of the soul. Compare that with the corresponding doctrine in the Gitâ. It will be found that the two are at one in rejecting the identity of the soul with the senses &c. The Gitâ then goes on to admit a soul separate from these. Buddhism rejects that also, and sees nothing but the senses.

would take up the position which Rammohun Roy took? Would he still rely on old authorities, but with sundry qualifications, and yet earnestly assail the current forms of orthodoxy? I do not think so. I think the true view to be, as already stated, very different. The Upanishads, with the Gîtâ, and the precepts of Buddha appear to me to be the successive[1] embodiments of the spiritual thought of the age, as it became more and more dissatisfied with the system of mere ceremonial then dominant.

There are several other points of much interest in the Bhagavadgîtâ, such as the reference to the Sâṅkhya and Yoga; the place assigned to the Mârga*s*îrsha month; the allusion to the doctrines of materialism; the nearly entire coincidence between a stanza of the Gîtâ and one in the Manu Sm*ri*ti. But in the present state of our knowledge, I do not think that we can extract any historical results from any of them. Without dwelling on them any further[2], therefore, I will only state it as my opinion, that the Sâṅkhya and Yoga of the Gîtâ are not identical with the systems known to us under those names, and that the Manu Sm*ri*ti has probably borrowed from the Gîtâ the stanza common to the two works.

We now proceed to a discussion of some of the external evidence touching the age of the Bhagavadgîtâ. It is, of course, unnecessary to consider any evidence of a date later than the eighth century A. C., that being the date generally received, though not on very strong grounds, as the date of *S*aṅkarâ*k*ârya, the celebrated commentator of the Gîtâ[3]. For the period prior to that limit, the first testimony to consider is that of Bâ*n*abha*tt*a, the author of the Kâdambarî. The date of Bâ*n*a is now fairly well settled as the

---

[1] The word Brahma-nirvâ*n*a, which occurs so often at the close of chapter V and also at chapter II, 72, seems to me to indicate that nirvâ*n*a had not yet become technically pinned down, so to say, to the meaning which Buddhism subsequently gave to it, as the name of what it deemed the summum bonum. Nirvâ*n*a by itself occurs at VI, 15.

[2] See some further remarks on these points in my Introduction to the Gîtâ in verse.

[3] Professor Tiele (History of Ancient Religions, p. 140) says *S*aṅkara was born in 788 A. D.; on the authority, I presume, of the Âryavidyâsudhâkara, p. 226.

middle of the seventh century A. C. The doubt which the late Dr. Bhâu Dâjî had cast upon its correctness[1], by impugning the received date of king Harshavardhana, appears to me to have been satisfactorily disposed of by the paper of my friend Professor R. G. Bhâ*nd*ârkar on the *K*âlukya dates[2]. In the Kâdambarî, then, we have testimony to the existence of the Bhagavadgîtâ in the middle of the seventh century A. C. For in that work, which, as is well known, abounds with equivoques, we have a passage which compares the royal palace to the Mahâbhârata, both being 'Anantagîtâkar*n*anânanditanaram[3],' which, as applied to the royal palace, means 'in which the people were delighted by hearing innumerable songs;' and as applied to the Mahâbhârata means 'in which Ar*g*una was delighted at hearing the Anantagîtâ.' Anantagîtâ is evidently only another name here for Bhagavadgîtâ. The conclusion deducible from this fact is not merely that the Gîtâ existed, but that it existed as a recognised portion of the Bhârata, in the seventh century A.C. Now the Kâdambarî shows, in numerous passages, in what high esteem the Mahâbhârata was held in its days. The queen Vilâsavatî used to attend at those readings and expositions of the Mahâbhârata, which have continued down to our own times; and it was even then regarded as a sacred work of extremely high authority, in the same way as it is now. It follows, therefore, that the Gîtâ must have been several centuries old in the time of Bâ*n*abha*tt*a.

Prior in time to Bâ*n*a is the Indian Shakespeare, Kâlidâsa, as he is referred to in Bâ*n*abha*tt*a's Harsha*k*arita[4], and also in a copperplate inscription of the early part of the seventh century, as a poet who had then already acquired a high reputation[5]. Unfortunately, it is not yet possible to fix exactly the date at which Kâlidâsa flourished. Still,

[1] Journal of the Bombay Branch of the Royal Asiatic Society, vol. viii, p. 250; and see, too, Indian Antiquary, vol. vi, p. 61 (Dr. Buhler).

[2] Journal of the Bombay Branch of the Royal Asiatic Society, vol. xiv, p. 16 seq.

[3] P. 182 (Târânâtha's ed.)

[4] See F. E. Hall's Vâsavadattâ, p. 14 note.

[5] See Indian Antiquary, vol. v, p. 70.

I think, we have pretty satisfactory evidence to show that the middle of the fifth century A.C. is the very latest date to which he can be referred. In a small tract (written by me in 1873), discussing Professor Weber's theory about the Râmâya*n*a, I have pointed out [1] that the Pa*ñk*atantra quotes from Kâlidâsa a passage which there is good reason to believe formed part of the Pa*ñk*atantra when it was translated for king Nushirvan of Persia about the beginning of the sixth century A.C. [2] Allowing for the time required to raise Kâlidâsa to the position of being cited as an authority, and for the time required for the spread of the fame of an Indian work to Persia in those early days, I think, that the middle of the fifth century is a date to which Kâlidâsa cannot well have been subsequent. Now in the works of Kâlidâsa we have some very remarkable allusions to the Bhagavadgîtâ. It is not necessary to go through all these allusions. I will only mention the most remarkable, one from the Raghuva*m*sa, and one from the Kumârasambhava. In Raghu, canto X, stanza 67, the gods addressing Vish*n*u say: 'There is nothing for you to acquire which has not been acquired. The one motive in your birth and work is the good of the worlds.' The first sentence here reminds one at once of Gîtâ, chapter III, stanza 22, the coincidence with which in sense as well as expression is very striking. The second sentence contains the words 'birth and work,' the precise words employed at Gîtâ IV, 9; and the idea of 'good of the worlds' is identical with the idea expressed in Gîtâ III, 20–24, the words only in which it is clothed being different. Couple this passage with the one from Kumârasambhava, canto VI, 67, where the seven *Ri*shis say to the Himâlaya mountain, 'Well hast thou been called Vish*n*u in a firmly-fixed form.' The allusion there to the Gîtâ, chapter X, stanza 25 (p. 89), is, I venture to think,

[1] 'Was the Râmâya*n*a copied from Homer?' See pp. 36–59.

[2] Cf. Colebrooke's Essays, vol. ii, p. 166 seq. It may be remarked that this argument is not affected by the attempt to distinguish the Kâlidâsa of the Sakuntalâ from the Kâlidâsa of the Raghuva*m*sa. Because the work cited in the Pa*ñk*atantra is the Kumârasambhava, which indisputably belongs to the same author as the Raghuva*m*sa.

unmistakable. The word 'firmly-fixed' is identical in both passages; the idea is identical, and Mallinâtha refers to the passage in the Gîtâ as the authority which Kâlidâsa had in view. It follows, therefore, that the Gîtâ must be prior to Kâlidâsa's time. It may be added, that Kâlidâsa in his Raghu XV, 67, cites Manu as an authority for the proposition that a king must protect all castes and all orders or âsramas. Manu, therefore, must have lived considerably earlier than Kâlidâsa, and the Gîtâ, as we have already argued, must be considerably earlier, not only than Manu, but also than his predecessor Âpastamba. The Gîtâ may, therefore, be safely said to belong to a period several centuries prior to the fifth century A. C.

The next piece of external evidence is furnished by the Vedânta-sûtras of Bâdarâya*n*a. In several of those Sûtras, references are made to certain Sm*ri*tis as authorities for the propositions laid down. Take, for instance, I, 2, 6, or I, 3, 23, and many others. Now three of these Sûtras are very useful for our present purpose. The first we have to consider is Sûtra II, 3, 45. The commentators *S*aṅkarâ*k*ârya, Râmânu*g*a, Madhva, and Vallabha[1] are unanimous in understanding the passage in Gîtâ, chapter XV, stanza 7 (p. 112), to be the one there referred to by the words of the Sûtra, which are, 'And it is said in a Sm*ri*ti.' Now a glance at the context of the Sûtra will, I think, satisfy us that the commentators, who are unanimous though representing different and even conflicting schools of thought, are also quite right. Sûtra 43, in the elliptical language characteristic of that branch of our literature, says, 'A part, from the statement of difference, and the reverse also; some lay down that it is a fisherman or a cheat.' Sûtra 44 runs thus, 'And also from the words of the Mantra.' And then comes Sûtra 45 as set out above. It is plain, that the Sûtra No. 45 indicates an authority for something not specified, being regarded as part of some other thing also not

---

[1] I am indebted to Professor M. M. Kunte for a loan of Vallabhâ*k*ârya's commentary on the Sûtras noted in the text. I had not seen it in 1875, when I last discussed this question.

specified. Now the discussion in previous Sûtras has been about the soul; so we can have little difficulty in accepting the unanimous interpretation of the commentators, that the proposition here sought to be made out is that the individual soul is part of the Supreme Soul, which is the proposition laid down in the Gîtâ in the passage referred to. The next Sûtra to refer to is IV, 1, 10. I shall not set forth the other relevant Sûtras here as in the preceding case. I only state that the three commentators, *S*aṅkara, Râmânu*g*a, and Madhva, agree that the Gîtâ is here referred to, namely, chapter VI, stanza 11 seq. Vallabha, however, I am bound to add, does not agree with this, as he interprets the Sûtra in question and those which precede and follow as referring to an entirely different matter. If I may be permitted to say so, however, I consider his interpretation not so satisfactory as that of the three other and older commentators. Lastly, we come to Sûtra IV, 2-19. On this, again, all the four commentators are unanimous, and they say that Gîtâ, chapter VIII, stanza 24 seq. (p. 80), is the authority referred to. And I think there can be very little doubt that they are right. These various pieces of evidence render it, I think, historically certain, that the Gîtâ must be considerably prior to the Vedânta-sûtras; and that the word Brahma-sûtras, which occurs at Gîtâ, chapter XIII, stanza 4 (p. 102), is correctly interpreted by the commentators as not referring to the Vedânta-sûtras, which are also called Brahma-sûtras, but to a different subject altogether[1]. When were the Vedânta-sûtras composed? The question must at once be admitted to be a difficult one; but I think the following considerations will show that the date of those Sûtras must, at the latest, be considerably earlier than the period which we have already reached in this part of our investigation. We may take it as fairly well settled, that Bha*tt*a Kumârila, the celebrated commentator of the Pûrva Mîmâ*m*sâ school, flourished not later than the end of the seventh century

[1] Cf. Weber's Indian Literature, p. 242. See also Lassen's Preface to his edition of Schlegel's Gîtâ, XXXV. Râmânuga takes the other view.

A.C.[1] A considerable time prior to him must be placed the great commentator on the Mîmâ*m*sâ-sûtras, namely, *S*abarasvâmin. If we may judge from the style of his great commentary, he cannot have flourished much later than Pata*ñg*ali, who may now be taken as historically proved to have flourished about 140 B.C.[2] Now a considerable time must have intervened between *S*abarasvâmin and another commentator on the Pûrva Mîmâ*m*sâ, whom *S*abara quotes with the highly honorific title Bhagavân, the Venerable, namely, Upavarsha. Upavarsha appears from *S*aṅkara's statement to have commented on the Vedânta-sûtras[3]. We have thus a long catena of works from the seventh century A.C., indicating a pretty high antiquity for the Vedânta-sûtras, and therefore a higher one for the Bhagavadgitâ. The antiquity of the Vedânta-sûtras follows also from the circumstance, which we have on the testimony of Râmânu*g*a, repeated by Mâdhavâ*k*ârya, that a commentary on the Sûtras was written by Baudhâyanâ*k*ârya[4], which commentary Râmânu*g*a says he followed. Baudhâyana's date is not accurately settled. But he appears to be older than Âpastamba, whose date, as suggested by Dr. Bühler, has already been mentioned[5]. The Vedânta-sûtras, then, would appear to be at least as old as the fourth century B.C.; if the information we have from Râmânu*g*a may be trusted. A third argument may be mentioned, bearing on the date of the Vedânta-sûtras. In Sûtra 110 of the third Pâda of the fourth Adhyâya of Pâ*n*ini's Sûtras, a Pârâ*s*arya is mentioned as the author of a Bhikshu-sûtra. Who is this Pârâ*s*arya, and what the Bhikshu-sûtra? Unluckily Pata*ñg*ali gives us no information on this head, nor

[1] See Burnell's Sâmavidhâna-brâhma*n*a, Introduction, p. vi note.

[2] The authorities are collected in our edition of Bhart*ri*hari (Bombay Series of Sanskrit Classics). Introd. p. xi note. See also Buhler's Âpastamba in this series, Introd. p. xxviii.

[3] See Colebrooke's Essays, vol. i, p. 332. An Upavarsha is mentioned in the Kathâsaritsâgara as living in the time of king Nanda, and having Pâ*n*ini, Kâtyâyana, and Vyâ*d*i for his pupils.

[4] See the Râmânu*g*a Bhâshya; and the Râmânu*g*a Dar*s*ana in Sarvadar*s*ana-saṅgraha.

[5] Âpastamba, p. xvi.

does the Kâsikâ Vritti. But a note of Professor Târânâtha Tarkavâkaspati, of Calcutta, says that Pârâsarya is Vyâsa, and the Bhikshu-sûtra is the Vedânta-sûtra[1]. If this is correct, the Vedânta-sûtras go very far indeed into antiquity. For Pânini can certainly not be assigned to a later date than the fourth century B.C., while that learned scholar, Professor Goldstücker, on grounds of considerable strength, assigned him to a much earlier date[2]. The question thus comes to this, Is the remark of Professor Târânâtha, above set out, correct? I find then, from enquiries made of my venerable and erudite friend Yagñesvar Sâstrin, the author of the Âryavidyâsudhâkara, that the note of Târânâtha is based on the works of Bhattogî Dikshita, Nâgogî Bhatta, and Gñânendra Sarasvatî, who all give the same interpretation of the Sûtra in question. It is certainly unfortunate that we have no older authority on this point than Bhattogî. The interpretation is in itself not improbable. Vyâsa is certainly by the current tradition[3] called the author of the Vedânta-sûtras, and also the son of Parâsara. Nor is Bhikshu-sûtra a name too far removed in sense from Vedânta-sûtra, though doubtless the former name is not now in use, at all events as applied to the Sûtras attributed to Bâdarâyana, and though, it must also be stated, a Bhikshu-sûtra Bhâshya Vârtika is mentioned eo nomine by Professor Weber as actually in existence at the present day[4]. Taking all things together, therefore, we may provisionally understand the Bhikshu-sûtra mentioned by Pânini to be identical with the Vedânta-sûtras. But even apart from that identification, the other testimonies we have adduced prove, I think, the high antiquity of those Sûtras, and consequently of the Bhagavadgîtâ.

We have thus examined, at what, considering the importance and difficulty of the subject, will not, I trust, be regarded as unreasonable length, some of the principal pieces of internal and external evidence touching the age

[1] See Siddhânta Kaumudî, vol. i, p. 592.

[2] See his Pânini; and see also Bühler's Âpastamba in this series, Introd. p. xxxii note.

[3] The correctness of this tradition is very doubtful.

[4] Indische Studien I, 470.

of the Bhagavadgîtâ and its position in Sanskrit literature. Although, as stated at the very outset, the conclusions we have deduced in the course of that examination are not all such as at once to secure acceptance, I venture to think that we have now adequate grounds for saying, that the various and independent lines of investigation, which we have pursued, converge to this point, that the Gîtâ, on numerous and essential topics, ranges itself as a member of the Upanishad group, so to say, in Sanskrit literature. Its philosophy, its mode of treating its subject, its style, its language, its versification, its opinions on sundry subjects of the highest importance, all point to that one conclusion. We may also, I think, lay it down as more than probable, that the latest date at which the Gîtâ can have been composed, must be earlier than the third century B.C., though it is altogether impossible to say at present how much earlier. This proposition, too, is supported by the cumulative strength of several independent lines of testimony.

Before closing this Introduction, it is desirable to add a word concerning the text of the Bhagavadgîtâ. The religious care with which that text has been preserved is very worthy of note. Schlegel and Lassen[1] have both declared it as their opinion, that we have the text now almost exactly in the condition in which it was when it left the hands of the author. There are very few real various readings, and some of the very few that exist are noted by the commentators. Considering that the Mahâbhârata must have been tampered with on numerous occasions, this preservation of the Gîtâ is most interesting. It doubtless indicates that high veneration for it which is still felt, and has for long been felt, by the Hindus, and which is embodied in the expression used in the colophons of the MSS. describing the Gîtâ as the 'Upanishad sung by God[2].' In view of the facts and deductions set forth in

---

[1] See the latter's edition of the Gîtâ, Preface, p. xxvii.

[2] In the edition of the Gîtâ published in Bombay in *S*aka 1782, there is a stanza which says that the Upanishads are the cows, K*ri*sh*n*a the milkman, Arguna the calf, and the milk is the nectar-like Gîtâ, which indicates the tradi-

this essay, that expression existing as, I believe, it does, almost universally in Indian MSS. of the Gîtâ, is not altogether devoid of historical value.

Schlegel draws attention to one other circumstance regarding the text of the Gîtâ, which is also highly interesting, namely, that the number of the stanzas is exactly 700. Schlegel concludes that the author must have fixed on that number deliberately, in order to prevent, as far as he could, all subsequent interpolations[1]. This is certainly not unlikely; and if the aim of the author was such as Schlegel suggests, it has assuredly been thoroughly successful. In the chapter of the Mahâbhârata immediately succeeding the eighteenth chapter of the Gîtâ, the extent of the work in *s*lokas is distinctly stated. The verses in which this is stated do not exist in the Gau*d*a or Bengal recension, and are doubtless not genuine. But, nevertheless, they are interesting, and I shall reproduce them here. 'Ke*s*ava spoke 620 *s*lokas, Ar*g*una fifty-seven, Sa*ñg*aya sixty-seven, and Dh*ri*tarâsh*t*ra one *s*loka; such is the extent of the Gîtâ.' It is very difficult to account for these figures. According to them, the total number of verses in the Gîtâ would be 745, whereas the number in the current MSS., and even in the Mahâbhârata itself, is, as already stated, only 700[2]. I cannot suggest any explanation whatever of this discrepancy.

In conclusion, a few words may be added regarding the general principles followed in the translation contained in this volume. My aim has been to make that translation as close and literal a rendering as possible of the Gîtâ, as interpreted by the commentators *S*ankarâ*k*ârya, *S*rîdharasvâmin, and Madhusûdana Sarasvatî. Reference has also been frequently made to the commentary of Râmânu*g*â*k*ârya, and also to that of Nîlaka*nth*a, which latter forms part of the author's general commentary on the Mahâbhârata.

tional view of the Gîtâ—a view in consonance with that which we have been led to by the facts and arguments contained in this Introduction.

[1] P. xl (Lassen's ed.)

[2] *S*ankara's commentary states in so many words that the Gîtâ he used contained only 700 *s*lokas.

In some places these commentators differ among themselves, and then I have made my own choice. The foot-notes are mainly intended to make clear that which necessarily remains obscure in a literal translation. Some of the notes, however, also point out the parallelisms existing between the Gîtâ and other works, principally the Upanishads and the Buddhistic Dhammapada and Sutta Nipâta. Of the latter I have not been able to procure the original Pâli; I have only used Sir M. C. Swamy's translation. But I may here note, that there are some verses, especially in the Salla Sutta (see pp. 124–127 of Sir M. C. Swamy's book), the similarity of which, in doctrine and expression, to some of the verses of the Gitâ is particularly striking. The analogies between the Gîtâ and the Upanishads have been made the basis of certain conclusions in this Introduction. Those between the Gitâ and these Buddhistic works are at present, to my mind, only interesting; I am unable yet to say whether they may legitimately be made the premises for any historical deductions.

There are two indexes: the first a general index of matters, the second containing the principal words in the Gitâ which may prove useful or interesting for philological, historical, or other kindred purposes.

BHAGAVADGÎTÂ.

Chapter I.

Dhritarâshtra said:

What did my (people) and the Pândavas do, O Sañgaya! when they assembled together on the holy field of Kurukshetra, desirous to do battle?

Sañgaya said:

Seeing the army of the Pândavas drawn up in battle-array[1], the prince Duryodhana approached his preceptor, and spoke (these) words: 'O preceptor! observe this grand army of the sons of Pându, drawn up in battle-array by your talented pupil, the son of Drupada. In it are heroes (bearing) large bows, the equals of Bhîma and Arguna in battle—(namely), Yuyudhâna, Virâta, and Drupada, the master of a great car[2], and Dhrishtaketu, Kekitâna, and the valiant king of Kâsî, Purugit and Kuntibhoga, and that eminent man Saibya; the heroic Yudhâmanyu, the valiant Uttamaugas, the son of Subhadrâ, and the sons of

[1] Several of these modes of array are described in Manu VII, 187, like a staff, like a wain, like a boar, &c. That of the Pândavas, here referred to, appears to have been like the thunderbolt, as to which see Manu VII, 191.

[2] This is a literal rendering; the technical meaning is 'a warrior proficient in military science, who single-handed can fight a thousand archers.'

Draupadî—all masters of great cars. And now, O best of Brâhma*n*as! learn who are most distinguished among us, and are leaders of my army. I will name them to you, in order that you may know them well. Yourself, and Bhîshma, and Kar*n*a, and K*ri*pa the victor of (many) battles; A*s*vatthâman, and Vikar*n*a, and also the son of Somadatta, and many other brave men, who have given up their lives for me, who fight with various weapons, (and are) all dexterous in battle. Thus our army which is protected by Bhîshma is unlimited; while this army of theirs which is protected by Bhîma is very limited. And therefore do ye all, occupying respectively the positions[1] assigned to you, protect Bhîshma[2] only.'

Then his powerful grandsire, Bhîshma, the oldest of the Kauravas, roaring aloud like a lion, blew his conch, (thereby) affording delight to Duryodhana. And then all at once, conchs, and kettledrums, and tabors, and trumpets were played upon; and there was a tumultuous din. Then, too, Mâdhava and the son of Pâ*nd*u (Ar*g*una), seated in a grand chariot to which white steeds were yoked, blew their heavenly conchs. H*ri*shîke*s*a[3] blew the Pâ*ñk*a*g*anya[4], and Dhana*ñg*aya the Devadatta, and Bhîma, (the doer) of fearful deeds, blew the great conch Pau*nd*ra. King Yudhish*th*ira, the son of Kuntî[5], blew the Anan-

[1] The original word means, according to *S*rîdhara, 'the ways of entrance into a Vyûha or phalanx.'

[2] Who, as generalissimo, remained in the centre of the army.

[3] Literally, according to the commentators, 'lord of the senses of perception.'

[4] Schlegel renders the names of these conchs by Gigantea, Theodotes, Arundinea, Triumphatrix, Dulcisona, and Gemmiflorea respectively.

[5] So called, par excellence, apparently.

tavigaya, and Nakula and Sahadeva (respectively) the Sughosha and Manipushpaka. And the king of Kâsî, too, who has an excellent bow, and Sikhandin, the master of a great car, and Dhrishtadyumna, Virâta, and the unconquered Sâtyaki, and Drupada, and the sons of Draupadî, and the son of Subhadrâ, of mighty arms, blew conchs severally from all sides, O king of the earth! That tumultuous din rent the hearts of all (the people) of Dhritarâshtra's (party), causing reverberations throughout heaven and earth. Then seeing (the people of) Dhritarâshtra's party regularly marshalled, the son of Pându, whose standard is the ape, raised his bow[1], after the discharge of missiles had commenced, and O king of the earth! spake these words to Hrishîkesa: 'O undegraded one! station my chariot between the two armies, while I observe those, who stand here desirous to engage in battle, and with whom, in the labours of this struggle, I must do battle. I will observe those who are assembled here and who are about to engage in battle, wishing to do service in battle[2] to the evil-minded son of Dhritarâshtra.'

Sañgaya said:

Thus addressed by Gudâkesa[3], O descendant of Bharata[4]! Hrishîkesa stationed that excellent chariot between the two armies, in front of Bhîshma

[1] I.e. to join in the fight.

[2] In the original, several derivatives from the root yudh, meaning 'to fight,' occur with the same frequency as 'battle' here.

[3] Generally interpreted 'lord of sleep,' i.e. not indolent. Nîlakantha also suggests, that it may mean 'of thick hair.'

[4] The son of Dushyanta and Sakuntalâ, after whom India is called 'Bhâratavarsha,' and from whom both Pândavas and Kauravas were descended.

and Dro*n*a and of all the kings of the earth, and said: 'O son of P*ri*thâ! look at these assembled Kauravas.' There the son of P*ri*thâ saw in both armies, fathers and grandfathers, preceptors, maternal uncles, brothers, sons[1], grandsons, companions, fathers-in-law, as well as friends. And seeing all those kinsmen standing (there), the son of Kuntî was overcome by excessive pity, and spake thus despondingly.

Arguna said:

Seeing these kinsmen, O K*ri*sh*n*a! standing (here) anxious to engage in battle, my limbs droop down; my mouth is quite dried up; a tremor comes over my body; and my hairs stand on end; the Gâ*nd*îva (bow) slips from my hand; my skin burns intensely. I am unable, too, to stand up; my mind whirls round, as it were; O Kesava! I see adverse omens[2]; and I do not perceive any good (likely to accrue) after killing (my) kinsmen in the battle. I do not wish for victory, O K*ri*sh*n*a! nor sovereignty, nor pleasures: what is sovereignty to us, O Govinda! what enjoyments, and even life? Even those, for whose sake we desire sovereignty, enjoyments, and pleasures, are standing here for battle, abandoning life and wealth—preceptors, fathers, sons as well as grandfathers, maternal uncles, fathers-in-law, grandsons, brothers-in-law, as also (other) relatives. These I do not wish to kill, though they kill (me), O destroyer of Madhu[3]! even for the sake of sovereignty over

[1] The words in this list include all standing in similar relationships to those directly signified.

[2] Such as the appearance of vultures, cars moving without horses, &c., mentioned in the Bhîshma Parvan II, 17. Cf. Sutta Nipâta, p. 100.

[3] A demon of this name.

the three worlds, how much less then for this earth (alone)? What joy shall be ours, O *G*anârdana! after killing Dh*ri*tarâsh*t*ra's sons? Killing these felons[1] we shall only incur sin. Therefore it is not proper for us to kill our own kinsmen, the sons of Dh*ri*tarâsh*t*ra. For how, O Mâdhava! shall we be happy after killing our own relatives? Although they have their consciences corrupted by avarice, they do not see the evils flowing from the extinction of a family, and the sin in treachery to friends; still, O *G*anârdana! should not we, who do see the evils flowing from the extinction of a family, learn to refrain from that sin? On the extinction of a family, the eternal rites of families are destroyed[2]. Those rites being destroyed, impiety predominates over the whole family[3]. In consequence of the predominance of impiety, O K*ri*sh*n*a! the women of the family become corrupt[4]; and the women becoming corrupt, O descendant of V*ri*sh*n*i! intermingling of castes results; that intermingling necessarily leads the family and the destroyers of the family to hell; for when the ceremonies of (offering) the balls of food and water (to them) fail[5], their ancestors fall down (to hell). By these transgressions of the destroyers of families, which occasion interminglings of castes, the eternal rites of castes and rites of families are

[1] Six classes are mentioned: an incendiary; one who administers poison; one who assaults another—weapon in hand; one who destroys property; one who robs another of his wife; or his fields.

[2] I.e. there being none to attend to the 'rites,' women being ineligible.

[3] I.e. the surviving members.

[4] I.e. either by the mere fact of relationship to such men, or by following their bad example.

[5] There being no qualified person to perform them; 'their ancestors'—that is to say, of the 'destroyers of families.'

subverted. And O *G*anârdana! we have heard that men whose family-rites are subverted, must necessarily live in hell. Alas! we are engaged in committing a heinous sin, seeing that we are making efforts for killing our own kinsmen out of greed of the pleasures of sovereignty. If the sons of Dh*ri*tarâsh*t*ra, weapon in hand, were to kill me in battle, me being weaponless and not defending (myself), that would be better for me.

Sa*ñg*aya said:

Having spoken thus, Ar*g*una cast aside his bow together with the arrows, on the battle-field, and sat down in (his) chariot, with a mind agitated by grief.

CHAPTER II.

Sa*ñg*aya said:

To him, who was thus overcome with pity, and dejected, and whose eyes were full of tears and turbid, the destroyer of Madhu spoke these words.

The Deity said:

How (comes it that) this delusion, O Ar*g*una! which is discarded by the good, which excludes from heaven, and occasions infamy, has overtaken you in this (place of) peril? Be not effeminate, O son of P*ri*thâ! it is not worthy of you. Cast off this base weakness of heart, and arise, O terror of (your) foes!

Ar*g*una said:

How, O destroyer of Madhu! shall I encounter with arrows in the battle Bhîshma and Dro*n*a—both, O destroyer of enemies! entitled to reverence?

Without killing (my) preceptors—(men) of great glory—it is better to live even on alms in this world. But if killing them, though they are avaricious of worldly goods, I should only enjoy blood-tainted enjoyments. Nor do we know which of the two is better for us—whether that we should vanquish them, or that they should vanquish us. Even those, whom having killed, we do not wish to live—even those sons of Dh*ri*tarâsh*t*ra stand (arrayed) against us. With a heart contaminated by the taint of helplessness[1], with a mind confounded about my duty, I ask you. Tell me what is assuredly good for me. I am your disciple; instruct me, who have thrown myself on your (indulgence). For I do not perceive what is to dispel that grief which will dry up my organs[2] after I shall have obtained a prosperous kingdom on earth without a foe, or even the sovereignty of the gods[3].

Sañ*g*aya said:

Having spoken thus to H*ri*shîke*s*a, O terror of (your) foes! Gu*d*âke*s*a said to Govinda, 'I shall not engage in battle;' and verily remained silent. To him thus desponding between the two armies, O descendant of Bharata! H*ri*shîke*s*a spoke these words with a slight smile.

The Deity said:

You have grieved for those who deserve no grief,

---

[1] The commentators say that 'heart' here signifies the dispositions which are stated in chapter XVIII infra, p. 126. The feeling of 'helplessness' is incompatible with what is there stated as the proper disposition for a Kshatriya.

[2] I.e. by the heat of vexation; the meaning is, 'which will cause constant vexation of spirit.'

[3] I.e. if the means employed are the sinful acts referred to.

and you speak words of wisdom[1]. Learned men grieve not for the living nor the dead. Never did I not exist, nor you, nor these rulers of men; nor will any one of us ever hereafter cease to be. As in this body, infancy and youth and old age (come) to the embodied (self)[2], so does the acquisition of another body; a sensible man is not deceived about that. The contacts of the senses[3], O son of Kuntî! which produce cold and heat, pleasure and pain, are not permanent, they are for ever coming and going. Bear them, O descendant of Bharata! For, O chief of men! that sensible man whom they[4] afflict not, (pain and pleasure being alike to him), he merits immortality. There is no existence for that which is unreal; there is no non-existence for that which is real. And the (correct) conclusion about both[5] is perceived by those who perceive the truth. Know that to be indestructible which pervades all this; the destruction of that inexhaustible (principle) none can bring about. These bodies appertaining to the embodied (self) which is eternal, indestructible, and indefinable, are declared[6] to be perishable; therefore do engage in battle, O descendant of Bharata! He who thinks one to be the killer and he who thinks

[1] Scil. regarding family-rites, &c., for, says Nîlaka*nth*a, they indicate knowledge of soul as distinct from body.

[2] A common word in the Gîtâ, that which presides over each individual body.

[3] Scil. with external objects.

[4] I.e. the 'contacts.'

[5] The sense is this—there are two things apparently, the soul which is indestructible, and the feelings of pain &c. which 'come and go.' The true philosopher knows that the former only is real and exists; and that the latter is unreal and non-existent. He therefore does not mind the latter.

[6] Scil. by those who are possessed of true knowledge.

one to be killed, both know nothing. He kills not, is not killed[1]. He is not born, nor does he ever die, nor, having existed, does he exist no more. Unborn, everlasting, unchangeable, and very ancient, he is not killed when the body is killed[2]. O son of Prithâ! how can that man who knows the self thus to be indestructible, everlasting, unborn, and imperishable, kill any one, or cause any one to be killed? As a man, casting off old clothes, puts on others and new ones, so the embodied (self), casting off old bodies, goes to others and new ones. Weapons do not divide the self (into pieces); fire does not burn it; waters do not moisten it; the wind does not dry it up. It is not divisible; it is not combustible; it is not to be moistened; it is not to be dried up. It is everlasting, all-pervading, stable, firm, and eternal[3]. It is said to be unperceived, to be unthinkable, to be unchangeable. Therefore knowing it to be such, you ought not to grieve. But even if you think that the self is constantly born, and constantly dies, still, O you of mighty arms! you ought not to grieve thus. For to one that is born, death is certain; and to one that dies, birth is certain[4]. Therefore about (this)

[1] Cf. *Katha*-upanishad, p. 104. [2] *Katha*-upanishad, pp. 103, 104.

[3] 'Eternal.' Nîlakantha explains this by 'unlimited by time, place,' &c. *S*ankara and others as 'uncreated,' 'without cause.' Stable = not assuming new forms; firm = not abandoning the original form. (*S*rîdhara.) The latter signifies a slight change; the former a total change.

[4] Cf. the following from the Sutta Nipâta (Sir M. C. Swamy's translation), pp. 124, 125: 'There is, indeed, no means by which those born could be prevented from dying.' 'Even thus the world is afflicted with death and decay; therefore wise men, knowing the course of things in the world, do not give way to grief.'

unavoidable thing, you ought not to grieve. The source of things, O descendant of Bharata! is unperceived; their middle state is perceived; and their end again is unperceived. What (occasion is there for any) lamentation regarding them[1]? One looks upon it[2] as a wonder; another similarly speaks of it as a wonder; another too hears of it as a wonder; and even after having heard of it, no one does really know it[3]. This embodied (self), O descendant of Bharata! within every one's body is ever indestructible. Therefore you ought not to grieve for any being. Having regard to your own duty also, you ought not to falter, for there is nothing better for a Kshatriya[4] than a righteous battle. Happy those Kshatriyas, O son of P*ri*thâ! who can find such a battle (to fight)—come of itself[5]—an open door to heaven! But if you will not fight this righteous battle, then you will have abandoned your own duty and your fame, and you will incur sin. All beings, too, will tell of your everlasting infamy; and to one who has been honoured, infamy is (a) greater (evil) than death. (Warriors who are) masters of great cars will think that you abstained from the battle through fear, and having been highly thought of by them, you will fall down to littleness. Your enemies, too, decrying your power, will speak much about you that should not be spoken. And what, indeed, more lamentable than that? Killed,

---

[1] Cf. Sutta Nipâta, p. 125. 'In vain do you grieve, not knowing well the two ends of him whose manner either of coming or going you know not.'

[2] I.e. the self spoken of above.

[3] Ka*th*a-upanishad, p. 96.

[4] One of the warrior caste.

[5] Without any effort, that is to say, of one's own.

you will obtain heaven; victorious, you will enjoy the earth. Therefore arise, O son of Kuntî! resolved to (engage in) battle. Looking on pleasure and pain, on gain and loss, on victory and defeat as the same, prepare for battle, and thus you will not incur sin. The knowledge here declared to you is that relating to the Sâṅkhya[1]. Now hear that relating to the Yoga. Possessed of this knowledge, O son of Pr*i*thâ! you will cast off the bonds of action. In this (path to final emancipation) nothing that is commenced becomes abortive; no obstacles exist; and even a little of this (form of) piety protects one from great danger[2]. There is here[3], O descendant of Kuru! but one state of mind consisting in firm understanding. But the states of mind of those who have no firm understanding are manifold and endless. The state of mind which consists in firm understanding regarding steady contemplation[4] does not belong to those, O son of Pr*i*thâ! who are strongly attached to (worldly) pleasures and power, and whose minds are drawn away by that flowery talk which is full of (the ordinances of) specific acts for the attainment of (those) pleasures and (that) power, and which promises birth as the fruit of acts[5]—(that flowery

[1] Sâṅkhya is explained in different modes by the different commentators, but the meaning here seems to be, that the doctrine stated is the doctrine of true knowledge and of emancipation by means of it. See infra, p. 52.

[2] Viz. this mortal mundane life.

[3] I.e. for those who enter on this 'path.'

[4] I.e. of the supreme Being; Yoga meaning really the dedication of all acts to that Being.

[5] See Sutta Nipâta, p. 4.

talk) which those unwise ones utter, who are enamoured of Vedic words, who say there is nothing else, who are full of desires, and whose goal is heaven[1]. The Vedas (merely) relate to the effects of the three qualities[2]; do you, O Arguna! rise above those effects of the three qualities, and be free from the pairs of opposites[3], always preserve courage[4], be free from anxiety for new acquisitions or protection of old acquisitions, and be self-controlled[5]. To the instructed Brâhma*n*a, there is in all the Vedas as much utility as in a reservoir of water into which waters flow from all sides[6]. Your business is with action alone; not by any means with fruit. Let not the fruit of action be your motive (to action). Let not your attachment be (fixed) on inaction[7]. Having recourse to devotion, O Dhana*ñg*aya! perform actions, casting off (all) attachment, and being equable in success or ill-success; (such) equability is called devotion. Action,

---

[1] This is a merely temporary good, and not therefore deserving to be aspired to before final emancipation.

[2] I.e. the whole course of worldly affairs. As to qualities, see chapter XIV.

[3] Heat and cold, pain and pleasure, and so forth. Cf. Manu I, 26.

[4] Cf. Sutta Nipâta, p. 17 and other places.

[5] Keeping the mind from worldly objects.

[6] The meaning here is not easily apprehended. I suggest the following explanation:—Having said that the Vedas are concerned with actions for special benefits, K*r*ish*n*a compares them to a reservoir which provides water for various special purposes, drinking, bathing, &c. The Vedas similarly prescribe particular rites and ceremonies for going to heaven, or destroying an enemy, &c. But, says K*r*ish*n*a, man's duty is merely to perform the actions prescribed for him, and not entertain desires for the special benefits named. The stanza occurs in the Sanatsugâtîya, too.

[7] Doing nothing at all.

O Dhanañgaya! is far inferior to the devotion of the mind. In that devotion seek shelter. Wretched are those whose motive (to action) is the fruit (of action). He who has obtained devotion in this world casts off both merit and sin[1]. Therefore apply yourself to devotion; devotion in (all) actions is wisdom. The wise who have obtained devotion cast off the fruit of action; and released from the shackles of (repeated) births[2], repair to that seat where there is no unhappiness[3]. When your mind shall have crossed beyond the taint of delusion, then will you become indifferent to all that you have heard or will hear[4]. When your mind, that was confounded by what you have heard[5], will stand firm and steady in contemplation[6], then will you acquire devotion.

Arguna said:

What are the characteristics, O Kesava! of one whose mind is steady, and who is intent on contemplation? How should one of a steady mind speak, how sit, how move?

The Deity said:

When a man, O son of Prithâ! abandons all the desires of his heart, and is pleased in his self only

---

[1] Merit merely leads to heaven, as to which see note on last page. Cf. Sutta Nipâta, pp. 4, 136, 145 note.

[2] Sutta Nipâta, pp. 3-7, &c.

[3] Sutta Nipâta, p. 21.

[4] This, according to Ânandagiri, means all writings other than those on the science of the soul.

[5] I.e. about the means for the acquisition of various desired things.

[6] I.e. of the soul (*S*añkara), of the supreme Being (*S*rîdhara). Substantially they both mean the same thing.

and by his self[1], he is then called of a steady mind. He whose heart is not agitated in the midst of calamities, who has no longing for pleasures, and from whom (the feelings of) affection, fear, and wrath[2] have departed, is called a sage of a steady mind. His mind is steady, who, being without attachments anywhere, feels no exultation and no aversion on encountering the various agreeable and disagreeable[3] (things of this world). A man's mind is steady, when he withdraws his senses from (all) objects of sense, as the tortoise (withdraws) its limbs from all sides. Objects of sense withdraw themselves from a person who is abstinent; not so the taste (for those objects). But even the taste departs from him, when he has seen the Supreme[4]. The boisterous senses, O son of Kuntî! carry away by force the mind even of a wise man, who exerts himself (for final emancipation). Restraining them all, a man should remain engaged in devotion, making me his only resort. For his mind is steady whose senses are under his control. The man who ponders over objects of sense forms an attachment to them; from (that) attachment is produced desire; and from desire anger is produced[5]; from anger results want of discrimination[6]; from want of dis-

[1] I.e. pleased, without regard to external objects, by self-contemplation alone.

[2] Cf. Sutta Nipâta, p. 3.

[3] The word *s*ubhâ*s*ubha in this sense also occurs in the Dhammapada, stanza 78, and in the Maitrî-upanishad, p. 34.

[4] See on this, Wilson's Essays on Sanskrit Literature, vol. iii, p. 130.

[5] I.e. when the desire is frustrated.

[6] I.e. between right and wrong. Confusion of memory = forgetfulness of *S*âstras and rules prescribed in them.

crimination, confusion of the memory; from confusion of the memory, loss of reason; and in consequence of loss of reason he is utterly ruined. But the self-restrained man who moves among[1] objects with senses under the control of his own self, and free from affection and aversion, obtains tranquillity[2]. When there is tranquillity, all his miseries are destroyed, for the mind of him whose heart is tranquil soon becomes steady. He who is not self-restrained has no steadiness of mind; nor has he who is not self-restrained perseverance[3] in the pursuit of self-knowledge; there is no tranquillity for him who does not persevere in the pursuit of self-knowledge; and whence can there be happiness for one who is not tranquil? For the heart which follows the rambling senses leads away his judgment, as the wind leads a boat astray upon the waters. Therefore, O you of mighty arms! his mind is steady whose senses are restrained on all sides from objects of sense. The self-restrained man is awake, when it is night for all beings; and when all beings are awake, that is the night of the right-seeing sage[4]. He into whom all objects of desire enter, as waters enter the ocean, which, (though) replenished, (still) keeps its position unmoved,—he only obtains tranquillity; not he who desires (those) objects of desire. The man who,

[1] Cf. Sutta Nipâta, p. 45.

[2] Cf. Maitrî-upanishad, p. 134, where the commentator explains it to mean freedom from desires.

[3] For a somewhat similar use of the word bhâvanâ in this sense, comp. Dhammapada, stanza 301.

[4] Spiritual matters are dark as night to the common run of men, while they are wide awake in all worldly pursuits. With the sage the case is exactly the reverse.

casting off all desires, lives free from attachments, who is free from egoism [1], and from (the feeling that this or that is) mine [2], obtains tranquillity. This, O son of Prithâ! is the Brahmic [3] state; attaining to this, one is never deluded; and remaining in it in (one's) last moments, one attains (brahma-nirvâna) the Brahmic bliss [4].

CHAPTER III.

Arguna said:

If, O Ganârdana! devotion is deemed by you to be superior to action, then why, O Kesava! do you prompt me to (this) fearful action? You seem, indeed, to confuse my mind by equivocal words. Therefore, declare one thing determinately, by which I may attain the highest good.

The Deity said:

O sinless one! I have already declared, that in this world there is a twofold path [5]—that of the Sâṅkhyas by devotion in the shape of (true) knowledge; and that of the Yogins by devotion in the shape of action. A man does not attain freedom from action [6] merely by not engaging in action; nor does he attain perfection [7] by mere [8] renunciation. For nobody ever remains even for an instant without

[1] Either pride or, better, the false notion mentioned infra, p. 55.

[2] An almost identical expression occurs in the Dhammapada, stanza 367, and Maitrî-upanishad, p. 37.

[3] The state of identification of oneself with the Brahman, which results from a correct knowledge of the Brahman.

[4] Infra, p. 66.

[5] Supra, p. 47.

[6] I.e., according to Sankara, identification of oneself with Brahman.

[7] Final emancipation.

[8] I.e. not coupled with knowledge and purity of heart.

performing some action; since the qualities of nature constrain everybody, not having free-will (in the matter), to some action [1]. The deluded man who, restraining the organs of action [2], continues to think in his mind about objects of sense, is called a hypocrite. But he, O Arguna! who restraining his senses by his mind [3], and being free from attachments, engages in devotion (in the shape) of action, with the organs of action, is far superior. Do you perform prescribed action, for action is better than inaction, and the support of your body, too, cannot be accomplished with inaction. This world is fettered by all action other than action for the purpose of the sacrifice [4]. Therefore, O son of Kuntî! do you, casting off attachment, perform action for that purpose. The Creator, having in olden times created men together with the sacrifice, said: 'Propagate with this. May it be the giver to you of the things you desire. Please the gods with this, and may those gods please you. Pleasing each other, you will attain the highest good. For pleased with the sacrifices, the gods will give you the enjoyments you desire. And he who enjoys himself without giving them what they have given, is, indeed, a thief.' The good, who eat the leavings of a sacrifice, are released from all sins. But the unrighteous ones, who prepare food for themselves only, incur sin [5].

---

[1] Cf. infra, pp. 122–128. [2] Hands, feet, &c.

[3] By means of true discrimination keeping the senses from attachments to worldly objects, which lead to sin and evil.

[4] Cf. infra, pp. 60, 61. Probably the 'sacrifices' spoken of in that passage must be taken to be the same as those referred to in the Creator's injunction mentioned in this passage.

[5] Cf. Maitrî-upanishad, p. 143.

From food are born (all) creatures; from rain is the production of food; rain is produced by sacrifices; sacrifices are the result of action; know that action has its source in the Vedas; the Vedas come from the Indestructible. Therefore the all-comprehending Vedas are always concerned with sacrifices[1]. He who in this world does not turn round the wheel revolving thus, is of sinful life, indulging his senses, and, O son of P*ri*thâ! he lives in vain. But the man who is attached to his self only, who is contented in his self, and is pleased with his self[2], has nothing to do. He has no interest at all in what is done, and none whatever in what is not done, in this world[3]; nor is any interest of his dependent on any being. Therefore[4] always perform action, which must be performed, without attachment. For a man, performing action without attachment, attains the Supreme. By action alone, did *G*anaka and the rest work for perfection[5]. And having regard also to the keeping of people (to their duties) you should perform action. Whatever a great man does, that other men also do. And people follow whatever he receives as authority. There is nothing, O son of P*ri*thâ! for me to do in (all) the three worlds,

---

[1] The commentators explain this to mean that though the Vedas elucidate all matters, their principal subject is the sacrifice.

[2] The distinctions here are rather nice,—an ordinary man is 'attached' to worldly objects, is 'contented' with goods &c., and is 'pleased' with special gains.

[3] No good or evil accrues to him from anything he does or omits to do.

[4] *S*rîdhara says that Ar*g*una is here told to perform action, as freedom from it is only for the man of true knowledge, which Ar*g*una is not as yet.

[5] I.e. final emancipation; cf. p. 59 infra, and Îsopanishad, p. 6.

nothing to acquire which has not been acquired. Still I do engage in action. For should I at any time not engage without sloth in action, men would follow in my path from all sides, O son of Prithâ! If I did not perform actions, these worlds would be destroyed, I should be the cause of caste-interminglings; and I should be ruining these people. As the ignorant act, O descendant of Bharata! with attachment to action, so should a wise man act without attachment, wishing to keep the people (to their duties). A wise man should not shake the convictions of the ignorant who are attached to action, but acting with devotion (himself) should make them apply themselves to all action. He whose mind is deluded by egoism thinks himself the doer of the actions, which, in every way, are done by the qualities of nature[1]. But he, O you of mighty arms! who knows the truth about the difference from qualities and the difference from actions[2], forms no attachments, believing that qualities deal with qualities[3]. But those who are deluded by the qualities of nature form attachments to the actions of the qualities[4]. A man of perfect knowledge should not shake these men of imperfect knowledge (in their convictions). Dedicating all actions to me with a mind knowing the relation of the supreme and individual self, engage in battle without

[1] The active principle is nature, the aggregate of the three qualities; the soul is only the looker-on; cf. inter alia, p. 104 infra.

[2] Scil. the difference of the soul from the collection of qualities, viz. the body, senses, &c., and from the actions of which they are the authors.

[3] Qualities (i.e. senses) deal with qualities, i.e. objects of sense.

[4] I.e. all mundane affairs.

desire, without (any feeling that this or that is) mine, and without any mental trouble[1]. Even those men who always act on this opinion of mine, full of faith, and without carping, are released from all actions. But those who carp at my opinion and do not act upon it, know them to be devoid of discrimination, deluded as regards all knowledge[2], and ruined. Even a man of knowledge acts consonantly to his own nature[3]. All beings follow nature. What will restraint effect? Every sense has its affections and aversions towards its objects fixed. One should not become subject to them, for they are one's opponents[4]. One's own duty, though defective, is better than another's duty well performed. Death in (performing) one's own duty is preferable; the (performance of the) duty of others is dangerous.

Arguna said:

But by whom, O descendant of V*ri*sh*n*i! is man impelled, even though unwilling, and, as it were, constrained by force, to commit sin?

---

[1] About the consequences of your actions.

[2] Of actions, or of the Brahman in its various forms.

[3] Which is the result of the virtues and vices of a preceding life. The sequence of ideas here is as follows:—The true view stated here about the 'difference from qualities and actions' is disregarded by some, owing to their 'nature' as now explained. Then the question is, If nature is so potent, what is the good of the *S*âstras? The answer is, Nature only acts through our likes and dislikes. Withstand them and then you can follow the *S*âstras. It is under the influence of these likes and dislikes, that some may say, we shall practise duties prescribed for others (our own being bad ones) as they are equally prescribed by the *S*âstras. That, as stated in the last sentence here, is wrong.

[4] Cf. Sutta Nipâta, p. 101, as to 'likings and dislikings.'

The Deity said:

It is desire, it is wrath[1], born from the quality of passion; it is very ravenous, very sinful. Know that that is the foe in this world. As fire is enveloped by smoke, a mirror by dust, the fœtus by the womb, so is this[2] enveloped by desire. Knowledge, O son of Kuntî! is enveloped by this constant foe of the man of knowledge, in the shape of desire, which is like a fire[3] and insatiable. The senses, the mind, and the understanding are said to be its seat[4]; with these it deludes the embodied (self) after enveloping knowledge. Therefore, O chief of the descendants of Bharata! first restrain your senses, then cast off this sinful thing which destroys knowledge and experience[5]. It has been said[6], Great are the senses, greater than the senses is the mind, greater than the mind is the understanding. What is greater than the understanding is that[7]. Thus knowing that which is higher than the understanding, and restraining (your)self by (your)self, O you of

---

[1] Vide p. 50 supra.

[2] I.e. knowledge, mentioned in the next sentence, for which construction p. 71 and p. 98 may be compared.

[3] Which becomes more powerful the more it is fed.

[4] The mind is that which ponders over things as such or such; the understanding is that which finally determines (cf. Lewes' History of Philosophy, II, 463–465). These and the senses are the 'seat' of desire, because the perception of an object by the sense, the pondering over it by the mind, and the determination about it by the understanding are the preliminaries to the awakening of the desire; supra, p. 50.

[5] Knowledge is from books or teachers, experience is the result of personal perception.

[6] Ka*th*opanishad, p. 114; and see also pp. 148, 149.

[7] I.e. the supreme Being, as in the Ka*th*opanishad.

mighty arms! destroy this unmanageable enemy in the shape of desire.

CHAPTER IV.

The Deity said:

This everlasting[1] (system of) devotion I declared to the sun, the sun declared it to Manu[2], and Manu communicated it to Ikshvâku. Coming thus by steps, it became known to royal sages. But, O terror of (your) foes! that devotion was lost to the world by long (lapse of) time. That same primeval devotion I have declared to you to-day, seeing that you are my devotee and friend, for it is the highest mystery.

Arguna said:

Later is your birth; the birth of the sun is prior. How then shall I understand that you declared (this) first?

The Deity said:

I have passed through many births, O Arguna! and you also. I know them all, but you, O terror of (your) foes! do not know them. Even though I am unborn and inexhaustible in (my) essence, even though I am lord of all beings, still I take up the control of my own nature[3], and am born by

[1] Because its fruit is imperishable, viz. final emancipation.

[2] In the *Kh*ândogya-upanishad, Manu is the channel of communication for some doctrine taught by Pragâpati, which Manu teaches the 'people,' interpreted by *S*ankara to mean Ikshvâku, &c. (p. 178; see too p. 625).

[3] Nature is what goes to the formation of the material form in which he is born; the 'power' includes knowledge, omnipotence, &c. It is delusive because he is still really 'unborn.'

means of my delusive power. Whensoever, O descendant of Bharata! piety languishes, and impiety is in the ascendant, I create myself. I am born age after age, for the protection of the good, for the destruction of evil-doers, and the establishment of piety. Whoever truly knows thus my divine birth and work, casts off (this) body and is not born again. He comes to me, O Arguna! Many from whom affection, fear[1], and wrath have departed, who are full of me, who depend on me, and who are purified by the penance of knowledge[2], have come into my essence. I serve men in the way in which they approach me[3]. In every way, O son of Prithâ! men follow in my path[4]. Desiring the success of actions[5], men in this world worship the divinities, for in this world of mortals, the success produced by action is soon obtained. The fourfold division of castes was created by me according to the apportionment of qualities and duties. But though I am its author, know me to be inexhaustible, and not the author. Actions defile me not. I have no attachment to the fruit of actions. He who knows me thus is not tied down by actions. Knowing this, the men of old who wished for final emancipation, performed action. Therefore do you, too, perform action as was done by men of old in olden times. Even sages are confused as to what is

[1] Cf. Sutta Nipâta, p. 73.
[2] Cf. infra, p. 61.
[3] I. e. I give to each worshipper what is proper for him.
[4] The original words used here occur before in a different sense (see p. 55). Here the meaning is that to whomsoever directly addressed, all worship is worship of me (see p. 84). In the whole passage, Krishna says that the Deity is not chargeable with partiality on account of the variety of human qualities and states.
[5] Such as acquisition of sons, cattle, &c.

action, what inaction. Therefore I will speak to you about action, and learning that, you will be freed from (this world of) evil. One must possess knowledge about action; one must also possess knowledge about prohibited action; and again one must possess knowledge about inaction. The truth regarding action is abstruse. He is wise among men, he is possessed of devotion, and performs all actions[1], who sees inaction in action, and action in inaction. The wise call him learned, whose acts are all free from desires and fancies, and whose actions are burnt down by the fire of knowledge. Forsaking all attachment to the fruit of action, always contented, dependent on none, he does nothing at all, though he engages in action. Devoid of expectations, restraining the mind and the self, and casting off all belongings[2], he incurs no sin, performing actions merely for the sake of the body[3]. Satisfied with earnings coming spontaneously[4], rising above the pairs of opposites, free from all animosity, and equable on success or ill-success, he is not fettered down, even though he performs (actions). The acts of one who is devoid of attachment, who is free[5], whose mind is fixed on knowledge, and who performs action for (the purpose of) the sacrifice[6] are all

[1] Devoted though performing all actions.

[2] 'Appropriating nothing,' at Sutta Nipâta, p. 101, seems to be the same idea. 'Self' just before this means senses.

[3] Preferably, perhaps, 'with the body only.' But *S*a*n*kara rejects this.

[4] Cf. infra, p. 101; and Sutta Nipâta, p. 12.

[5] The commentators vary in their interpretations of this word (mukta), but the common point appears to be 'free from attachment to worldly concerns.' Cf. Sutta Nipâta, p. 8.

[6] Sacrifice here apparently means every act for the attainment of

destroyed. Brahman is the oblation; with Brahman (as a sacrificial instrument) it is offered up; Brahman is in the fire; and by Brahman it is thrown; and Brahman, too, is the goal to which he proceeds who meditates on Brahman in the action[1]. Some devotees perform the sacrifice to the gods, some offer up the sacrifice by the sacrifice itself in the fire of Brahman[2]. Others offer up the senses, such as the sense of hearing and others, in the fires of restraint[3]; others offer up the objects of sense, such as sound and so forth, into the fires of the senses[4]. Some again offer up all the operations of the senses and the operations of the life-breaths into the fire of devotion by self-restraint[5], kindled by knowledge. Others perform the sacrifice of wealth, the sacrifice of penance, the sacrifice of concentration of mind, the sacrifice of Vedic study[6], and of knowledge, and others are ascetics of rigid vows. Some offer up the upward life-breath into the downward life-breath, and the downward life-breath into the upper life-breath, and stopping up the motions of the upward and downward life-breaths, devote themselves to the restraint of the life-breaths[7]. Others, who (take)

---

the supreme; cf. supra, p. 53. In Âsvalâyana Grihya-sûtra I, 1, 5, a text is cited meaning 'salutation verily is a sacrifice.'

[1] This thorough identification with the Brahman explains why the action is 'destroyed' and does not 'fetter' the doer.

[2] I. e. all acts, religious and other, offered up to the Brahman in the mode above stated.

[3] Practise 'yoga' and other like exercises.

[4] Remaining unattached to sensuous enjoyments.

[5] Stopping the bodily operations mentioned, and engaging in contemplation.

[6] This is called Brahmayagña, Âsvalâyana Grihya-sûtra III, 1, 3.

[7] Maitrî-upanishad, p. 129.

limited food, offer up the life-breaths into the life-breaths. All of these, conversant with the sacrifice, have their sins destroyed by the sacrifice. Those who eat the nectar-like leavings of the sacrifice repair to the eternal Brahman[1]. This world is not for those who perform no sacrifice, whence (then) the other, O best of the Kauravas! Thus sacrifices of various sorts are laid down in the Vedas. Know them all to be produced from action[2], and knowing this you will be released (from the fetters of this world). The sacrifice of knowledge, O terror of (your) foes! is superior to the sacrifice of wealth, for action, O son of P*ri*thâ! is wholly and entirely comprehended in knowledge. That[3] you should learn by salutation, question, and service[4]. The men of knowledge who perceive the truth will teach knowledge to you. Having learnt that, O son of Pâ*nd*u! you will not again fall thus into delusion; and by means of it, you will see all beings, without exception, first in yourself, and then in me[5]. Even if you are the most sinful of all sinful men, you will cross over all trespasses by means of the boat of knowledge alone. As a fire well kindled, O Ar*g*una! reduces fuel to ashes, so the fire of knowledge reduces all actions to ashes[6]. For there is in this world no means of sanctification like knowledge[7], and that one perfected by devotion finds

[1] Supra, p. 53.
[2] Operations of mind, senses, &c.; cf. supra, p. 54.
[3] I. e. knowledge.
[4] Addressed to men of knowledge. Cf. Mu*nd*akopanishad, p. 282.
[5] The essential unity of the supreme and individual soul and the whole universe. Cf. Îsopanishad, pp. 13, 14.
[6] Supra, p. 60.
[7] Sutta Nipâta, p. 48.

within one's self in time. He who has faith, whose senses are restrained, and who is assiduous, obtains knowledge[1]. Obtaining knowledge, he acquires, without delay, the highest tranquillity. He who is ignorant and devoid of faith, and whose self is full of misgivings, is ruined. Not this world, not the next, nor happiness, is for him whose self is full of misgivings. Actions, O Dhanañgaya! do not fetter one who is self-possessed[2], who has renounced action by devotion, and who has destroyed misgivings by knowledge. Therefore, O descendant of Bharata! destroy, with the sword of knowledge, these misgivings of yours which fill your mind, and which are produced from ignorance. Engage in devotion. Arise!

Chapter V.

Arguna said:

O Krishna! you praise renunciation of actions and also the pursuit (of them). Tell me determinately which one of these two is superior.

The Deity said:

Renunciation and pursuit of action are both instruments of happiness. But of the two, pursuit of action is superior to renunciation of action. He should be understood to be always an ascetic[3], who has no aversion and no desire. For, O you of mighty arms! he who is free from the pairs of opposites is easily released from (all) bonds. Children—not wise men—talk of sâṅkhya and yoga as dis-

[1] Sutta Nipâta, p. 49. [2] Cautious, free from heedlessness.
[3] I.e. one who has performed 'renunciation.'

tinct. One who pursues either well obtains the fruit of both. The seat which the sâṅkhyas obtain is reached by the yogas[1] also. He sees (truly), who sees the sâṅkhya and yoga as one. Renunciation, O you of mighty arms! is difficult to reach without devotion; the sage possessed of devotion attains Brahman[2] without delay. He who is possessed of devotion, whose self is pure, who has restrained his self[3], and who has controlled his senses, and who identifies his self with every being, is not tainted though he performs (actions). The man of devotion, who knows the truth, thinks he does nothing at all, when he sees[4], hears, touches, smells, eats, moves, sleeps, breathes, talks, throws out[5], takes, opens or closes the eyelids; he holds that the senses deal with the objects of the senses. He who, casting off (all) attachment, performs actions dedicating them to Brahman, is not tainted by sin, as the lotus-leaf[6] (is not tainted) by water. Devotees, casting off attachment, perform actions for attaining purity of self, with the body, the mind, the understanding, or even the senses[7]—(all) free (from

[1] Those who follow the yoga 'path.' The form is noteworthy, grammatically.

[2] I.e. 'attains true renunciation,' says *S*aṅkara; *S*ridhara says, 'attains Brahman, after becoming a "renouncer."'

[3] Here self is explained as body; in the line which goes before it is explained as heart.

[4] These are the various operations of the organs of perception, action, &c.

[5] Excretions, &c.

[6] A very common simile. Cf. inter alia *K*h*â*ndogya-upanishad, p. 276; Sutta Nipâta, pp. 107-134; and Davids' Buddhism, p. 158 note.

[7] Body = bathing, &c.; mind = meditation, &c.; understanding = ascertainment of truth; senses = hearing and celebrating God's name.

egoistic notions). He who is possessed of devotion, abandoning the fruit of actions, attains the highest tranquillity. He who is without devotion, and attached to the fruit (of action), is tied down by (reason of his) acting in consequence of (some) desire. The self-restrained, embodied (self) lies at ease within the city of nine portals[1], renouncing all actions by the mind, not doing nor causing (anything) to be done. The Lord is not the cause of actions, or of the capacity of performing actions amongst men, or of the connexion of action and fruit. But nature only works. The Lord receives no one's sin, nor merit either. Knowledge is enveloped by ignorance, hence all creatures are deluded[2]. But to those who have destroyed that ignorance by knowledge of the self, (such) knowledge, like the sun, shows forth that supreme (principle). And those whose mind is (centred) on it, whose (very) self it is, who are thoroughly devoted to it, and whose final goal it is, go never to return, having their sins destroyed by knowledge. The wise look upon a Brâhma*n*a possessed of learning and humility, on a cow, an elephant, a dog, and a *S*vapâka, as alike[3]. Even here, those have conquered the material world, whose mind rests in equability[4]; since Brahman is free from defects and equable, therefore they rest in

[1] Cf. Pra*s*nopanishad, p. 202; *S*vetâ*s*vatara, p. 332; Sutta Nipâta, p. 52. The Ka*th*opanishad has eleven portals (p. 132). The nine are the eyes, nostrils, ears, mouth, and the two for excretions.

[2] As regards the Lord's relation to man's merit or sin.

[3] As manifestations of Brahman, though of different qualities and classes. As to *S*vapâka, a very low caste, see Sutta Nipâta, p. 36.

[4] As stated in the preceding words.

Brahman. He who knows Brahman, whose mind is steady, who is not deluded, and who rests in Brahman, does not exult on finding anything agreeable, nor does he grieve on finding anything disagreeable[1]. One whose self is not attached to external objects, obtains the happiness that is in (one's) self; and by means of concentration of mind, joining one's self (with the Brahman), one obtains indestructible happiness. For the enjoyments born of contact (between senses and their objects) are, indeed, sources of misery; they have a beginning as well as an end[2]. O son of Kuntî! a wise man feels no pleasure in them. He who even in this world, before his release from the body, is able to bear the agitations produced from desire and wrath, is a devoted man, he is a happy man. The devotee whose happiness is within (himself), whose recreation is within (himself), and whose light (of knowledge) also is within (himself), becoming (one with) the Brahman[3], obtains the Brahmic bliss[4]. The sages whose sins have perished, whose misgivings are destroyed, who are self-restrained, and who are intent on the welfare of all beings[5], obtain the Brahmic bliss. To the ascetics, who are free from desire and wrath[6], and whose minds are restrained, and who have knowledge of the self, the Brahmic bliss is on both sides (of death). The sage who excludes (from his mind)

[1] Ka*th*opanishad, p. 100. [2] Cf. supra, p. 44.

[3] He is one with the Brahman as he is intent exclusively on the Brahman.

[4] The bliss of assimilation with the Brahman, or, as Râmânuga puts it, the bliss of direct knowledge of the self.

[5] Sutta Nipâta, p. 39; also Davids' Buddhism, p. 109.

[6] Cf. Sutta Nipâta, p. 3.

external objects, (concentrates) the visual power between the brows[1], and making the upward and downward life-breaths even, confines their movements within the nose, who restrains senses, mind, and understanding[2], whose highest goal is final emancipation, from whom desire, fear, and wrath have departed, is, indeed, for ever released (from birth and death). He knowing me to be the enjoyer of all sacrifices and penances, the great Lord of all worlds, and the friend of all beings, attains tranquillity.

CHAPTER VI.

The Deity said:

He who, regardless of the fruit of actions, performs the actions which ought to be performed, is the devotee and renouncer; not he who discards the (sacred) fires[3], nor he who performs no acts. Know, O son of Pându! that what is called renunciation is devotion; for nobody becomes a devotee who has not renounced (all) fancies[4]. To the sage who wishes to rise to devotion, action is said to be a means, and to him, when he has risen to devotion, tranquillity[5] is said to be a means. When one does not attach oneself to objects of sense, nor to action, renouncing all fancies, then one is said to have risen to devotion. (A man) should elevate his self by his self[6]; he should not debase his self, for even (a man's) own self is his

[1] Cf. infra, p. 78. [2] P. 57 and Ka*th*opanishad, p. 157.

[3] Which are required for ordinary religious rites.

[4] Which are the cause of desires; see supra, p. 50.

[5] Abandonment of distracting actions; means scil. to perfect knowledge, says *S*rîdhara.

[6] I. e. by means of a mind possessed of true discrimination.

friend, (a man's) own self is also his enemy[1]. To him who has subjugated his self by his self[2], his self is a friend; but to him who has not restrained his self, his own self behaves inimically, like an enemy. The self of one who has subjugated his self and is tranquil, is absolutely concentrated (on itself), in the midst of cold and heat, pleasure and pain, as well as honour and dishonour. The devotee whose self is contented with knowledge and experience[3], who is unmoved[4], who has restrained his senses, and to whom a sod, a stone, and gold are alike, is said to be devoted. And he is esteemed highest, who thinks alike[5] about well-wishers, friends, and enemies, and those who are indifferent, and those who take part with both sides, and those who are objects of hatred, and relatives, as well as about the good and the sinful. A devotee should constantly devote his self to abstraction, remaining in a secret place[6], alone, with his mind and self[7] restrained, without expectations, and without belongings. Fixing his seat firmly in a clean[8] place, not too high nor too low, and covered over with a sheet of cloth, a deer-skin, and (blades of) Kusa (grass),—and there seated on (that) seat, fixing his mind exclusively on one

[1] Self is here explained as mind, the unsteadiness of which prevents the acquisition of devotion, p. 71.

[2] This means restraining senses by mind. See Maitrî-upanishad, p. 180.

[3] Supra, p. 57.

[4] By any of the vexations of the world.

[5] I. e. is free from affection or aversion towards them.

[6] 'Release from society' is insisted on at Sutta Nipâta, p. 55.

[7] Self is here explained as senses; in the previous clause as mind.

[8] This requisite is prescribed by many authorities. Cf. *Kh*ândogya-upanishad, p. 626; Maitrî, p. 156; *S*vetâsvatara, pp. 318, 319; and Âsvalâyana (*Gri*hya-sûtra) III, 2, 2, for Vedic study too.

point, with the workings of the mind and senses restrained, he should practice devotion for purity of self. Holding his body, head, and neck even and unmoved, (remaining) steady, looking at the tip of his own nose[1], and not looking about in (all) directions, with a tranquil self, devoid of fear, and adhering to the rules of Brahmakârins[2], he should restrain his mind, and (concentrate it) on me, and sit down engaged in devotion, regarding me as his final goal. Thus constantly devoting his self to abstraction, a devotee whose mind is restrained, attains that tranquillity which culminates in final emancipation, and assimilation with me. Devotion is not his, O Arguna! who eats too much, nor his who eats not at all; not his who is addicted to too much sleep, nor his who is (ever) awake. That devotion which destroys (all) misery is his, who takes due food and exercise[3], who toils duly in all works, and who sleeps and awakes (in) due (time)[4]. When (a man's) mind well restrained becomes steady upon the self alone, then he being indifferent to all objects of desire, is said to be devoted. As a light standing in a windless (place) flickers not, that is declared to be the parallel for a devotee, whose mind is restrained, and who devotes his self to abstraction. That (mental condition), in which the mind restrained by practice of abstraction, ceases to work; in which

[1] Cf. Kumârasambhava, Canto III, 47. This is done in order to prevent the sight from rambling—a total closing of the eyes being objectionable as leading to sleep.

[2] See these in Âpastamba (p. 7 in this series); and cf. Sutta Nipâta, pp. 159, 160; and Max Müller's Hibbert Lectures, p. 158.

[3] Cf. Sutta Nipâta, pp. 28, 95.

[4] Buddhism shows similar injunctions. Cf. Sutta Nipâta, pp. 21, 28, 95; and Dhammapada, stanza 8.

too, one seeing the self by the self[1], is pleased in the self; in which one experiences that infinite happiness which transcends the senses, and which can be grasped by the understanding only; and adhering to which, one never swerves from the truth; acquiring which, one thinks no other acquisition higher than it; and adhering to which, one is not shaken off even by great misery; that should be understood to be called devotion in which there is a severance of all connexion with pain. That devotion should be practised with steadiness and with an undesponding heart. Abandoning, without exception, all desires[2], which are produced from fancies, and restraining the whole group of the senses on all sides by the mind only[3], one should by slow steps become quiescent[4], with a firm resolve coupled with courage[5]; and fixing the mind upon the self, should think of nothing. Wherever the active and unsteady mind breaks forth[6], there one should ever restrain it, and fix it steadily on the self alone. The highest happiness comes to such a devotee, whose mind is fully tranquil, in whom the quality of passion has been suppressed, who is free from sin, and who is become (one with) the Brahman. Thus constantly devoting his self to abstraction, a devotee, freed from sin, easily obtains that supreme happiness—contact with the Brahman[7]. He who has devoted his self to abstraction, by devotion, looking alike on everything,

[1] Sees the highest principle by a mind purified by abstraction.

[2] Cf. Sutta Nipâta, p. 62.

[3] Cf. supra, p. 53.

[4] I. e. cease to think of objects of sense. Cf. supra, p. 69.

[5] I. e. an undespairing and firm resolution that devotion will be achieved ultimately.

[6] Cf. Sutta Nipâta, p. 106.

[7] Assimilation with the Brahman.

sees the self abiding in all beings, and all beings in the self[1]. To him who sees me in everything, and everything in me, I am never lost, and he is not lost to me[2]. The devotee who worships me abiding in all beings, holding that all is one[3], lives in me, however he may be living[4]. That devotee, O Arguna! is deemed to be the best, who looks alike on pleasure or pain, whatever it may be, in all (creatures), comparing all with his own (pleasure or pain)[5].

Arguna said:

I cannot see, O destroyer of Madhu! (how) the sustained existence (is to be secured) of this devotion by means of equanimity which you have declared—in consequence of fickleness. For, O Krishna! the mind is fickle, boisterous[6], strong, and obstinate; and I think that to restrain it is as difficult as (to restrain) the wind.

The Deity said:

Doubtless, O you of mighty arms! the mind is difficult to restrain, and fickle[7]. Still, O son of Kuntî! it may be restrained by constant practice and by indifference (to worldly objects). It is my belief, that devotion is hard to obtain for one who does not restrain his self. But by one who is self-restrained

[1] Realises the essential unity of everything.

[2] He has access to me, and I am kind to him.

[3] Cf. Îsopanishad, p. 13.

[4] 'Even abandoning all action,' says Srîdhara; and cf. infra, p. 105.

[5] Who believes that pleasure and pain are as much liked or disliked by others as by himself, and puts himself in fact in the place of others.

[6] Troublesome to the body, senses, &c.

[7] Cf. Dhammapada, stanza 33 seq.

and assiduous, it can be obtained through (proper) expedients.

Arguna said:

What is the end of him, O Krishna! who does not attain the consummation of his devotion, being not assiduous[1], and having a mind shaken off from devotion, (though) full of faith? Does he, fallen from both (paths)[2], go to ruin like a broken cloud, being, O you of mighty arms! without support, and deluded on the path (leading) to the Brahman? Be pleased, O Krishna! to entirely destroy this doubt of mine, for none else than you can destroy this doubt.

The Deity said:

O son of Prithâ! neither in this world nor the next, is ruin for him; for, O dear friend! none who performs good (deeds) comes to an evil end. He who is fallen from devotion attains the worlds of those who perform meritorious acts, dwells (there) for many a year, and is afterwards born into a family of holy and illustrious[3] men. Or he is even born into a family of talented devotees; for such a birth as that in this world is more difficult to obtain. There he comes into contact with the knowledge which belonged to him in his former body, and then again, O descendant of Kuru! he works for perfection[4]. For even though reluctant[5], he is led away by the

---

[1] Cf. p. 73 infra.

[2] The path to heaven, and that to final emancipation.

[3] 'Kings or emperors,' says Madhusûdana.

[4] I.e. final emancipation.

[5] 'As Arguna himself,' says Madhusûdana, 'receives instruction in knowledge, though he comes to the battle-field without any such object; hence it was said before, "nothing is here abortive."' See p. 47.

self-same former practice, and although he only wishes to learn devotion, he rises above the (fruits of action laid down in the) divine word. But the devotee working with great efforts [1], and cleared of his sins, attains perfection after many births, and then reaches the supreme goal. The devotee is esteemed higher than the performers of penances, higher even than the men of knowledge, and the devotee is higher than the men of action; therefore, O Arguna! become a devotee. And even among all devotees, he who, being full of faith, worships me, with his inmost self intent on me, is esteemed by me to be the most devoted.

CHAPTER VII.

The Deity said:

O son of Prithâ! now hear how you can without doubt know me fully, fixing your mind on me, and resting in me, and practising devotion. I will now tell you exhaustively about knowledge together with experience; that being known, there is nothing further left in this world to know. Among thousands of men, only some [2] work for perfection [3]; and even of those who have reached perfection, and who are assiduous, only some know me truly. Earth, water, fire, air, space, mind, understanding,

[1] As distinguished from the others who work half-heartedly, so to say. See p. 72.

[2] 'Some one' in the original.

[3] I.e. knowledge of the self. *Sankara* says, as to the next clause, that those even who work for final emancipation must be deemed to have 'reached perfection.'

and egoism[1], thus is my nature divided eightfold. But this is a lower (form of my) nature. Know (that there is) another (form of my) nature, and higher than this, which is animate, O you of mighty arms! and by which this universe is upheld. Know that all things have these (for their) source[2]. I am the producer and the destroyer of the whole universe. There is nothing else, O Dhanañgaya! higher than myself; all this is woven upon me, like numbers of pearls upon a thread[3]. I am the taste in water, O son of Kuntî! I am the light of the sun and moon. I am 'Om[4]' in all the Vedas, sound[5] in space, and manliness in human beings; I am the fragrant smell in the earth, refulgence in the fire; I am life in all beings, and penance[6] in those who perform penance. Know me, O son of Prithâ! to be the eternal seed of all beings; I am the discernment of the discerning ones, and I the glory of the glorious[7]. I am also the strength, unaccompanied by fondness or desire[8], of the strong. And, O chief of the descendants of Bharata! I am love unopposed to piety[9] among all

[1] This accords with the Sânkhya philosophy. See chapter I, sutra 61 of the current aphorisms.

[2] Cf. infra, p. 105.

[3] Cf. Mundakopanishad, p. 298.

[4] Infra, p. 79. Cf. Goldstücker's Remains, I, 14, 122; Yoga-sûtras I, 27.

[5] I. e. the occult essence which underlies all these and the other qualities of the various things mentioned.

[6] I. e. power to bear the pairs of opposites.

[7] Glory here seems to mean dignity, greatness.

[8] Desire is the wish to obtain new things; fondness is the anxiety to retain what has been obtained. The strength here spoken of, therefore, is that which is applied to the performance of one's own duties only.

[9] I. e. indulged within the bounds allowed by the rules of the Sâstras, namely, for the procreation of sons &c. only.

beings. And all entities which are of the quality of goodness, and those which are of the quality of passion and of darkness, know that they are, indeed, all from me; I am not in them, but they are in me [1]. The whole universe deluded by these three states of mind, developed from the qualities, does not know me, who am beyond them and inexhaustible; for this delusion of mine, developed from the qualities, is divine and difficult to transcend. Those who resort to me alone cross beyond this delusion. Wicked men, doers of evil (acts), who are deluded, who are deprived of their knowledge by (this) delusion, and who incline to the demoniac state of mind [2], do not resort to me. But, O Arguna! doers of good (acts) of four classes worship me: one who is distressed, one who is seeking after knowledge, one who wants wealth, and one, O chief of the descendants of Bharata! who is possessed of knowledge. Of these, he who is possessed of knowledge, who is always devoted, and whose worship is (addressed) to one (Being) only, is esteemed highest. For to the man of knowledge I am dear above all things, and he is dear to me. All these are noble. But the man possessed of knowledge is deemed by me to be my own self. For he with (his) self devoted to abstraction, has taken to me as the goal than which there is nothing higher. At the end of many lives, the man possessed of knowledge approaches me, (believing) that Vâsudeva is everything. Such a high-souled man is very hard to find. Those who are deprived of knowledge by various desires approach other

[1] They do not dominate over me, I rule them.

[2] Infra, p. 115.

divinities, observing various regulations [1], and controlled by their own natures [2]. Whichever form (of deity) any worshipper wishes to worship with faith, to that form I render his faith steady. Possessed of that faith, he seeks to propitiate (the deity in) that (form), and obtains from it those beneficial things which he desires, (though they are) really given by me. But the fruit thus (obtained) by them, who have little judgment, is perishable. Those who worship the divinities go to the divinities [3], and my worshippers, too, go to me. The undiscerning ones, not knowing my transcendent and inexhaustible essence, than which there is nothing higher, think me, who am unperceived, to have become perceptible [4]. Surrounded by the delusion of my mystic power [5], I am not manifest to all. This deluded world knows not me unborn and inexhaustible. I know, O Arguna! the things which have been, those which are, and those which are to be. But me nobody knows. All beings, O terror of (your) foes! are deluded at the time of birth by the delusion, O descendant of Bharata! caused by the pairs of opposites arising from desire and aversion. But the men of meritorious actions, whose sins have terminated, worship me, being released from the delusion (caused) by the pairs of

[1] Fasts and so forth.

[2] Which are the result of the actions done in previous lives.

[3] And the divinities are not eternal, so the fruit obtained is ephemeral.

[4] The ignorant do not know the real divinity of Vishnu, thinking him to be no higher than as he is seen in the human form. This gives them an inadequate notion of the purity and eternity of the happiness to be obtained by worshipping him; cf. infra, p. 83.

[5] The veil surrounding me is created by my mysterious power, and that everybody cannot pierce through; cf. Ka*th*a, p. 117.

opposites, and being firm in their beliefs[1]. Those who, resting on me, work for release from old age and death[2], know the Brahman[3], the whole Adhyâtma, and all action. And those who know me with the Adhibhûta, the Adhidaiva, and the Adhiyag*ñ*a, having minds devoted to abstraction, know me at the time of departure (from this world).

CHAPTER VIII.

Arg*u*na said:

What is that Brahman, what the Adhyâtma, and what, O best of beings! is action? And what is called the Adhibhûta? And who is the Adhiyag*ñ*a, and how in this body, O destroyer of Madhu? And how, too, are you to be known at the time of departure (from this world) by those who restrain their selfs?

The Deity said:

The Brahman is the supreme, the indestructible. Its manifestation (as an individual self) is called the Adhyâtma. The offering (of an oblation to any divinity), which is the cause of the production and development of all things, is named action. The Adhibhûta is all perishable things. The Adhidaivata is the (primal) being. And the Adhiyag*ñ*a, O best of embodied (beings)! is I myself in this body[4].

---

[1] Concerning the supreme principle and the mode of worshipping it.

[2] Cf. infra, p. 109.

[3] See the next chapter.

[4] Adhyâtma where it occurs before (e.g. p. 55) has been rendered 'the relation between the supreme and individual soul.' As to

And he who leaves this body and departs (from this world) remembering me in (his) last moments, comes into my essence. There is no doubt of that. Also whichever form[1] (of deity) he remembers when he finally leaves this body, to that he goes, O son of Kuntî! having been used to ponder on it. Therefore, at all times remember me, and engage in battle. Fixing your mind and understanding on me, you will come to me, there is no doubt. He who thinks of the supreme divine Being, O son of Prithâ! with a mind not (running) to other (objects), and possessed of abstraction in the shape of continuous meditation (about the supreme), goes to him. He who, possessed of reverence (for the supreme Being) with a steady mind, and with the power of devotion, properly concentrates the life-breath between the brows[2], and meditates on the ancient Seer, the ruler, more minute than the minutest atom[3], the supporter of all, who is of an unthinkable form, whose brilliance is like that of the sun, and who is beyond all darkness[4], he attains to that transcendent and divine Being. I[5] will tell you briefly about the seat, which those who know the Vedas declare to be indestructible; which is entered by ascetics from whom all desires have departed; and wishing for which, people pursue the

action, cf. pp. 53, 54. Adhibhûta is apparently the whole inanimate creation, and Adhidaivata is the being supposed to dwell in the sun. Adhiyagña is Krishna. Cf. too pp. 113, 114.

[1] Some commentators say 'whatever thing' generally. The 'form' remembered in one's last moments would be that which had been most often meditated on during life.

[2] Cf. supra, p. 67.

[3] Katha, p. 105; Svetâsvatara, p. 333.

[4] Cf. Svetâsvatara-upanishad, p. 327.

[5] Kathopanishad, p. 102.

mode of life of Brahma*k*ârins[1]. He who leaves the body and departs (from this world), stopping up all passages[2], and confining the mind within the heart[3], placing the life-breath in the head, and adhering to uninterrupted meditation[4], repeating the single syllable 'Om,' (signifying) the eternal Brahman[5], and meditating on me, he reaches the highest goal. To the devotee who constantly practises abstraction, O son of P*ri*thâ! and who with a mind not (turned) to anything else, is ever and constantly meditating on me, I am easy of access. The high-souled ones, who achieve the highest perfection, attaining to me, do not again come to life, which is transient, a home of woes[6]. All worlds, O Ar*g*una! up to the world of Brahman, are (destined) to return[7]. But, O son of Kuntî! after attaining to me, there is no birth again. Those who know a day of Brahman to end after one thousand ages, and the night to terminate after one thousand ages, are the persons

---

[1] As to Brahma*k*ârins, see supra, p. 69.

[2] 'The senses,' say the commentators. Might it not refer to the 'nine portals' at p. 65 supra? See also, however, p. 108.

[3] I.e. thinking of nothing, making the mind cease to work. Cf. Maitrî-upanishad, p. 179.

[4] Cf. Maitrî-upanishad, p. 130, uninterrupted, like 'oil when poured out,' says the commentator.

[5] Cf. *Kh*ândogya-upanishad, p. 151; Mândukya, pp. 330–388 (Om is all—past, present, and future); N*ri*si*m*ha Tâpinî, pp. 110, 117, 171; Maitrî, p. 140; Prasna, p. 220. On the opening passage of the *Kh*ândogya, *S*a*n*kara says, 'Om is the closest designation of the supreme Being. He is pleased when it is pronounced, as people are at the mention of a favourite name.' See also Max Müller, Hibbert Lectures, p. 84; Goldstücker's Remains, I, 122.

[6] See infra, p. 86; and cf. Sutta Nipâta, p. 125.

[7] They are only temporary, not the everlasting seats of the soul.

who know day and night[1]. On the advent of day, all perceptible things are produced from the unperceived; and on the advent of night they dissolve in that same (principle) called the unperceived. This same assemblage of entities, being produced again and again, dissolves on the advent of night, and, O son of P*ri*thâ! issues forth on the advent of day, without a will of its own[2]. But there is another entity, unperceived and eternal, and distinct from this unperceived (principle), which is not destroyed when all entities are destroyed. It is called the unperceived, the indestructible; they call it the highest goal. Attaining to it, none returns[3]. That is my supreme abode. That supreme Being, O son of P*ri*thâ! he in whom all these entities dwell[4], and by whom all this is permeated, is to be attained to by reverence not (directed) to another. I will state the times, O descendant of Bharata! at which devotees departing (from this world) go, never to return, or to return. The fire, the flame[5], the day,

---

[1] Cf. Manu I, 73. *S*aṅkara says, that this explains why the abodes of Brahmâ and others are said to be not lasting. They are limited by time. As to ages, *S*rîdhara says, a human year is a day and night of the gods. Twelve thousand years made of such days and nights make up the four ages: one thousand such 'quaternions of ages' make up a day, and another thousand a night of Brahmâ. Of such days and nights Brahmâ has a hundred years to live. At the close of his life, the universe is destroyed.

[2] Cf. p. 82 infra; also Manu-sm*ri*ti I, 52; and Kâlidâsa's Kumârasambhava II, 8.

[3] Cf. Ka*th*opanishad, p. 149; and also p. 112 infra.

[4] I.e. by whom, as the cause of them, all these entities are supported; cf. p. 82 infra.

[5] *S*rîdhara understands 'the time when,' in the sentence preceding this, to mean 'the path indicated by a deity presiding over

the bright fortnight, the six months of the northern solstice, departing (from the world) in these, those who know the Brahman go to the Brahman. Smoke, night, the dark fortnight, the six months of the southern solstice, (dying) in these, the devotee goes to the lunar light and returns[1]. These two paths, bright and dark, are deemed to be eternal in this world[2]. By the one, (a man) goes never to return, by the other he comes back. Knowing these two paths, O son of P*ri*thâ! no devotee is deluded[3]. Therefore at all times be possessed of devotion, O Arguna! A devotee knowing all this[4], obtains all the holy fruit which is prescribed for (study of) the Vedas, for sacrifices, and also for penances and gifts, and he attains to the highest and primeval seat.

CHAPTER IX.

Now I will speak to you, who are not given to carping, of that most mysterious knowledge, accompanied by experience, by knowing which you will be released from evil. It is the chief among the sciences, the chief among the mysteries. It is the best means of sanctification. It is imperishable, not

---

time, by which;' and the fire-flame as included in this, though having no connexion with time. *S*aṅkara agrees, though he also suggests that fire means a deity presiding over time. I own I have no clear notion of the meaning of these verses. Cf. *Kh*ândogya, p. 342; Br*i*had-âra*n*yaka-upanishad, p. 1057 seq.

[1] Cf. Prasna-upanishad, p. 64; and *S*ârîraka Bhâshya, p. 747 seq.

[2] I.e. for those who are fitted for knowledge or action.

[3] I.e. does not desire heaven, but devotes himself to the supreme Being, seeing that heavenly bliss is only temporary.

[4] All that is stated in this chapter.

opposed to the sacred law. It is to be apprehended directly[1], and is easy to practise. O terror of your foes! those men who have no faith in this holy doctrine, return to the path of this mòrtal world, without attaining to me. This whole universe is pervaded by me in an unperceived form. All entities live in me, but I do not live in them[2]. Nor yet do all entities live in me. See my divine power. Supporting all entities and producing all entities, my self lives not in (those) entities. As the great and ubiquitous atmosphere always remains in space, know that similarly all entities live in me[3]. At the expiration of a Kalpa, O son of Kuntî! all entities enter my nature; and at the beginning of a Kalpa, I again bring them forth. Taking the control of my own nature[4], I bring forth again and again this whole collection of entities, without a will of its own[5], by the power of nature. But, O Arguna! these actions do not fetter[6] me, who remain like one unconcerned, and who am unattached to those actions. Nature gives birth to movables and immovables through me, the supervisor, and by reason of that[7], O son of Kuntî! the universe revolves. Deluded people of vain hopes, vain acts, vain know-

[1] I.e. by immediate consciousness, not mediately; 'not opposed to the sacred law,' i.e. like the *S*yena sacrifice for destroying a foe.

[2] Because he is untainted by anything. And therefore also the entities do not live in him, as said in the next sentence. See p. 80 supra.

[3] As space is untainted and unaffected by the air which remains in it, so am I by the entities.

[4] Supra, p. 58. Nature=the unperceived principle.

[5] Cf. p. 80 supra.

[6] I am not affected by the differences in the conditions of these entities.

[7] Viz. the supervision.

ledge[1], whose minds are disordered, and who are inclined to the delusive nature of Asuras and Râkshasas, not knowing my highest nature as great lord of all entities, disregard me as I have assumed a human body[2]. But the high-souled ones, O son of P*ri*thâ! who are inclined to the godlike nature, knowing me as the inexhaustible source of (all) entities, worship me with minds not (turned) elsewhere. Constantly glorifying me, and exerting themselves[3], firm in their vows[4], and saluting me with reverence, they worship me, being always devoted. And others again, offering up the sacrifice of knowledge, worship me as one, as distinct, and as all-pervading in numerous forms[5]. I am the Kratu[6], I am the Ya*gñ*a, I am the Svadhâ, I the product of the herbs. I am the sacred verse. I too am the sacrificial butter, and I the fire, I the offering[7]. I am the father of this universe, the mother, the creator, the grandsire, the thing to be known, the means of sanctification, the syllable Om[8], the *Rik*, Sâman, and Ya*g*us also; the goal, the sustainer, the lord, the supervisor, the

[1] Hope, viz. that some other deity will give them what they want; acts, vain as not offered to the supreme; knowledge, vain as abounding in foolish doubts, &c.

[2] Cf. p. 76 supra.

[3] For a knowledge of the supreme, or for the means of such knowledge.

[4] Vows = veracity, harmlessness, &c.

[5] Sacrifice of knowledge, viz. the knowledge that Vâsudeva is all; as one = believing that all is one; as distinct = believing that sun, moon, &c. are different manifestations of 'me.'

[6] Kratu is a Vedic sacrifice; Ya*gñ*a, a sacrifice laid down in Sm*ri*tis. Svadhâ = offering to the manes; 'product of the herbs' = food prepared from vegetables, or medicine.

[7] Cf. p. 61 supra.

[8] P. 79 supra.

residence[1], the asylum, the friend, the source, and that in which it merges, the support, the receptacle, and the inexhaustible seed. I cause heat and I send forth and stop showers. I am immortality and also death; and I, O Arguna! am that which is and that which is not[2]. Those who know the three (branches of) knowledge, who drink the Soma juice, whose sins are washed away, offer sacrifices and pray to me for a passage into heaven; and reaching the holy world of the lord of gods, they enjoy in the celestial regions the celestial pleasures of the gods. And having enjoyed that great heavenly world, they enter the mortal world when (their) merit is exhausted[3]. Thus those who wish for objects of desire, and resort to the ordinances of the three (Vedas), obtain (as the fruit) going and coming. To those men who worship me, meditating on me and on no one else, and who are constantly devoted, I give new gifts and preserve what is acquired by them[4]. Even those, O son of Kuntî! who being devotees of other divinities worship with faith, worship me only, (but) irregularly[5]. For I am the enjoyer as well as the lord[6] of all sacrifices. But they know me not truly, therefore do they fall[7]. Those who make vows[8] to the gods go to the gods;

[1] I.e. the seat of enjoyment; receptacle = where things are preserved for future use, say the commentators.

[2] The gross and the subtle elements, or causes and effects.

[3] Cf. Mundakopanishad, p. 279; and *Kh*ândogya, p. 344.

[4] Cf. Dhammapada, stanza 23. I.e. attainment to the Brahman and not returning from it.—Râmânuga.

[5] Because in form they worship other divinities.

[6] Giver of the fruit. As to enjoyer, cf. p. 67 supra.

[7] I.e. return to the mortal world.

[8] I.e. some regulation as to mode of worship. Cf. also p. 76 supra.

those who make vows to the manes go to the manes; those who worship the Bhûtas go to the Bhûtas; and those likewise who worship me go to me. Whoever with devotion offers me leaf, flower, fruit, water, that, presented with devotion, I accept from him whose self is pure. Whatever you do, O son of Kuntî! whatever you eat, whatever sacrifice you make, whatever you give, whatever penance you perform, do that as offered to me [1]. Thus will you be released from the bonds of action, the fruits of which are agreeable or disagreeable. And with your self possessed of (this) devotion, (this) renunciation [2], you will be released (from the bonds of action) and will come to me. I am alike to all beings; to me none is hateful, none dear. But those who worship me with devotion (dwell) in me [3], and I too in them. Even if a very ill-conducted man worships me, not worshipping any one else, he must certainly be deemed to be good, for he has well resolved [4]. He soon becomes devout of heart, and obtains lasting tranquillity. (You may) affirm, O son of Kuntî! that my devotee is never ruined. For, O son of P*ri*thâ! even those who are of sinful birth [5], women, Vaisyas, and *S*ûdras likewise, resorting to me, attain the supreme goal. What then (need

[1] Cf. p. 55 supra, and other passages.

[2] This mode of action is at once devotion and renunciation: the first, because one cares not for fruit; the second, because it is offered to the supreme.

[3] 'They dwell in me' by their devotion to me; I dwell in them as giver of happiness to them.

[4] Viz. that the supreme Being alone should be reverenced.

[5] *S*ankara takes Vaisyas &c. as examples of this; not so *S*rîdhara. Cf. as to women and *S*ûdras, N*ri*simha-tâpinî, p. 14. 'Of sinful birth' = of low birth (*S*rîdhara) = birth resulting from sins (*S*ankara).

be said of) holy Brâhma*n*as and royal saints who are (my) devotees? Coming to this transient unhappy[1] world, worship me. (Place your) mind on me, become my devotee, my worshipper; reverence me, and thus making me your highest goal, and devoting your self to abstraction, you will certainly come to me.

Chapter X.

Yet again, O you of mighty arms! listen to my excellent[2] words, which, out of a wish for your welfare, I speak to you who are delighted (with them). Not the multitudes of gods, nor the great sages know my source; for I am in every way[3] the origin of the gods and great sages. Of (all) mortals, he who knows me to be unborn, without beginning, the great lord of the world, being free from delusion, is released from all sins. Intelligence, knowledge, freedom from delusion, forgiveness, truth, restraint of the senses, tranquillity, pleasure, pain, birth, death, fear, and also security, harmlessness, equability, contentment, penance, (making) gifts, glory, disgrace, all these different tempers[4] of living beings are from me alone. The seven great sages, and likewise the four ancient Manus[5], whose descendants are (all) these people in the world, were all born from my

[1] Cf. p. 79 supra.

[2] As referring to the supreme soul.

[3] As creator, as moving agent in workings of the intellect, &c.

[4] The names are not always names of 'tempers,' but the corresponding 'temper' must be understood.

[5] The words are also otherwise construed, 'The four ancients (Sanaka, Sanandana, Sanâtana, Sanatkumâra) and the Manus.' According to the later mythology the Manus are fourteen.

mind[1], (partaking) of my powers. Whoever correctly knows these powers and emanations of mine, becomes possessed of devotion free from indecision; of this (there is) no doubt. The wise, full of love[2], worship me, believing that I am the origin of all, and that all moves on through me. (Placing their) minds on me, offering (their) lives to me, instructing each other, and speaking about me, they are always contented and happy. To these, who are constantly devoted, and who worship with love, I give that knowledge by which they attain to me. And remaining in their hearts, I destroy, with the brilliant lamp of knowledge, the darkness born of ignorance in such (men) only, out of compassion for them.

Ar*g*una said:

You are the supreme Brahman, the supreme goal, the holiest of the holy. All sages, as well as the divine sage Nârada, Asita[3], Devala, and Vyâsa, call you the eternal being, divine, the first god, the unborn, the all-pervading. And so, too, you tell me yourself, O Kesava! I believe all this that you tell me (to be) true; for, O lord! neither the gods nor demons understand your manifestation[4]. You only know your self by your self. O best of beings! creator of all things! lord of all things! god of gods! lord of the universe! be pleased to declare without

[1] By the mere operation of my thought. As to ancients, cf. Aitareya-âranyaka, p. 136.

[2] *S*añkara renders the word here by perseverance in pursuit of truth.

[3] Ânandagiri calls Asita father of Devala. See also Davids' Buddhism, p. 185; Max Müller's Anc. Sansk. Lit., p. 463.

[4] Scil. in human form for the good of the gods and the destruction of demons.

exception your divine emanations, by which emanations you stand pervading all these worlds. How shall I know you, O you of mystic power! always meditating on you? And in what various entities [1], O lord! should I meditate on you? Again, O *G*anârdana! do you yourself declare your powers and emanations; because hearing this nectar, I (still) feel no satiety.

The Deity said:

Well then, O best of Kauravas! I will state to you my own divine emanations; but (only) the chief (ones), for there is no end to the extent of my (emanations). I am the self, O Gu*d*âke*s*a! seated in the hearts of all beings [2]. I am the beginning and the middle and the end also of all beings. I am Vish*n*u among the Âdityas [3], the beaming sun among the shining (bodies); I am Mari*k*i among the Maruts [4], and the moon among the lunar mansions [5]. Among the Vedas, I am the Sâma-veda [6]. I am Indra among the gods. And I am mind among the senses [7]. I am consciousness in (living) beings. And I am *S*ankara [8] among the Rudras, the lord of wealth [9] among Yakshas and Rakshases. And I am fire among the Vasus, and Meru [10] among the high-

---

[1] To know you fully being impossible, what special manifestation of you should we resort to for our meditations?

[2] P. 129 infra.

[3] 'Âditya is used in the Veda chiefly as a general epithet for a number of solar deities.' Max Müller, Hibbert Lectures, p. 264.

[4] The storm-gods, as Max Müller calls them.

[5] Cf. Sutta Nipâta, p. 121.

[6] As being, probably, full of music.

[7] Cf. *Kh*ândogya, p. 121, where *S*ankara says, 'Mind is the chief of man's inner activities.'

[8] Now the third member of our Trinity.

[9] Kubera.

[10] The Golden Mount.

topped (mountains). And know me, O Arguna! to be Brihaspati, the chief among domestic priests. I am Skanda among generals. I am the ocean among reservoirs of water [1]. I am Bhrigu among the great sages. I am the single syllable (Om [2]) among words. Among sacrifices I am the *G*apa sacrifice [3]; the Himâlaya among the firmly-fixed (mountains); the Asvattha [4] among all trees, and Nârada among divine sages; *K*itraratha among the heavenly choristers, the sage Kapila among the Siddhas [5]. Among horses know me to be U*kk*aissravas [6], brought forth by (the labours for) the nectar; and Airâvata among the great elephants, and the ruler of men among men [7]. I am the thunderbolt among weapons, the wish-giving (cow) among cows. And I am love which generates [8]. Among serpents I am Vâsuki. Among Nâga [9] snakes I am Ananta; I am Varu*n*a among aquatic beings. And I am Aryaman among the manes, and Yama [10] among rulers. Among demons, too, I am Pralhâda. I am the king of death (Kâla, time) among those that count [11]. Among beasts

[1] Cf. Sutta Nipâta, p. 121. [2] Vide p. 79 supra.

[3] *G*apa is the silent meditation. Madhusûdana says it is superior owing to its not involving the slaughter of any animal, &c.

[4] The fig tree. It is the symbol of 'life' in chapter XV infra.

[5] Those who even from birth are possessed of piety, knowledge, indifference to the world, and superhuman power. Cf. *S*vetâsvatara-upanishad, p. 357.

[6] This is Indra's horse, brought out at the churning of the ocean. Airâvata is Indra's elephant. [7] Cf. Sutta Nipâta, p. 121.

[8] I.e. not the merely carnal passion. Cf. p. 74 supra.

[9] Nâgas are without poison, says *S*rîdhara. Varu*n*a is the sea-god.

[10] Yama is death, and Pralhâda the virtuous demon for whom Vish*n*u became incarnate as the man-lion. As to manes, see Goldstücker's Remains, I, 133.

[11] 'Counts the number of men's sins,' Râmânuga; *S*ridhara says

I am the lord of beasts, and the son of Vinatâ[1] among birds. I am the wind among those that blow[2]. I am Râma[3] among those that wield weapons. Among fishes I am Makara[4], and among streams the *G*âhnavî[5]. Of created things I am the beginning and the end and the middle also, O Ar*g*una! Among sciences, I am the science of the Adhyâtma, and I am the argument of controversialists. Among letters I am the letter A[6], and among the group of compounds the copulative[7] compound. I myself am time inexhaustible, and I the creator whose faces are in all directions. I am death who seizes all, and the source of what is to be. And among females, fame[8], fortune, speech, memory, intellect, courage, forgiveness. Likewise among Sâman hymns, I am the B*ri*hat-sâman[9], and I the Gâyatrî[10] among metres. I am Mârga*s*îrsha among the months, the

this refers to 'time, with its divisions into years, months,' &c.; while a little further on it means 'time eternal.'

[1] I.e. the Garu*d*a or eagle, who is the vehicle of Vish*n*u in Hindu mythology.

[2] 'Those who have the capacity of motion,' says Râmânu*g*a.

[3] The hero of the Hindu epos, Râmâya*n*a, translated into verse by Mr. R. T. H. Griffiths.

[4] The dolphin.

[5] The Ganges.

[6] That letter is supposed to comprehend all language. Cf. Aitareya-âra*n*yaka, p. 346, and another text there cited by Mâdhava in his commentary (p. 348).

[7] This is said to be the best, because all its members are co-ordinate with one another, not one depending on another.

[8] I.e. the deities of fame, &c.

[9] See, as to this, Muir, Sanskrit Texts, vol. i, p. 16. *S*aṅkara says this hymn relates to final emancipation.

[10] Cf. *Kh*ândogya-upanishad, p. 181, where *S*aṅkara says, 'Gâyatrî is the chief metre, because it is the means to a knowledge of the Brahman.' It is the metre of the celebrated verse 'Om Tatsavitur,' &c.

spring among the seasons[1]; of cheats, I am the game of dice; I am the glory of the glorious; I am victory, I am industry, I am the goodness of the good. I am Vâsudeva among the descendants of V*ri*sh*n*i[2], and Ar*g*una among the Pâ*nd*avas. Among sages also, I am Vyâsa[3]; and among the discerning ones, I am the discerning U*s*anas[4]. I am the rod of those that restrain, and the policy[5] of those that desire victory. I am silence respecting secrets. I am the knowledge of those that have knowledge. And, O Ar*g*una! I am also that which is the seed of all things. There is nothing movable or immovable which can exist without me. O terror of your foes! there is no end to my divine emanations. Here I have declared the extent of (those) emanations only in part. Whatever thing (there is) of power, or glorious, or splendid, know all that to be produced from portions of my energy. Or rather, O Ar*g*una! what have you to do, knowing all this at large? I stand supporting all this by (but) a single portion (of myself)[6].

---

[1] Cf. *Kh*ândogya-upanishad, p. 126. Mârga*s*îrsha is November–December. Madhusûdana says this is the best month, as being neither too hot nor too cold; but see Schlegel's Bhagavadgîtâ, ed. Lassen, p. 276.

[2] One of K*ri*sh*n*a's ancestors.

[3] The compiler of the Vedas.

[4] The preceptor of the Daityas or demons. A work on politics is ascribed to him.

[5] Making peace, bribing, &c.

[6] Cf. Purusha-sûkta (Muir, Sanskrit Texts, vol. i, p. 9).

Chapter XI.

Arguna said:

In consequence of the excellent and mysterious words concerning the relation of the supreme and individual soul, which you have spoken for my welfare, this delusion of mine is gone away. O you whose eyes are like lotus leaves! I have heard from you at large about the production and dissolution of things, and also about your inexhaustible greatness. O highest lord! what you have said about yourself is so. I wish, O best of beings! to see your divine form. If, O lord! you think that it is possible for me to look upon it, then, O lord of the possessors of mystic power[1]! show your inexhaustible form to me.

The Deity said:

In hundreds and in thousands see my forms, O son of Prithâ! various, divine, and of various colours and shapes. See the Âdityas, Vasus, Rudras, the two Asvins, and Maruts likewise. And O descendant of Bharata! see wonders, in numbers, unseen before. Within my body, O Gudâkesa! see to-day the whole universe, including (everything) movable and immovable, (all) in one, and whatever else you wish to see. But you will not be able to see me with merely this eye of yours. I give you an eye divine. (Now) see my divine power.

Sañgaya said:

Having spoken thus, O king! Hari, the great

[1] Madhusûdana takes power to mean capacity of becoming small or great, of obtaining what is wanted, &c.; the so-called eight Bhûtis.

lord of the possessors of mystic power, then showed to the son of P*ri*thâ his supreme divine form, having many mouths and eyes, having (within it) many wonderful sights, having many celestial ornaments, having many celestial weapons held erect, wearing celestial flowers and vestments, having an anointment of celestial perfumes, full of every wonder, the infinite deity with faces in all directions[1]. If in the heavens, the lustre of a thousand suns burst forth all at once, that would be like the lustre of that mighty one. There the son of Pâ*nd*u then observed in the body of the god of gods the whole universe (all) in one, and divided into numerous[2] (divisions). Then Dhana*ñg*aya filled with amazement, and with hair standing on end, bowed his head before the god, and spoke with joined hands.

Ar*g*una said:

O god! I see within your body the gods, as also all the groups of various beings; and the lord Brahman seated on (his) lotus seat, and all the sages and celestial snakes. I see you, who are of countless forms, possessed of many arms, stomachs, mouths, and eyes on all sides. And, O lord of the universe! O you of all forms! I do not see your end or middle or beginning. I see you bearing a coronet and a mace and a discus—a mass of glory, brilliant on all sides, difficult to look at, having on

---

[1] Cf. p. 90 supra. *S*ankara explains it as meaning 'pervading everything.' The expression occurs in the N*ri*si*m*ha-tâpinî-upanishad, p. 50, where it is said, 'as, without organs, it sees, hears, goes, takes from all sides and pervades everything, therefore it has faces on all sides.'

[2] Gods, manes, men, and so forth.

all sides the effulgence of a blazing fire or sun, and indefinable. You are indestructible, the supreme one to be known. You are the highest support[1] of this universe. You are the inexhaustible protector of everlasting piety. I believe you to be the eternal being. I see you void of beginning, middle, end—of infinite power, of unnumbered arms, having the sun and moon for eyes, having a mouth like a blazing fire, and heating the universe with your radiance. For this space between heaven and earth and all the quarters are pervaded by you alone. Looking at this wonderful and terrible form of yours, O high-souled one! the three worlds are affrighted. For here these groups of gods are entering into you. Some being afraid are praying with joined hands, and the groups of great sages and Siddhas are saying 'Welfare[2]!' and praising you with abundant (hymns) of praise. The Rudras, and Âdityas, the Vasus, the Sâdhyas, the Visvas, the two Asvins, the Maruts, and the Ushmapas, and the groups of Gandharvas, Yakshas, demons, and Siddhas are all looking at you amazed. Seeing your mighty form, with many mouths and eyes, with many arms, thighs, and feet, with many stomachs, and fearful with many jaws, all people, and I likewise, are much alarmed, O you of mighty arms! Seeing you, O Vishnu! touching the skies, radiant, possessed of many hues, with a gaping mouth, and with large blazing eyes, I am much alarmed in my inmost self, and feel no courage, no tranquillity. And seeing your mouths terrible by the jaws, and

[1] The words are the same as at p. 97 infra, where see the note.

[2] Seeing signs of some great cataclysm, they say, 'May it be well with the universe,' and then proceed to pray to you.

resembling the fire of destruction, I cannot recognise the (various) directions, I feel no comfort. Be gracious, O lord of gods! who pervadest the universe. And all these sons of Dh*ri*tarâsh*t*ra, together with all the bands of kings, and Bhîshma and Dro*n*a, and this charioteer's son[1] likewise, together with our principal warriors also, are rapidly entering your mouths, fearful and horrific[2] by (reason of your) jaws. And some with their heads smashed are seen (to be) stuck in the spaces between the teeth. As the many rapid currents of a river's waters run towards the sea alone, so do these heroes of the human world enter your mouths blazing all round. As butterflies, with increased velocity, enter a blazing fire to their destruction, so too do these people enter your mouths with increased velocity (only) to their destruction. Swallowing all these people, you are licking them over and over again from all sides, with your blazing mouths. Your fierce splendours, O Vish*n*u! filling the whole universe with (their) effulgence, are heating it. Tell me who you are in this fierce form. Salutations be to thee, O chief of the gods! Be gracious. I wish to know you, the primeval one, for I do not understand your actions.

The Deity said:

I am death, the destroyer of the worlds, fully developed, and I am now active about the over-

---

[1] I.e. Kar*n*a, who was really the eldest brother of the Pâ*nd*avas, but having been immediately on birth abandoned by Kuntî, was brought up by a charioteer. Kar*n*a was told of his true origin by Bhîshma on his deathbed, and advised to join the Pâ*nd*avas, but he declined.

[2] By reason of the ruggedness and distortion of face.

throw of the worlds. Even without you, the warriors standing in the adverse hosts, shall all cease to be. Therefore, be up, obtain glory, and vanquishing (your) foes, enjoy a prosperous kingdom. All these have been already killed by me. Be only the instrument, O Savyasâkin[1]! Drona, and Bhishma, and Gayadratha, and Karna, and likewise other valiant warriors also, whom I have killed, do you kill. Be not alarmed. Do fight. And in the battle you will conquer (your) foes.

Sañgaya said:

Hearing these words of Kesava, the wearer of the coronet[2], trembling, and with joined hands, bowed down; and sorely afraid, and with throat choked up, he again spoke to Krishna after saluting him.

Arguna said:

It is quite proper, O Hrishîkesa! that the universe is delighted and charmed by your renown, that the demons run away affrighted in all directions, and that all the assemblages of Siddhas bow down (to you). And why, O high-souled one! should they not bow down to you (who are) greater than Brahman, and first cause? O infinite lord of gods! O you pervading the universe! you are the indestructible, that which is, that which is not, and what is beyond them[3]. You are the primal

---

[1] Arguna, as he could shoot with his left hand as well as the right.—Srîdhara.

[2] Arguna, who had this coronet given him by Indra.—Madhusûdana.

[3] The commentators interpret this to mean the perceptible, the unperceived, and the higher principle. Cf. p. 84 supra, and also pp. 103, 113 infra and notes there.

god, the ancient being, you are the highest support of this universe[1]. You are that which has knowledge, that which is the object of knowledge, you are the highest goal. By you is this universe pervaded, O you of infinite forms! You are the wind, Yama, fire, Varu*n*a, the moon, you Pra*g*âpati, and the great grandsire[2]. Obeisance be to thee a thousand times, and again and again obeisance to thee! In front and from behind obeisance to thee! Obeisance be to thee from all sides, O you who are all! You are of infinite power, of unmeasured glory; you pervade all, and therefore you are all! Whatever I have said contemptuously,—for instance, 'O K*ri*sh*n*a!' 'O Yâdava!' 'O friend!'—thinking you to be (my) friend, and not knowing your greatness (as shown in) this (universal form), or through friendliness, or incautiously; and whatever disrespect I have shown you for purposes of merriment, on (occasions of) play, sleep, dinner, or sitting (together), whether alone or in the presence (of friends),—for all that, O undegraded one! I ask pardon of you who are indefinable[3]. You are the father of the world—movable and immovable—you its great and venerable master; there is none equal to you, whence can there be one greater, O you whose power is unparalleled in all the three worlds? Therefore I bow and prostrate myself, and would propitiate you, the praiseworthy lord. Be pleased,

[1] See p. 94 supra. Here the commentators say the words mean 'that in which the universe is placed at deluge-time.'

[2] Professor Tiele mentions great-grandfather as a name for the Creator among Kaffirs (History of Religion, p. 18). Cf. p. 83 supra.

[3] I.e. of whom it is impossible to ascertain whether he is such or such. Cf. p. 94 supra.

O god! to pardon (my guilt) as a father (that of his) son, a friend (that of his) friend, or a husband (that of his) beloved. I am delighted at seeing what I had never seen before, and my heart is also alarmed by fear. Show me that same form, O god! Be gracious, O lord of gods! O you pervading the universe! I wish to see you bearing the coronet and the mace, with the discus in hand, just the same (as before)[1]. O you of thousand arms! O you of all forms! assume that same four-handed form.

The Deity said:

O Arguna! being pleased (with you). I have by my own mystic power shown you this supreme form, full of glory, universal, infinite, primeval, and which has not been seen before by any one else but you, O you hero among the Kauravas! I cannot be seen in this form by any one but you, (even) by (the help of) the study of the Vedas, or of[2] sacrifices, nor by gifts, nor by actions, nor by fierce penances. Be not alarmed, be not perplexed, at seeing this form of mine, fearful like this. Free from fear and with delighted heart, see now again that same form of mine.

Sañgaya said:

Having thus spoken to Arguna, Vâsudeva again showed his own form, and the high-souled one becoming again of a mild form, comforted him who had been affrighted.

---

[1] This is the ordinary form of Krishna.

[2] This is the original construction. One suspects that sacrifices and study of the Vedas are meant. Cf. the speech of Krishna on the next page.

Arguna said:

O *G*anardana! seeing this mild, human form of yours, I am now in my right mind, and have come to my normal state.

The Deity said:

Even the gods are always desiring to see this form of mine, which it is difficult to get a sight of, and which you have seen. I cannot be seen, as you have seen me, by (means of) the Vedas, not by penance, not by gift, nor yet by sacrifice. But, O Arguna! by devotion to me exclusively, I can in this form be truly known, seen, and assimilated[1] with, O terror of your foes! He who performs acts for (propitiating) me, to whom I am the highest (object), who is my devotee, who is free from attachment, and who has no enmity towards any being, he, O son of Pâ*nd*u! comes to me.

Chapter XII.

Arguna said:

Of the worshippers, who thus, constantly devoted, meditate on you, and those who (meditate) on the unperceived and indestructible, which do best know devotion?

The Deity said:

Those who being constantly devoted, and possessed of the highest faith, worship me with a mind fixed on me, are deemed by me to be the most devoted. But those, who, restraining the (whole) group of the senses, and with a mind at all times

[1] Literally, 'entered into;' it means final emancipation. See p. 128.

equable, meditate on the indescribable, indestructible, unperceived (principle) which is all-pervading, unthinkable, indifferent [1], immovable, and constant, they, intent on the good of all beings, necessarily attain to me. For those whose minds are attached to the unperceived, the trouble is much greater. Because the unperceived goal [2] is obtained by embodied (beings) with difficulty. As to those, however, O son of Prithâ! who, dedicating all their actions to me, and (holding) me as their highest (goal), worship me, meditating on me with a devotion towards none besides me, and whose minds are fixed on me, I, without delay, come forward as their deliverer from the ocean of this world of death. Place your mind on me only; fix your understanding on me. In me you will dwell [3] hereafter, (there is) no doubt. But if you are unable to fix your mind steadily on me, then, O Dhanañgaya! endeavour [4] to obtain me by the abstraction of mind (resulting) from continuous meditation [5]. If you are unequal even to continuous meditation, then let acts for (propitiating) me be your highest (aim). Even performing actions for (propitiating) me, you will attain perfection. If you are unable to do even this, then resort to devotion [6] to me, and, with self-restraint, abandon all fruit of action. For knowledge is better than continuous meditation; concentration [7]

---

[1] Passively looking on what occurs on earth; immovable = changeless; constant = eternal.

[2] Viz. the indestructible.

[3] I.e. assimilated with me, as expressed before.

[4] Literally, 'wish.'

[5] Cf. p. 78 supra.

[6] Performing actions, but dedicating them to me.

[7] Fixing the mind with effort on the object of contemplation. Cf. Maitri-upanishad, p. 130.

is esteemed higher than knowledge; and the abandonment of fruit of action than concentration; from (that) abandonment, tranquillity soon (results). That devotee of mine, who hates no being, who is friendly and compassionate, who is free from egoism, and from (the idea that this or that is) mine, to whom happiness and misery are alike, who is forgiving, contented, constantly devoted, self-restrained, and firm in his determinations, and whose mind and understanding are devoted to me, he is dear to me. He through whom the world is not agitated[1], and who is not agitated by the world, who is free from joy and anger and fear and agitation, he too is dear to me. That devotee of mine, who is unconcerned[2], pure, assiduous[3], impartial, free from distress[4], who abandons all actions (for fruit[5]), he is dear to me. He who is full of devotion to me, who feels no joy and no aversion, who does not grieve and does not desire, who abandons (both what is) agreeable and (what is) disagreeable, he is dear to me. He who is alike to friend and foe, as also in honour and dishonour, who is alike in cold and heat, pleasure and pain, who is free from attachments, to whom praise and blame are alike, who is taciturn[6], and contented with anything whatever (that comes), who is homeless[7], and of a steady mind, and full of

[1] No disturbance results from him to other men, or from other men to him. Cf. Sutta Nipâta, p. 56.

[2] Indifferent to worldly objects.

[3] Ready to do work as it arises.

[4] Not feeling afflicted by other people's doing an injury to him.

[5] 'For fruit' must be understood here.

[6] I. e. governs his tongue properly. Cf. Sutta Nipâta, p. 55, and Dhammapada, stanza 96.

[7] Cf. Sutta Nipâta, pp. 94, 101, 122; Âpastamba, Dharma-sûtra,

devotion, that man is dear to me. But those devotees who, imbued with faith, and (regarding) me as their highest (goal), resort to this holy (means for attaining) immortality, as stated, they are extremely dear to me.

Chapter XIII.

The Deity said:

This body, O son of Kuntî! is called Kshetra [1], and the learned call him who knows it the Kshetra*gñ*a [2]. And know me also, O descendant of Bharata! to be the Kshetra*gñ*a in all Kshetras. The knowledge of Kshetra and Kshetra*gñ*a is deemed by me (to be real) knowledge. Now hear from me in brief what that Kshetra (is), what (it is) like, what changes (it undergoes), and whence (it comes), and what is he [3], and what his powers, (all which) is sung in various ways by sages in numerous hymns [4], distinctly, and in well-settled texts full of argument, giving indications or full instruction about the Brahman. The great elements [5], egoism, the understanding, the unperceived also, the ten senses, and the one, and the five objects of sense, desire,

p. 86 (p. 152 in this series); and Dhammapada, stanzas 40–91 (where the identical word is used).

[1] I retain the original for want of a good equivalent.

[2] Cf. *S*vetâsvataropanishad, p. 368, and Maitrî, pp. 25–72.

[3] I. e. the Kshetra*gñ*a.

[4] Hymns=scil. from the Vedas about ordinary or special actions and so forth. Argument=e.g. in texts like 'How can entity come from non-entity?' 'Who could breathe, if &c.?'

[5] Cf. Aitareya-âra*n*yaka, p. 97. The subtle elements, earth, fire, &c., are meant. The unperceived=nature; the one=mind; courage=that by which the drooping body and senses are supported; egoism=self-consciousness—the feeling 'this is I.'

aversion, pleasure, pain, body, consciousness, courage, thus in brief has been declared the Kshetra with changes[1]. Absence of vanity, absence of ostentatiousness, absence of hurtfulness, forgiveness, straightforwardness, devotion to a preceptor, purity[2], steadiness, self-restraint, indifference towards objects of sense, and also absence of egoism; perception of the misery and evil of birth, death[3], old age, and disease; absence of attachment, absence of self-identifying regard for son, wife[4], home, and so forth; and constant equability on the approach of (both what is) agreeable and (what is) disagreeable; unswerving devotion to me, without meditation on any one else; resorting to clean places, distaste for assemblages of men[5], constancy in knowledge of the relation of the individual self to the supreme, perception of the object[6] of knowledge of the truth, this is called knowledge; that is ignorance which is opposed to this. I will declare that which is the object of knowledge, knowing which, one reaches immortality; the highest Brahman, having no beginning nor end, which cannot be said to be existent or non-existent[7]. It has hands and feet on all sides, it has eyes, heads, and faces on all sides, it has ears on all sides, it

[1] See the last page. Changes = development.

[2] Internal as well as external; as to devotion to a preceptor, cf. Âpastamba, p. 11 (p. 23 in this series); Taittirîya-upanishad, p. 38; *S*vetâ*s*vatara, p. 117; and Sutta Nipâta, p. 87; as to egoism, see p. 52 supra.

[3] Cf. Sutta Nipâta, pp. 18–95.

[4] Cf. Sutta Nipâta, p. 12.

[5] Cf. Sutta Nipâta, p. 11.

[6] Viz. removal of ignorance and acquisition of happiness.

[7] Words indicate a class, a quality, an action, or a relation, says *S*aṅkara. None of these can be predicated of the Brahman; so you cannot apply either of these words to it. Cf. pp. 84, 96 supra, also *S*vetâ*s*vatara, p. 346.

stands pervading everything in the world. Possessed of the qualities of all the senses, (but) devoid of all senses[1], unattached, it supports all, is devoid of qualities, and the enjoyer[2] of qualities. It is within all things and without them; it is movable and also immovable; it is unknowable through (its) subtlety; it stands afar and near[3]. Not different in (different) things[4], but standing as though different, it should be known to be the supporter of (all) things, and that which absorbs and creates (them). It is the radiance even of the radiant (bodies); it is said (to be) beyond darkness. It is knowledge, the object of knowledge, that which is to be attained to by knowledge, and placed in the heart of all[5]. Thus in brief have Kshetra, knowledge, and the object of knowledge been declared. My devotee, knowing this, becomes fit for assimilation with me. Know nature and spirit both (to be) without beginning, and know all developments and qualities[6] (to be) produced from nature. Nature is said to be the origin of the capacity of working (residing) in the body and the senses; and spirit is said (to be) the origin of the capacity of enjoying pleasures and

---

[1] Cf. *S*vetâ*s*vatara, p. 331. He has no ears, but has the quality of hearing, and so forth; unattached = really out of relation to everything, though seeming to be connected with other things through delusion.

[2] I.e. he perceives them.

[3] Î*s*opanishad, p. 12; Mu*nd*aka, p. 313.

[4] Everything being really one. Cf. inter alia, p. 124 infra. The various manifestations of the Brahman are really one in essence, though apparently different, like foam and water.

[5] Cf. p. 88.

[6] Developments = body, senses, &c. Qualities = pleasure, pain, &c.; altogether the expression means the body and feelings and so forth.

pains[1]. For spirit with nature joined, enjoys the qualities born of nature. And the cause of its birth in good or evil wombs is the connexion with the qualities[2]. The supreme spirit in this body is called supervisor, adviser[3], supporter, enjoyer, the great lord, and the supreme self also. He who thus knows nature and spirit, together with the qualities, is not born again, however living[4]. Some by concentration see the self in the self by the self; others by the Sâṅkhya-yoga; and others still by the Karma-yoga[5]; others yet, not knowing this, practise concentration, after hearing from others[6]. They, too, being (thus) devoted to hearing (instruction) cross beyond death. Whatever thing movable or immovable comes into existence, know that to be from the connexion of Kshetra and Kshetrag*ñ*a, O chief of the descendants of Bharata! He sees (truly),

[1] *S*rîdhara says that 'is said to be' means by Kapila and others. For the notion that activity is not a function of the soul, see inter alia. p. 55 supra. Enjoyment, however, is, according to this passage, the function of the soul, not of nature. See also Maitrî-upanishad, pp. 107, 108.

[2] I.e. 'the senses,' says *S*rîdhara; good=gods, &c.; evil=beasts, &c.

[3] Scil. concerning the operations of the body and senses. Cf. N*ri*si*m*ha-tâpinî, p. 224. He is adviser because, though he does not interfere, he sees and therefore may be said to sanction the operations alluded to. Supporter, i. e. of body &c. in their workings.

[4] I. e. though he may have trangressed rules.

[5] Concentration=fixing of the mind exclusively on the soul, the senses being quiescent. 'See the self,' i.e. the soul; 'in the self,' i.e. within themselves; 'by the self,' i.e. by the mind. Sâṅkhya-yoga=belief that qualities are distinct from the self, which is only a passive spectator of their operations. Cf. *S*vetâsvatara, p. 109. Karma-yoga=dedication of actions to the supreme. Cf. as to this the gloss on *S*aṅkara's Bhâshya on Vedânta-sûtra IV, 2, 21.

[6] Cf. Sutta Nipâta, p. 49.

who sees the supreme lord abiding alike in all entities, and not destroyed though they are destroyed. For he who sees the lord abiding everywhere alike, does not destroy himself[1] by himself, and then reaches the highest goal. He sees (truly), who sees (all) actions (to be) in every way done by nature alone, and likewise the self (to be) not the doer. When a man sees all the variety of entities as existing in one[2], and (all as) emanating from that, then he becomes (one with) the Brahman. This inexhaustible supreme self, being without beginning and without qualities, does not act, and is not tainted, O son of Kuntî! though stationed in the body. As by (reason of its) subtlety the all-pervading space is not tainted, so the self stationed in every body is not tainted. As the sun singly lights up all this world, so the Kshetragña, O descendant of Bharata! lights up the whole Kshetra. Those who, with the eye of knowledge, thus understand the difference between Kshetra and Kshetragña, and the destruction of the nature of all entities[3], go to the supreme.

CHAPTER XIV.

The Deity said:

Again I will declare (to you) the highest knowledge, the best of (all sorts of) knowledge, having

[1] Not to have true knowledge is equivalent to self-destruction. Cf. Îsopanishad, pp. 9, 15, 16.

[2] I.e. absorbed at the time of the deluge in nature, one of the energies of the supreme; 'emanating,' i.e. at the time of creation.

[3] Nature, which is the material cause from which all entities are produced; the destruction of it results from true knowledge of the soul. See the third note on p. 107 infra.

learnt which, all sages have reached perfection beyond (the bonds of) this (body). Those who, resorting to this knowledge, reach assimilation with my essence, are not born at the creation, and are not afflicted [1] at the destruction (of the universe). The great Brahman [2] is a womb for me, in which I cast the seed. From that, O descendant of Bharata! is the birth of all things. Of the bodies, O son of Kuntî! which are born from all wombs, the (main) womb is the great Brahman, and I (am) the father, the giver of the seed. Goodness, passion, darkness, these qualities [3] born from nature, O you of mighty arms! bind down the inexhaustible soul in the body. Of these, goodness, which, in consequence of being untainted, is enlightening and free from (all) misery, binds the soul, O sinless one! with the bond of pleasure and the bond of knowledge [4]. Know that passion consists in being enamoured, and is produced from craving and attachment. That, O son of Kuntî! binds down the embodied (self) with the

[1] I.e. 'are not destroyed,' Madhusûdana; 'do not fall,' *S*ankara; 'are not born,' *S*rîdhara, and apparently Râmânuga.

[2] I.e. the 'nature' spoken of before.

[3] These constitute nature. We must understand nature, with Professor Bhâ*nd*ârkar, as the hypothetical cause of the soul's feeling itself limited and conditioned. If nature is understood, as it usually is, to mean matter, its being made up of the qualities is inexplicable. Interpreted idealistically, as suggested by Professor Bhâ*nd*ârkar, the destruction of it spoken of at the close of the last chapter also becomes intelligible. By means of knowledge of the soul, the unreality of these manifestations is understood and nature is destroyed.

[4] Pleasure and knowledge appertain to the mind, not the self, hence they are described as constituting bonds, when erroneously connected with the self, *S*ankara and *S*rîdhara. They constitute 'bonds,' because the self when brought into contact with them, strives to obtain them, Râmânuga.

bond of action. Darkness (you must) know to be born of ignorance, it deludes all embodied (selfs). And that, O descendant of Bharata! binds down (the self) with heedlessness [1], indolence, and sleep. Goodness unites (the self) with pleasure; passion, O descendant of Bharata! with action; and darkness with heedlessness, after shrouding up knowledge. Passion and darkness being repressed, goodness stands, O descendant of Bharata! Passion and goodness (being repressed), darkness; and likewise darkness and goodness (being repressed), passion [2]. When in this body at all portals [3] light (that is to say) knowledge prevails, then should one know goodness to be developed. Avarice, activity [4], performance of actions, want of tranquillity, desire, these are produced, O chief of the descendants of Bharata! when passion is developed. Want of light, want of activity [5], heedlessness, and delusion, these are produced, O descendant of Kuru! when darkness is developed. When an embodied (self) encounters death, while goodness is developed, then he reaches the untainted worlds of those who know the highest [6]. Encountering death during (the preva-

[1] Carelessness about duty, owing to being intent on something else. Cf. Sutta Nipâta, pp. 51–91; Dhammapada, stanza 21; Ka*th*opanishad, p. 152.

[2] The effects of each quality assert themselves, when the other two are held in check. [3] I.e. the senses of perception.

[4] Activity = always doing something or another; performance, &c. = rearing large mansions, &c.; want of tranquillity = perpetual agitation of mind, 'this I will do now, then that, and next the other;' desire = to obtain everything that one comes across.

[5] I.e. doing absolutely nothing.

[6] The highest manifestations of Brahman, viz. the Hira*n*yagarbha, &c., say *S*rîdhara and Madhusûdana. Nîlaka*n*/*h*a also suggests that 'those who know the highest' means gods.

lence of) passion, he is born among those attached to action. Likewise, dying during (the prevalence of) darkness, he is born in the wombs of the ignorant[1]. The fruit of meritorious action is said to be good, untainted; while the fruit of passion is misery; and the fruit of darkness ignorance. From goodness is produced knowledge, from passion avarice[2], and from darkness heedlessness and delusion and ignorance also. Those who adhere to (the ways of) goodness go up[3]; the passionate remain in the middle; while those of the qualities of darkness, adhering to the ways of the lowest quality, go down. When a right-seeing person sees none but the qualities (to be) the doers (of all action), and knows what is above the qualities[4], he enters into my essence. The embodied (self), who transcends these three qualities, from which bodies are produced[5], attains immortality, being freed from birth and death and old age and misery.

Arguna said:

What are the characteristics, O lord! of one who has transcended these three qualities? What is his conduct, and how does he transcend these three qualities[6]?

---

[1] Lower creation, such as birds, beasts, &c.

[2] Cf. Sutta Nipâta, p. 15.

[3] I.e. are born as gods, &c.; 'middle,' as men, &c.; 'down,' as brutes, &c.

[4] I.e. what has been called Kshetragña before, the supervising principle within one.

[5] Bodies are developments of the qualities, say the commentators, which is not incompatible with the explanation of qualities given above. As to transcending qualities, cf. p. 48 supra.

[6] Cf. as to what follows what is said in chapter II about 'one whose mind is steady.'

The Deity said:

He is said to have transcended the qualities, O son of Pându! who is not averse to light and activity and delusion (when they) prevail, and who does not desire (them when they) cease[1]; who sitting like one unconcerned is never perturbed by the qualities[2]; who remains steady and moves[3] not, (thinking) merely that the qualities[4] exist; who is self-contained[5]; to whom pain and pleasure are alike; to whom a sod and a stone and gold are alike; to whom what is agreeable and what is disagreeable are alike; who has discernment; to whom censure and praise of himself are alike; who is alike in honour and dishonour; who is alike towards the sides of friends and foes; and who abandons all action[6]. And he who worships me with an unswerving devotion, transcends these qualities, and becomes fit for (entrance into) the essence of the Brahman. For I am the embodiment of the Brahman[7], of indefeasible immortality, of eternal piety, and of unbroken happiness.

---

[1] I.e. who does not feel troubled, for instance, thinking now I am actuated by a motive of passion or darkness, and so forth.

[2] So as to lose all discrimination.

[3] I.e. from his determination to pursue truth, by worldly pleasures or pains.

[4] Cf. p. 55 supra.

[5] Intent on the self only.

[6] For the whole passage, cf. p. 101 supra.

[7] Nîlakantha interprets this to mean 'the ultimate object of the Vedas.' I here means Krishna. Srîdhara suggests this parallel, as light embodied is the sun, so is the Brahman embodied identical with Vâsudeva.

Chapter XV.

The Deity said:

They say the inexhaustible Asvattha[1] has (its) roots above, (its) branches below; the *Kh*andas are its leaves. He who knows it knows the Vedas. Upwards and downwards extend its branches, which are enlarged by the qualities, and the sprouts of which are sensuous objects. And downwards to this human world are continued its roots which lead on to action. Its form is not thus known here, nor (its) end, nor beginning, nor support. But having with the firm weapon of unconcern, cut this Asvattha, whose roots are firmly fixed, then should one seek for that seat from which those that go there never return, (thinking) that one rests on that same primal being from whom the ancient course (of worldly life) emanated. Those who are free from pride and delusion, who have overcome the evils of attachment, who are constant in (contemplating) the relation of the supreme and individual self, from whom desire has departed, who are free from the pairs (of opposites) called pleasure and pain, go undeluded to that imperishable seat[2]. The sun

---

[1] Cf. Ka*th*opanishad, p. 70, and Sutta Nipâta, p. 76.

[2] Asvattha stands here for the course of worldly life. Its roots are above, viz. the supreme being; its boughs are Hira*n*yagarbha and others of the higher beings. The Vedas are its leaves, preserving it as leaves preserve trees (another interpretation is that they are the causes of the fruit which the tree bears, i.e. salvation, &c.) Upwards and downwards, from the highest to the lowest of created things. Enlarged = the qualities manifesting themselves, as body, senses, &c.; objects of sense are sprouts as they are attached to the senses, which are the tips of the branches above stated. The roots which extend downwards are the desires for various

does not light it, nor the moon, nor fire [1]. That is my highest abode, going to which none returns. An eternal portion of me it is, which, becoming an individual soul in the mortal world, draws (to itself) the senses with the mind as the sixth [2]. Whenever the ruler (of the bodily frame) obtains or quits a body, he goes taking these (with him) as the wind (takes) perfumes from (their) seats [3]. And presiding over the senses of hearing and seeing, and touch, and taste, and smell, and the mind, he enjoys sensuous objects. Those who are deluded do not see (him) remaining in or quitting (a body), enjoying or joined to the qualities [4]; they see, who have eyes of knowledge. Devotees making efforts perceive him abiding within their selfs [5]. But those whose selfs have not been refined, and who have no discernment, do not perceive him even (after) making efforts. Know that glory (to be) mine which, dwelling in the sun, lights up the whole world, or in the moon or fire [6].

---

enjoyments. Its form not thus known here, i.e. to those who live and move in this world, thus viz. as above described. The man who knows the tree thus is said to know the Vedas, because knowledge of it is knowledge of the substance of the Vedas, which is, that the course of worldly life springs from the supreme, is kept up by Vedic rites, and destroyed by knowledge of the supreme. As to freedom from pride, cf. Sutta Nipâta, p. 4.

[1] Cf. Ka*th*opanishad, p. 142; Mu*nd*aka, p. 304; N*ri*si*m*hatâpinî, p. 106; *S*vetâ*s*vatara, p. 110.

[2] Five senses and the mind issue from nature, in which they are absorbed during sleep or at a dissolution of the world. Cf. Sutta Nipâta, p. 44.

[3] Cf. Kaushîtaki-upanishad, pp. 86, 87.

[4] Perceiving objects of sense, or feeling pleasure, pain, &c.

[5] 'Selfs'=bodies, Râmânuga and *S*ridhara; 'understandings,' *S*añkara. In the next sentence 'self' means mind.

[6] Cf. Maitrî-upanishad, p. 142. This sentence continues what has been stated at the top of the page. The intervening

Entering the earth[1], I by my power support all things; and becoming the juicy moon, I nourish all herbs. I becoming the fire, and dwelling in the bodies of (all) creatures, and united with the upward and downward life-breaths, cause digestion of the fourfold food[2]. And I am placed in the heart of all[3]; from me (come) memory, knowledge, and their removal; I alone am to be learnt from all the Vedas; I am the author of the Vedântas[4]; and I alone know the Vedas. There are these two beings in the world, the destructible and the indestructible[5]. The destructible (includes) all things. The unconcerned one is (what is) called the indestructible. But the being supreme is yet another, called the highest self, who as the inexhaustible lord, pervading the three worlds, supports (them). And since I transcend the destructible, and since I am higher also than the indestructible[6], therefore

portion explains how souls do come back in some cases. As a general rule, 'all going ends in returning.' But the soul is an exception in some cases, as the 'going' to the Brahman is going to the fountain-head. Then the question arises, How does the severance come off at all? And that is what the lines up to this explain.

[1] 'Entering in the form of the goddess earth,' say Ânandagiri and Madhusûdana. Support, i.e. by keeping the earth from falling or crumbling away. The moon is said to nourish herbs by communicating to them some of her 'juice.' The moon, it may be noted, is called 'watery star' by Shakespeare. As to her relation to the vegetable kingdom, see Matsya-purâ*n*a XXIII, stanza 10 seq.

[2] I.e. what is drunk, what is licked, what is powdered with the teeth, and what is eaten without such powdering.

[3] Cf. p. 104 supra.

[4] See Introduction, p. 18.

[5] Cf. *S*vetâ*s*vatara, p. 294.

[6] The two are the whole collection of things as they appear and their material cause. The supreme being is a third principle.

am I celebrated in the world and in the Vedas as the best of beings. He who, undeluded, thus knows me the best of beings, worships me every way[1], O descendant of Bharata! knowing everything. Thus, O sinless one! have I proclaimed this most mysterious science. He who knows this, has done all he need do, and he becomes possessed of discernment.

CHAPTER XVI.

Freedom from fear, purity of heart, perseverance in (pursuit of) knowledge and abstraction of mind, gifts[2], self-restraint[2], and sacrifice, study of the Vedas, penance, straightforwardness, harmlessness, truth[2], freedom from anger, renunciation[3], tranquillity, freedom from the habit of backbiting[4], compassion for (all) beings, freedom from avarice, gentleness, modesty, absence of vain activity, noblemindedness, forgiveness, courage, purity, freedom from a desire to injure others, absence of vanity, (these), O descendant of Bharata! are his who is born to godlike endowments. Ostentatiousness, pride, vanity[5], anger, and also harshness and ignorance (are) his, O son of Pr*i*thâ! who is born to demoniac[6] endowments. Godlike endowments are deemed to be (means) for

---

[1] Cf. p. 129 infra. Here *S*ankara paraphrases it by 'thinking me to be the soul of everything.'

[2] Cf. Sutta Nipâta, p. 49.

[3] See next chapter.

[4] Sutta Nipâta, pp. 15, 101.

[5] Ostentatiousness = making a show of piety; pride = scil. of wealth and learning; vanity = esteeming oneself too highly; harshness = mercilessness.

[6] Cf. *Kh*ândogya-upanishad, p. 585, and Max Müller's Hibbert Lectures, p. 322.

final emancipation, demoniac for bondage[1]. Grieve not, O descendant of Bharata! you are born to godlike endowments. (There are) two classes of created beings in this world, the godlike and the demoniac; the godlike (class) has been described at length; now hear from me, O son of P*ri*thâ! about the demoniac. Demoniac persons know not action or inaction[2], neither purity nor yet (correct) conduct nor veracity are in them. They say the universe is devoid of truth[3], devoid of fixed principle[4], and devoid of a ruler, produced by union (of male and female) caused by lust[5], and nothing else. Holding this view, (these) enemies of the world, of ruined[6] selfs, of little knowledge, and of ferocious actions, are born for the destruction (of the world). Entertaining insatiable desire, full of vanity, ostentatiousness, and frenzy, they adopt false notions[7] through delusion, and engage in unholy observances. Indulging in boundless thoughts ending with death[8], given up to the enjoyment of objects of desire, being resolved that that is all, bound down by nets of hopes in hundreds, given up to anger and desire, they wish

[1] Scil. to birth and death in this world.

[2] What should be done for the attainment of real good, and what should not be done as productive of mischief. See too p. 125.

[3] I.e. contains nothing that is entitled to belief, as the Vedas, &c.

[4] No principle based on virtue and vice in the government of the world.

[5] They do not believe in any unseen cause, but say the lust of mankind is the cause of the universe.

[6] I.e. who have none of the means of reaching the next world.

[7] Such as that by propitiating a certain divinity by a certain rite they may obtain treasure and so forth.

[8] Till their last moments, thinking of making new acquisitions and preserving old ones.

to obtain heaps of wealth unfairly for enjoying objects of desire. 'This have I obtained to-day; this wish I will obtain; this wealth is mine; and this also shall be mine; this foe I have killed; others too I will destroy; I am lord, I am the enjoyer, I am perfect [1], strong, happy; I have wealth; I am of noble birth; who else is like me? I will sacrifice [2]; I will make gifts; I will rejoice.' Thus deluded by ignorance, tossed about by numerous thoughts, surrounded by the net of delusion, and attached to the enjoyment of objects of desire, they fall down into impure hell. Honoured (only) by themselves, void of humility, and full of the pride and frenzy of wealth, these calumniators (of the virtuous) perform sacrifices, which are sacrifices only in name, with ostentatiousness and against prescribed rules [3]; indulging (their) vanity, brute force, arrogance, lust, and anger; and hating me in their own bodies and in those of others [4]. These enemies [5], ferocious, meanest of men, and unholy, I continually hurl down to these worlds [6], only into demoniac wombs. Coming into demoniac wombs, deluded in every birth, they go down to the vilest state, O son of Kuntî! without ever coming to me. Threefold is this way to hell,—

---

[1] Blessed with children, &c. *S*rîdhara takes it to mean, 'one who has done all he need do,' and Râmânuga 'sufficient in himself.'

[2] I. e. get higher renown for sacrifices than others.

[3] That is, because of indulgence in vanity, &c. Vanity = believing oneself to have virtues which one has not; arrogance = proud disdain of others.

[4] There is trouble to oneself in sacrifices and to the animals killed for them.

[5] I. e. of God.

[6] The commentators render the original here by 'the paths of life and death,' or 'path to hell.'

ruinous to the self[1],—lust, anger, and likewise avarice; therefore one should abandon this triad. Released from these three ways to darkness, O son of Kuntî! a man works out his own salvation, and then proceeds to the highest goal. He[2] who abandoning scripture ordinances, acts under the impulse of desire, does not attain perfection[3], nor happiness, nor the highest goal. Therefore in discriminating between what should be done and what should not be done, your authority (must be) scripture. And knowing what is declared by the ordinances of scripture, you should perform action in this world.

CHAPTER XVII.

Arguna said:

What is the state of those, O Krishna! who worship with faith, (but) abandoning scripture ordinances—goodness, passion, or darkness?

The Deity said:

Faith is of three kinds in embodied (beings), it is produced from dispositions[4]. It is of the quality of goodness, of the quality of passion, and of the quality of darkness. Hear about it. The faith of all, O descendant of Bharata! is conformable to the

---

[1] I.e. rendering the self unfit for any of the highest ends of man.

[2] Here, says Srîdhara, it is laid down that the triad is not to be got rid of save by following scripture rules.

[3] I.e. fitness for the attainment of the summum bonum. As to acting from desire, see also p. 65.

[4] I.e. the result of the actions in a former birth, cf. p. 56 supra.

heart[1]. A being here is full of faith, and whatever is a man's faith, that is a man himself[2]. Those of the quality of goodness worship the gods; those of the quality of passion the Yakshas and Rakshases[3]; and the others, the people of the quality of darkness, worship departed (spirits) and the multitudes of Bhûtas. Know those to be of demoniac convictions, who practise fierce penance[4] not ordained by scripture; who are full of ostentatiousness and egoism, and of desire, attachment, and stubbornness; who are without discernment; and who torment the groups of organs in (their) bodies, and me also seated within (those) bodies. The food also, which is liked by all, and likewise the sacrifice, the penance, and gifts, are of three kinds. Listen to the distinctions regarding them as follows. The kinds of food which increase life, energy, strength, health, comfort, and relish, which are savoury, oleaginous, full of nutrition, and agreeable, are liked by the good. The kinds of food which are bitter, acid, saltish, too hot, sharp, rough, and burning, and which cause pain, grief, and disease, are desired by the passionate. And the food[5] which is cold, tasteless, stinking, stale, impure, and even leavings, are liked by the dark. That sacrifice is good which, being prescribed in (scripture) ordinances, is performed by persons

[1] The hearts of gods are said to be good, those of Yakshas &c. passionate, those of men mixed, and so forth.

[2] Faith is the dominant principle in man, and he is good, passionate, or dark, as his faith is.

[3] Goldstücker, Remains, I, 154.

[4] Troublesome to oneself and others, as standing on heated stones, &c. 'Egoism' (Ahankâra)=the feeling that one is worthy of honour, Nîlakantha.

[5] Cf. Sutta Nipâta, p. 109, and Âpastamba, p. 31 (p. 62 in this series).

not wishing for the fruit (of it), and after determining (in their) mind that the sacrifice must needs be performed. But when a sacrifice is performed, O highest of the descendants of Bharata! with an expectation of fruit (from it), and for the purpose of ostentation, know that sacrifice (to be) passionate. They call that sacrifice dark, which is against the ordinances (of scripture), in which no food is dealt out (to Brâhma*n*as, &c.), which is devoid of Mantras [1], devoid of Dakshi*n*â presents, and which is without faith. Paying reverence to gods, Brâhma*n*as, preceptors, and men of knowledge; purity [2], straightforwardness, life as Brahma*k*ârin, and harmlessness, (this) is called the penance bodily. The speech which causes no sorrow, which is true, agreeable, and beneficial, and the study [3] of the Vedas, (this) is called the penance vocal. Calmness of mind, mildness, taciturnity [4], self-restraint, and purity of heart, this is called the penance mental. This threefold penance, practised with perfect faith, by men who do not wish for the fruit, and who are possessed of devotion, is called good. The penance which is done for respect, honour, and reverence [5], and with ostenta-

---

[1] Texts from the Vedas which ought to be recited on such occasions. Presents (Dakshi*n*â) to Brâhma*n*as are insisted on in B*ri*had-âra*n*yaka-upanishad, p. 661; Â*s*valâyana G*ri*hya I, 23, 14.

[2] Cleanliness of body; straightforwardness = not doing prohibited acts; harmlessness = not injuring any living beings. These are 'bodily,' because the body is the main insurument in these actions.

[3] I.e. recitation of the Vedas.

[4] This is part of the 'mental penance,' because the government of the tongué is a consequence of mental restraint; the effect being, according to *S*aṅkara, put here for the cause.

[5] Respect = people rising to receive one, &c.; honour = people saying 'this is a holy man,' &c.; reverence = people washing one's feet, &c.

tiousness, and which is uncertain and transient[1], is here called passionate. And that penance is described as dark, which is performed under a misguided conviction, with pain to oneself, or for the destruction of another. That gift is said (to be) good, which is given, because it ought to be given, to one who (can) do no service (in return), at a (proper) place and time, and to a (proper) person. But that gift which is given with much difficulty, for a return of services, or even with an expectation of fruit[2], is said to be passionate. And that gift is described as dark, which is given to unfit persons, at un unfit place and time, without respect, and with contempt. Om, Tad, and Sat, this is said (to be) the threefold designation of the Brahman. By that[3], the Brâhma*n*as and the Vedas and sacrifices were created in olden times. Hence, the performance by those who study the Brahman, of sacrifices, gifts, and penances, prescribed by the ordinances (of scripture), always commence after saying 'Om[4].' Those who desire final emancipation perform the various acts of sacrifice and penance, and the various acts of gift, without expectation of fruit, after (saying) 'Tad[5].' 'Sat' is employed to express existence and goodness; and likewise, O son of P*ri*thâ! the word 'Sat' is used to express an auspicious act. Constancy in

[1] The fruit of which is uncertain or perishable.

[2] Heaven &c. as a reward for liberality.

[3] I.e. the Brahman, according to *S*rîdhara.

[4] Cf. Âpastamba, p. 21 (p. 49 in this series). Nîlaka*nth*a cites texts to show that this and the other two words are used to designate the Brahman. The texts are from the Taittirîya, Aitareya, and *Kh*ândogya-upanishads.

[5] Nîlaka*nth*a says, 'after "Tad"' means considering the act and all are Brahman, and cites p. 61 supra.

(making) sacrifices, penances, and gifts, is called 'Sat;' and (all) action, too, of which that[1] is the object, is also called 'Sat.' Whatever oblation is offered, whatever is given, whatever penance is performed, and whatever is done, without faith[2], that, O son of Prithâ! is called 'Asat,' and that is nought, both after death and here[3].

Chapter XVIII.

Arguna said:

O you of mighty arms! O Hrishîkesa! O destroyer of Kesin! I wish to know the truth about renunciation and abandonment distinctly.

The Deity said:

By renunciation the sages understand the rejection of actions done with desires. The wise call the abandonment of the fruit of all actions (by the name) abandonment. Some wise men say, that action should be abandoned as being full of evil; and others, that the actions of sacrifice, gift, and penance

[1] I.e. either the Brahman itself, or sacrifice, penance, and gift.

[2] Cf. Sutta Nipâta, p. 69.

[3] The meaning of this whole passage seems to be that these three words, which designate the Brahman, have distinct uses, as specified. 'Om,' says Nilakantha, is employed whether the action is done with any special desire or not. Those who study the Brahman there means 'study the Vedas.' 'Tad' is employed in case of actions without desires only. 'Sat' is employed, according to Sankara, in case of existence, such as the birth of a first son; 'goodness,' the reclamation of a bad man; 'auspicious acts,' marriage, &c. The intelligent use of these terms as here specified is said to cure any defects in the actions, the various classes of which are mentioned before.

should not be abandoned. As to that abandonment, O best of the descendants of Bharata! listen to my decision; for abandonment, O bravest of men! is described (to be) threefold. The actions of sacrifice, gift, and penance should not be abandoned; they must needs be performed; for sacrifices, gifts, and penances are means of sanctification to the wise. But even these actions, O son of P*ri*thâ! should be performed, abandoning attachment and fruit; such is my excellent and decided opinion. The renunciation of prescribed action is not proper. Its abandonment through delusion [1] is described as of the quality of darkness. When a man abandons action, merely as being troublesome, through fear of bodily affliction, he does not obtain the fruit [2] of abandonment by making (such) passionate abandonment. When prescribed action is performed, O Ar*g*una! abandoning attachment and fruit also, merely because it ought to be performed, that is deemed (to be) a good abandonment. He who is possessed of abandonment [3], being full of goodness, and talented, and having his doubts destroyed, is not averse from unpleasant actions, is not attached to pleasant [4] (ones). Since no embodied (being) can abandon actions without exception [5], he is said to be possessed of abandonment, who abandons the fruit of action. The threefold fruit of action, agreeable, disagreeable, and mixed, accrues after death to those who are not possessed of abandonment, but never to

[1] Without delusion no such abandonment will occur.

[2] Namely, final emancipation, by means of purity of heart.

[3] I.e. who has the frame of mind necessary for a good abandonment.

[4] Such as bathing at midday in summer.

[5] Cf. p. 53 supra.

renouncers[1]. Learn from me, O you of mighty arms! these five causes of the completion of all actions, declared in the Sânkhya system[2]. The substratum, the agent likewise, the various sorts of organs, and the various and distinct movements, and with these the deities, too, as the fifth. Whatever action, just or otherwise, a man performs with his body, speech, and mind, these five are its causes. That being so, the undiscerning man, who being of an unrefined understanding, sees the agent in the immaculate self, sees not (rightly)[3]. He who has no feeling of egoism[4], and whose mind is not tainted, even though he kills (all) these people, kills not, is not fettered[5] (by the action). Knowledge[6], the object of knowledge, the knower—threefold is the prompting to action. The instrument, the action, the agent, thus in brief is action threefold. Knowledge and action and agent

[1] The original is sannyâsî, but *S*rîdhara is probably right in taking it to mean one who has command of 'abandonment.' *S*ankara and Madhusûdana, however, take the word in its ordinary sense of 'ascetic.' What follows explains, says *S*rîdhara, why 'the fruit does not accrue to renouncers.'

[2] *S*ankara and Madhusûdana say this means Vedânta-*s*âstra. *S*rîdhara suggests also the alternative Sânkhya-*s*âstra. Substratum = the body, in which desire, aversion, &c. are manifested; agent = one who egoistically thinks himself the doer of actions; organs = senses of perception, action, &c.; movements = of the vital breaths in the body; deities = the deities which preside over the eye and other senses (as to this cf. Aitareya-upanishad, p. 45; Prasna, pp. 216, 217; Mun*d*aka, p. 314; Aitareya-âra*n*yaka, pp. 88–270; and Max Müller's Hibbert Lectures, p. 204, note). [3] Cf. p. 106.

[4] Egoism = the feeling that he is the doer of the action; taint = the feeling that the fruit of the action must accrue to him.

[5] Cf. p. 45, and Dhammapada, stanza 294.

[6] Knowledge, i.e. that something is a means to what is desired; object is the means; the knower is he who has this knowledge. When these co-exist we have action. The instrument = senses, &c.

are declared in the enumeration of qualities[1] (to be) of three classes only, according to the difference of qualities. Hear about these also as they really are. Know that knowledge to be good, by which (a man) sees one entity, inexhaustible, and not different in all things (apparently) different[2] (from one another). Know that knowledge to be passionate, which is (based) on distinctions[3] (between different entities), which sees in all things various entities of different kinds. And that is described as dark, which clings to one created (thing) only as everything, which is devoid of reason, devoid of real principle, and insignificant[4]. That action is called good, which is prescribed, which is devoid of attachment, which is not done from (motives of) affection or aversion, (and which is done) by one not wishing for the fruit. That is described as passionate, which (occasions) much trouble, is performed by one who wishes for objects of desire, or one who is full of egotism[5]. The action is called dark, which is commenced through delusion, without regard to consequences, loss, injury, or strength[6]. That agent is called good, who has cast off attachment, who is free from egotistic talk, who is possessed of courage and energy, and unaffected by success or ill-success. That agent is called passionate, who is full of affections[7],

[1] The system of Kapila.

[2] Cf. p. 104.

[3] Cf. Ka*th*opanishad, p. 129.

[4] Reason=argument in support; real principle=truth, view of things as they are; insignificant, i.e. in comprehensiveness.

[5] I.e. 'pride of learning,' &c., *S*ankara; 'egoism,' Râmânuga.

[6] Consequences=good or evil resulting; loss=of wealth or strength; injury=to others; strength=one's own capacity.

[7] I.e. 'for children,' &c., according to *S*rîdhara; 'for the action,' according to others.

who wishes for the fruit of actions, who is covetous, cruel, and impure, and feels joy and sorrow. That agent is called dark, who is without application[1], void of discernment, headstrong, crafty, malicious, lazy, melancholy, and slow. Now hear, O Dhana*ñg*aya! the threefold division of intelligence[2] and courage, according to qualities, which I am about to declare exhaustively and distinctly. That intelligence, O son of P*ri*thâ! is good which understands action and inaction[3], what ought to be done and what ought not to be done, danger and the absence of danger, emancipation and bondage. That intelligence, O son of P*ri*thâ! is passionate, by which one imperfectly understands piety and impiety, what ought to be done and also what ought not to be done. That intelligence, O son of P*ri*thâ! is dark, which shrouded by darkness, understands impiety (to be) piety, and all things incorrectly. That courage, O son of P*ri*thâ! is good courage, which is unswerving[4], and by which one controls the operations of the mind, breath, and senses, through abstraction. But, O Ar*g*una! that courage is passionate, by which one adheres to piety, lust, and wealth[5], and through attachment[6] wishes,

---

[1] I.e. attention to work; melancholy=always desponding and wanting in energy.

[2] The nature of the faculty of understanding; and courage is the firmness of that faculty.

[3] See p. 115. *Sañkara* takes these to mean the 'paths' of action and knowledge, and Nîlaka*nth*a takes the next expression to mean that which is constant and that which is not constant—nitya, anitya.

[4] Always co-existing with mental abstraction and supporting it.

[5] Three of the aims of mankind, the highest being final emancipation. In the view of the Gîtâ, piety, leading only to heaven, is of doubtful benefit.

[6] I.e. to the action for attaining them, in the belief that one is

O son of P*ri*thâ! for the fruit. That courage is dark, O son of P*ri*thâ! by which an undiscerning man does not give up sleep, fear, sorrow, despondency, and folly. Now, O chief of the descendants of Bharata! hear from me about the three sorts of happiness. That happiness is called good, in which one is pleased after repetition[1] (of enjoyment), and reaches the close of all misery, which is like poison first and comparable to nectar in the long run, and which is produced from a clear knowledge of the self[2]. That happiness is called passionate, which (flows) from contact between the senses and their objects, and which is at first comparable to nectar and in the long run like poison. That happiness is described as dark, which arises from sleep, laziness, heedlessness, which deludes the self, both at first and in its consequences. There is no entity either on earth or in heaven among the gods, which is free from these three qualities born of nature. The duties of Brâhma*n*as, Kshatriyas, and Vai*s*yas, and of *S*ûdras, too, O terror of your foes! are distinguished according to the qualities born of nature[3]. Tranquillity[4], restraint of the senses, penance, purity, forgiveness, straightforwardness, also knowledge, experience, and belief (in a future world), this is the natural duty of Brâhma*n*as. Valour, glory, courage,

---

the doer of it; the 'fruit' scil. of the action performed with an eye to the three things named.

[1] Not at once, as in the case of sensuous pleasures.

[2] Cf. p. 51. The original has also been rendered by 'tranquillity of one's own mind.'

[3] Cf. p. 59.

[4] I.e. resulting from control of the mind, purity here is both external and internal. And see p. 119.

dexterity[1], not slinking away from battle, gifts, exercise of lordly power[2], this is the natural duty of Kshatriyas. Agriculture, tending cattle, trade, (this) is the natural duty of Vaisyas. And the natural duty of *S*ûdras, too, consists in service. (Every) man intent on his own respective duties obtains perfection[3]. Listen, now, how one intent on one's own duty obtains perfection. Worshipping, by (the performance of) his own duty, him from whom all things proceed, and by whom all this is permeated, a man obtains perfection. One's duty, though defective, is better than another's duty well performed[4]. Performing the duty prescribed by nature, one does not incur sin. O son of Kuntî! one should not abandon a natural duty though tainted with evil; for all actions are enveloped by evil, as fire by smoke[5]. One who is self-restrained, whose understanding is unattached everywhere, from whom affections have departed, obtains the supreme perfection of freedom from action[6] by renunciation. Learn from me, only in brief, O son of Kuntî! how one who has obtained perfection attains the Brahman, which is the highest culmination of knowledge. A man possessed of a pure understanding, controlling his self by courage, discarding sound and other objects of sense, casting off

---

[1] I.e. in battle, Nîlaka*nth*a seems to say. *S*aṅkara says it means ready resource whenever occasion arises.

[2] I.e. 'power to restrain people from going astray,' Nîlaka*nth*a.

[3] Eligibility for the path of knowledge.

[4] Cf. p. 56.

[5] Cf. p. 121; the evil appears to be the quality of 'fettering' the soul.

[6] *S*rîdhara compares p. 65 (V, 13) and distinguishes this from p. 64 (V, 8 seq.) *S*aṅkara says the perfection here spoken of is emancipation, and it is obtained by true knowledge.

affection and aversion; who frequents clean places, who eats little, whose speech, body, and mind are restrained, who is always intent on meditation and mental abstraction[1], and has recourse to unconcern, who abandoning egoism[2], stubbornness, arrogance, desire, anger, and (all) belongings, has no (thought that this or that is) mine, and who is tranquil, becomes fit for assimilation with the Brahman. Thus reaching the Brahman[3], and with a tranquil self, he grieves not, wishes not; but being alike to all beings, obtains the highest devotion to me. By (that) devotion he truly understands who I am and how great. And then understanding me truly, he forthwith enters into my (essence). Even performing all actions, always depending on me, he, through my favour, obtains the imperishable and eternal seat. Dedicating in thought[4] all actions to me, be constantly given up to me, (placing) your thoughts on me, through recourse to mental abstraction. (Placing) your thoughts on me, you will cross over all difficulties by my favour. But if you will not listen through egotism[5], you will be ruined. If entertaining egotism, you think that you may not fight, vain, indeed, is that resolution of yours. Nature[6] will constrain you. That, O son of Kuntî! which through delusion you do not wish to do, you will do involuntarily,

---

[1] Abstraction is concentrated and exclusive meditation, *S*ankara. The other commentators take dhyânayoga as meditation simply,—as treated of in chapter VI, says Nîlaka*nt*h*a.

[2] See p. 52.

[3] I. e. comprehending his identity with the Brahman.

[4] Cf. p. 55.

[5] Pride of learning and cleverness, or of piety. See p. 124, note 5.

[6] The nature of a Kshatriya, *S*ankara.

tied down by your own duty, flowing from your nature. The lord, O Arguna! is seated in the region of the heart[1] of all beings, turning round all beings (as though) mounted on a machine, by his delusion. With him, O descendant of Bharata! seek shelter in every way[2]; by his favour you will obtain the highest tranquillity, the eternal seat. Thus have I declared to you the knowledge more mysterious than any mystery. Ponder over it thoroughly, and then act as you like. Once more, listen to my excellent words—most mysterious of all. Strongly I like you, therefore I will declare what is for your welfare. On me (place) your mind, become my devotee, sacrifice to me, reverence me, and you will certainly come to me. I declare to you truly, you are dear to me. Forsaking all duties[3], come to me as (your) sole refuge. I will release you from all sins. Be not grieved. This[4] you should never declare to one who performs no penance[5], who is not a devotee[6], nor to one who does not wait on (some preceptor)[7], nor yet to one who calumniates me. He who, with the highest devotion[8] to me, will proclaim this supreme mystery among my devotees, will come to me, freed from (all) doubts. No one

---

[1] *S*vetâsvatara-upanishad, pp. 333–345; Ka*th*opanishad, p. 157.

[2] Cf. p. 114; by thought, word, and deed.

[3] Of caste or order, such as Agnihotra and so forth.

[4] All that has been taught in the Gîtâ.

[5] *S*ridhara renders this to mean, 'who performs no pious acts.'

[6] I. e. of God and a preceptor. Cf. last stanza of *S*vetâsvataropanishad.

[7] Cf. p. 62. *S*aṅkara says all these elements must co-exist to give eligibility.

[8] I. e. belief that in disseminating it, he is serving me. Cf. Ka*th*opanishad, p. 120.

amongst men is superior to him in doing what is dear to me. And there will never be another on earth dearer to me than he. And he who will study this holy dialogue of ours, will, such is my opinion, have offered to me the sacrifice of knowledge [1]. And the man, also, who with faith and without carping will listen (to this), will be freed (from sin), and attain to the holy regions of those who perform pious acts [2]. Have you listened to this, O son of P*ri*thâ! with a mind (fixed) on (this) one point only? Has your delusion (caused) by ignorance been destroyed, O Dhana*ñg*aya?

Ar*g*una said:

Destroyed is my delusion; by your favour, O undegraded one! I (now) recollect [3] myself. I stand freed from doubts [4]. I will do your bidding.

Sa*ñg*aya said:

Thus did I hear this dialogue between Vâsudeva and the high-minded son of P*ri*thâ, (a dialogue) wonderful and causing the hair to stand on end. By the favour of Vyâsa, I heard this highest mystery, (this) devotion [5], from K*ri*sh*n*a himself, the lord of the possessors of mystic power, who proclaimed it in person. O king! remembering and (again) remembering this wonderful and holy dialogue of Ke*s*ava and Ar*g*una, I rejoice over and over again. And remembering and (again) remembering that

---

[1] Which is the best of sacrifices; see p. 62.

[2] Cf. p. 72.

[3] I.e. understand my real essence, what I am, &c.

[4] As to whether the battle was right or not.

[5] The work is so called, as it refers to devotion.

excessively wonderful form of Hari also, great is my amazement, O king! and I rejoice over and over again. Wherever (is) K*ri*sh*n*a, the lord of the possessors of mystic power, wherever (is) the (great) archer, the son of P*ri*thâ, there in my opinion (are) fortune, victory, prosperity[1], and eternal justice.

[1] Prosperity is the greater development of fortune.

SANATSU*G*ÂTÎYA.

INTRODUCTION

TO

SANATSU*G*ÂTÎYA.

THE Sanatsu*g*âtîya is, like the Bhagavadgîtâ, one of the numerous episodes of the Mahâbhârata[1]. It is true, that it has never commanded anything like that unbounded veneration which has always been paid in India to the Bhagavadgîtâ. Still it is sometimes studied even in our days, and it has had the high distinction of being commented on by the great leader of the modern Vedântic school—*S*aṅkarâ*k*ârya[2]. The Sanatsu*g*âtîya purports to be a dialogue mainly between Sanatsu*g*âta on the one side and Dh*ri*tarâsh*t*ra on the other. Sanatsu*g*âta, from whom it takes its name, is said to be identical with Sanatkumâra, a name not unfamiliar to students of our Upanishad literature. And Dh*ri*tarâsh*t*ra is the old father of those Kauravas who formed one of the belligerent parties in the bellum plusquam civile which is recorded in the Mahâbhârata. The connexion of this particular episode with the main current of the narrative of that epos is one of the loosest possible character—much looser, for instance, than that of the Bhagavadgîtâ. As regards the latter, it can fairly be contended that it is in accordance with poetical justice for Ar*g*una to feel despondent and unwilling to engage in battle, after actual sight of 'teachers, fathers, sons,' and all the rest of them, arrayed in opposition to him; and that therefore it was necessary for the poet to adduce some specific explanation as to how Ar*g*una was ultimately enabled to get over such natural scruples. But as regards the Sanatsu*g*âtîya, even such a contention as this

---

[1] Mahâbhârata, Udyoga Parvan, Adhyâya 41–46.

[2] Mâdhavâ*k*ârya, in speaking of *S*aṅkara's works, describes him as having commented on the Sanatsu*g*âtîya, which is 'far from evil (persons,' [asatsudûram]. *S*aṅkara-vi*g*aya, chapter VI, stanza 62.

can have no place. For this is how the matter stands. In the course of the negotiations for an amicable arrangement[1] between the Pâ*nd*avas and the Kauravas, Sañ*g*aya, on one occasion, came back to Dh*ri*tarâsh*t*ra with a message from the Pâ*nd*avas. When he saw Dh*ri*tarâsh*t*ra, however, he said that he would deliver the message in the public assembly of the Kauravas the next morning, and went away after pronouncing a severe censure on Dh*ri*tarâsh*t*ra for his conduct. The suspense thus caused was a source of much vexation to the old man, and so he sent for Vidura, in order, as he expresses it, that Vidura might by his discourse assuage the fire that was raging within him. Vidura accordingly appears, and enters upon an elaborate prelection concerning matters spiritual, or, perhaps, more accurately quasi-spiritual, and at the outset of the Sanatsu*g*âtîya he is supposed to have reached a stage where, as being born a *S*ûdra, he hesitates to proceed. After some discussion of this point, between Vidura and Dh*ri*tarâsh*t*ra, it is determined to call in the aid of Sanatsu*g*âta, to explain the spiritual topics which Vidura felt a delicacy in dealing with; and Sanatsu*g*âta is accordingly introduced on the scene in a way not unusual in our epic and purâ*n*ic literature, viz. by Vidura engaging in some mystic process of meditation, in response to which Sanatsu*g*âta appears. He is received then with all due formalities, and after he has had some rest, as our poem takes care to note, he is catechised by Dh*ri*tarâsh*t*ra; and with one or two exceptions, all the verses which constitute the Sanatsu*g*âtîya are Sanatsu*g*âta's answers to Dh*ri*tarâsh*t*ra's questions[2].

This brief statement of the scheme of this part of the Mahâbhârata shows, as already pointed out, that the connexion of the Sanatsu*g*âtiya with the central story of that epic is very loose indeed; and that it might have been entirely omitted without occasioning any æsthetical or other defect. And therefore, although there is nothing positive

[1] See p. 3 supra.

[2] After this dialogue is over, the dawn breaks, and Dh*ri*tarâsh*t*ra and the Kaurava princes meet in general assembly.

tending to prove the Sanatsugâtîya to be a later addition to the original epos, still the misgivings which are often entertained upon such points may well, in this case, be stronger than in the case of the Bhagavadgîtâ. The text, too, of the Sanatsugâtîya is not preserved in nearly so satisfactory a condition as that of the Gîtâ. I have had before me, in settling my text, the editions of the Mahâbhârata respectively printed and published at Bombay [1], Calcutta, and Madras, and three MSS., one of which was most kindly and readily placed at my disposal by my friend Professor Râmkrishna Gopâl Bhândârkar; the second by another friend, Professor Âbâgî Vishnu Kâthavate; and the third was a copy made for me at Sâgar in the Central Provinces, through the good offices of a third friend, Mr. Vâman Mahâdeva Kolhatkar. The copy lent me by Professor Bhândârkar comes from Puna, and that lent by Professor Kâthavate also from Puna. This last, as well as the Sâgar copy, and the edition printed at Madras, contains the commentary of Sankarâkârya. And the text I have adopted is that which is indicated by the commentary as the text which its author had before him. But the several copies of the commentary differ so much from one another, that it is still a matter of some doubt with me, whether I have got accurately the text which Sankara commented upon. For instance, the Sâgar copy entirely omits chapter V, while the other copies not only give the text of that chapter, but also a commentary upon it which calls itself Sankarâkârya's commentary [2]. Again, take the stanzas which stand within brackets at pp. 167, 168 [3] of our translation. There is in none of the copies we have, any commentary of Sankarâkârya on them. And yet the stanzas exist in the text of the Mahâbhârata as given in those copies which do contain Sankara's commentary. The matter is evidently one for further investigation. I have not, however, thought it

[1] This contains Nîlakantha's commentary, but his text avowedly includes the text of Sankara, and verses and readings contained in more modern copies.

[2] The commentary on the sixth chapter, however, takes up the thread from the end of the fourth chapter.

[3] See p. 182, where one of the lines recurs.

absolutely necessary to make such an investigation for the purposes of the present translation. But to be on the safe side, I have retained in the translation everything which is to be found in those copies of the Sanatsugâtîya which also contain *S*aṅkara's commentary. As to other stanzas—and there are some of this description—which other MSS. or commentators vouch for, but of which no trace is to be found in the MSS. containing *S*aṅkara's commentary [1], I have simply omitted them.

These facts show that, in the case of the Sanatsugâtîya. the materials for a trustworthy historical account of the work are not of a very satisfactory character. The materials for ascertaining its date and position in Sanskrit literature are, indeed, so scanty, that poor as we have seen the materials for the Bhagavadgîtâ to be, they must be called superlatively rich as compared with those we have now to deal with. As regards external evidence on the points now alluded to, the first and almost the last fact falling under that head, is the fact of the work being quoted from and commented upon by *S*aṅkarâ*k*ârya. In his commentary on the *S*vetâ*s*vatara-upanishad [2], *S*aṅkara cites the passage about the flamingo at p. 189, introducing it with the words, 'And in the Sanatsugâta also.' In the same [3] commentary some other passages from the Sanatsugâtîya are also quoted, but without naming the work except as a Sm*ri*ti, and mixing up together verses from different parts of the work.

This is really all the external evidence, that I am aware of, touching the date of the Sanatsugâtîya. There is, however, one other point, which it is desirable to notice, though not, perhaps, so much because it is of any very great value in itself, as because it may hereafter become useful, should further research into the Mahâbhârata and other works yield the requisite information. There are, then, eight stanzas in the thirty-sixth, thirty-seventh, thirty-ninth, and fortieth chapters of the Udyoga Parvan of the Mahâbhâ-

[1] See note 1, p. 137.

[2] P. 283.

[3] P. 252. See, too, *S*ârîraka Bhâshya, p. 818.

rata (the Sanatsu*g*âtîya commencing at the forty-first chapter), seven of which are quoted in the Pa*ñk*atantra [1], and the eighth in the Mahâbhâshya [2] of Pata*ñg*ali. Of course, it almost goes without saying, that neither the Pa*ñk*atantra nor the Mahâbhâshya mentions the source from which they derive the verses in question. But I do not think it unallowable to make the provisional assumption, that they were derived from the Mahâbhârata, so long as we cannot produce any other, and more likely, source. It is true, that Professor Weber has, in another connexion, impugned the cogency of this argument. He seems to think, that the probability—in the case he was actually dealing with—of the Râmâya*n*a having borrowed from the Mahâbhâshya, is quite as strong as the probability of the Mahâbhâshya having borrowed from the Râmâya*n*a [3]. And doubtless, he would by parity of reason contend, in the case before us, that the probabilities, as between the Mahâbhârata on the one hand, and the Mahâbhâshya and the Pa*ñk*atantra on the other, bear the same mutual relation. I cannot accept this view. I am not now concerned to discuss the merits of the conclusion in support of which Professor Weber has advanced this argument [4]. I am only considering, how far it affects the question now before us. And as to that question, I may say, that the Pa*ñk*atantra expressly introduces the stanzas now under consideration with some such expression as, 'For it has been said,' indicating clearly that it was there quoting the words of another [5]. And so, too, does the Mahâbhâshya,

[1] Cf. Kosegarten's Pa*ñk*atantra, p. 28 (I, 28, Bombay S. C. ed.), with Udyoga Parvan, chap. XL, st. 7 (Bombay ed.); Pa*ñk*atantra, pp. 112 and 209 (II, 10; IV, 5, Bombay ed.), with Udyoga Parvan, chap. XXXVIII, 9; p. 35 I, 37, Bombay ed.) with chap. XXXVI, st. 34; p. 140 (II, 40, Bombay ed.) with chap. XXXVII, st. 15; p. 160 (III, 62, Bombay ed.) with chap. XXXVII, st. 17, 18; p. 106 (II, 2, Bombay ed.) with chap. XXXVI, st. 59.

[2] Udyoga Parvan, chap. XXXVIII, st. 1, and Mahâbhâshya VI, 1–4, p. 35 (Banâras ed.)

[3] See Indian Antiquary IV, 247. The parallel from Mâdhava which Professor Weber adduces is quite inconclusive, and as far as it goes appears to me to militate against the Professor's own view.

[4] I may, however, admit at once, that I ought not to have expressed myself as strongly as I did in the note which Professor Weber criticises.

[5] See p. 203 infra.

where the passage we refer to runs as follows: '(It is) laid down, (that there is) a sin in one of tender age not rising to receive (an elderly person), and (that there is) merit in rising to receive. How? Thus, "The life-winds of a youth depart upwards, when an elderly man approaches (him). By rising to receive (him), and salutation, he obtains them again."' It appears to me, that the indications of this being a quotation in the Bhâshya are very strong. But apart from that, I do demur to the proposition, that the probabilities are equal, of a work like the Mahâbhârata or Râmâyana borrowing a verse from the Mahâbhâshya, and vice versa. It appears to me perfectly plain, I own, that the probability of a grammatical work like the Bhâshya borrowing a verse from a standard work like the Bhârata or Râmâyana for purposes of illustration is very much the stronger of the two. And this, quite independently of any inquiry as to whether the Bhâshya does or does not show other indications of acquaintance with the Bhârata or the Râmâyana.

If these arguments are correct, it seems to me that they carry us thus far in our present investigation—namely, that we may now say, that we have reason to believe some parts, at all events, of the thirty-sixth, thirty-seventh, thirty-eighth, and fortieth chapters of the Udyoga Parvan of the Mahâbhârata to have probably been in existence prior to the sixth century A.C.[1]; and that some parts of the thirty-seventh chapter were probably extant in the time of Patañgali, viz. the second century B.C.[2] Now, internal evidence does not yield any indications tending to show that the several chapters here referred to must have been prior in time to the chapters composing the Sanatsugâtîya, which come so soon after them in the Mahâbhârata. On the contrary, it is not too much to maintain, that to a certain extent the style and language of the Sanatsugâtîya is, if anything, rather indicative of its priority in time over the five chapters immediately preceding it. And, therefore, so far as this argument goes, it enables us—provisionally only, it must be

[1] See p. 29 supra. [2] See p. 32 supra.

remembered—to fix the second century B.C. as a terminus ad quem for the date of the Sanatsugâtîya.

This is all the external evidence available for a discussion of the question—when the Sanatsugâtîya was composed. We now turn to the internal evidence. Standing by itself, internal evidence is not, in my opinion, of much cogency in any case. Still in ascertaining, as best we can, the history of our ancient literature, even this species of evidence is not to be despised; it must only be used and received with caution. Under this head, then, we may note first the persons who are supposed to take part in the dialogue. Sanatsugâta[1]—or Sanatkumâra—as already pointed out, is a name already familiar to the readers of one of our older Upanishads—the *Kh*ândogya. Dh*ri*tarâsh*t*ra is not known in the Upanishads, but he is an important personage in the epic literature. And it is to be remarked, that his character as disclosed in the Sanatsugâtîya is not at all similar to that which has attached itself to his name, alike in the later literature of our country, and in that popular opinion which was probably formed by this later literature. In the dialogue before us, he figures as an earnest inquirer after truth; he is described as the 'talented king Dh*ri*tarâsh*t*ra;' and is addressed by Sanatsugâta as, 'O acute sir!' 'O learned person!' True it is, that Nîlaka*nt*ha in one place, as we have noticed in our note there[2], endeavours to bring out the later view of Dh*ri*tarâsh*t*ra's character[3]; but it seems to me that that endeavour, based as it is on a forced and far-fetched interpretation of a single word in our poem, is an unsuccessful one. None of the questions, which Dh*ri*tarâsh*t*ra puts to Sanatsugâta in the course of their dialogue, indicates the avaricious old man who wished to deprive his innocent nephews of their just rights in the interests of his own wicked and misguided sons. They rather indicate the bona fide student of spiritual lore, and thus point to what is, perhaps, an earlier view of Dh*ri*tarâsh*t*ra's character.

---

[1] See Hall's Sâṅkhyasâra, preface, pp. 14, 15. [2] P. 151, note 2.

[3] Nîlaka*nt*ha himself, however, treats Dh*ri*tarâsh*t*ra's question later on as showing that he had attained indifference to worldly concerns. That question does not occur in *Sa*ṅkara's text, but is given at p. 158 infra.

If we look next to the general style of this poem, we find that it has none of that elaboration which marks what I have called the age of Kâvyas and Nâ*t*akas. The remarks on this topic in the Introduction to the Gîtâ apply pretty accurately to this work also. We observe here the same paucity of long-drawn compounds, the same absence of merely ornamental adjectives, the same absence of figures and tropes[1]; in one word, the same directness and simplicity of style. Furthermore, there is a somewhat greater want of finish about the syntax of our poem than there is even in the Gîtâ. Such constructions as we find inter alia at chapter II, stanza 2, or 25, or at chapter III, stanza 14, or chapter IV, stanza 12, or in the early verses of the last chapter, indicate a period in the history of the language, when probably the regulations of syntax were not quite thoroughly established in practice.

If we turn to the metre of the poem, an analogous phenomenon strikes us there. Similar irregularities in the collocation of long and short syllables, similar superfluities and deficiencies of syllables, meet us in the Sanatsu*g*âtîya and the Bhagavadgîtâ. And in the former work, as in the latter, the irregularities are less observable in the Anush*t*ubh[2] than in the other metres used. Probably the explanation, apart from the great elasticity of that metre, is that the Anush*t*ubh had been more used, and had in consequence become comparatively more settled in its scheme even in practical composition.

Looking now more particularly to the language of the work before us, we find one word to be of most frequent occurrence, namely, the word vai, which we have rendered 'verily.' It is not a common word in the later literature, while in the Upanishad literature we meet with great frequency, not merely vai, but the words, which I think are cognate with it, vâ and vâva. The former word, indeed,

---

[1] The five similes which occur, and which are nearly all that occur, in the poem, are the very primitive ones—of the hunter, of water on grass, the tiger of straw, death eating men like a tiger, dogs eating what is vomited, a branch of a tree and the moon, and birds and their nests.

[2] Cf. as to this the N*ri*si*m*ha Tâpinî, p. 105.

appears to me to stand in some passages of the Upanishads for vai by euphonic alterations. Thus in the passage tva*m* vâ aham asmi bhagavo devate, aha*m* vai tvam asi, it is difficult not to suppose that the vâ of the first part of the sentence is the same word as the vai of the second part, only altered according to the rules of Sandhi in Sanskrit.

A second point of similarity between the language of the Upanishads and that of the Sanatsu*g*âtîya is to be found in the phrase, 'He who knows this becomes immortal.' This sentence, or one of like signification, is, as is well known, of common occurrence in the Upanishads and in the Brâhma*n*as. In the Bhagavadgîtâ, the verses towards the end, which come after K*r*ish*n*a's summing-up of his instruction. seem to be of a somewhat analogous, though in some respects different, nature. And in the Purâ*n*as we meet sometimes with elaborate passages extolling the merits of a particular rite, or a particular pilgrimage, and so forth. This form of the Phala*s*ruti, as it is called, appears to have been developed in process of time from the minute germ existing in the Brâhma*n*as and the Upanishads. In the Sanatsu*g*âtîya, however, we are almost at the beginning of those developments; indeed, the form before us is identically the same as that which we see in the works where it is first met with. It is a short sentence, which, though complete in itself, still appears merely at the end of another passage, and almost as a part of such other passage.

There is one other point of a kindred nature which it may be well to notice here. As in the Gîtâ, so in the Sanatsu*g*âtîya, we meet with a considerable number of words used in senses not familiar in the later literature. They are collected in the Index of Sanskrit words in this volume; but a few remarks on some of them will not, it is thought, be entirely out of place here. The word mârga[1]—in the sense of 'worldly life'—is rather remarkable. *S*aṅkara renders it by 'the path of sa*m*sâra' or worldly life. And he quotes as a parallel the passage from the *Kh*ândogya-

[1] I give no references here, as they can be found in the Index of Sanskrit words at the end of this volume.

upanishad which speaks of returning to the 'path.' There, however, *S*aṅkara explains it to mean the 'path by which the self returns to worldly life,' namely, from space to the wind and so forth into vegetables, and food, ultimately appearing as a fœtus. Another remarkable word is 'varga,' which occurs twice in the Sanatsu*g*âtîya. *S*aṅkara and Nîlaka*nth*a differ in their explanations of it, and Nîlaka*nth*a indeed gives two different meanings to the word in the two passages where it occurs. We may also refer here specially to utsa, *ri*tvi*g*, and matvâ. In Boehtlingk and Roth's Lexicon the only passages cited under 'utsa' are from Vedic works, except two respectively from Su*s*ruta and the Da*s*akumâra*k*arita. One passage, however, there cited, viz. Vish*n*o*h* pade parame madhva utsa*h*, is plainly the original of the passage we are now considering. As to *ri*tvi*g* in the sense it bears here, we see, I think, what was the earlier signification of that word before it settled down into the somewhat technical meaning in which it is now familiar. And matvâ in the sense of 'meditating upon' is to be found in the Upanishads, but not, I think, in any work of the classical literature. These words, therefore, seem to indicate that the Sanatsu*g*âtîya was composed at a stage in the development of the Sanskrit language which is a good deal earlier than the stage which we see completely reached in the classical literature.

Coming now to the matter of the Sanatsu*g*âtîya, it appears to me, that we there see indications pointing in a general way to the same conclusion as that which we have here arrived at. There is, in the first place, a looseness and want of rigid system in the mode of handling the subject, similar to that which we have already observed upon as characterising the Bhagavadgîtâ. There is no obvious bond of connexion joining together the various subjects discussed, nor are those subjects themselves treated after any very scientific or rigorous method. Again, if the fourth chapter is a genuine part of the Sanatsu*g*âtîya, we have an elaborate repetition in one part, of what has been said in another part of the work, with only a few variations in words, and perhaps fewer still in signification. As, however, I am not at present prepared to stand finally by the genuineness of that chapter, I do not consider it desirable to further labour this argument than to point out, that similar repetitions, on a smaller scale, perhaps, are not uncommon in our older literature[1].

Coming now to the manner in which the Vedas are spoken of in the work before us, there are, we find, one or two noteworthy circumstances proper to be considered here. In the first place, we have the reference to the four Vedas together with Âkhyânas as the fifth Veda. This is in conformity with the old tradition recorded in the various works to which we have referred in our note on the passage. The mention of the Atharva-veda, which is implied in this passage, and expressly contained in another, might be regarded as some mark of a modern age. But without dwelling upon the fact, that the Atharva-veda, though probably modern as compared with the other Vedas, is still old enough to date some centuries before the Christian era[2], it must suffice to draw attention here to the fact that the *Kh*ândogya-upanishad mentions that Veda, and it is not here argued that the Sanatsu*g*âtîya is older than the *Kh*ândogya-upanishad. We have next to consider the reference to the Sâman hymns as 'vimala,' or pure. The point involved in this reference has been already sufficiently discussed in the Introduction to the Gîtâ[3]; and it is not necessary here to say more than that, of the two classes of works we have there made, the Sanatsu*g*âtîya appears from the passage under discussion to rank itself with the class which is prior in date.

The estimate of the value of the Vedas which is implied in the Sanatsu*g*âtîya appears to coincide very nearly with that which we have shown to be the estimate implied in the Bhagavadgîtâ. The Vedas are not here cast aside as useless any more than they are in the Bhagavadgîtâ. For, I do not think the word An*rik*as which occurs in one passage of the work can be regarded really as referring to those

[1] See p. 181, note 1 infra. [2] P. 19 supra. [3] Pp. 19, 20.

who entirely reject the Vedic revelation. But without going as far as that, the Sanatsugâtîya seems certainly to join the Bhagavadgîtâ in its protest against those men of extreme views, who could see nothing beyond the rites and ceremonies taught in the Vedas. A study of the Vedas is, indeed, insisted on in sundry passages of the Sanatsugâtîya. But it is equally maintained, that the performance of the ceremonies laid down in the Vedas is not the true means of final emancipation. It is maintained, that action done with any desire is a cause of bondage to worldly life; that the gods themselves are ordinary creatures who have reached a certain high position owing to the practice of the duties of Brahma*k*ârins, but that they are not only not superior to, but are really under the control of, the man who has acquired the true knowledge of the universal self. On all these points, we have opinions expressed in the Sanatsu*g*âtîya, which conclusively establish an identity of doctrine as between the Upanishads and the Bhagavadgîtâ [1] on the one hand, and the Sanatsu*g*âtîya on the other. Lastly, we have an explicit statement, that the mere study of Vedic texts avails nothing, and that sin is not to be got rid of by one who merely 'studies the *Rik* and the Ya*g*us texts, and the Sâma-veda.' It is not necessary to repeat here the chronological deductions which may be based upon this relation between the Sanatsugâtîya and the Vedas. We have already argued in the Introduction to the Bhagavadgîtâ, that such a relation points to a period of Indian religious history prior to the great movement of Gautama Buddha [2].

There is, however, this difference, perhaps, to be noted between the Gîtâ and the Sanatsu*g*âtîya—namely, that the latter work seems to afford more certain indications of the recognition, at the date of its composition, of a *G*ñânakâ*nd*a as distinguished from a Karmakâ*nd*a in the Vedas, than, we have seen, are contained in the Bhagavadgîtâ [3]. The passage, for instance, which speaks of the *Kh*andas as

[1] Cf. p. 16 supra. [2] Cf. pp. 25, 26. [3] P. 17.

referring 'of themselves' to the Brahman, and the passage which refers to an understanding of the Brahman by means of the Vedas, according to the principle of the moon and the branch—these seem rather to point to a portion of the Vedas which was regarded as giving instruction in true knowledge, as distinguished from merely laying down various sacrifices and ceremonials for special purposes. In fact, in one passage we have the germ of the whole Vedântic theory as afterwards settled. For there we are told, that sacrifices and penances are laid down as the preliminary steps towards the acquisition of true knowledge. By those sacrifices one is purified of one's sins, and then acquires a knowledge of the supreme self as described in the Vedas—which, I apprehend, must mean the Upanishads.

There is but one other point on which we need say anything further. And that is connected with the definition of a Brâhma*n*a. That definition appears to me, to point to an earlier stage in religious progress than is indicated in Âpastamba and Manu. The true Brâhma*n*a is he who is attached to the Brahman. Perhaps, this marks some little advance beyond the more general doctrine of the Gîtâ, but it is still very far short of the petrified doctrine, if I may so call it, of the later law-givers. The Brâhma*n*a has not yet degenerated into the mere receiver of fees and presents, but is still in possession of the truth.

We thus see, that the external and internal evidence bearing upon the question of the position of the Sanatsu*g*âtîya in Sanskrit literature, seems to point to nearly the same period and place for it as for the Bhagavadgîtâ. It is plain enough, that the evidence under both heads is extremely scanty and meagre. But such as it is, it appears to us to justify a provisional conclusion, that the Sanatsu*g*âtîya dates from a period prior to the rise of Buddhism, and forms part of that same movement in the religious history of ancient India of which the Gîtâ is another embodiment. More than this, we are not at present in a position to assert. To this extent, the evidence enables us, I think, to go. And we accordingly hold, that unless other and further evidence requires a reversal of this judgment, the Sanatsugâtîya may be treated as a work nearly contemporary with the Bhagavadgîtâ, and occupying generally the same point of view.

One word, finally, about the translation. As stated already, the text adopted is that which appears to have been before *S*ankarâ*k*ârya. And the translation follows mainly his interpretations in his commentary. Sometimes we have followed Nîlaka*nth*a, whose commentary has been consulted as well as a very incorrect copy of another commentary by one Sarva*gñ*a Nârâya*n*a, contained in the MS. from Pu*n*a lent me by Professor Bhâ*nd*ârkar. In some places even the commentators have failed to clear up obscurities, and there we have given the best translation we could suggest, indicating the difficulties. There has been an endeavour made here, as in the case of the Bhagavadgîtâ, to keep the translation as close and faithful to the text as the exigencies of the English language permitted. The exegetical notes are mostly taken from the commentaries, even where the name of the commentator is not specified; while the references to parallel passages have been collected, mostly by myself, in the same way as in the case of the Bhagavadgîtâ.

SANATSUGÂTÎYA.

CHAPTER I.

Dhritarâshtra said:

If, O Vidura! there is anything not (yet) said by you in (your) discourse, then do impart it to me who wish to hear, for you have spoken marvellous (things).

Vidura said:

O Dhritarâshtra! the ancient youth Sanatsugâta, (otherwise called) Sanâtana[1], who declared that death exists not—he, O descendant of Bharata! the best of all talented men, will explain all the doubts of your mind, both those (which are) secret[2], and those openly declared.

Dhritarâshtra said:

What, do you not yourself know more about this (subject), that Sanâtana should explain (it) to me? Explain (it) yourself, O Vidura! if there is any remnant of intelligence (left) in you.

---

[1] So Nîlakantha. *Sankara* says Sanatsugâta is Sanatkumâra, and the component parts of the name he paraphrases by 'born from Brahman.' For Sanâtana, see Brihadâranyaka, p. 506, and note 1, p. 141 supra.

[2] I.e. relating to subjects which may be freely discussed by all, and those which may not. Nîlakantha adopts a different reading, which he interprets to mean 'doctrines exoteric and esoteric,' e.g. self-restraint, &c., and the acquisition of mystic power, &c., respectively. The expression 'doubts of the mind' occurs, however, further on.

Vidura said:

I am born of a *S*ûdra womb, and do not like to say more than what (I have said). But the intelligence of that youth, I believe to be eternal[1]. He who has come of a Brâhma*n*a womb, even though he may proclaim a great mystery, does not thereby become liable to the censure of the gods. Therefore do I say this to you.

Dh*ri*tarâsh*t*ra said:

Do you, O Vidura! speak to the ancient Sanâtana for me, so that there may be a meeting even here, between (myself in) this body (and him).

Vai*s*ampâyana[2] said:

(Then) Vidura meditated on that sage whose vows are laudable[3]. And he, too, O descendant of Bharata! knowing of such meditation, made his appearance. And he[4], too, received him with the ceremonies prescribed in the ordinances. After he had been comfortably seated, and had taken rest, Vidura then spoke to him: 'Venerable sir! there is some doubt in Dh*ri*tarâsh*t*ra's mind, which cannot

---

[1] I.e., I suppose, never-failing, and such as can deal with all sorts of topics. Sanatkumâra, it need scarcely be stated, is the teacher of Nârada in the famous dialogue in the *Kh*ândogyopanishad, p. 473.

[2] Vai*s*ampâyana is the narrator of the grand story of which pieces like the present form parts.

[3] The reading is sometimes different, so as to mean 'of rigid vows,' as at Gîtâ, p. 61 supra.

[4] The pronouns here are too numerous. Does 'he' here refer to Dh*ri*tarâsh*t*ra? Vidura seems more likely, though the express mention of him in the next sentence might be treated as pointing the other way.

be explained by me. Do you be pleased to explain (it) to him. Hearing it (explained), this lord of men may cross beyond all misery, so that gain and loss [1], (what is) agreeable and (what is) odious, old age and death, fear and vindictiveness, hunger and thirst, frenzy and worldly greatness, disgust and also laziness, desire and wrath, ruin and prosperity, may not trouble him.'

Chapter II.

Vaisampâyana said:

Then the talented king, Dhritarâshtra, bowed [2] to those words uttered by Vidura, and, in a secluded place [3], interrogated Sanatsugâta regarding the highest knowledge [4], wishing to become (a) high-souled (man) [5].

Dhritarâshtra said:

O Sanatsugâta! which of the two is correct, your teaching [6], about which I have heard, that death exists not, or that [7] the gods and demons practised

[1] Comp. Gîtâ passim; disgust, scil. that resulting from a general dissatisfaction with everything. As to 'ruin and prosperity,' Nîlakantha adds, 'and their causes, sin and merit.'

[2] Literally 'respected.' Nîlakantha says it means 'rejoiced over,' for Dhritarâshtra thought, that in spite of his treachery he was safe, as death was taught by Sanatsugâta to have no existence.

[3] I.e. free from the presence of ignorant and vulgar people. Cf. Gîtâ, p. 68 supra.

[4] I.e. knowledge concerning the supreme Self.

[5] *Sankara's* construction seems different, but is not quite clear. He says, 'wishing to become—Brahman—the meaning is wishing to acquire the self lost through ignorance.'

[6] I.e. imparted to your pupils, *Sankara* adds; 'heard,' scil. from Vidura.

[7] The construction is imperfect, but the sense is clear. Is your

the life of Brahma*k*ârins[1], for freedom from death?

Sanatsu*g*âta said:

Some (say), that freedom from death (results) from action[2]; and others that death exists not. Hear me explain (this), O king! have no misgiving about it[3]. Both truths, O Kshatriya! have been current from the beginning[4]. The wise maintain what (is called) delusion (to be) death. I[5] verily call heedlessness death, and likewise I call freedom from heedlessness immortality. Through heedlessness, verily, were the demons[6] vanquished; and through freedom

---

view correct, or the view involved in the practice of gods and demons?

[1] See Gîtâ, p. 69 supra; Ka*th*opanishad, p. 102; Prasna, p. 162. As to the gods being afraid of death, see *Kh*ândogya, p. 50; and N*ri*si*m*ha Tâpinî, p. 32; and as to gods and demons practising the life of Brahma*k*ârins, see *Kh*ândogya, p. 571; and cf. B*ri*had-âra*n*yaka, p. 964.

[2] I.e. action prescribed in the Vedas.

[3] I.e. as to how I shall be able to reconcile the seeming contradiction between the 'two truths.'

[4] I.e. of creation.

[5] Sanatsu*g*âta says he differs from 'the wise;' delusion = thinking the not-self to be the self; heedlessness = falling off from one's natural condition as the Brahman—which is the cause of delusion (*S*aṅkara). See p. 153 infra; Ka*th*a, p. 152; and Taittirîya-upanishad, p. 80.

[6] *S*aṅkara suggests that demons might mean creatures attached to worldly objects; and gods those who are pleased in their own self; and he cites a stanza in support of this suggestion. The allusion, however, seems to be plainly to the story at *Kh*ândogya, p. 571 seq., where the idea and expression of 'being vanquished' also occurs (p. 583). That word *S*aṅkara interprets in connexion with his suggested interpretation to mean 'are born in lower species.' See *Kh*ândogya, p. 585, and Maitrî, p. 211, about asuras or demons. It is interesting to note that in the Introduction to the Mahâbhâshya, there is an allusion to a story of the 'demons' being 'vanquished' in consequence of their grammatical blunders.

from heedlessness the gods attained to the Brahman. Death, verily, does not devour living creatures like a tiger; for, indeed, his form is not to be perceived. Some[1] say that death is different from this, (named) Yama, who dwells in the self[2]; the (practice of the) life of Brahma*k*ârins (being) immortality. That god governs his kingdom in the world of the Pit*ri*s, (being) good to the good, and not good to (those who are) not good. That death, (or) heedlessness, develops in men as desire, and afterwards as wrath, and in the shape of delusion[3]. And then travelling in devious paths[4] through egoism, one does not attain to union[5] with the self. Those who are deluded by it[6], and who remain under its influence, depart from this (world), and there again fall down[7]. Then the deities[8] gather around them. And then he undergoes death after death[9]. Being attached to the fruit of action, on action presenting itself, they follow after it[10], and do not cross

---

[1] Those deluded by worldly objects; 'this' means 'heedlessness.'

[2] *S*ankara cites a stanza from Manu, which says that king Yama Vaivasvata dwells in the heart of every one. Cf. Aitareya-upanishad, p. 187. The following clause he understands to contain two epithets of Yama, meaning 'immortal, and intent on the Brahman.' I follow Nîlaka*n*t*h*a, but not very confidently.

[3] Cf. Gîtâ, p. 57. Here we have the developments, the varying forms, of death or heedlessness.

[4] I.e. paths contrary to *S*rutis and Sm*ri*tis.

[5] Concentration of mind on the self or Brahman.

[6] I.e. the egoism spoken of before.

[7] I.e. to this mortal world. Cf. Gîtâ, p. 84, and B*ri*hadâra*n*yaka, pp. 855, 856. There = from the next world. *S*ankara says, 'having lived there.'

[8] I.e. the senses. Cf. Gîtâ, p. 123, and inter alia Î*s*opanishad, p. 10.

[9] Cf. Ka*th*a, p. 129, and B*ri*hadâra*n*yaka, p. 889.

[10] I.e. the fruit. Cf. Ka*th*a, p. 155, and Mu*nd*aka, p. 317.

beyond death. And the embodied (self), in consequence of not understanding union[1] with the real entity, proceeds on all hands[2] with attachment to enjoyments. That[3], verily, is the great source of delusion to the senses; for by contact[4] with unreal entities, his migrations[5] are (rendered) inevitable; because having his inner self contaminated by contact with unreal entities, he devotes himself to objects of sense on all sides, pondering on them (only). (That) pondering, verily, first ruins[6] him; and soon afterwards desire and wrath, after attacking him. These[7] lead children to death. But sensible men cross beyond death by their good sense. He who pondering (on the self) destroys[8] (the) fugitive (objects of sense), not even thinking of them through contempt (for them), and who being possessed of knowledge destroys desires in this way, becomes, as it were, the death of death (itself), and swallows (it) up[9]. The being who

---

[1] I.e. its identity with the Brahman.

[2] I.e. in various forms of life, Nîlakantha.

[3] The going about in search of enjoyments.

[4] The contact leads to pondering on them, and that to desire, &c., as described further on.

[5] Through various lives. Birth and death are certain for him.

[6] I.e. causes oblivion of his real nature, Sankara. Cf. the whole train of cause and effect at Gîtâ, p. 50 supra.

[7] I.e. the pondering, desire, wrath, &c. As to 'children,' cf. Katha, pp. 96 and 123, where bâla is contrasted with dhîra, as here. The 'good sense' is of help in withstanding the temptations of worldly objects.

[8] Destroys = abandons; pondering, just before this, is rendered by Sankara to mean 'thinking of the objects as transient, impure,' &c.

[9] Sankara cites on this a stanza of unknown authorship, which says, 'The learned and clever man who knows the self, and by discrimination destroys all objects of sense, is said to be the death of death.' See too p. 178 infra.

pursues desires, is destroyed (in pursuing) after the desires[1]. But casting away desires, a being gets rid of all taint[2] whatever. This body, void of enlightenment[3], seems (to be) a hell for (all) beings. Those who are avaricious run about[4], going headlong to a ditch. A man, O Kshatriya! who contemns everything else[5] learns nothing. To him (the body is) like a tiger made of straw[6]. And this internal self (joined to) delusion and fear[7] in consequence of wrath and avarice, within your body,—that verily is death[8]. Understanding death[9] to be thus produced, and adhering to knowledge, one is not afraid of death[10] in this (world). In his province death is destroyed, as a mortal (is destroyed) on arriving in the province of death.

Dh*ri*tarâsh*t*ra said:

The good, eternal, and most holy worlds[11], which

[1] On this Nîlaka*nth*a quotes these lines, 'The antelope, elephant, butterfly, bee, and fish—these five are destroyed by the five,' i.e. the five objects of sense, sound, &c. See *S*ânti Parvan (Moksha Dharma), chap. 174, st. 45.

[2] I.e. misery, Nîlaka*nth*a; merit or sin, *S*ankara.

[3] I.e. void of discrimination between the real and unreal, Nîlaka*nth*a; result of ignorance, *S*ankara. 'A hell, as being full of filth,' says *S*ankara, 'such as phlegm, blood, excretions.' Cf. Maitrî, p. 48.

[4] As blind men groping about fall into a ditch, so do these, *S*ankara.

[5] I.e. other than the sensuous objects he loves; 'learns nothing' about the supreme Self which he disregards.

[6] Useless for any good purpose.

[7] Cf. Taittirîya-upanishad, p. 102.

[8] As being ruinous to oneself. *S*ankara compares Gîtâ, p. 68. Cf. also Taittirîya-upanishad, p. 103, and see B*ri*hadâra*n*yaka, p. 61.

[9] I.e. heedlessness and its developments as stated.

[10] *S*ankara cites on this Taittirîya-upanishad, p. 78.

[11] Such as Satyaloka, &c.

are mentioned (as attainable) by the twice-born by means of worship [1], those, say the Vedas, are the highest aim [2]. How is it, then, that one who understands this does not resort to action?

Sanatsugâta said:

(Thinking) so, an ignorant man does resort to action. The Vedas likewise do lay down various benefits [3] (for him). But that [4] (man) comes not hither [5]. (Becoming) the supreme self [6], he attains the supreme, by the (right) path destroying the wrong paths [7].

Dhritarâshtra said:

Who [8] is it that constrains this unborn primeval (self), if it is (itself) all this severally [9]? And what

[1] *G*yotish*t*oma, Asvamedha, and other rites.

[2] As leading to final emancipation.

[3] I.e. objects for which various ceremonies (or 'actions') should be performed.

[4] I.e. the man of knowledge.

[5] I.e. into the sphere of action. Cf. Gîtâ, p. 48.

[6] Knowing the supreme self is identical with becoming the supreme self, Mu*nd*aka, p. 323.

[7] I.e. getting rid of the paths which keep one away from the Brahman by means of contemplation of the Brahman, &c. Nîlaka*nth*a renders 'right path' to mean the Sushum*n*â passage by which the soul proceeds to final emancipation, see *Kh*ândogya, p. 570; Ka*th*a, p. 157.

[8] *S*aṅkara says: 'Having shown that true death is heedlessness, and having shown that heedlessness in its forms of anger &c. is the cause of all evil, and having also shown that death is destroyed by true knowledge, and having shown further that heaven &c. are really not man's highest goal; the author has also implied the unity of the supreme and individual self. On that arises a doubt which is stated in this passage.'

[9] All this = all the developments of the Brahman, i.e. space, wind, fire, water, earth, vegetation, food, living creatures; see Taittirîyopanishad, p. 68.

has it to do, or what is its unhappiness[1]? Tell me all that accurately, O learned person!

Sanatsu*g*âta said:

There is great danger[2] in attributing distinctions to it. The everlasting[3] (principles) exist by connexion with the beginningless[4] (principle). So that his greatness is not lost at all[5], and beings exist by connexion with the beginningless[4] (principle). That which is the real—the supreme Being[6]—is eternal. He creates the universe by means of changes[7], for such is his power held to be; and for such connexions of things the Vedas are (authority)[8].

[1] What is the purpose of its existence, and what misery does it undergo on entering the course of worldly life?

[2] 'The danger,' says *S*aṅkara, 'is that of contravening Vedic texts such as "I am the Brahman," "Thou art that," &c.' May it not rather be that pointed out at Ka*th*opanishad, p. 129, viz. never attaining final emancipation? Cf. also N*ri*si*m*ha Tâpinî, p. 223.

[3] The individual selfs, *S*aṅkara.

[4] Nature or mâyâ.

[5] The appearance of degradation to an inferior state being delusive.

[6] The original word implies the possession of ai*s*varya, dharma, ya*s*as, *s*rî, vairâgya, moksha. See *S*vetâ*s*vatara, p. 329 (where the list is slightly different). For another definition, see Maitri, p. 6 (gloss).

[7] See note 9, p. 156.

[8] *S*aṅkara says: 'The question of Dh*ri*tarâsh*t*ra having suggested a difference between two principles, one of which constrains, and the other of which is constrained, the answer is—Such a difference ought not to be alleged, as it involves "danger." Then the question arises, How is the difference, which does appear, to be explained? The reply is, It is due to the beginningless principle—delusion or ignorance. The next sentence shows that the universe as it appears is also a result of delusion.' Nîlaka*nth*a says expressly, changes = delusion. He renders the original which we have translated by 'beginningless' first, to mean 'collection of objects of enjoyments.' *S*aṅkara's explanation seems tautological as regards the words 'connexion with the beginningless,' which occur twice in the above. Nîla-

Dhritarâshtra said:

Since some practise piety[1] in this world, and some likewise practise impiety in this world; is the piety destroyed by the sin, or else does the piety destroy sin?

Sanatsugâta said:

Whichever[2] he adheres to, the man of understanding always destroys both by means of knowledge; (that is) settled[3]. Likewise, in the other case[4], the embodied (self) obtains merit; and to such a one sin (also) accrues; (that too is) settled[3]. Departing (from this world), he enjoys by his actions both (kinds of) fruit, which are not enduring[5]—of actions (which are) pure, and of (those which are) sinful. The man of understanding casts aside sin by piety in this (world), for know that his piety is more powerful[6]. Those Brâhmanas, in whom there is emulation[7] about (their) piety, as there is in strong men about (their) strength, after departing from this world, become glorious in heaven[8]. And

kantha's is not quite clear. May the expression on the second occasion mean, that the connexion by which beings are stated before to exist has had no beginning—has existed from eternity? The translation should then run thus: 'And beings exist by a connexion which had no beginning;' (see Sârîraka Bhâshya, p. 494.) Connexions of things=creation of universe by his power.

[1] E.g. Agnishtoma, &c., Sankara.

[2] I.e. impiety or piety, sin or merit.

[3] In Srutis and Smritis, which Sankara quotes. Khândogya, p. 622; Mundaka, p. 309; Brihadâranyaka, p. 911. See, too, Maitrî, p. 131.

[4] Of the man devoid of knowledge.

[5] Cf. Gîtâ, p. 76, and Brihadâranyaka, p. 636.

[6] See p. 164, note 9 infra.

[7] The feeling of one's own superiority over others in piety.

[8] 'In the shape of Nakshatras,' says Sankara, which is not quite intelligible. See Khândogya, p. 258, and Anugîtâ infra, p. 240.

to those in whom there is no emulation about (their) piety, that (piety) is a means of (acquiring) knowledge [1]. Such Brâhma*n*as released from this (world), go to the heaven which is free from the threefold source of pain [2]. People who understand the Vedas call his conduct good. (But) people closely connected [3], as well as strangers, do not pay much regard to him. Wherever he may believe food and drink for a Brâhma*n*a to exist in abundance, like water on grass in the autumn, there would he live and not be vexed [4]. (To him) only that person is good, and no other (as a companion), who does nothing in excess, and who occasions fear and injury to a taciturn man [5]. And his food is acceptable to the good, who does not vex the self of a taciturn man, and who does not destroy the property of a Brâhma*n*a [6]. A Brâhma*n*a should hold, that living in the midst of kinsmen, his actions should be always unknown [7]; and he should not

[1] According to the Vedântic theory, the acts of piety purify the inner man, and are thus a stepping-stone to knowledge. See Introduction, p. 147 supra. Cf. Gîtâ, p. 122; and B*ri*hadâra*n*yaka, p. 899.

[2] I.e. physical, mental, and such as is caused by superhuman agency. This is *S*aṅkara's explanation. It is somewhat far-fetched, but I can find none better. Cf. Gîtâ, p. 49. And see also B*ri*hadâra*n*yaka, p. 876, and the commentary of *S*aṅkara there with Ânandagiri's gloss.

[3] E.g. wife, children, &c.

[4] I.e. vexed as to how his livelihood is to be earned, &c.

[5] Excess, e.g. too much obsequiousness towards a 'taciturn man,' owing to his holiness, &c. Taciturn man = ascetic. Injury = disrespect, &c. Perhaps the protest against worldliness is here carried to an extreme. *S*aṅkara cites Manu as a parallel, 'A Brâhma*n*a should be afraid of (worldly) respect as of poison.'

[6] E.g. the Ku*s*a grass, deerskin, &c., mentioned at Gîtâ, p. 68.

[7] I.e. he should not parade his actions. *S*aṅkara compares Vasish*th*a and a Vedic text. See, too, the quotation at Taitt. Âra*n*. p. 902.

think[1] (about them). What Brâhmana ought to think of the inner self, which is void of symbols[2], immovable, pure, and free from all pairs of opposites, in this way[3]? What sin is not committed by that thief, who steals away his own self[4], who regards his self as one thing, when it is a different thing. The far-seeing Brâhmana, who knows the Brahman, is not wearied[5], he receives nothing[6]; he is honoured, free from trouble[7], and wise, but acts as if he was not wise[8]. As dogs eat what is vomited, so do they, enjoying their own bravery[9], eat what is vomited, always with disaster (to themselves). Those twice-born persons, who are not

---

[1] Cf. Gitâ, p. 103. Sankara suggests an alternative explanation of this stanza, which will make it mean that one performing the operations of the senses, should devote oneself nevertheless to the unknown principle, and not consider the senses to be the self.

[2] I. e. beyond the reach of inference; 'subtle,' says Sankara. Cf. Svetâsvatara, p. 364; Brihadâranyaka, p. 855; Maitrî, p. 182; and Katha, p. 149, where Sankara suggests a somewhat different meaning. As to immovable, cf. Îsa, p. 10, and Gitâ, p. 104. Sankara renders it by 'void of activity;' and pure he paraphrases by 'free from ignorance and other taints.'

[3] It is difficult to say what 'in this way' refers to. Sankara renders it by 'as possessing qualities appertaining to the two kinds of body.' On Sankara's suggested meaning of the stanza preceding (see note 1), it would refer to the confusion of the senses with the self.

[4] Such a person is called a destroyer of his own self at Îsopanishad, p. 9.

[5] I. e. by the troubles of worldly life.

[6] Cf. 'without belongings' at Gitâ, p. 128.

[7] Anger and other obstacles to concentration of mind.

[8] I. e. unintelligent. The text of Vasishtha referred to in note 7, p. 159, says he should act like an unintelligent man. Cf. also Gaudapâda-kârikâs, p. 443, and Sârîraka Bhâshya, p. 1041.

[9] I. e. singing the praises of their own greatness and worth, instead of keeping their 'conduct unknown.'

first[1] in respect of human wealth, but who are first in the Vedas[2], are unconquerable, not to be shaken[3]; they should be understood to be forms of the Brahman. Whosoever may in this (world) know all the gods[4]—doers of favours—he is not equal to a Brâhma*n*a, (nor even) he[5] for whom he exerts himself. The man who makes no efforts[6], and is respected, does not, being respected, think himself respected[7], nor does he become vexed in consequence of disrespect. One who is respected[8] should think it to be a natural operation of people, like their opening or closing of the eyelids, that the learned respect him in this world. One who is not respected should think, that the deluded people who do not understand piety, and who are devoid of (knowledge of) the world and the *S*âstras, will never respect one who is worthy of respect. Respect and taciturnity[9], verily, never dwell together; for this world is (the field) for respect, the next for taciturnity, as is understood[10]. For worldly wealth dwells in the

[1] Highly esteemed for or strongly attached to, *S*aṅkara. Human wealth = wife, offspring, property, &c. Cf. *Kh*ândogya, p. 319; B*r*ihadâra*n*yaka, p. 262.

[2] I.e. veracity and other duties taught by the Vedas.

[3] 'They need fear nought,' says Nîlaka*n*tha.

[4] I.e. may sacrifice to them, *S*aṅkara.

[5] Not even the deity to whom the sacrifice is offered is equal to one who knows the Brahman. Cf. Taittirîya, p. 23, and Anugîtâ, p. 250.

[6] I.e. one who is 'taciturn' and does not parade his greatness.

[7] He does not care for the respect shown him.

[8] Because he knows the Brahman.

[9] I.e. restraint of all senses, not of speech only. For the contrast compare that between *s*reya and preya at Ka*th*a, p. 92.

[10] I.e. by all men of understanding. *S*aṅkara's rendering is different: 'The next, which is known as Tad, is for taciturnity.' He cites for this Gîtâ, p. 120.

sphere of respect[1], and that, too, is an obstacle[2]. While the Brahmic wealth[3], O Kshatriya! is difficult to be attained by any one devoid of knowledge. The ways (to it) are stated by the good to be of various descriptions, and difficult to reach—truth, straightforwardness, modesty[4], restraint (of senses), purity, knowledge, which are the six impediments (in the way) of respect and delusion.

CHAPTER III.

Dh*ri*tarâsh*t*ra said:

Who possesses this taciturnity[5], and which of the two[6] is taciturnity? Describe, O learned person! the condition of taciturnity here. Does a learned man reach taciturnity[7] by taciturnity? And how, O sage! do they practise taciturnity in this world?

---

[1] I. e. they both follow on devotion to worldly life.

[2] I. e. in the way to final emancipation.

[3] The enjoyment of supreme felicity, Brahmânanda (*S*ankara); the greatness consisting of a knowledge of *Rik*, Yagus, Sâman, and the substance of their teaching, which is worthy of a Brâhma*n*a (Nîlaka*nth*a). See, too, Anugîtâ, p. 232.

[4] Modesty = being ashamed of doing wrong; restraint (of senses) = mental restraint; and purity is both internal and external,—*S*ankara; knowledge is, of course, knowledge of the Brahman.

[5] I. e. that spoken of in the last chapter.

[6] Viz. mere silence, or the contemplation of the self after restraining all the senses. In the B*ri*hadâra*n*yaka-upanishad, *S*ankara (p. 605) renders the original word, mauna, to mean, 'The fruit of the destruction of the consciousness of anything other than the self.' And his commentator makes it clearer thus: 'The conviction in the mind that one is the self—the supreme Brahman—and that there is nothing else existing but oneself.'

[7] I. e. the highest seat—the Brahman; for mind, sense, &c. are all non-existent there. Cf. Ka*th*a, p. 151, and Maitrî, p. 161.

Sanatsugâta said:

Since the Vedas, together with the mind[1], fail to attain to him, hence (is he) taciturnity[2]—he about whom the words of the Vedas were uttered[3], and who, O king! shines forth as consubstantial[4] with them.

Dhritarâshtra said:

Does[5] the twice-born person who studies the *Rik* and the Yagus texts, and the Sâma-veda, committing sinful (acts), become tainted, or does he not become tainted?

Sanatsugâta said:

Not the Sâman texts, nor yet the *Rik* texts, nor the Yagus texts[6] save him, O acute sir! from sinful

[1] Cf. Kenopanishad, p. 39; Katha, p. 152; Taittirîya, p. 119.

[2] 'Taciturnity is his name,' says Nîlakantha.

[3] Or, says *S*ankara, 'who is the author of the Vedas.'

[4] I. e. 'with the Vedas,' says Nîlakantha, Om, the quintessence of the Vedas, being a name of the Brahman (as to which cf. Gîtâ, p. 79, and Maitrî, p. 84). *S*ankara takes the whole expression to mean *g*yotirmaya, consisting of light. Nîlakantha says this stanza answers the five following questions put in the stanza preceding, viz. of what use is taciturnity? which of the two is taciturnity? &c., as above. The first four questions are answered by the first two lines of this stanza—the substance of the answer being, that the use of taciturnity is to attain the seat which is not to be grasped even by the mind, that taciturnity includes both restraint of mind and of the external senses. By means of such restraint, the external and internal worlds cease to be perceived as existing, and the highest goal is attained.

[5] This question arises naturally enough on Nîlakantha's interpretation of the preceding stanza, the meaning of which is in substance that the Vedas cannot grasp the Brahman fully, but they are of use towards a rudimentary comprehension of it, as is said further on, see p. 172 infra.

[6] Cf. *S*vetâ*s*vatara-upanishad, p. 339; see, too, Nrisimha Tâpinî, pp. 81–98.

action. I do not tell you an untruth. The *Kh*andas do not save a sinful deceitful[1] man who behaves deceitfully[2]. At the time of the termination (of his life), the *Kh*andas abandon[3] him, as birds who have got wings (abandon their) nest.

Dh*ri*tarâsh*t*ra said:

If, O acute sir! the Vedas are not able to save one who understands the Vedas, then whence is this eternal talk[4] of the Brâhma*n*as?

Sanatsu*g*âta said:

O you of great glory! this universe becomes manifest through his special forms—names[5] and the rest. The Vedas proclaim (his form) after describing (it) well[6], and (they[7] also) state his difference from the universe. For that[8] are this penance and sacrifice prescribed. By these a learned man acquires merit, and afterwards destroying sin by merit[9], he has his self illuminated by knowledge. By knowledge the learned man attains

---

[1] I.e. one who parades his piety.

[2] I.e. hypocritically.

[3] I.e. do not rise to his memory—Nîlaka*nt*ha, citing Gîtâ, p. 78 supra.

[4] Scil. about the veneration due to one who has studied the Vedas—Nîlaka*nt*ha, citing one or two passages in point.

[5] The universe consists of 'names and forms,' the reality being the Brahman only. Cf. *Kh*ândogya, p. 407 seq.

[6] *S*aṅkara refers to Taittirîya-upanishad, p. 68; *Kh*ândogya, p. 596 seq. &c.

[7] *S*aṅkara takes this to mean 'sages,' who, according to him, state the difference. He quotes Parâsara for this.

[8] I.e. the Brahman, that is to say, for attaining to it. Penance=*K*ândrâya*n*a and other observances; sacrifice=*G*yotish*t*oma, &c.

[9] Cf. p. 158 supra, and Taittirîya-âra*n*yaka, p. 888.

the self[1]. But, on the other hand, one who wishes for the fruit—heaven[2]—takes with him[3] all that he has done in this (world), enjoys it in the next, and then returns to the path[4] (of this world). Penance is performed in this world; the fruit is enjoyed elsewhere. But the penance of Brâhma*n*as is further developed[5]; that of others remains only as much (as when first performed).

Dh*ri*tarâsh*t*ra said:

How does the pure penance become developed and well developed[6]? O Sanatsu*g*âta! tell (me) how I should understand that, O Lord!

Sanatsu*g*âta said:

This penance, free from sin[7], is called pure[8]; and this pure penance becomes developed and well developed, not otherwise[9]. All this[10], O Kshatriya!

---

[1] Cf. *S*vetâ*s*vatara, p. 327; Mu*nd*aka, p. 323.

[2] So *S*a*n*kara. Nîlaka*nt*ha takes the original word to mean 'the group of the senses,' and the whole phrase to mean 'enjoyments of sense.' Nîlaka*nt*ha is supported by a passage further on, p. 167. But as to 'those who wish for heaven,' cf. Gîtâ, pp. 48–84.

[3] I.e. in the form of merit, &c.

[4] Cf. Gîtâ, p. 84.

[5] Cf. *Kh*ândogya, p. 23. Brâhma*n*as=those that know the Brahman. See p. 171 infra.

[6] I am not quite sure about the meaning of the original here. *Ri*ddha, which I have rendered 'developed,' Nîlaka*nt*ha understands to mean 'what is performed merely for show.' What has been rendered 'well developed' in the text, Nîlaka*nt*ha takes to mean 'performed from some desire,' &c.

[7] Anger, desire, &c.

[8] The original is kevala. Nîlaka*nt*ha says it is so called as being a means of kaivalya, 'final emancipation.'

[9] I.e. not that which is not free from sin, which latter is not developed at all.

[10] All objects of enjoyment, Nîlaka*nt*ha.

has for its root that penance about which you question me. By penance[1], those conversant with the Vedas attained immortality, after departing from this world.

Dhritarâshtra said:

I have heard about penance free from sin, O Sanatsugâta! Tell me what is the sin (connected) with penance, so that I may understand the eternal mystery[2].

Sanatsugâta said:

The twelve beginning with wrath, and likewise the seven cruelties, are the defects (connected) with it; and there are (stated) in the Sâstras twelve merits (connected) with it, beginning with knowledge, which are known to the twice-born, and may be developed. Wrath, desire[3], avarice, delusion[4], craving[5], mercilessness, censoriousness, vanity, grief[6], attachment[7], envy[8], reviling others—these twelve should always be avoided by a man of high quali-

[1] Cf. Brihadâranyaka, p. 899. Tapas is variously rendered. See inter alia, Prasna, pp. 162–170; Svetâsvatara, p. 307; Mundaka, pp. 270–280, 311–314; Khândogya, p. 136; Anugîtâ, pp. 247, 339.

[2] I.e. Brahma-vidyâ, or science of the Brahman, Nîlakantha; the Brahman itself, Sankara.

[3] I.e. lust.

[4] Want of discrimination between right and wrong.

[5] Desire to taste worldly objects.

[6] For the loss of anything desired.

[7] Desire to enjoy worldly objects. The difference between this and craving, according to Sankara, appears to be between merely tasting and continual enjoyment. According to Nîlakantha, the former is a desire which is never contented; the latter is merely a general liking.

[8] Impatience of other people's prosperity; censoriousness being the pointing out of flaws in other people's merits; and reviling being an ignoring of the merits and merely abusing.

fications[1]. These, O king of kings! attend each and every man, wishing to find some opening[2], as a hunter (watches) animals. [Boastful, lustful, haughty, irascible, unsteady[3], one who does not protect (those dependent[4] on him), these six sinful acts are performed by sinful men who are not afraid (even) in the midst of great danger[5].] One whose thoughts are (all) about enjoyments, who prospers by injuring (others), who repents of generosity, who is miserly, who is devoid of the power[6] (of knowledge), who esteems the group[7] (of the senses), who hates his wife[8]—these seven, different (from those previously mentioned), are the seven forms of cruelty. Knowledge, truth, self-restraint, sacred learning, freedom from animosity (towards living beings), modesty[9], endurance[10], freedom from censoriousness, sacrifice, gift, courage[11], quiescence[12],—these are the twelve great observances[13] of a Brâhmana. Whoever is not devoid of these twelve can govern this whole world, and those who are

---

[1] Scil. for attaining to the Brahman.

[2] Some weak point by which they may attack a man.

[3] Fickle in friendship, &c.

[4] Such as a wife, &c.

[5] Connected with this or the next world, Nîlakantha. This and a stanza further on I place within brackets, as it is not quite certain whether *S*ankara's copy had them, though they are now in some of our copies of the text with his commentary. See Introduction.

[6] Cf. Mundaka, p. 319; *Kh*ândogya, p. 494.

[7] See note 2, at page 165.

[8] The wife having no other protector.

[9] See note 4, at page 162.

[10] Of pairs of opposites, such as heat and cold, &c.

[11] Restraint of senses in presence of their objects.

[12] Cf. Gîtâ, pp. 69, 70.

[13] Which are serviceable in attaining the highest goal.

possessed of three, two, or even one (of these) become, in (due) course, distinguished (for knowledge) and identified with the Brahman[1]. [Self-restraint, abandonment[2], and freedom from heedlessness—on these depends immortality. And the talented Brâhma*n*as say that truth is chief over them.] Self-restraint has eighteen defects; if (any one of them is) committed, it is an obstacle (to self-restraint). They are thus stated. Untruthfulness, backbiting, thirst[3], antipathy (to all beings), darkness[4], repining[5], hatred[6] of people, haughtiness, quarrelsomeness, injuring living creatures, reviling others, garrulity, vexation[7], want of endurance[8], want of courage[9], imperfection[10], sinful conduct, and slaughter. That is called self-restraint by the good, which is free from these defects. Frenzy has eighteen defects[11]; and abandonment is of six kinds. The contraries of those which have been laid down[12] are stated to be the defects of frenzy. Abandonment of six kinds is excellent. Of those six, the third is hard to achieve. With it one certainly crosses

[1] The original is the word 'taciturnity' as at p. 162 supra.

[2] Offering one's acts to God (Nilaka*nth*a), as to which cf. Gîtâ, p. 64. See also p. 182 infra for this stanza.

[3] I. e. for objects of sense.

[4] Ignorance.

[5] Discontent even when one obtains much.

[6] This is active; antipathy is passive only.

[7] Of oneself, by brooding on evil. Cf. Taittirîya, p. 119. One copy of *S*aṅkara's commentary says this means 'thinking ill of others without cause.'

[8] Of pairs of opposites.

[9] Restraint of senses in presence of their objects.

[10] I. e. of piety, knowledge, and indifference to worldly objects.

[11] I. e. qualities which destroy it.

[12] Scil. as defects of self-restraint, viz. untruthfulness, &c.

beyond all misery without distinction[1]. That being achieved, (everything) is accomplished[2]. The (first is the) giving away of sons and wealth to a deserving man who asks (for them); the second is gifts at Vedic ceremonies, and gifts at ceremonies laid down in the Smritis[3]. The abandonment of desires, O king of kings! by means of indifference (to worldly objects) is laid down as the third[4]. With these one should become free from heedlessness. That freedom from heedlessness, too, has eight characteristics, and is (a) great (merit). Truthfulness, concentration, absorbed contemplation, reflexion[5], and also indifference (to worldly objects), not stealing[6], living the life of a Brahmakârin, and

---

[1] Scil. any distinction as to physical, mental, or that which is caused by superhuman agency.

[2] Literally, 'all is conquered.' Everything that needs to be done is done. Cf. Kathopanishad, p. 155; Mundaka, p. 317.

[3] Another interpretation of ishtâpûrta is 'offerings to gods, and offerings to the manes;' a third 'sacrifices, &c., and works of charity, such as digging tanks and wells;' for a fourth, see Sankara on Mundaka, p. 291.

[4] Each of the three classes mentioned contains two sub-classes, and so the six are made up. It is not quite easy to see the two heads under the third class; but perhaps indifference, and the consequent abandonment of desire, may be the two intended. To indicate that, I have adopted the construction which takes the words 'by means of indifference' with abandonment, instead of with 'gifts at Vedic ceremonies,' &c. Sankara seems to understand 'giving away of wealth' with the words 'by means of indifference,' and thus to constitute the second head under the third class. But he is not quite clear.

[5] Concentration = fixing the mind continuously on some object, such as the being in the sun, &c.; contemplation is that in which one identifies oneself with the Brahman; reflexion as to what one is, whence one comes, and so forth.

[6] Sankara says this may refer to the 'stealing' mentioned at p. 160. The life of a Brahmakârin is here taken to mean con-

likewise freedom from all belongings[1]. Thus have the defects of self-restraint been stated; one should avoid those defects. Freedom from (those) defects is freedom from heedlessness; and that, too, is deemed to have eight characteristics[2]. Let truth be your (very) self, O king of kings! On truth all the worlds rest[3]. Truth is said to be their main (principle). Immortality depends on truth[4]. Getting rid of (these) defects, one should practise the observance of penance. This is the conduct prescribed by the Creator. Truth is the solemn vow of the good. The pure penance, which is free from these defects, and possessed of these characteristics, becomes developed, and well developed[5]. I will state to you, in brief, O king of kings! what you ask of me. This (observance)[6] is destructive of sin, and pure, and releases (one) from birth and death and old age[7]. If one is free from the five senses, and also from the mind[8], O descendant of Bharata! also from (thoughts regarding) the past and the future[9], one becomes happy.

Dh*ri*tarâsh*t*ra said:

Some people make great boasts in consequence of (their knowing) the Vedas with the Âkhyânas as

---

tinence by the commentators, as also at Mu*nd*aka, p. 311 inter alia. See also *Kh*ândogya, p. 533.

[1] Son, wife, home, &c.; as to which cf. Gîtâ, p. 103, and N*ri*si*m*ha Tâpinî, p. 198, commentary.

[2] The eight mentioned already. [3] Cf. Taitt. Âra*n*. p. 885.

[4] Cf. Mu*nd*aka, p. 312; *S*ânti Parvan (Moksha), chap. 199, st. 64 seq. Immortality = final emancipation.

[5] P. 165 supra. [6] Of penance, that is to say.

[7] Cf. Gîtâ, p. 109 for the collocation.

[8] Ka*th*opanishad, p. 151; Maitrî, p. 161. *S*aṅkara seems to take the five and the senses separately; the five meaning the five classes of sensuous objects. [9] Past losses and future gains, Nîlaka*nth*a.

the fifth[1]; others, likewise, are (masters) of four Vedas; others, too, of three Vedas; others are (masters) of two Vedas, and of one Veda; and others of no Veda[2]. Tell me which of these is the greatest, whom I may know (to be) a Brâhma*n*a.

Sanatsu*g*âta said:

Through ignorance of the one Veda[3]—the one truth—O king of kings! numerous Vedas came into existence. Some[4] only adhere to the truth. The fancies of those who have fallen away from the truth are abortive, and through ignorance of the truth, ceremonies become amplified[5]. One should understand a Brâhma*n*a, who (merely) reads much, to be a man of many words[6]. Know him only to be the (true) Brâhma*n*a, who swerves not from the truth[7]. O you who are the highest among men[8]! the *Kh*andas, indeed, refer of themselves[9] to it. There-

[1] Cf., as to this, Max Müller's Ancient Sanskrit Literature, p. 38 seq.; and *Kh*ândogya, pp. 164, 474, 493; B*ri*hadâra*n*yaka, pp. 456, 687, 926; Maitrî, p. 171; N*ri*si*m*ha Tâpinî, p. 105.

[2] The original is 'void of *Rik*s.' The commentators give no explanation. Does it mean those who abandon the karma-mârga? Heretics who reject all Vedas are scarcely likely to be referred to in this way. Nîlaka*n*t*h*a's interpretation of all this is very different. See his gloss.

[3] *S*a*n*kara gives various interpretations of this. Perhaps the best is to take it as meaning knowledge. 'The one knowledge—the one truth'—would then be like the famous text—Taittirîya, p. 56—'The Brahman is truth, knowledge,' &c.

[4] For this phrase cf. Gîtâ, p. 73.

[5] Those who do not understand the Brahman lose their natural power of obtaining what they wish, and so go in for various ceremonies for various special benefits. Cf. *Kh*ândogya, p. 541; Gîtâ, p. 47; and p. 184 infra.

[6] Cf. B*ri*hadâra*n*yaka, p. 893.

[7] Ibid. p. 636.

[8] Literally, 'highest among bipeds,' a rather unusual expression.

[9] Nîlaka*n*t*h*a says, 'The part of the Vedas which teaches the

fore, studying them, the learned persons who understand the *Kh*andas, attain to the Veda, not that which is to be known[1]. Among the Vedas, there is none which understands[2]. By the unintelligent[3], one understands not the Veda, nor the object of knowledge[4]. He who knows the Veda knows the object of knowledge. He who knows the object of knowledge[5] knows not the truth. He who understands the Vedas understands also the object of knowledge; but that[6] is not understood by the Vedas or by those who understand the Vedas. Still the Brâhma*n*as who understand the Vedas, understand the Veda by means of the Vedas[7]. As the branch of a tree with regard to the part of a portion of the glorious[8] one, so, they declare, are the Vedas with

knowledge of the supreme is enough by itself for its purpose; it is not like the part about rites, &c., which rites must be performed before they serve any useful purpose.' The *G*ñânakânda is enough by itself for understanding the Brahman. *S*aṅkara compares Gîtâ, p. 113, and Ka*th*a, p. 102.

[1] The Veda = the Brahman, as above, cf. *S*vetâ*s*vatara, p. 372 and commentary; that which is to be known = the material world, which is a subject for human knowledge.

[2] Scil. understands the Veda—the Brahman.

[3] 'The mind,' says Nîlaka*nth*a; literally, 'that which is to be understood.'

[4] Because a real knowledge of it requires a knowledge of the Brahman. As to the next clause cf. inter alia *Kh*ândogya, p. 384; B*ri*hadâra*n*yaka, p. 450.

[5] This is the converse of the last sentence, as to which cf. B*ri*hadâra*n*yaka, p. 925.

[6] The supreme.

[7] The apparent contradiction is explained in the next sentence.

[8] I.e. the moon. This refers to the well-known *s*âkhâ*k*andranyâya. As the small digit of the moon, which cannot be perceived by itself, is pointed out as being at the tip of a branch of a tree pointing towards the moon, so the Vedas are of use as pointing towards the Brahman, though inaccurately and imperfectly.

regard to the subject of understanding the supreme self. I understand him to be a Brâhma*n*a who is ingenious, and explains[1] (Vedic texts). He who apprehends (those texts) thus[2], does verily know that supreme (principle). One should not go in search of it among (things) antagonistic[3] to it at all. Not looking (for him there) one sees that Lord by means of the Veda[4]. Remaining quiet, one should practise devotion, and should not even form a wish in the mind[5]. To him the Brahman presents[6] itself, and directly afterwards he attains to the perfect[7] (one). By taciturnity[8], verily, does one become a sage; (one does) not (become) a sage by dwelling in a forest[9]. And he is called the highest sage, who understands that indestructible (principle). One is called an analyser[10] (also) in consequence of

---

[1] Scil. in the manner just indicated.

[2] As giving an idea of the Brahman. The first step to a knowledge of the Brahman is to 'hear' about it from Vedic texts. Cf. B*ri*hadâra*n*yaka, p. 925.

[3] Such as the body, the senses, &c., which must be distinguished as quite distinct from the self, though most often confounded with it.

[4] Such passages, namely, as 'Thou art that, I am the Brahman,' &c.

[5] About the objects of the senses.

[6] Cf. Ka*th*a, p. 155.

[7] Cf. *Kh*ândogya, p. 516. The Bhûman there is the same as the Bahu here, viz. the Brahman. *S*aṅkara says expressly in his comment on the Upanishad text, that Bahu and Bhûman, among other words, are synonyms.

[8] Self-restraint, as explained before at p. 163.

[9] Though this is not unimportant, as may be seen from the contrast between town and forest at *Kh*ândogya, p. 340. See also Maitrî, p. 100; Mu*nd*aka, p. 240. As to the 'highest sage,' see B*ri*hadâra*n*yaka, p. 899, where the passage about 'sacrifice, gift, penance' should be compared with Gîtâ, p. 122.

[10] The construction in the original is not quite clear. I understand the sense to be as follows: In the science of the soul, the

analysing all objects. The analysis (is) from that as the root; and as he makes (such an) analysis, hence is he so (called). The man who sees the worlds directly sees everything[1]. A Brâhma*n*a, verily, adhering to the truth, understands it, and becomes omniscient. I say to you, O learned man! that adhering to knowledge and the rest[2] in this way, one sees the Brahman, O Kshatriya! by means of a course (of study) in the Vedas[3].

CHAPTER IV.

Dh*ri*tarâsh*t*ra said:

O Sanatsu*g*âta! since you have spoken these words of highest significance, relating to the Brahman, and of numerous forms[4], give me that advice which is excellent, and difficult to obtain in the

---

analyser (the word is the same as the word for grammarian) is he who analyses objects, not words merely. Now the true analysis of objects reduces them all to the Brahman (cf. *Kh*ândogya, p. 407; B*ri*hadâra*n*yaka, p. 152); and the sage understands this, and makes the analysis accordingly, so he is rightly called an analyser.

[1] This again is not clear, and the discrepancies of the MSS. make it more perplexing. The meaning, I take to be, that a man may perceive all material things, such as the worlds, Bhûr, &c. (as the commentators put it), but to be really omniscient, you must have knowledge of the truth—the Brahman. See Sabhâ Parvan, chapter V, stanza 7. And see, too, B*ri*hadâra*n*yaka, p. 613.

[2] P. 167 supra.

[3] 'Hearing the Vedântas—Upanishads,' &c., says *S*a*n*kara. See note 2 supra, p. 173.

[4] Does this mean referring to many aspects of the Brahman? *S*a*n*kara merely says nânârûpâ. Nîlaka*n*t*h*a takes it differently, and as meaning that in which everything is elucidated; 'relating to the Brahman' Nîlaka*n*t*h*a takes to mean 'leading to the Brahman,' or 'instrument for attaining to the Brahman.'

midst of these created objects[1]. Such is my request, O youth!

Sanatsugâta said:

This Brahman, O king! about which you question me with such perseverance, is not to be attained by anybody who is in a hurry. When the mind is absorbed in the understanding[2], then can that knowledge, which must be deeply pondered over, be attained by living the life of a Brahmakârin[3]. For you are speaking of that primordial knowledge[4], which consists in the truth; which is obtained by the good by living the life of Brahmakârins[5]; which being obtained, men cast off this mortal world; and which knowledge, verily, is to be invariably (found) in those who have been brought up under preceptors[6].

Dhritarâshtra said:

Since that knowledge is capable of being truly acquired by living the life of a Brahmakârin, therefore tell me, O Brâhmana! of what description the life of a Brahmakârin is[7].

Sanatsugâta said:

Those who entering (as it were) the womb[8] of a

---

[1] In this material world, the highest knowledge is not to be got. Cf. Katha, p. 96.

[2] I.e. withdrawn from objects and fixed on the self only. Cf. Gitâ, p. 79, and Maitrî, p. 179, where, however, we have hrid for buddhi.

[3] Virokana and Indra do so according to the Khândogya, p. 570. See also Mundaka, p. 311.

[4] The object of which is the primal Brahman.

[5] Cf. Khândogya, p. 534; and Gîtâ, pp. 78, 79, and the passage from the Katha there cited.

[6] Khândogya, pp. 264–459.

[7] See Khândogya, p. 553 seq.

[8] I.e. attending closely upon him; fœtus=pupil.

preceptor, and becoming (as it were) a fœtus, practise the life of Brahma*k*ârins, become even in this world authors of *S*âstras[1], and they repair to the highest truth[2] after casting off (this) body. They subjugate desires here in this world, practising forbearance in pursuit of the Brahmic state[3]; and with courage, they even here remove the self out of the body[4], like the soft fibres from the Mu*ñg*a. Father and mother, O descendant of Bharata! only form the body. But the birth[5] obtained from the preceptor, that verily is true[6], and likewise immortal. He perfects[7] (one), giving (one) immortality. Recognising what he has done (for one), one should not injure him. The disciple should always make obeisance to the preceptor[8]; and, free from heedlessness, should always desire sacred instruction. When the pure man obtains knowledge by this same course of discipleship[9], that is the first quarter of his life as a Brahma*k*ârin. As (is) his conduct

---

[1] Learned, men of knowledge, *S*ankara.

[2] The supreme, which is described as 'truth, knowledge,' &c. In our ancient works the truth often means the real.

[3] The state of being absorbed in the Brahman. Cf. Gîtâ, p. 52.

[4] Cf. Ka*th*a, p. 158.

[5] *S*ankara cites Âpastamba (p. 11) in support of this, and Pra*s*na-upanishad, p. 256. The consciousness of being one with the Brahman is a new birth. See, too, Mu*nd*aka, p. 282.

[6] That birth is not merely delusive, and does not result in death.

[7] Immortality or final emancipation is not to be achieved without knowledge, which can only be got from a preceptor. And one is not perfect without that immortality; one is limited by the conditions of human existence. See Nirukta (Roth's ed.), p. 41.

[8] *S*ankara compares *S*vetâ*s*vatara, p. 374; see also p. 203 infra. The necessity of having a Guru is often insisted on even in the Upanishads. Cf. Mu*nd*aka, p. 282; *Kh*ândogya, p. 264.

[9] Stated at the beginning of this speech, *S*ankara.

always towards his preceptor, so likewise should he behave towards the preceptor's wife, and so likewise should he act towards the preceptor's son—(that) is said to be the second quarter. What one, recognising what the preceptor has done for one, and understanding the matter[1] (taught), feels with a delighted heart regarding the preceptor—believing that one has been brought into existence[2] by him—that is the third quarter of life as a Brahma*k*ârin. One should do what is agreeable to the preceptor, by means of one's life and riches, and in deed, thought, and word[3]—that is said to be the fourth quarter. (A disciple) obtains a quarter by time[4], so likewise a quarter by associating with the preceptor, he also obtains a quarter by means of his own energy; and then he attains to a quarter by means of the *S*âstras. The life as a Brahma*k*ârin of that man, whose beauty[5] consists in the twelve beginning with knowledge, and whose limbs are the other (qualifications mentioned), and who has

---

[1] The meaning of the Vedic texts, &c., *S*aṅkara in one copy; the highest aim of man, according to another copy.

[2] See note 5 on p. 176.

[3] I keep the order of the original, though I do not translate quite literally; 'thought and word' should be literally 'mind and speech.' See, on the collocation, Gîtâ, p. 123 inter alia.

[4] Time=maturity of understanding which comes by time; energy=intellectual power; *S*âstras=consultation about *S*âstras with fellow-students—*S*aṅkara, who adds that the order is not material as stated, and quotes a stanza which may be thus rendered, 'The pupil receives a quarter from the preceptor, a quarter by his own talent; he receives a quarter by time; and a quarter through fellow-Brahma*k*ârins.

[5] The body being disregarded, these qualities are attributed to the self in this way. For the twelve, see p. 167; the others are abandonment, truthfulness, &c., p. 169.

strength[1], bears fruit, they say, by association with a preceptor, in (the shape of) contact with that entity—the Brahman. Whatever wealth may come to a man who lives in this way, he should even pay that over to the preceptor. He would thus be adopting the conduct of the good which is of many merits; and the same conduct is (to be adopted) towards the preceptor's son. Living thus, he prospers greatly[2] on all sides in this world; he obtains sons and position; the quarters[3] and sub-quarters shower (benefits[4]) on him, and men pass their lives as Brahma*k*ârins under him. By this life as a Brahma*k*ârin, the divinities obtained their divinity. And the sages, too, became great by living the life of Brahma*k*ârins. By this same (means), too, the Apsarasas, together with the Gandharvas, achieved for themselves beautiful forms. And by this life as a Brahma*k*ârin, the sun illuminates (the universe). That man of knowledge, O king! who practising penance, may by penance pierce through or tear off his body, crosses beyond childhood[5] by means of this (life as a Brahma*k*ârin), and at the time of the termination (of life) overcomes death[6]. Those who understand this (life as a Brahma*k*ârin) attain to a

[1] To observe the duties referred to, *S*aṅkara. But see, too, p. 167, note 6.

[2] 'Obtains wealth, learning, and greatness,' says a commentator. For similar benefits, cf. *Kh*ândogya, p. 122.

[3] Cf. *Kh*ândogya, p. 132.

[4] 'Wealth,' says Nîlaka*nth*a, as well as another commentator.

[5] Ignorance; cf. note 7 at p. 154 supra. Nîlaka*nth*a reads 'reaches' instead of 'crosses beyond,' and interprets 'bâlya' to mean 'freedom from affection, aversion,' &c. Cf. B*ri*hadâra*n*yaka, p. 605. As to the divinity of divinities, cf. Taitt. Âra*n*. p. 886.

[6] Nîlaka*nth*a reads 'vanquishes death.' The meaning is, he reaches final emancipation. Cf. p. 154 supra.

condition like that of those who ask (for what they want) from the wish-granting stone[1], when they obtain the thing desired. By performing action, O Kshatriya! people conquer (for themselves only) perishable worlds[2]. (But) the man of understanding attains by knowledge to the everlasting glory—for there is no other way to it[3].

Dh*ri*tarâsh*t*ra said:

Where a Brâhma*n*a possessed of knowledge, perceives it, does it appear as white[4], as red, or again as black, or again as grey or tawny? What is the colour of that immortal, indestructible goal?

Sanatsu*g*âta said:

It appears not as white, as red, nor again as black, nor again as grey, nor tawny[5]. It dwells not on earth, nor in the sky; nor does it bear a body in this ocean[6](-like world). It is not in the stars, nor does it dwell in the lightning; nor is its form[7] to be seen in the clouds, nor even in the air, nor in the deities; it is not to be seen in the moon, nor in the sun. It is not to be seen in *Rik* texts, nor in

---

[1] Called *K*intâma*n*i. The effect of Brahma*k*arya is that those who practise it can get what they desire.

[2] Cf. Gîtâ, p. 76; *Kh*ândogya, p. 538; Mu*nd*aka, p. 279.

[3] Cf. *S*vetâ*s*vatara, p. 327. [4] Cf. B*r*ihadâra*n*yaka, p. 877.

[5] Cf. Ka*th*a, p. 119; and Mu*nd*aka, p. 267. As to its not dwelling in earth, sky, &c., *S*a*n*kara refers to *Kh*ândogya, p. 518, as implying that.

[6] Literally, 'it bears no water in the ocean.' 'Water' is said by the commentators to mean the five elements of which the body is composed. See Manu I, 5, and *Kh*ândogya, p. 330. In the *S*vetâ*s*vatara it signifies mind (see p. 388). For ocean meaning world, or *s*a*m*sâra; cf. Aitareya-upanishad, p. 182.

[7] Here I do not render rûpa by colour, as before.

Yagus texts; nor yet in the Atharvan texts, nor in the pure Sâman texts; nor yet, O king, in the Rathantara or Brihadratha[1] hymns. It is seen in the self of a man of high vows[2]. It is invincible, beyond darkness[3], it comes forth from within[4] at the time of destruction. Its form is more minute than the most minute (things), its form is larger even than the mountains[5]. That is the support[6] (of the universe); that is immortal; (that is) all things perceptible[7]. That is the Brahman, that is glory[8]. From that all entities were produced[9], in that they are dissolved. All this shines forth as dwelling in it in the form of light[10]. And it is perceived by means of knowledge[11] by one who understands the self; on it depends this whole universe. Those who understand this become immortal.

---

[1] See Muir, Sanskrit Texts, vol. i, p. 16; Tândya-brâhmana, p. 838; Gîtâ, p. 90; and Kaushîtaki, p. 21. Brihadratha = Brihat-sâman (?).

[2] The twelve great vows—knowledge, &c., mentioned above, see p. 167. Nîlakantha takes Mahâvrata to refer to the sacrifice of that name. It is described in the Aitareya Âranyaka.

[3] See Gîtâ, p. 78, note 4.

[4] Cf. Gîtâ, p. 82, and Îsopanishad, p. 12.

[5] See Gîtâ, p. 78, note 3.

[6] Cf. Gîtâ, p. 113; Katha, p. 99.

[7] So Nîlakantha. The original word ordinarily means 'worlds.'

[8] Cf. Svetâsvatara, p. 347.

[9] Cf. the famous passage in the Taittirîya, p. 123: and also Mundaka, p. 289.

[10] The explanations of the commentators are not quite clear as to the word ahnâ, 'in the form of light.' Probably the meaning is: The universe depends on the Brahman, and is, as it were, the light of the Brahman. Sankara compares the passages referred to at Gîtâ, p. 112, note 1.

[11] 'Not by means of action,' says Sankara.

CHAPTER V[1].

Grief and wrath, and avarice, desire, delusion, laziness, want of forgiveness, vanity, craving, friendship[2], censoriousness, and reviling others—these twelve great enormities are destructive of a man's life. These, O king of kings! attend on each and every man. Beset by these, a man, deluded in his understanding, acts sinfully. A man full of attachments, merciless, harsh (of speech), talkative, cherishing wrath in his heart, and boastful—these are the men of cruel qualities; (such) persons, even obtaining wealth, do not always enjoy (it)[3]. One

[1] The whole of this chapter is wanting in one of our copies of *S*ankara's commentary. In the copy published in the Mahâbhârata (Madras edition) there is, however, this passage: 'Wrath &c. have been already explained, still there are some differences here and there, and those only are now explained.' The chapter is for the most part a repetition of what we have already had. For such repetitions cf. B*ri*hadâra*n*yaka, pp. 317–1016; 444–930. The same copy of *S*ankara's commentary gives this general statement of the object of this and the next chapter: 'The course of study of the science of the Brahman, in which knowledge is the principal thing, and concentration of mind &c. are subsidiary, has been described. Now is described the course of study in which concentration of mind is principal, and knowledge subsidiary. The first mode consists in understanding the meaning of the word "you" by means of concentration of mind, and then identifying it with the Brahman by means of a study of the Upanishads; the second, in first intellectually understanding the identity of the individual self and Brahman, by such study of the Upanishads, and then realising the identity to consciousness by contemplation, &c. In both modes the fruit is the same, and the means are the same; and to show this, the merits and defects already stated are here again declared.' This explanation is verbatim the same in Nilaka*n*t*h*a's commentary.

[2] The original is 'pity,' which is explained to mean 'friendship' by *S*ankara and Nilaka*n*t*h*a.

[3] 'Owing to there being in it no enjoyment for the self,' says one

whose thoughts are fixed on enjoyments, who is partial[1], proud[2], boastful when he makes a gift, miserly, and devoid of power[3], who esteems the group (of the senses), and who hates (his) wife—thus have been stated the seven (classes of) cruel persons of sinful dispositions. Piety, and truthfulness, and penance, and self-restraint, freedom from animosity, modesty, endurance, freedom from censoriousness, liberality, sacred learning, courage, forgiveness—these are the twelve great observances of a Brâhma*n*a. Whoever does not swerve from these twelve may govern this whole world. And one who is possessed of three, two, or even one, of these, must be understood to have nothing of his own[4]. Self-restraint, abandonment, freedom from delusion, on these immortality depends[5]. These are possessed by those talented Brâhma*n*as to whom the Brahman is the principal[6] (thing). A Brâhma*n*a's speaking ill of others, whether true or false, is not commended.

copy of *S*ankara's commentary. Another reading, which is in the Madras edition and in Nîlaka*n*t*h*a, may be rendered, 'even obtaining benefits, they do not respect one (from whom they obtain them).'

[1] The commentary says the meaning is the same as that of the expression used in the corresponding place before, viz. one who prospers by injuring others.

[2] One copy of *S*ankara's commentary takes this to mean one who thinks the not-self to be the self. I adopt the other meaning, however, as agreeing with that of atimânî, which is the reading of some copies instead of abhimânî.

[3] Nîlaka*n*t*h*a reads durbala and does not explain it. See p. 167.

[4] One commentator says this means that he should not be supposed to have incurred the demerit of having any attachment to this world. Nîlaka*n*t*h*a says, he gives up everything in the pursuit of even one of these observances.

[5] See p. 168.

[6] I.e. the goal to be reached. The commentary takes Brahman to mean the Vedas, and the whole phrase to mean those who devote themselves to the performance of actions stated in the Vedas.

The men who act thus have their places in hell. Frenzy has eighteen defects—as already described here—hatred of men, factiousness [1], censoriousness, untruthful speech, lust, wrath, want of self-control [2], speaking ill of others, backbiting, mismanagement in business [3], quarrelsomeness, animosity, troubling living creatures, want of forgiveness, delusion, flippancy, loss of reason [4], censoriousness [5]; therefore a wise man should not be subject to frenzy, for it is always censured. Six characteristics should be understood as (belonging) to friendship—that one should rejoice at (anything) agreeable; and feel grieved at (anything) disagreeable; that with a pure heart one, when asked by a deserving (man), should give to him who asks what can [6] certainly be given, (though it) may be beneficial to oneself, and even though it ought not to be asked, (namely) one's favourites, sons, wealth, and one's own wife; that one should not dwell there where one has bestowed (all one's) wealth, through a desire (to get a return for one's liberality); that one should enjoy

[1] One copy of *S*añkara's commentary says this means 'obstructing other people's acts of piety,' &c.

[2] One copy of *S*añkara's commentary says this means 'being given up to intoxicating drinks,' &c.; another copy says, 'doing another's bidding without thought.'

[3] One copy says this means 'inattention to any work undertaken;' another renders the original by 'destruction of property, i.e. squandering it on dancers,' &c.

[4] I.e. discrimination between right and wrong.

[5] This seems to be some error, for 'censoriousness' has occurred before. But neither the texts nor the commentaries give any help to correct the error. Perhaps the latter is to be distinguished as referring to the habit, and the former only to sporadic acts, of censoriousness. These qualities, I presume, constitute frenzy; they are not the 'defects.'

[6] I.e. where the power to give exists.

(the fruit of one's[1] own) toils (only); and that one should forego one's own profit[2]. Such a man, possessed of wealth, and possessed of merits, is a liberal man of the quality of goodness[3]; such a one diverts the five elements from the five[4] (senses). This[5] pure penance, acquired out of desire[6] by those who are fallen off from the truth, even though developed, leads upwards[7]; since sacrifices are performed owing to a misapprehension of the truth[8]. (The

[1] Not a friend's. [2] For a friend. [3] See Gîtâ, p. 120.

[4] The commentators take this to mean objects of sense, and they interpret 'elements' before to mean senses.

[5] 'Viz. the turning away of the senses from their objects,' says one copy of *S*añkara.

[6] Scil. to enjoy the higher enjoyments of superior worlds.

[7] I. e. to the higher worlds; it does not lead to emancipation here.

[8] Cf. Mu*nd*aka, p. 277. I must own that I do not quite understand this passage, nor its explanation as given in the commentaries. I do not quite see what the penance here mentioned has to do with sacrifice, and yet the commentators seem to take the words 'since sacrifices,' &c., with what precedes them, not with what follows. Taking them, however, with what follows, it is difficult to explain the word 'since.' As far as I can understand the passage I take the sense of it to be as follows: The author having said that penance performed out of a particular motive does not lead to final emancipation, he then proceeds to point out that all 'action' or 'sacrifice' is due to an imperfect understanding of the truth (cf. p. 171 supra), being mostly due to some particular motive. Then he goes on to show the different classes of sacrifice, and finally points out that he who is free from desires is superior to one who is actuated by desires. The original for 'misapprehension' is avabodha, which commonly means 'apprehension,' but *S*añkara finally makes it mean moha or 'delusion.' The original for truth is rendered by Nilaka*nth*a to mean 'fancies.' Nîlaka*nth*a says that the sacrifice by the mind is the highest; that by speech, viz. Brahmaya*gñ*a, *G*apa, &c., is middling; and that by deed, viz. with clarified butter and other offerings, of the lowest class. 'Perfected by fancies'= one whose fancies are always fulfilled 'through a knowledge,' says Nîlaka*nth*a, 'of the Brahma as possessing qualities.'

sacrifices) of some are by the mind, of others by speech, and also by deed. The man void of fancies takes precedence over the man perfected by fancies, —especially among Brâhma*n*as[1]. And hear this further from me. One should teach this great and glorious[2] (doctrine); (other doctrines) the wise call mere arrangements of words. On this concentration of mind[3], all this[4] depends. Those who know this become immortal. Not by meritorious action only, O king! does man conquer the truth[5]. One may offer offerings, or sacrifice. By that the child(-like man) does not cross beyond death; nor, O king! does he obtain happiness in his last moments[6]. One should practise devotion quietly, and should not be active even in mind[7]; and then one should avoid delight and wrath (resulting) from praise and censure[8]. I say to you, O learned person! that adhering to this[9], one attains the Brahman and perceives it, O Kshatriya! by a course (of study) of the Vedas.

[1] This also is far from clear. Should it be, 'and a Brâhma*n*a more especially?' This might be taken as referring to one who knows the Brahman as devoid of qualities, as Nîlaka*n*/*h*a does take it. But his construction is not quite clear.

[2] As serviceable in attaining to 'the glory,' the Brahman; see p. 180.

[3] See note 1 at p. 181. As to 'arrangements of words,' cf. Maitrî, p. 179.

[4] 'Everything,' says one copy of *S*ankara's commentary; 'all that is good and desirable,' says another.

[5] Cf. inter alia, Mu*nd*aka, pp. 281–314.

[6] For he has got to undergo migration from one life to another as the result of the action. Cf. B*ri*hadâra*n*yaka, p. 856; Mu*nd*aka, p. 278.

[7] Cf. Gîtâ, p. 70.

[8] Ibid. pp. 101–110.

[9] I.e. the yoga or concentration of mind here described. This stanza, like many others in this chapter, occurs in chapter III with slight variations.

CHAPTER VI.

That pure[1], great light[2], which is radiant; that great glory[3]; that, verily, which the gods worship[4]; that by means of which the sun shines forth[5]—that eternal divine being is perceived by devotees. From (that) pure (principle) the Brahman[6] is produced; by (that) pure (principle) the Brahman is developed[7]; that pure (principle), not illumined among all radiant (bodies), is (itself) luminous and illuminates (them)[8]. That eternal divine being is perceived by devotees. The perfect is raised out of the perfect. It (being raised) out of the perfect is called the perfect. The perfect is withdrawn from the perfect, and the perfect only remains[9]. That eternal divine being is perceived by devotees.

---

[1] Free from ignorance and other taints. See Ka*th*a, p. 144.

[2] *S*aṅkara compares Ka*th*a, p. 142. See, too, Mu*nd*aka, p. 303; and note 4 infra.

[3] *S*vetâ*s*vatara, p. 347, and p. 180 supra.

[4] *S*aṅkara refers to B*ri*hadâra*n*yaka, p. 887.

[5] Cf. Gîtâ, p. 112, note 1.

[6] 'Named Hira*n*yagarbha,' *S*aṅkara. Cf. Gîtâ, p. 107; *S*vetâ*s*vatara, p. 354; Mu*nd*aka, p. 309; Maitrî, p. 130; Taitt. Âra*n*. p. 894.

[7] 'In the form of Virâ*g*,' says *S*aṅkara. As to these two, cf. Mu*nd*aka, pp. 270–272; and *S*aṅkara's and Ânandagiri's notes there. See also *S*vetâ*s*vatara, pp. 324, 325; and N*ri*si*m*ha Tâpinî, pp. 233, 234; Colebrooke, Essays, pp. 344, 368 (Madras reprint). The Virâ*g* corresponds rather to the gross material world viewed as a whole; the Hira*n*yagarbha to the subtle elements similarly viewed, an earlier stage in the development. Cf. the Vedântasâra.

[8] Cf. Mu*nd*aka, p. 303, and Gîtâ, p. 112.

[9] The individual self is part of the supreme (Gîtâ, p. 112); perfect = not limited by space, time, &c.; as being part of a thing perfect in its essence, the individual soul also is perfect. The individual self is withdrawn from the perfect, viz. the whole aggregate of body, senses, &c. presided over by the self, and when so withdrawn it appears to be the pure self only. Cf. B*ri*hadâra*n*yaka, p. 948.

(From the Brahman), the waters[1] (are produced); and then from the waters, the gross body. In the space within that[2], dwelt the two divine (principles). Both enveloping the quarters and sub-quarters, support earth and heaven[3]. That eternal divine being is perceived by devotees. The horse[4](-like senses) lead towards heaven him, who is possessed of knowledge and divine, (who is) free from old age, and who stands on the wheel of this chariot(-like body), which is transient, but the operations of which are imperishable[5]. That eternal divine being[6] is perceived by devotees. His form has no parallel[7]; no one sees him with the eye[8]. Those who apprehend him by means of the understanding, and also the mind and heart, become immortal[9]. That eternal

---

[1] 'The five elements,' says *S*a*n*kara, cf. Aitareya, p. 189; and for 'gross body,' the original is literally 'water;' see supra, p. 179, note 6; and see, too, Îsopanishad, p. 11, and *S*vetâsvatara, p. 368, for different but kindred meanings.

[2] Viz. the lotus-like heart. Cf. *Kh*ândogya, p. 528.

[3] The two principles between them pervade the universe, the individual self being connected with the material world, the other with heaven; 'divine' is, literally, 'the brilliant,' says *S*a*n*kara, who quotes Ka*th*a, p. 305, as a parallel for the whole passage.

[4] Cf. Ka*th*a, p. 111; Maitrî, pp. 19–34; and Mahâbhârata Strî Parvan, chap. VII, st. 13. Heaven = the Brahman here (see B*ri*hadâra*n*yaka, p. 876); divine = not vulgar, or unrefined—*S*a*n*kara, who adds that though the senses generally lead one to sensuous objects, they do not do so when under the guidance of true knowledge.

[5] The body is perishable, but action done by the self while in the body leaves its effect.

[6] To whom, namely, the man of knowledge goes, as before stated.

[7] Cf. *S*vetâsvatara, p. 347.

[8] Cf. Ka*th*a, p. 152, and comment there, where the eye is said to stand for all the senses.

[9] Ka*th*a, p. 149; *S*vetâsvatara, pp. 346–348, also p. 330 (should it be manîshâ there instead of manviro?). The meanings of the three words are difficult to fix accurately. *S*a*n*kara varies in his interpre-

divine being is perceived by devotees. The currents of twelve collections[1], supported by the Deity, regulate the honey[2]; and those who follow after it move about in (this) dangerous (world). That eternal divine being[3] is perceived by devotees. The bee[4] drinks that accumulated honey for half a month[5]. The Lord created the oblation for all beings[6]. That eternal divine being is perceived by devotees. Those who are devoid of wings[7], coming

tations. Probably the meaning he gives here is the best. Mind and understanding have been explained at Gîtâ, p. 57. The heart is the place within, where the self is said to be, and it may be taken as indicating the self, the meaning would then be—a direct consciousness in the self of its unity with the Supreme. See, too, Taitt. Âra*n*. p. 896.

[1] The five organs of action, the five senses of perception, the mind and understanding make the twelve.

[2] Each current has its own honey regularly distributed to it under the supervision of the Deity, the Supreme. Honey = material enjoyment. Cf. Ka*th*a, p. 126, where *S*aṅkara renders it by karmaphala, 'fruit of action.'

[3] Who supervises the distribution as stated. Cf. Vedânta-sûtra III, 2, 28–31.

[4] Bhramara, which the commentators interpret to mean 'one who is given to flying about—the individual self.'

[5] I. e. in one life in respect of actions done in a previous life.

[6] *S*aṅkara says this is in answer to a possible difficulty that action performed here cannot have its fruit in the next world, as the fruit is so far removed in time from the action. The answer is, The Lord, the Supreme, can effect this, and taking his existence into account there is no difficulty. Oblation = food, &c., *S*aṅkara. The meaning of the whole passage, which is not very clear, seems to be that the Lord has arranged things so that each being receives some of this honey, this food, which is the fruit of his own action. Then the question arises, Do these beings always continue taking the honey and 'migrating,' or are they ever released? That is answered by the following sentence.

[7] 'The wings of knowledge,' says *S*aṅkara, citing a Brâhma*n*a text, 'those, verily, who have knowledge are possessed of wings, those who are not possessed of knowledge are devoid of wings.'

to the Asvattha of golden leaves[1], there become possessed of wings, and fly away happily[2]. That eternal divine being[3] is perceived by devotees. The upward life-wind swallows up the downward life-wind; the moon swallows up the upward life-wind; the sun swallows up the moon[4]; and another[5] swallows up the sun. Moving about above the waters, the supreme self[6] does not raise one leg[7]. (Should he raise) that, which is always performing sacrifices[8], there will be no death, no immortality[9]. That eternal divine being[10] is perceived by devotees.

[1] So, literally; Sankara explains 'golden' to mean 'beneficial and pleasant,' by a somewhat fanciful derivation of the word hiranya. He refers to Gitâ, p. 111, about the leaves of the Asvattha. Nilakantha takes the leaves to be son, wife, &c., which are 'golden,' attractive at first sight. 'Coming to the Asvattha,' Sankara says, 'means being born as a Brâhmana,' &c. 'Flying away' = obtaining final emancipation.

[2] The 'selfs' are compared to birds in the famous passage at Mundaka, p. 306 (also Svetâsvatara, p. 337). See also Brihadâranyaka, p. 499.

[3] Knowledge of whom leads to 'flying away happily.'

[4] Cf. Khândogya, p. 441. Sankara says that the author here explains the yoga by which the Supreme is to be attained. As to the life-winds, cf. Gitâ, p. 61. 'The moon,' says Sankara, 'means the mind, and the sun the understanding, as they are the respective deities of those organs' (cf. Brihadâranyaka, pp. 521-542, and Aitareya, p. 187, where, however, the sun is said to appertain to the eye).

[5] I. e. the Brahman; the result is, one remains in the condition of being identified with the Brahman.

[6] Literally, flamingo. Cf. Svetâsvatara, pp. 332, 367; see also p. 289; Maitrî, p. 99; and the commentary on Svetâsvatara, p. 283.

[7] Viz. the individual self, Sankara; that is, as it were, the bond of connexion between the Supreme and the world. Cf. Gitâ, p. 112.

[8] This is the meaning, though the word in the original is Ritvig, which in the later literature only means priest.

[9] As the whole of the material world is dissolved, when the self is dissevered from the delusion which is the cause of it.

[10] Viz. who moves about on the waters, as above stated.

The being which is the inner self, and which is of the size of a thumb[1], is always migrating in consequence of the connexion with the subtle body[2]. The deluded ones do not perceive that praiseworthy lord, primeval and radiant, and possessed of creative power[3]. That eternal divine being is perceived by devotees. Leading mortals to destruction by their own action[4], they conceal themselves like serpents in secret recesses[5]. The deluded men then become more deluded[6]. The enjoyments afforded by them cause delusion, and lead to worldly life[7]. That eternal divine being[8] is perceived by devotees. This[9] seems to be common to all mankind—whether possessed of resources[10] or not possessed of resources—it is common to immortality and the other[11]. Those who are possessed (of them)[12] attain there to the source of the honey[13]. That eternal divine being is perceived by devotees. They go,

---

[1] *S*vetâ*s*vatara, pp. 330–355; Taitt. Âra*n*. p. 858, and comments there.

[2] The life-winds, the ten organs or senses, mind, and understanding. See the same word similarly interpreted at *S*vetâ*s*vatara, p. 306, and Sâṅkhya-sûtra III, 9.

[3] According to *S*aṅkara, he who makes the distinct entities, after entering into them; he alludes apparently to *Kh*ândogya, p. 407.

[4] Namely, that of giving the poison of sensuous objects.

[5] I. e. the eye, ear, &c., like the holes of serpents.

[6] I. e. can appreciate nought but those sensuous objects.

[7] One reading is, 'lead to danger'=which means 'to hell,' according to Nîlaka*n*t*h*a.

[8] Scil. delusion about whom leads to 'danger' or 'worldly life.'

[9] The quality of being one with the Brahman in essence.

[10] Self-restraint, tranquillity, &c.

[11] I. e. whether in the midst of worldly life, or in the state of perfect emancipation.

[12] Viz. the resources spoken of before.

[13] Viz. the supreme Brahman. 'There' *S*aṅkara takes to mean 'in the supreme abode of Vish*n*u.' See Introduction.

pervading both worlds by knowledge[1]. Then the Agnihotra though not performed is (as good as) performed[2]. Your (knowledge) of the Brahman, therefore, will not lead you to littleness[3]. Knowledge is (his)[4] name. To that the talented ones attain. That eternal divine being is perceived by devotees. The self of this description absorbing the material cause[5] becomes great. And the self of him who understands that being is not degraded here[6]. That eternal divine being is perceived by devotees. One should ever and always be doing good. (There is) no death, whence (can there be) immortality[7]? The real and the unreal have both the same real (entity) as their basis. The source of the existent and the non-existent is but one[8]. That eternal divine being is perceived by devotees. The

[1] *S*añkara does not explain this. Nîlaka*n*/*h*a says pervading = fully understanding; both worlds = the self and the not-self. Is the meaning something like that of the passage last cited by *S*añkara under Vedânta-sûtra IV, 2, 14?

[2] He obtains the fruit of it, *S*añkara. See as to Agnihotra, *Kh*ândogya, p. 381 seq.; and Vedânta-sûtra IV, 1, 16.

[3] I.e. this mortal world, as action &c. would do.

[4] I.e. of one who understands himself to be the Brahman. See Aitareya-upanishad, p. 246.

[5] *S*añkara says, 'the cause in which all is absorbed.' Cf. a similar, but not identical, meaning given to Vais*v*ânara at *Kh*ândogya, p. 264; and see Vedânta-sûtra I, 2, 24. Becomes great = becomes the Brahman, *S*añkara.

[6] Even in this body, *S*añkara; degradation he takes to mean departure from the body, citing B*ri*hadâra*n*yaka, p. 540.

[7] There is no worldly life with birth and death for one who does good, and thinks his self to be the Brahman; hence no emancipation from such life either.

[8] The Brahman is the real, and on that the unreal material world is imagined. Cf. Taittirîya, p. 97, and *S*añkara's comments there, which are of use in understanding this passage.

being who is the inner self, and who is of the size of a thumb, is not seen, being placed in the heart[1]. He is unborn, is moving about day and night, without sloth. Meditating on him, a wise man remains placid[2]. That eternal divine being is perceived by devotees. From him comes the wind[3]; in him, likewise, is (everything) dissolved. From him (come) the fire and the moon; and from him comes life[4]. That is the support (of the universe); that is immortal; that is all things perceptible[5]; that is the Brahman, that glory. From that all entities were produced; and in that (they) are dissolved[6]. That eternal divine being is perceived by devotees. The brilliant (Brahman) supports the two divine principles[7] and the universe, earth and heaven, and the quarters. He from whom the rivers flow in (various) directions, from him were created the great oceans[8]. That eternal divine being is perceived by devotees. Should one fly, even after furnishing oneself with thousands upon thousands of wings, and even though one should have the velocity of thought[9], one would never reach the end of the (great) cause[10]. That eternal divine

[1] Cf. Ka*th*a, pp. 130, 157; and B*ri*hadâra*n*yaka, p. 360.

[2] Cf. *S*vetâ*s*vatara, p. 342; Ka*th*a, pp. 100, 107; Maitrî, p. 134.

[3] Cf. Taittirîya, p. 67; Ka*th*a, p. 146; Mu*nd*aka, p. 293.

[4] Ka*th*a, p. 298; Mu*nd*aka, p. 288.

[5] See p. 180, note 7.

[6] See p. 180 supra.

[7] 'The individual soul, and God,' say the commentators, the latter being distinct from the supreme self. 'The universe,' says Nîlaka*nt*ha, 'means earth,' &c., by which I suppose he means earth, heaven, quarters, mentioned directly afterwards.

[8] Ka*th*a, p. 293.

[9] This figure is implied in the Î*s*opanishad, p. 10.

[10] 'Therefore it is endless,' says *S*a*n*kara; and as to this, cf. Taittirîya, p. 51.

being is perceived by devotees. His form dwells in the unperceived[1]; and those whose understandings are very well refined[2] perceive him. The talented man who has got rid (of affection and aversion) perceives (him) by the mind. Those who understand him[3] become immortal. When one sees this self in all beings stationed in various places[4], what should one grieve for after that[5]? The Brâhma*n*a has (as much interest) in all beings, as in a big reservoir of water, to which waters flow from all sides[6]. I alone am your mother[7], father;

[1] 'In a sphere beyond the reach of perception,' says *S*ankara, who also quotes Ka*th*a, p. 149, or *S*vetâ*s*vatara, p. 347, where the same line also occurs.

[2] The original for understandings is sattva, which *S*ankara renders to mean anta*h*kara*n*a. 'Refined,' he says, 'by sacrifices and other sanctifying operations.' In the Ka*th*a at p. 148 sattva is rendered by *S*ankara to mean buddhi—a common use of the word.

[3] 'As being,' says *S*ankara, 'identical with themselves.' It will be noted that the form of expression is slightly altered here. It is not 'those who understand this.'

[4] I.e. in different aggregates of body, senses, &c. Cf. Gîtâ, pp. 104 and 124; also *Kh*ândogya, pp. 475–551.

[5] Cf. B*ri*hadâra*n*yaka, p. 882; *S*ankara also refers to Î*s*opanishad, p. 14.

[6] The words are pretty nearly the same as at Gîtâ, p. 48. *S*ankara says, the Brâhma*n*a 'who has done all he need do' has no interest whatever in any being, as he has none in a big reservoir, and he cites Gîtâ, p. 54, in support of this. One copy of *S*ankara, however, differs from this; that runs thus: 'As a person who has done all he need do, has no interest in a big reservoir of water, so to a Brâhma*n*a who sees the self in all beings, there is no interest in all the actions laid down in the Vedas, &c.; as he has obtained everything by mere perception of the self.' Nîlaka*nth*a's reading is exactly the same as at Gîtâ, p. 48.

[7] *S*ankara says that Sanatsugâta states here his own experiences, like Vâmadeva (about whom there is a reference at B*ri*hadâra*n*yaka, p. 216) and others, to corroborate what he has already said. Cf. also Gîtâ, p. 83, as to the whole passage.

and I too am the son. And I am the self of all this—that which exists and that which does not exist[1]. (I am) the aged grandfather of this, the father, and the son, O descendant of Bharata! You dwell in my self only[2]. You are not mine, nor I (yours). The self only is my seat[3]; the self too is (the source of) my birth[4]. I am woven through and through[5] (everything). And my seat is free from (the attacks of) old age[6]. I am unborn, moving about day and night, without sloth. Knowing (me), verily, a wise man remains placid[7]. More minute than an atom[8], possessed of a good mind[9], I am stationed within all beings[10]. (The wise) know the father of all beings to be placed in the lotus[11](-like heart of every one).

[1] See Gitâ, p. 84. Nîlaka*nth*a takes what exists to mean 'present,' and what does not exist to mean 'past and future.' Cf. *Kh*ândogya, p. 532.

[2] See Gitâ, p. 82, where there is also a similar apparent contradiction.

[3] Cf. *Kh*ândogya, p. 518.

[4] That is to say he is 'unborn,' says Nîlaka*nth*a. *S*aṅkara seems to take 'my' with 'seat' only, and not with birth; for he says, 'everything has its birth from the self.'

[5] Cf. Mu*nd*aka, p. 298; Maitrî, p. 84, and comment there.

[6] Cf. Gitâ, pp. 77, 109, and *Kh*ândogya, pp. 535, 550.

[7] See p. 192, note 2.

[8] Cf. Gitâ, p. 78, and note 3 there.

[9] I.e. a mind free from affection and aversion, hatred, &c., *S*aṅkara.

[10] Cf. Gîtâ, p. 113, and note 3; and also Îsopanishad, p. 12.

[11] *Kh*ândogya, p. 528; and cf. Gîtâ, p. 113.

ANUGÎTÂ.

INTRODUCTION

TO

ANUGÎTÂ.

Like the Bhagavadgîtâ and the Sanatsugâtîya, the Anugîtâ is one of the numerous episodes of the Mahâbhârata. And like the Sanatsugâtîya, it appears here for the first time in an English, or, indeed, it is believed, in any European garb. It forms part of the Asvamedha Parvan of the Mahâbhârata, and is contained in thirty-six chapters of that Parvan. These chapters—being chapters XVI to LI—together with all the subsequent chapters of the Asvamedha Parvan, form by themselves what in some of our copies is called the Anugîtâ Parvan—a title which affords a parallel to the title Bhagavadgîtâ Parvan, which we have already referred to. The Anugîtâ is not now a work of any very great or extensive reputation. But we do find some few quotations from it in the Bhâshyas of *S*ankarâ*k*ârya, and one or two in the Sâṅkhya-sâra of Vig*ñ*âna Bhikshu, to which reference will be made hereafter. And it is included in the present volume, partly because it affords an interesting glimpse of sundry old passages of the Upanishad literature in a somewhat modified, and presumably later, form; and partly, perhaps I may say more especially, because it professes to be a sort of continuation, or rather recapitulation, of the Bhagavadgîtâ. At the very outset of the work, we read, that after the great fratricidal war of the Mahâbhârata was over, and the Pâ*nd*avas had become sole and complete masters of their ancestral kingdom, K*ri*sh*n*a and Arguna—the two interlocutors in the Bhagavadgîtâ—happened to take a stroll together in the great magical palace built for the Pâ*nd*avas by the demon Maya. In the course of the conversation which they held on the occasion, K*ri*sh*n*a communicated to Arguna his wish to return to his own people at Dvârakâ, now that the business which had called him away from them was happily terminated. Ar*g*una, of course, was unable to resist the execution of this wish; but he requested K*r*ish*n*a, before leaving for Dvârakâ, to repeat the instruction which had been already conveyed to him on 'the holy field of Kurukshetra,' but which had gone out of his 'degenerate mind.' K*r*ish*n*a thereupon protests that he is not equal to a verbatim recapitulation of the Bhagavad-gîtâ, but agrees, in lieu of that, to impart to Ar*g*una the same instruction in other words, through the medium of a certain 'ancient story'—or purâtana itihâsa. And the instruction thus conveyed constitutes what is called the Anugîtâ, a name which is in itself an embodiment of this anecdote.

Now the first question which challenges investigation with reference to this work is, if we may so call it, the fundamental one—how much is properly included under the name? The question is not one quite easy of settlement, as our authorities upon it are not all reconcilable with one another. In the general list of contents of the A*s*vamedha Parvan, which is given at the end of that Parvan in the edition printed at Bombay, we read that the first section is the Vyâsa Vâkya, and the second the Sa*m*vartamaruttîya. With neither of these have we aught to do here. The list then goes on thus: 'Anugîtâ, Vâsudevâgamana, Brâhma*n*a Gîtâ, Guru*s*ishyasa*m*vâda, Uttankopâkhyâna,' and so forth. With the later sections, again, we are not here concerned. Now let us compare this list with the list which may be obtained from the titles of the chapters in the body of the work itself. With the sixteenth chapter, then, of the A*s*vamedha Parvan, begins what is here called the Anugîtâ Parvan; and that chapter and the three following chapters are described as the sixteenth, seventeenth, eighteenth, and nineteenth chapters respectively of the Anugîtâ Parvan, which forms part of the A*s*vamedha Parvan. The title of the twentieth chapter contains a small, but important, addition. It runs thus, 'Such is the twentieth chapter of the Anugîtâ Parvan, forming part of the A*s*vamedha Parvan—being the Brahma Gîtâ.' This form is continued down to the thirty-fourth chapter, only Brâhma*n*a

Gîtâ being substituted for Brahma Gîtâ. At the close of the thirty-fifth chapter, there is another alteration caused by the substitution of Gurusishyasamvâda for Brâhmana Gîtâ; and this continues down to the fifty-first chapter, where the thread of the narrative is again taken up—the philosophical parenthesis, if I may so say, having come to an end. With the fifty-first chapter our present translation also ends. Now it appears from the above comparison, that the list of contents set out above is accurate, save in so far as it mentions Vâsudevâgamana as a distinct section of the Asvamedha Parvan. No such section seems to be in existence. And there appears to be nothing in the Asvamedha Parvan to which that title could be appropriately allotted. The edition printed at Madras agrees in all essential particulars with the Bombay edition; with this difference, that even at the close of the twentieth chapter, the name is Brâhmana Gîtâ, and not Brahma Gîtâ as it is in the Bombay edition. The Calcutta edition also agrees in these readings. Turning now to a MS. procured for me by my excellent friend Professor Âbâgî Vishnu Kâthavate at Ahmedabad, and bearing date the 15th of Phâlguna Vadya 1823, Sunday, we find there at the end of the Asvamedha Parvan a list of contents like that which we have seen in the printed edition. The relevant portion of that list is as follows: 'Samvartamaruttîya, Anugîtâ, Gurusishyasamvâda, and Uttankopâkhyâna.' Here we find neither the erroneous entry of Vâsudevâgamana, nor the correct entry of Brahma Gîtâ, which are both contained in the other list. In another MS. which I have now before me, and which has been lent me by Professor Bhândârkar, who purchased it in Puna for the Government of Bombay—in this MS., which contains the commentary of Arguna Misra, the earlier chapters are described not as chapters of the Anugîtâ Parvan, but of the Anugîtâ contained in the Asvamedha Parvan, and they are numbered there as they are numbered in our translation, not continuously with the numbering of the previous chapters of the Asvamedha Parvan. At the close of chapter IV, we have an explicit statement that the Anugîtâ ends there. Then the Brahma Gîtâ begins. And the first chapter is described as a chapter of the Brahma Gîtâ in the Asvamedha Parvan. The numbering of each of these chapters of the Brahma Gîtâ is not given in the copy before us—the titles and descriptions of the various chapters being throughout incomplete. Some of the later chapters are described as chapters of the Brâhma Gîtâ, and some as chapters of the Brâhmana Gîtâ; but this discrepancy is probably to be put to the account of the particular copyist who wrote out the copy used by us. With what is chapter XX in our numbering the Gurusishyasamvâda begins. This MS. omits all reference to any Anugîtâ Parvan, and fails to number the various chapters. Its list of sections agrees with that in the Bombay edition. It bears no date.

So much for what may be described as our primary sources of information on this subject. Let us now glance at the secondary sources. And, first, Nîlakantha in commenting on what is, according to his numbering, chapter XV, stanza 43, apparently distinguishes that chapter from what he speaks of as the Brâhmana Gîtâ and Gurusishyasamvâda, which, as he implies, follow after that chapter—thus indicating that he accepted in substance the tradition recorded in the passages we have already set forth, viz. that the first four chapters of our translation form the Anugîtâ, the next fifteen the Brâhmana Gîtâ, and the last seventeen the Gurusishyasamvâda. This is also the view of Arguna Misra. At the close of his gloss on chapter IV, he distinctly states that the Anugîtâ ends at that chapter; and again at the close of the gloss on chapter XIX, he explicitly says that the Brâhmana Gîtâ ends there. He also adds the following interesting observation: 'The feminine form (Gîtâ, namely) is used in consequence of (the word) Upanishad being feminine.' The full title of that part of the Mahâbhârata would then be, according to this remark of Arguna Misra, 'the Upanishads sung by the Brâhmana,' a title parallel to that of the Bhagavadgîtâ, 'the Upanishads sung by the Deity.' It is to be further remarked, that the last chapter of the Gurusishyasamvâda is called in this commentary the eighteenth chapter of the Gurusishyasamvâda, a fact which seems to indicate that Arguna Misra either found in the MS. which he used, or himself established, a separate numbering for the chapters in the several sections[1] of which the A*s*vamedha Parvan is made up.

Although the information here set out from these various sources is not easily to be harmonised in all its parts, the preponderance of testimony seems to be in favour of regarding the portion of the A*s*vamedha Parvan embraced in our translation as containing three distinct sections, viz. the Anugîtâ, the Brâhma*n*a Gîtâ, and the Guru*s*ishyasa*m*vâda. And some indirect support for this conclusion may be derived from one or two other circumstances. In the Sâṅkhya-sâra of Vig*ñ*âna Bhikshu—a work which, as we shall see in the sequel, expressly mentions the Anugîtâ—we have a passage cited as from the 'Bhârata[2]' which coincides almost precisely with a passage occurring in chapter XXVII of our translation (see p. 335). And in the Bhâshya of *S*aṅkarâ*k*ârya on the Bhagavadgîtâ, chapter XV, stanza 1, we have a citation as from a 'Purâ*n*a' of a passage which coincides pretty closely with one which occurs in chapter XX of our translation (see p. 313). If the discrepancies between the quotations as given by Vig*ñ*âna Bhikshu and *S*aṅkara, and the passages occurring in our text, may be treated merely as various readings—and there is nothing inherently improbable in this being the case—it may be fairly contended, that neither *S*aṅkara nor Vig*ñ*âna Bhikshu would have used the vague expressions, 'a Purâ*n*a,' or even 'the Bhârata,' if they could have correctly substituted in lieu of them the specific name Anugîtâ. And this, it may be said, is a contention of some weight, when it is remembered, that both *S*aṅkara and Vig*ñ*âna show, in other parts of their writings, an acquaintance with this very Anugîtâ. If this reasoning is correct,

[1] In the beginning of his gloss on the Anugîtâ he says, that he proposes to explain difficult passages in the Anugîtâ, &c.—Anugîtâdishu. And at the outset of his gloss on the whole Parvan he says, that in the Anugîtâ we have a statement of the miseries of birth, &c. as a protest against worldly life; in the Brahma Gîtâ we have a recommendation of Prâ*n*âyâma, &c.; and in the Guru*s*ishyasa*m*vâda we have a eulogium on the perception of the self as distinct from Pra*kri*ti or nature, and incidentally a protest against Prav*ri*tti or action.

[2] P. 21.

the conclusion to be derived from it must be, that *S*ankara and Vig*ñ*âna must have considered the chapters of the A*s*vamedha Parvan from which their respective quotations are taken as not forming part of the Anugîtâ.

The testimony we have thus collected is apparently of considerable weight. Against it, however, we have to weigh some testimony which appears to me to be entitled, upon the whole, to even greater weight. In the Sâṅkhya-sâra of Vig*ñ*âna Bhikshu, to which we have already referred, we have two quotations[1] from the Anugîtâ which are distinctly stated to be taken from that work. The first occurs in our translation at p. 332, the second at p. 313. Now, if we adopt the conclusion above referred to, regarding the correct titles of the thirty-six chapters which we have translated, it is a mistake to attribute the passages in question to the Anugîtâ. They would, on that view, form part of the Guru*s*ishyasa*m*vâda. Again, in his commentary on the Sanatsu*g*âtîya, *S*aṅkara refers to sundry passages which he expressly says are taken from the Anugîtâ, but which are not contained in the Anugîtâ as limited by the evidence we have considered above. One of the passages referred to is taken from chapter XI of our translation, and others are contained in the comments on Sanatsu*g*âtîya I, 6, and on I, 20 and I, 41[2]. It is difficult to resist the conclusion to which this positive evidence leads. One cannot possibly explain this evidence upon the view which we have first stated; while, on the other hand, the points which apparently support that view are capable of some explanation on the theory that the Anugîtâ includes all the chapters here translated. And that in this wise. The passages which we have referred to as cited by *S*aṅkara and Vig*ñ*âna from a Purâ*n*a and from the Bhârata may have been actually taken from some other work than the Anugîtâ. Even waiving the fact that the readings are different,—though in regard especially to the quotation given by *S*aṅkara it is not one to be entirely lost sight of,—there is this fact which is of great and almost conclusive weight on such a point as

[1] Pp. 15, 21. The latter corresponds to *S*aṅkara's quotation above referred to.
[2] See p. 206 note.

this, namely, that we have many instances of passages common, almost verbatim et literatim, to the Mahâbhârata and other works. For one instance, take the very passage on which a chronological argument has been founded by us in the Introduction to the Sanatsugâtîya[1]. It ought to have been there pointed out, that the stanza about a young man being bound to rise to receive an elderly person, occurs in the Manu Smriti[2] also in exactly the same words. The omission to note this circumstance in its proper place in the Introduction to the Sanatsugâtîya was due to a mere inadvertence. But the conclusion there hinted at was expressed in very cautious language, and with many qualifications, out of regard to circumstances such as those which we are now considering. Similar repetitions may be pointed out in other places. The passage about the Kshetragña and Sattva and their mutual relations (see p. 374) occurs, as pointed out in the note there, in at least two other places in the Mahâbhârata. The passage likewise which occurs in Gîtâ, p. 103, about the 'hands, feet, &c., on all sides,' is one which may be seen, to my own knowledge, in about half a dozen places in the Mahâbhârata. Such cases, I believe, may be easily multiplied; and they illustrate and are illustrated by Mr. Freeman's proposition respecting the epic age in Greece, to which we have already alluded. It follows, consequently, that the quotations from Sankara and Vigñâna, to which we have referred above, do not militate very strongly against the final conclusion at which we have arrived. The testimony of the MSS. and the commentators is of considerably greater force. But Nîlakantha, whatever his merits as an exegete—and even these are often marred by a persistent effort to read his own foregone conclusions into the text he comments on—Nîlakantha is but an indifferent authority in the domain of historical criticism. In his commentary on the Sanatsugâtîya, for instance, he tells us that he has admitted into his text sundry verses which were not in the copy used by Sankara, and for which he had none but a very modern voucher, and he very naively adds that he has done so on the principle of collecting all

[1] P. 139, and cf. p. 176 with Vishnu XXX, 44 seq.

[2] See II, 120.

good things to a focus. Arguna Misra is a very much more satisfactory commentator. But he is not likely to be a writer of a very remote date. I assume, that he must be more recent than Saṅkarâkârya, though I cannot say that I have any very tenable ground for the assumption. But assuming that, I think it more satisfactory to adopt Saṅkarâkârya's nomenclature, and to treat the thirty-six chapters here translated as constituting the Anugîtâ. It is not improbable, if our assumption is correct, that the division of the thirty-six chapters in the manner we have seen may have come into vogue after the date of Vigñâna Bhikshu, who, according to Dr. F. E. Hall, 'lived in all probability in the sixteenth or seventeenth century, and whom there is some slight reason for carrying back still further[1].'

Do these thirty-six chapters, then, form one integral work? Are they all the work of one and the same author? These are the questions which next present themselves for consideration. The evidence bearing upon them, however, is, as might be expected, excessively scanty. Of external evidence, indeed, we have really none, barring Saṅkara's statement in his commentary on the Brihadâranyaka-upanishad[2] that the verse which he there quotes from the Anugîtâ has Vyâsa for its author. That statement indicates that Saṅkara accepted the current tradition of Vyâsa's authorship of the Anugîtâ; and such acceptance, presumably, followed from his acceptance of the tradition of Vyâsa's authorship of the entire Mahâbhârata. If that tradition is incorrect, and Vyâsa is not the author of the Anugîtâ, we have no means of ascertaining who is the author. And as to the tradition in question, it is difficult, in the present state of our materials, to form any satisfactory judgment. We therefore proceed at once to consider whether the Anugîtâ is really one work. And I must admit at the outset that I find it difficult to answer this question. There are certainly some circumstances connected with the work which might be regarded as indicating a different authorship of different parts of it. Thus

[1] See Preface, Sâṅkhya-sâra, p. 37.

[2] P. 234.

in an early portion of the work, we find the first personal pronoun is used, where the Supreme Being is evidently intended to be signified, and yet the passage is not put into the mouth of K*ri*sh*n*a, but of the Brâhma*n*a. A similar passage occurs a little later on also. Now it must be taken to be a somewhat strained interpretation of the words used in the passages in question to suppose that the speaker there used the first personal pronoun, identifying himself for the nonce with the Supreme Being[1]. Again, in a passage still further on, we have the vocative O Pârtha! where the person addressed is not Ar*g*una at all, but the Brâhma*n*a's wife. Now these lapses are susceptible of two explanations—either we are to see in them so many cases of 'Homer nodding,' or we may suppose that they are errors occasioned by one writer making additions to the work of a previous writer, without a vivid recollection of the framework of the original composition into which his own work had to be set[2]. I own, that on balancing the probabilities on the one side and the other, my mind rather leans to the hypothesis of one author making a slip in the plexus of his own story within story, rather than the hypothesis of a deliberate interpolator forgetting the actual scheme of the original work into which he was about to foist his own additions[3]. And this the rather, that we find a similar slip towards the very beginning of the work, where we have the Brâhma*n*a Kâ*s*yapa addressed as Parantapa, or destroyer of foes—an epithet which, I think, is exclusively reserved for Kshatriyas, and is, in any case, a very inappropriate one to apply to a humble seeker for spiritual light. This slip appears to me to be incapable of explanation on any theory of interpolation[4]. And hence the other slips above noted can hardly be regarded as supporting any such theory. Another circumstance, not indeed bearing

[1] In fact the Brâhma*n*a is not identified with the Supreme Being afterwards. But that fact has not much bearing on the question here.

[2] Cf. Wilson's Da*s*akumâra*k*arita, Introd. p. 22.

[3] The third alternative, that a work independently written was afterwards bodily thrown into the Mahâbhârata, is one which in the circumstances here seems to me improbable.

[4] See also pp. 235, 252, 299.

out that theory, but rendering interpolations possible, deserves to be noted. The scheme of the Anugîtâ certainly lends itself to interpolations. A story might without much difficulty be added to the series of story joined to story which it contains. Against this, however, it must not be forgotten, that the *S*ânti Parvan of the Mahâbhârata and the Yogavâsish*th*a exhibit a precisely similar framework of contents, and that the Pa*ñk*atantra and the Kathâsaritsâgara, among other works, follow the same model. And from this fact it may be fairly argued, that while there is, doubtless, room for suspecting interpolations in such cases, there is this to be remembered, that with respect to any particular one of these cases, such suspicion can carry us but a very short way. And further, it is to be observed, valeat quantum, that the connexion of the several chapters of the Anugîtâ one with the other is not altogether a loose one, save at one or two points only, while they are all linked on to the main body of the narrative, only in what we have treated as the last chapter of the Anugîtâ, without any trace of any other connecting link anywhere else. Upon the whole, therefore, we here conclude, though not without doubt, that the whole of the Anugîtâ is the work of one author.

The next question to be discussed is the important one of the age of the work. The quotations already given above from *S*ankarâ*k*ârya's works, and one other which is referred to in the note below[1], suffice to show that the Anugîtâ must have been some few centuries old in the time of *S*ankarâ*k*ârya. For whether we treat the Anugîtâ as a part of the original Mahâbhârata or not, it is not likely that such a scholar as *S*ankara would have accepted the book as a genuine part of the Mahâbhârata, and as a work of Vyâsa, if it had not been in his day of some respectable antiquity, of antiquity sufficient to have thrown the real author into oblivion, and to have substi-

[1] See *S*ankara, *S*ârîraka Bhâshya, p. 726. That, however, may be a quotation from some other work. It may be noted that the passages quoted in the Bhâshya on Sanatsugâtîya I, 20 and I, 41 are not to be traced in our copies, though expressly stated there to have been taken from the Anugîtâ.

tuted in his place Vyâsa, who lived at the junction of the Dvâpara and Kali ages[1], upwards of thirty centuries before the Christian era. The calculation is avowedly a very rough one, but I think we may, as the result of it, safely fix the third century of the Christian era as the latest date at which the Anugîtâ can have been composed. Let us now endeavour to find out whether we can fix the date as lying within any better defined period. It is scarcely needful to say, that the Anugîtâ dates from a period considerably subsequent to the age of the Upanishads. The passages relating to the Prâ*n*asa*m*vâda and so forth, which occur originally in the Upanishads, are referred to in the Anugîtâ as 'ancient stories'—an indication that the Upanishads had already come to be esteemed as ancient compositions at the date of the latter work. It is not necessary, therefore, to go through an elaborate examination of the versions of the ancient stories alluded to above, as contained in the Upanishads and in the Anugîtâ, more especially because it is possible for us to show that the Anugîtâ is later than the Bhagavadgîtâ, which latter work, as we have seen, is later than the Upanishads. And to this point we shall now address ourselves. We have already observed upon the story referred to at the opening of this Introduction, which, historically interpreted, indicates the priority of the Bhagavadgîtâ to the Anugîtâ. This conclusion is confirmed by sundry other circumstances, which we must now discuss in some detail, as they are also of use in helping to fix the position of the work in the history of Sanskrit literature and philosophy. First, then, it seems to me, that the state of society mirrored in the Anugîtâ indicates a greater advance in social evolution than we have already seen is disclosed in the Bhagavadgîtâ. Not to mention decorations of houses and so forth, which are alluded to in one passage of the Anugîtâ, we are here told of royal oppressions, of losses of wealth accumulated with great difficulty, and of fierce captivities; we are told, to adapt the language of a modern English poet, of laws grinding the weak, for strong men rule the

[1] Cf. *S*ârîraka Bhâshya, p. 913.

law; we have references to the casting of images with liquefied iron, and to the use of elephants as vehicles[1]; and we meet with protests against the amusements of music and dancing, and against the occupation of artisans[2]. True it is, that all these indications put together, fail to constitute what, according to the standard of modern times, would be called a highly artificial state of society. But it seems to me to mark a very perceptible and distinct advance beyond the social condition when mankind was divided into four castes or classes, with such a division of duties, to put it briefly, as that of preparation for a future world, government of this world, agriculture and trade, and service respectively[3]. Artisans, it will be observed, are not even referred to in the Bhagavadgîtâ, nor is there any trace of royal oppressions, or unequal laws. Then as regards music, it may be noted, that there are references to it in the B*ri*hadâra*n*yaka and Kaushîtaki-upanishads[4], without any indications of disapprobation. The protest against music, therefore, and the sister art of dancing, is probably to be explained as evoked by some abuses of the two arts which must have come into prevalence about the time of the composition of the Anugîtâ. A similar protest is found recorded in the Dharma*s*âstras of Manu and Âpastamba and Gautama[5]. We shall consider in the sequel the chronological positions of the Anugîtâ with reference to those Dharma*s*âstras. But we have already pointed out that the Gîtâ stands prior to them both[6].

Look again at the views on caste which are embodied in the Anugîtâ and the Bhagavadgîtâ respectively. The reference to the Kshatriya as representing the quality of passion, while the Brâhma*n*a represents the quality of goodness[7], seems to place a considerably larger distance between the Brâhma*n*a and the Kshatriya than is suggested by the Bhagavadgîtâ, and thus marks an advance in the direction of the later doctrine on the subject. And in connexion

[1] Cf. Lalita Vistara, p. 17. [2] See pp. 325–365. [3] See Gîtâ, p. 126.
[4] See B*ri*hadâra*n*yaka, p. 454, and Kaushîtaki, p. 68.
[5] See Bühler's Âpastamba I, 1, 3, 11, Gautama II, 13, and Manu II, 178.
[6] P. 21 seq. [7] P. 329.

with this, perhaps, the discrepancy between the reading of the Bhagavadgîtâ at p. 85, and that of the Anugîtâ at p. 255, is not entirely without significance, though much weight would not be due to it, if it stood alone. The expression 'devoted royal sages,' which we find in the one work, makes way for 'well-read Kshatriyas who are intent on their own duties' in the other. Again, although the passage at p. 353 is undoubtedly susceptible of a different interpretation, it seems to me, that the word 'twice-born' there employed, was meant to be interpreted as meaning the Brâhma*n*as, and not the three twice-born castes; and if this interpretation is correct, we have here the very proposition upon the absence of which in the Bhagavadgîtâ we have already made some observations[1]. That twice-born in the passage in question means Brâhma*n*a only, is, of course, not a proved fact. But having regard to the passages noted above and to the passage at p. 320, where reference is made to disparagement of Brâhma*n*as—it is not twice-born there—and in the same clause with disparagement of gods and Vedas, it seems to me that the interpretation we have suggested must be taken to be the true one. And it is to be further noted, that this conclusion is corroborated by a comparison of the passage now under consideration with a passage occurring in the *S*ânti Parvan[2], in the Râ*g*adharma section of it, where we read that 'the cow is the first among quadrupeds, gold among metals, a mantra among words, and the Brâhma*n*a is the first among bipeds.' The cow and gold occur in the passage in the Anugîtâ also, very near the clause we are now discussing. And it is allowable to argue, that reading the two together, twice-born in the Anugîtâ must be interpreted to be synonymous with Brâhma*n*a in the Râ*g*adharma. And the same conclusion is, to my mind, confirmed indirectly by comparing the clause 'the twice-born among men' of the Anugîtâ with 'the ruler of men among men' of that Bhagavadgîtâ, the teaching of which the former work professes to recapitulate.

[1] P. 24 supra.

[2] See note at p. 353.

A similar inference seems to be derivable from a comparison of the specific doctrines as to the duties of Brâhma*n*as which are enunciated in the Gîtâ and the Anugîtâ. In the latter work, the famous six duties are expressly mentioned. We have already argued in our Introduction to the Gîtâ, that a comparison of the teaching of that work upon this point with the teaching of Âpastamba and Manu shows the former to have been older than the latter. The six duties mentioned in the Anugîtâ are those also mentioned by Manu and Âpastamba. It follows, therefore, that the Gîtâ is prior to the Anugîtâ also. Whether the Anugîtâ is prior or subsequent to Manu and Âpastamba, is a question which will have to be discussed in the sequel.

The net result of the whole of this comparison appears to me to clearly show the Anugîtâ to be a work of considerably more recent date than the Bhagavadgîtâ. What interval of time lay between the two, is a most interesting, but also a most difficult, question. The differences we have noted appear to me to indicate a pretty wide interval. If I am right in regarding the Gîtâ as a work of what may be called, for practical purposes, the age of the older Upanishads, I am inclined to think that the interval between the Gîtâ and the Anugîtâ must have been one of larger extent than even three or four centuries. For as we have already pointed out, the description of the various 'Itihâsas' mentioned in the Anugîtâ as 'purâtana'—ancient—points to at least three or four centuries having elapsed between the close of the Upanishad period and the composition of the Anugîtâ. It is obvious, however, that this result is not one with which we can rest satisfied. Even if it were more precise and accurate, it would only fix the age of the Anugîtâ with reference to the age of another work itself of unknown and unascertained date. We must therefore endeavour to compare the Anugîtâ with some other work, the date of which is better known. For this purpose, it seems to be not of any great use to refer to the Sâṅkhya and Yoga-sûtras, although it is not improbable that some materials might be forthcoming for a useful comparison between them and the Anugîtâ. Neither the Sâṅkhya nor the Yoga-sûtras can be said to have their ages fixed with even any approach to accuracy. And in the case of the Sânkhya-sûtras, there is the further difficulty presented by the circumstance, that there is room for very serious doubts as to whether the current Sûtras are really of the authorship of Kapila, or whoever else was the original founder of the system. With regard to the Yoga, one or two observations from a different point of view may not, however, be entirely out of place. At p. 248 the Yoga *S*âstra is referred to eo nomine. What *S*âstra is here alluded to? Is it Patañ*g*ali's, or some other *S*âstra dealing with similar topics? Or, again, is it an entirely different matter that is alluded to, and are we not to see in the expression in question an allusion to any system formally propounded? I own, as stated in the note on the passage, that my mind inclines to the last view. There is not very much to say on either side of the question, as far as I am able to understand it. But the view I incline to appears to have one small circumstance in its favour. At p. 249 we have an allusion to persons who understand the Yoga, and to a certain illustration propounded by them. Now who are these persons? My limited knowledge of Yoga literature has not enabled me to trace the illustration anywhere else than in the Ka*th*opanishad, and in the Sanatsu*g*âtîya. It seems to me very unlikely, that the illustration can have been put forward in any work older than the Ka*th*opanishad. And we may, I think, assume it as most probable that the Sanatsu*g*âtîya borrowed it from that work. If so, it is not likely that the Anugîtâ can have referred to any other master of the Yoga than the author of the Ka*th*opanishad. And then it would seem to follow, that the Anugîtâ must have been composed at a time when, although the Upanishads were looked on with reverence and as works of authority, they were not yet regarded as part and parcel of the Vedic revelation[1]. It is impossible not to perceive, that the train of reasoning here is at every stage hedged round with difficulties and doubts. And the inference therefore to which we are led by it must be accepted with proportionate

[1] This seems to be also the implication of the passage at p. 309, where the rules for final emancipation are alluded to.

caution. But if the reasoning is correct, it seems to be certain, that the Anugîtâ belongs to some period prior to the second, and probable, that it belongs to some period prior to the third century, before Christ. For in the second century before Christ was composed the Mahâbhâshya of Patañgali, in which Rahasyas—which is another name for Upanishads—are mentioned as forming part of the Vedic literature. And in Âpastamba's Dharma-sûtras, which are older than Patañgali, Upanishads[1] are mentioned in the same way. I am aware that it may be said, that because Upanishads as a class of works are mentioned by Patañgali and Âpastamba, it does not follow that any particular Upanishad, such as the Ka*th*a, for instance, also existed at that time. This is quite true. But without going now into the general question, it is sufficient to point out, that our argument here is concerned merely with the recognition of the Upanishads as a class of works forming part of the Vedic canon. Such recognition must have come later than the period at which the Anugîtâ could speak of a passage in the Ka*th*a-upanishad as the utterance of Yogavids, or persons who understood the Yoga.

Turning now to the materials available for ascertaining the relative chronological positions of the Anugîtâ and the rise of Buddhism, we have again to complain of their unsatisfactory character. We will briefly note the two or three circumstances which appear to have a bearing upon this question. In the first place, we have the word Nirvâ*n*a used in one passage of the Anugîtâ in the sense of the highest tranquillity, and there the simile of the extinction of the fire is expressly adduced. On this it may be argued, that if the term Nirvâ*n*a had become the well-understood property of Buddhism, such a use of it as we find here would probably not have occurred. Again, we have the injunction that an ascetic must dwell in a town only for one day and no more, while he may stay at one place during the rains. This is very similar to an injunction prescribed by the Buddhistic teachers also. But

[1] They are also referred to in the Buddhistic Lalita Vistara, p. 65.

this fact furnishes, I think, no safe ground for a chronological inference, more especially because, as pointed out by Dr. Bühler, the Buddhistic injunction is itself only borrowed from the Brahminical rules on the subject[1]. It is impossible, therefore, to say that the Anugîtâ borrowed its doctrine from Buddhism. It is, of course, equally impossible on the other hand to say, that Buddhism borrowed its rule from the Anugîtâ. And, therefore, we can build no safe inference upon this fact either. We have next the very remarkable passage at chapter XXXIV, where various contradictory and mutually exclusive views of piety are stated, or rather passingly and briefly indicated—a passage which one most devoutly wishes had been clearer than it is. In that passage I can find no reference to Buddhism. True it is that Nîlaka*n*/*h*a's commentary refers some of the doctrines there stated to Buddhistic schools[2]. But that commentary, unsatisfactory enough in other places, is particularly unsatisfactory here. And its critical accuracy may be judged from its reference to Saugatas and Yogâ*k*âras apparently as two distinct schools, whereas in truth the Saugatas are Buddhists, and Yogâ*k*âras one of the four principal Buddhist sects. And it must be further remembered, that the interpretations of Nîlaka*n*/*h*a, upon which his specifications of the different schools are based, are by no means such as necessarily claim acceptance. If then we do not find any reference to Buddhism in this passage, that fact becomes certainly a remarkable one. Still, on the other hand, I am not prepared to apply the 'negative argument' here, and to say that inasmuch as Buddhism is not referred to where so many different opinions are referred to, Buddhism cannot have come into existence at the date of the Anugîtâ. It seems to me that the argument will here be a very hazardous one, because if the author of the Anugîtâ was, as we may assume he was, an orthodox Hindu, he might well have declined, although not unacquainted with Buddhism, to put into the mouths of the seven sages even as a possible view, that

[1] See Gautama, pp. lv and 191. [2] See also the gloss on chap. XXXIV, st. 14.

which was the view of a school esteemed heretical by the author and his co-religionists. This passage, therefore, also fails to furnish any tangible ground for a chronological inference, at all events in the present state of our knowledge. Lastly, we come to the allusion to those who indulge in constant talk in disparagement of Vedas and Brâhma*n*as, the two being thus bracketed together in the original. That seems, at the first blush, to be a somewhat more distinct allusion to Buddhism than any of those we have noted above. But even that is not unambiguous. If the stanzas quoted by Mâdhavâ*k*ârya, in his Sarvadar*s*anasaṅgraha in its first section, are the composition of the original founder of the *K*ârvâka school, or even if they correctly represent the earliest opinions of that school, it is at least quite as likely that the *K*ârvâkas were the target for the denunciations of the Anugîtâ in the passage in question as that the Buddhists were so. To me, indeed, it appears to be more likely. For Buddha's opinion with regard to the Vedas is, that they are inadequate; with regard to the Brâhma*n*as, that they are in no sense the chosen of God as they claim to be. The opinion of the *K*ârvâkas, on the other hand, is a far more aggressive one, so to say. According to Mâdhavâ*k*ârya, they taught that the Vedas were either simple fatuity or imposture, and that the Brâhma*n*as were impostors. It seems to me much more likely, that this, which I have called a comparatively aggressive attitude, was the one at which the remarks of the Anugîtâ were levelled; and more especially does this appear to be correct when we remember, that the view taught by Gautama Buddha regarding the Vedas and the Brâhma*n*as was propounded by him only in its strongest form; and that even before his time, the doctrine of the inadequacy of the Vedas for the purpose of securing the summum bonum of humanity had been taught by other teachers. It is further to be recollected, that we have evidence showing that other thinkers also than Buddha, or B*ri*haspati, had in early days attacked the authority of the Vedas. Kautsa is the name of one who was probably the most distinguished among them. It is certainly possible that his followers were the people branded as of 'the dark quality' by the Anugîtâ in the passage in question. We have, therefore, at least two different recognised bodies of thinkers, and one individual thinker, to whom the words under discussion may apply, and it is plainly unsafe, under these circumstances, to draw any chronological inference based on the hypothesis of one particular body out of those three being the one intended by the author. Before closing this part of the investigation, it may be interesting to note, that the phrase 'turning the wheel,' a phrase now so familiar to us as one of the household words of Buddhism, is used in the Anugîtâ with respect to king *G*anaka. I do not think, however, that either alone, or even coupled with the word Nirvâ*n*a, that phrase can be made the basis of any legitimate deduction in favour of the priority of the Anugîtâ to Buddhism. At the outside, the only deduction admissible, if any deduction were admissible, would be, that the Anugîtâ was composed prior to the recognition, of Nirvâ*n*a and *K*akrapravartana as specially Buddhistic words. But priority to such recognition is not, I apprehend, necessarily synonymous with priority to the rise of Buddhism.

The net result of this part of the investigation appears to be, that we have pretty strong grounds for holding the Anugîtâ to belong to a period very considerably removed from the period of the Upanishads and the Bhagavadgîtâ; but that we have no tangible grounds on which to base any deduction regarding its priority or otherwise to the Sâṅkhya and Yoga systems of philosophy, or to the great movement of Gautama Buddha. There is only one other point, which we can establish in a not entirely unsatisfactory way, and which enables us to draw closer the limits within which the Anugîtâ must have been composed. That point is the position of the Anugîtâ with reference to Âpastamba's Dharma-sûtra. I need not say again, that I accept here the proposition about the age of Âpastamba which has been laid down by Dr. Bühler, as a sufficiently satisfactory working hypothesis. And accepting that proposition, I venture to suggest the fourth century B.C. as a not unlikely date for the Anugîtâ. It appears to me, that a comparison of the Anugîtâ and the rules of Âpastamba upon one important point which they both deal with shows the priority of the former work. I allude to the rules and regulations touching the four Âsramas or orders contained in the Anugîtâ and in the Dharma-sûtra of Âpastamba. One circumstance strikes us at once on comparing the two works on this point. Âpastamba goes into a very great deal of minute details more than the Anugîtâ, although the latter work does not deal with the topic in any very summary mode. Taking all the differences between the two works together, and the fact that the Anugîtâ sets about the discussion of the topic in a manner which seems intended to be—not, indeed, absolutely exhaustive, but still—very full, I am very strongly inclined to attribute the differences to an actual development and progress of doctrine. I will endeavour to illustrate this view by means of a few detailed instances [1]. And let us first take the order of householders to which the Anugîtâ gives precedence over the others. One of the injunctions laid down by the Anugîtâ is that the householder should always be devoted to his wife. Against this simple precept, we have a very minute series of rules prescribed by Âpastamba, which it is not necessary to refer to specifically, but which may be seen in several of the Sûtras contained in the first Khan*d*a of the first Pa*t*ala of the second Prasna. Compare again the excessive minuteness of the rules regarding the Bali-offering or the reception of guests, as given by Âpastamba, with the simple statement of the Anugîtâ that the five great sacrifices should be performed. There again, I think, we are to see in this difference of treatment the result of a pretty long course of ceremonial progress. Proceeding to the rules regarding the Brahma*k*ârin or student, an analogous phenomenon meets us there. Taking first the subject of food, we have a considerable number of detailed injunctions in Âpastamba, compared with the simple rule of the Anugîtâ, that the student should, with the leave of his preceptor, eat his food without decrying it. Again with regard to alms, whereas the Anugîtâ simply

[1] Cf. pp. 358, 360 infra with Âpastamba, pp. 9 seq., 103 seq., 114 seq.

says that the student should take his food out of the alms received by him, Âpastamba has an elaborate catena of rules as to how the alms are to be collected, and from whom, and so forth. Take again the provisions in the two works regarding the description of the cloth, staff, and girdle of the student. Âpastamba refers to various opinions on this subject, of which there is not even a trace in the Anugîtâ[1]. It appears that even before Âpastamba's time, distinctions had been laid down as to the description of girdle staff and cloth to be used by the different castes—distinctions of which there is no hint in the Anugîtâ, where all students, of whatever caste, are spoken of under the generic name. These distinctions appear to me to point very strongly to that ceremonial and doctrinal progress of which we have spoken above. The tendency is visible in them to sever the Brâhma*n*as from the other castes—by external marks. And that tendency, it seems to me, must have set in, as the merits which had given the Brâhma*n*a caste its original position at the head of Hindu society were ceasing to be a living reality, and that caste was intrenching itself, so to say, more behind the worth and work of the early founders of its greatness, than the worth and work of their degenerating representatives. These comparisons, taken together, appear to me to warrant the proposition we have already laid down with regard to the priority of the Anugîtâ to Âpastamba. If we have not referred to the rules relating to the two other orders of forester and ascetic, it is because the scope for a comparison of those is very limited. Those rules alone would scarcely authorise the inference drawn above; but I can perceive nothing in them to countervail the effect of the comparisons already made. And it must be remembered, that the rules as to foresters and ascetics would be less apt to undergo change than those as to students and householders.

It appears to me that the view we have now expressed may be also supported by a comparison of the doctrines of the Anugîtâ and Âpastamba touching the duties of Brâhma*n*as. According to Âpastamba, the occupations lawful

[1] Cf. also Bühler's Gautama, p. 175.

to Brâhma*n*as are the famous six referred to in our Introduction to the Bhagavadgîtâ, and two others superadded, namely, inheritance and gleaning corn in the fields. These last are not mentioned in the Anugîtâ, or in Manu either, and are, even according to Âpastamba, common to Brâhma*n*as with Kshatriyas and Vai*s*yas. But as regards the six above referred to, it is worthy of note, that the Anugîtâ apparently groups them into two distinct sets of three. The first set of three consists of those which, in our Introduction to the Bhagavadgîtâ, we have characterised as constituting rather the rights than the duties of Brâhma*n*as, and which the Anugîtâ describes as 'means of livelihood for Brâhma*n*as.' The other set of three consists of real duties, and these the Anugîtâ speaks of as 'pious duties.' This grouping appears to me to furnish powerful corroboration of the view put forward in our Introduction to the Bhagavadgîtâ. It would seem, that the possession of the moral and spiritual merits which, according to the Gîtâ, constituted the duty of Brâhma*n*as, in the simple and archaic society there disclosed, was developed, in a more advanced and artificial state of society, into the performance of the 'pious duties' of the Anugîtâ and the duties which are 'the means of livelihood.' Then in the further social evolution, in the course of which the old spiritual view began to be forgotten, and the actual facts of the past began to be transmuted into the dogmatic rules of the future, the occupations of receiving presents, imparting instruction, and officiating at sacrifices, became the special occupations of the Brâhma*n*as, and the distinction between these occupations from their higher duties was thrown into the background; and accordingly we find no allusion to any such distinction in Âpastamba or Manu, or, as far as I know, in any other later embodiment of the current ideas on the subject[1]. If all this has been correctly argued, the conclusion derivable from it is in entire accord with that which we have already drawn, namely, that the Bhagavadgîtâ, the Anugîtâ, and the Dharma-sûtra of Âpastamba, belong to different

[1] In Gautama X, 1 3, the 'pious duties' are called 'obligatory,' the others 'additional for Brâhma*n*as.' See the note on the passage in Bühler's edition, and cf. Gautama VIII, 9, 10.

stages of ancient Indian history, and that the stage to which the Gîtâ belongs is the earliest, and that to which Âpastamba belongs, the latest of such stages.

I am unable to find anything else in the way of internal evidence bearing upon the date of the Anugîtâ. It appears to me, that the date to which the investigation we have now gone through leads us, is one which, in the present state of our information, may be fairly accepted as a provisional hypothesis. It does not appear to me to conflict with any ascertained dates, while it is pointed to as probable by the various lines of testimony which we have here considered. We now proceed to discuss one or two other points which may have a bearing upon this topic, but which at present cannot yield us any positive guidance in our search for the date of the Anugîtâ. And first among these, let us consider the various names of deities that occur in different parts of the work. We have, then, Vish*n*u, *S*ambhu, *G*ish*n*u, Soma, Âditya, Sûrya, Mitra, Agni, *K*andra, Rudra, *S*iva, Varu*n*a, Pra*g*âpati, Maghavat, Purandara, Indra, Brahman, *S*atakratu, Dharma, Nârâya*n*a, Vâyu, Yama, Tvash*t*ri, Hari, Î*s*vara, and lastly Umâ under three different names, namely, Umâ, Mâhe*s*varî, and Pârvatî. Now, leaving aside for the moment the three names of Umâ, which appear from the passage where they are used to be all three the names of the same goddess, there is no doubt that in the list above set out, some of the names are merely used in different passages, but still to indicate the same being. Thus, Indra, *S*atakratu, Purandara, and Maghavat are really the names of one and the same deity. But when Soma is mentioned as the deity presiding over the tongue, and *K*andramas as the deity presiding over the mind, it becomes doubtful whether the two names do really indicate the same deity, albeit in later Sanskrit Soma and *K*andramas both signify the moon. Similarly, when Arka is said to be the deity presiding over the eye, and Mitra over another organ, it seems open to question whether Arka and Mitra both signify the sun there, as they undoubtedly do in classical Sanskrit. True it is, that even in such a recent work as the Sâṅkhya-sâra, this mention of Arka and Mitra as presiding deities of two several organs does occur. But it is plain, that that circumstance can have no bearing on the inquiry before us, for the Sâṅkhya-sâra is avowedly a compilation based on older authorities, and in the particular part under consideration, really reproduces a passage from some older work. It cannot, therefore, be argued, that because Arka and Mitra were identified with one another at the time of the Sâṅkhya-sâra, and yet are mentioned as deities of two separate organs, therefore, they must have also been regarded as one in the older original work where they are also mentioned as deities of two separate organs. And it may, perhaps, be remarked here in passing, that the Vedânta Paribhâshâ has M*ri*tyu instead of Mitra, which would get rid of the difficulty here altogether; while as regards Soma and *K*andramas, the passage in the Sâṅkhya-sâra reads Pra*k*etas instead of Soma, which would get rid of the other difficulty above pointed out. Whether these discrepancies are owing to any tampering with the lists of organs and deities, at a time when the later identifications between different deities took place, or whether they are to be explained on some other theory, it is impossible at present to say. And, therefore, it is also unnecessary to pursue the inquiry here any further. It must suffice for the present to have drawn attention to the matter.

Akin to this point, though quite distinct from it, is one which arises on a passage where the emancipated being is identified with Vish*n*u, Mitra, Agni, Varu*n*a, and Pragâpati[1]. Now it is reasonable to suppose, that the deities thus specified here must have been among those held in highest repute at the time, the whole significance of the passage where they are mentioned requiring that that should be so. But in our Pantheon as disclosed by our later literature, Mitra and Agni and Varu*n*a occupy but a very subordinate position. Even in Kâlidâsa[2], the subordination of these deities to our celebrated Trinity seems to be quite

[1] See p. 345.

[2] See inter alia, Kumâra II, 20 seq., and VII, 44 seq., and cf. our Bhart*ri*hari (Bombay Sanskrit Classics), Introd. p. xix.

fully established. But, on the other hand, in the Vedic theogony, they are among the most prominent deities. In the Taittirîya-upanishad, we have in the very first sentence Mitra, Varuna, Vishnu, and Brahman (who may be identified with Pragâpati) all mentioned together, and their blessings invoked. This does not help in fixing a date for the Anugîtâ; but it lends some support to the conclusion already arrived at on that point, by showing that the theogony of the Anugîtâ is not yet very far removed from the theogony of the Vedic times, while it is separated by a considerable interval from the theogony disclosed in the works of even such an early writer of the classical period as Kâlidâsa.

Another point of similar bearing on our present investigation is the mode in which the story of Parasurâma is dealt with in the Anugîtâ. There is in the first place no allusion to his being an incarnation of Vishnu, nor to the encounter between him and his namesake, the son of Dasaratha and the hero of the Râmâyana. We have, on the contrary, an explicit statement, that after the advice of the '*Pitris*' he entirely abandons the slaughter of the Kshatriyas, and resorting to penance thereby achieves final emancipation. We have elsewhere argued [1], that the theory of Parasurâma being an incarnation of Vishnu, must have probably originated prior to the time of Bhartrihari, but later than the time of Kâlidâsa. The allusion to Parasurâma in the work before us does not, however, enable us to judge of its chronological position with reference to Kâlidâsa. But the last point discussed renders it unnecessary to consider this question further. It may be noted, by the way, that the Anugîtâ represents Parasurâma, although living in the Âsrama or hermitage of his father, who was a *Ri*shi, as mounting a chariot for the purpose of sweeping away the kinsmen of Kârtavîrya. Whence he obtained a chariot in a hermitage, the Anugîtâ does not explain.

In connexion with the episode of Parasurâma, may be noted the list which occurs in the course of it, of the

[1] See 'Was the Râmâyana copied from Homer?' pp. 56, 57.

degraded Kshatriya tribes, of Dravi*das*, *S*abaras, &c. I am unable to see that those names can give us any further help in our present investigation than in so far as they show that, at the time of the Anugîtâ, there must have been some information about the south of India available in the districts where the author of the Anugîtâ lived. Some of the tribes mentioned appear to have been located far in the south of the Indian peninsula. But this is a point on which we shall have to say something more in discussing the next item of internal evidence to which we shall refer. Here it is enough to point out that some of the tribes mentioned in the Anugîtâ are also referred to in no less a work than the Aitareya-brâhma*n*a [1].

We come next to the enumeration of the principal mountains which is contained in one passage of the Anugîtâ. Those mountains are the Himâlaya, the Pâriyâtra, the Sahya, the Vindhya, the Trikû*t*avat, the *S*veta, the Nîla, the Bhâsa, the Kosh*th*avat, the Mahendra, the Mâlyavat, and perhaps the Guruskandha. I am not sure whether the last name is intended to be taken as a proper name, or only as an epithet of Mahendra. Now compared with the mountains mentioned in the Bhagavadgîtâ, this is certainly a remarkable list. The Gîtâ mentions only Meru [2] and Himâlaya; while here we have in the Anugîtâ the Sahya, and Malaya, and Trikû*t*avat, and Nîla (the same, I presume, with the modern Nîlgiri, the Sanatorium of the Madras Presidency), which take us far to the west and south of the Indian peninsula; and the Mahendra and Mâlyavat, which, coupled with the mention of the river Ganges, cover a considerable part of the eastern districts. The Pariyâtra and Vindhya occupy the regions of Central India. The Anugîtâ, therefore, seems to belong to that period in the history of India, when pretty nearly the whole,

[1] Haug's ed., p. 183. And see generally on these tribes, Wilson's Vish*n*u Purâ*n*a (Hall's ed., vol. ii, p. 170 seq., and *S*ânti Parvan (Moksha), chap. 207, st. 42.

[2] This is also mentioned in the Anugîtâ, but in a different passage. The Nîla is said by Professor Wilson to be a mountain in Orissa. But our suggestion has, I find, been already made by Dr. F. E. Hall also: see on this, and generally, Wilson's Vish*n*u Purâ*n*a, vol. ii, p. 141 seq. (ed. Hall). See also Indian Antiquary, VI, 133 seq.

if not absolutely the whole, of the Indian continent was known to the Sanskrit-speaking population of the country. When was this knowledge reached? It is difficult to fix the precise period; and even if it could be fixed, it would not help us to fix satisfactorily any point of time to which the Anugîtâ could be attributed. But it may be pointed out here, that in Patañgali's Mahâbhâshya we have evidence of such knowledge having been possessed by the Âryas in the second century B.C. In truth, the evidence available in the Mahâbhâshya is even fuller than this in the Anugîtâ. For Patañgali tells us of a town or city in the south named Kâñkîpura[1]; he speaks of the dominions of the Pâ*nd*ya kings, and of the *K*ola and Kerala districts[2]; he refers also to the large tanks of the south; and he makes allusions to linguistic usages current in the southern and other provinces[3]. Before Patañgali's time there had taken place Mahendra's invasion of Ceylon, and the invading army must have penetrated through the southern provinces. And there had been also put up the great Inscriptions of Asoka, which have attracted so much interest, and are proving such prolific sources of information in various departments of knowledge. One of these inscriptions was at Gañgam, which is not very far from the Mahendra mountain alluded to in the Anugîtâ[4]. All these facts support the conclusion drawn by General Cunningham from the correctness of the information given to Alexander the Great by the Hindus of his time, namely, that 'the Indians, even at that early date in their history, had a very accurate knowledge of the form and extent of their native land[5].' And not only do they support that conclusion, they show that the knowledge covered other facts regarding

---

[1] Banâras ed., p. 74 (IV, 2, 2).

[2] P. 60 (IV, 1, 4). See also p. 65.

[3] See Mahâbhâshya, p. 82 (I, 1, 5), p. 16 (I, 1, 1); and cf. Muir, Sanskrit Texts, vol. ii, pp. 152, 355.

[4] See Cunningham's Corpus Inscriptionum, I, p. 1.

[5] See Ancient Geography of India, p. 3. And compare also the information collected in the Periplus of the Erythraean Sea (translated by Mr. McKindle), pp. 112–136, where a large number of ports is mentioned as existing on the Indian coasts. The Periplus seems to date from about 90 A.D. see ibid. p. 5).

their native land than its form and extent. It follows consequently that this enumeration of mountains does not require the date of the Anugîtâ to be brought down to a later period than the fourth century B.C., and leaves it open to us, therefore, to accept whatever conclusion the other evidence available may seem to justify. On the other hand, it is plain also, that it affords no positive information as to when the Anugîtâ was composed, and therefore we need not dwell any further upon the point on the present occasion.

There are a few other points which arise upon the contents of the Anugîtâ, but which are not, in the present condition of our knowledge, capable of affording any certain guidance in our present investigation. Thus we have the story of Dharma appearing before king *G*anaka disguised as a Brâhma*n*a. I am not aware of any case of such disguises occurring in any of the Upanishads, although there are numerous parallel instances throughout the Purânik literature[1]. It is, however, difficult to draw any definite chronological inference from this fact. There is further the reference to the attack of Râhu on the sun. It is difficult, in the present state of our knowledge, to say for certain, when the theory of eclipses there implied was prevalent. In the *Kh*ândogya-upanishad[2] we have the emancipated self compared to the moon escaped from the mouth of Râhu. And a text of the Rig-veda, quoted by Mr. Ya*gñ*esvara *S*âstrin in his Âryavidyâsudhâkara[3], speaks of the demon Râhu attacking the sun with darkness. Here again we have another matter of some interest; but I cannot see that any safe deduction can be derived from it, without a more ample knowledge of other relevant matters than is at present accessible. Take again the references to certain practices which look very much like the practices of the *G*ainas of the present day. Is the Anugîtâ, then, earlier or later than the rise of the *G*aina system? It is not safe, I think, to found an answer to this question upon the very narrow basis afforded by the

[1] And see, too, Kâlidâsa Kumâra V, st. 84. [2] P. 622.
[3] P. 26. In Kâlidâsa's Raghuva*m*sa the true explanation of eclipses is alluded to. See Canto XIV, 40.

passage referred to. But it may be observed, that the precepts laid down in the passage in question are laid down as precepts for orthodox Hindus, and not as the doctrines of a heretical sect. They are also very general, and not so minute as those which the *G*ainas of the present day observe as binding upon them. If, therefore, any conclusion is to be drawn from these precepts, it must be that the Anugîtâ must have been composed prior to the rise of *G*ainism; and that *G*ainism must have appropriated and developed this doctrine which it obtained from the current Brâhmanism[1]. If this is so, the Anugîtâ must be a very ancient work indeed. It is not, however, necessary to further work out this line of argument, having regard to the opinions recently expressed by Mr. Thomas[2], rehabilitating the views enunciated long ago by Colebrooke and others. If those views are correct, and if *G*ainism was a dominant system in this country prior even to the time of Gautama Buddha, and if, further, we are right in the suggestion—for it is no more, it must be remembered—that the Anugîtâ dates from a period prior to the rise of *G*ainism, then it would seem to follow that the Anugîtâ belongs to some period prior to the sixth century B.C. All this, however, is at present very hypothetical, and we draw attention to it only that the question may be hereafter considered when fuller materials for expressing a final judgment upon it become accessible. Meanwhile, having regard to the views above alluded to as so elaborately put forward by Mr. Thomas, it is possible for us still to hold that, in the present state of our knowledge, the third or fourth century B.C. is not too early a date to assign to the Anugîtâ, even on the assumption that the precepts contained in that work regarding the care to be taken of worms and insects were borrowed by it from the *G*aina system. With this negative result, we must for the present rest contented.

One other fact of similar nature to those we have now

[1] As the Buddhists did in sundry instances. Cf. inter alia Buhler's Gautama, pp. lv and 191. And cf. also 'Was the Râmâya*n*a copied from Homer?' pp. 48, 49.

[2] See Mr. Thomas's very elaborate discussion of the whole subject in the Journal of the Royal Asiatic Society (New Series), vol. ix, p. 155 seq.

dealt with may, perhaps, be also noticed here. We allude to the stanzas which we find in the Anugîtâ and also in the *S*ânti Parvan of the Mahâbhârata and in the Manusm*ri*ti. There is also one which the Anugîtâ has in common with the Pari*s*ish*t*a of Yâska's Nirukta[1]. It is not possible, I conceive, to say finally whether one of these works borrowed these stanzas from the other of them; while, on the other hand, it is quite possible, as already argued by us in the Introduction to the Gîtâ, that all these works were only reproducing from some entirely different work, or that the stanzas in question were the common property of the thinkers of the time. We have no means available for deciding between these conflicting hypotheses.

We have thus noticed all the salient points in the evidence, external and internal, which is available for determining the position of the Anugîtâ in our ancient literature. Nobody who has seen even a little of the history of that literature will be surprised at the quantity or quality of that evidence, or the nature of the conclusions legitimately yielded by it. We have endeavoured to express those conclusions in language which should not indicate any greater certainty attaching to them than can fairly be claimed for them. The net result appears to be this. The Anugîtâ may be taken with historical certainty to have been some centuries old in the time of the great *S*añkarâ*k*ârya. It was very probably older than the Dharma-sûtras of Âpastamba, but by what period of time we are not in a position at present to define. It was, perhaps, older also than the rise of Buddhism and *G*ainism, and of the Yoga philosophy; but on this it is impossible to say anything with any approach to confidence. It is, on the other hand, almost certain that it belongs to a period very considerably removed from the older Upanishads; probably removed by a distance of some centuries, during which 'stories' not contained in the Upanishads had not only obtained currency, but also come to be regarded as belonging to antiquity[2]. And yet the period to

[1] Cf. Anugîtâ I, 36 with Yâska (ed. Roth), p. 190.

[2] Some of the Purâtana Itihâsas, e.g. that of Nârada and Devamata, are not traceable in any Vedic work known to us. Devamata's name I do not find referred to anywhere else.

which the work belongs was one in which the Upanishads were only reverenced as the authoritative opinions of eminent men, not as the words of God himself[1]. In this respect, it may be said that the Anugîtâ seems rather to belong to an earlier stratum of thought than even the Sanatsugâtîya, in which a *G*ñânakâ*nd*a, as forming a part of the Vedic canon, seems to be recognised[2]. But it is abundantly clear, that the Anugitâ stands at a very considerable chronological distance from the Bhagavadgîtâ.

Such are the results of our investigation. We have not thought it necessary to discuss the verse or the language of the work. But it must in fairness be pointed out, that upon the whole, the verse and language are both pretty near the classical model. There are, it is true, a few instances of the metrical anomalies we have noticed elsewhere, but having regard to the extent of the work, those instances are far from being very numerous. The language and style, too, are not quite smooth and polished; though, judging from them alone, I should rather be inclined to place the Sanatsu*g*âtîya prior to the Anugîtâ. But that suggests a question which we cannot now stop to discuss.

One word, in conclusion, about the translation. The text used has been chiefly that adopted in the commentary of Ar*g*una Mi*s*ra, a commentary which on the whole I prefer very much to that of Nîlaka*nth*a, which has been printed in the Bombay edition of the Mahâbhârata. Ar*g*una Mi*s*ra, as a rule, affords some explanation where explanation is wanted, and does not endeavour to suit his text to any foregone conclusion. His comments have been of the greatest possible help to me; and my only regret is that the only copy of his commentary which was available to me, and the use of which I owe to the kindness of my friend Professor Bhâ*nd*ârkar, was not as correct a one as could be desired. I have also looked into the Vishama*s*lokî, a short work containing notes on difficult passages of the Mahâbhârata.

[1] See p. 211 supra.

[2] See p. 146 supra. The Buddhists seem to have borrowed the division of Karma and *G*ñânakâ*nd*a. See Dr. Ragendralâla Mitra's Lalita Vistara (transl.), p. 21. The division, therefore, was probably older than the first century B.C.

The MS. of it belonging to the Government Collection of MSS. deposited in Deccan College was lent me also by Professor Bhâ*nd*ârkar. The principles adopted in the translation and notes have been the same as those followed in the other pieces contained in this volume.

P. S. I take this opportunity of stating that it is not at all certain that Ar*g*una Mi*s*ra is the name of the author of the commentary which I have used. I find that in supposing Ar*g*una Mi*s*ra to be the author, I confounded that commentary, which does not mention its author's name, with the commentary on another section of the Mahâbhârata which does give its author's name as Ar*g*una Mi*s*ra, and which is also among the MSS. purchased by Professor Bhâ*nd*ârkar for the Government of Bombay. (See with regard to these MSS. Professor Bhâ*nd*ârkar's Report on the Search for Sanskrit MSS. of 7th July, 1880.)

ANUGÎTÂ.

CHAPTER I.

*G*anamegaya[1] said:

What conversation, O twice-born one[2]! took place between the high-souled Kesava and Arguna, while they dwelt in that palace[3] after slaying their enemies?

Vaisampâyana said:

The son of Prithâ, after becoming possessed of his kingdom (in an) undisturbed (state), enjoyed himself in the company of Krishna, full of delight in that heavenly palace. And once, O king! they happened to go, surrounded by their people, and rejoicing, to a certain portion of the palace which resembled heaven. Then Arguna, the son of Pându, having surveyed with delight that lovely palace, in the company of Krishna, spoke these words: 'O you of mighty arms! O you whose mother is Devakî[4]! when the battle was about to commence, I became aware of your greatness, and that divine

---

[1] This is the prince to whom the Mahâbhârata, as we have it, purports to have been related.

[2] I.e. Vaisampâyana, who relates the Mahâbhârata to *G*anamegaya.

[3] This appears to have been situated at Indraprastha, and to have been the one built for the Pândavas by the demon Maya, as related in the Sabhâ Parvan.

[4] This is a rather unusual form of address.

form of yours[1]. But that, O Kesava! which through affection (for me) you explained before[2], has all disappeared, O tiger-like man! from my degenerate mind. Again and again, however, I feel a curiosity about those topics. But (now), O Mâdhava! you will be going at no distant date to Dvârakâ.'

Vaisampâyana said:

Thus addressed, that best of speakers, K*ri*sh*n*a, possessed of great glory, replied in these words after embracing Ar*g*una.

Vâsudeva said:

From me, O son of P*ri*thâ! you heard a mystery, and learnt about the eternal[3] (principle), about piety in (its true) form, and about all the everlasting worlds[4]. It is excessively disagreeable to me, that you should not have grasped it through want of intelligence. And the recollection (of it) now again is not possible (to me). Really, O son of Pâ*nd*u! you are devoid of faith and of a bad intellect. And, O Dhana*ñg*aya! it is not possible for me to repeat in full (what I said before). For that doctrine was perfectly adequate for understanding the seat[5] of the Brahman. It is not possible for me to state it again in full in that way. For then accompanied by my mystic power[6], I declared to you the Supreme Brahman. But I shall relate an ancient story upon

[1] Cf. Bhagavadgîtâ, chapters X and XI passim.

[2] I.e. in the Bhagavadgîtâ.

[3] This may also be taken with piety thus: 'and learnt about the eternal piety in (its true) form.'

[4] As to the plural, see *S*aṅkara on Mu*nd*aka, p. 320.

[5] Cf. Gîtâ, p. 78. For 'understanding' here we might, perhaps, substitute 'attaining.' The original word means both understanding and attaining.

[6] Cf. Gîtâ, p. 82.

that subject, so that adhering to this knowledge, you may attain the highest goal. O best of the supporters of piety! listen to all that I say. (Once), O restrainer of foes! there came from the heavenly world and the world of Brahman[1], a Brâhmana difficult to withstand[2], and he was (duly) honoured by us. (Now) listen, without entertaining any misgivings, O chief of the descendants of Bharata! O son of Prithâ! to what he said on being interrogated by us according to heavenly rules[3].

The Brâhmana said:

O Krishna! O destroyer of Madhu! I will explain to you accurately what you, out of compassion for (all) beings[4], have asked me touching the duties (to be performed) for final emancipation. It is destructive of delusion, O Lord! Listen to me with attention[5], as I relate it, O Mâdhava! A certain Brâhmana named Kâsyapa, who had performed (much) penance, and who best understood piety, approached a certain twice-born (person) who had learnt the Scriptures relating to (all) duties[6], having heard (of him, as one) who had over and over again gone through all knowledge and experience about coming and going[7], who was well versed in the true nature of all worlds[8],

---

[1] This seems to mean not the Supreme Brahman, but the Creator.

[2] Cf. Sanatsugâtîya, p. 161, 'not to be shaken.'

[3] I suppose this to mean according to the forms proper in the case of such a being as the one in question. Cf. Gîtâ, p. 62, and note there.

[4] This is not easy to understand. Perhaps the allusion is to the doctrine at Gîtâ, pp. 54, 55.

[5] Cf. Brihadâranyaka, p. 447.

[6] I.e. all prescribed acts of piety.

[7] As to knowledge and experience, cf. Gîtâ, p. 57; and as to coming and going, cf. ibid. p. 84.

[8] I.e. as stated, for instance, at Gîtâ, p. 79, or Brihadâranyaka, p. 613.

who knew about happiness and misery [1], who knew the truth about birth and death [2], who was conversant with merit and sin, who perceived the migrations of embodied (souls) of high and low (degrees) in consequence of (their) actions, who moved about like an emancipated being, who had reached perfection [3], who was tranquil, whose senses were restrained, who was illumined with the Brahmic splendour [4], who moved about in every direction, who understood concealed movements [5], who was going in company of invisible Siddhas and celestial singers [6], and conversing and sitting together (with them) in secluded (places), who went about as he pleased, and was unattached (anywhere) like the wind. Having approached him, that talented ascetic possessed of concentration (of mind), that best of the twice-born, wishing to acquire piety, fell at his feet, after seeing that great marvel. And amazed on seeing that marvellous man, the best of the twice-born, Kâsyapa, pleased the preceptor by his great devotion. That was all appropriate [7], (being) joined to sacred learning and correct conduct. And, O terror of your foes! he pleased that (being) by (his purity of) heart and behaviour (suitable) towards a preceptor [8]. Then being satisfied and pleased, he spoke to the pupil these words, referring to the

[1] Cf. infra, p. 245. [2] Cf. Gîtâ, pp. 48, 103.
[3] Cf. Gîtâ, passim. [4] Cf. Sanatsugâtîya, p. 162.
[5] I. e. moving about so as not to be seen by everybody.
[6] Literally, 'holders of wheels,' which Arguna Misra interprets to mean '*K*âra*n*as.' At *S*ânti Parvan (Moksha Dharma) CCXLIV, 26 Nîlaka*n*tha renders *K*akradhara by *K*akravartin or Emperor.
[7] I. e. as Kâsyapa was possessed of Vedic lore, and behaved as he ought to behave in his capacity of pupil, it was natural that the other should be pleased. [8] See p. 176 seq. supra.

highest perfection. Hear (them) from me, O *G*anârdana!

The Siddha said:

Mortals, O dear friend[1]! by their actions which are (of) mixed (character), or which are meritorious and pure, attain to this world as the goal, or to residence in the world of the gods[2]. Nowhere is there everlasting happiness; nowhere eternal residence[3]. Over and over again is there a downfall from a high position attained with difficulty. Overcome by lust and anger, and deluded by desire, I fell into uncomfortable and harassing states (of life), in consequence of (my) committing sin. Again and again death, and again and again birth[4]. I ate numerous (kinds of) food, sucked at various breasts, saw various mothers, and fathers of different sorts; and, O sinless one! (I saw) strange pleasures and miseries. Frequently (I suffered) separation from those I loved, association with those I did not love. Loss of wealth also came on me, after I had acquired that wealth with difficulty; ignominies full of affliction from princes and likewise from kinsmen; excessively poignant pain, mental and bodily. I also underwent frightful indignities, and fierce deaths and captivities; (I had a) fall into hell, and torments in the house of Yama[5]. I also suffered much from old age, continual ailments, and numerous misfortunes flowing from the pairs of opposites[6]. Then on one occasion, being much afflicted with misery, I abandoned the whole

[1] The same word as at Gîtâ, p. 72.
[2] Cf. *Kh*ândogya-upanishad, pp. 356–359, and Gîtâ, p. 84.
[3] See Gîtâ, p. 76, and cf. Ka*th*a, p. 90.
[4] For the whole of this passage, cf. Maitrî-upanishad, p. 8.
[5] See Manu VI, 61.
[6] See Gîtâ, p. 48.

course of worldly life, through indifference (to worldly objects), and taking refuge with the formless (principle)[1]. Having learnt about this path in this world, I exercised myself (in it), and hence, through favour of the self[2], have I acquired this perfection[3]. I shall not come here again[4]; I am surveying the worlds, and the happy migrations[5] of (my) self from the creation of beings to (my attaining) perfection. Thus, O best of the twice-born! have I obtained this highest perfection. From here I go to the next[6] (world), and from there again to the still higher (world)—the imperceptible seat of the Brahman. Have no doubt on that, O terror of your foes[7]! I shall not come back to this mortal world. I am pleased with you, O you of great intelligence! Say, what can I do for you? The time is now come for that which you desired in coming to me. I know for what you have come to me. But I shall be going away in a short time, hence have I given

[1] Taking refuge, says Nilaka*nth*a, in the belief of my being identical with the Brahman, which is to be comprehended by means of the profound contemplation called Asampra*gñ*âta Samâdhi.

[2] I.e., says Nîlaka*nth*a, the mind, and he cites Maitrî, p. 179. Cf. Ka*th*a, p. 108. The rendering at p. 192 supra will also suit (through the self becoming placid). This placidity is defined at *S*ânti Parvan (Moksha Dharma) CCXLVII, 11, with which cf. Gîtâ, p. 69. See Gîtâ, p. 51.

[3] As above described.

[4] Cf. *Kh*ândogya, p. 628; see also ibid. p. 282.

[5] He calls them happy because they have ended happily, I presume. 'Surveying the worlds' Nîlaka*nth*a takes to be an index of omniscience. Cf. Sanatsugâtiya, p. 174. See also Yoga-sûtras III, 25, and commentary there.

[6] I.e. the world of Brahman, or the Satyaloka; and the next step is assimilation into the Brahman.

[7] So read all the copies I have seen, though Kâsyapa is the person addressed.

this hint to you. I am exceedingly pleased, O clever one! with your good conduct. Put (your) questions without uneasiness, I will tell (you) whatever you desire. I highly esteem your intelligence, and greatly respect it, inasmuch as you have made me out[1]; for, O Kâsyapa! you are (a) talented (man).

CHAPTER II.

Vâsudeva[2] said:

Then grasping his feet, Kâsyapa asked questions very difficult to explain, and all of them that (being), the best of the supporters of piety, did explain.

Kâsyapa said:

How does the body perish, and how, too, is it produced? How does one who moves in this harassing course of worldly life become freed? And (how) does the self, getting rid of nature, abandon the body (produced) from it[3]? And how, being freed from the body, does he attain to the other[4]? How does this man enjoy the good and evil acts done by himself? And where do the acts of one who is released from the body remain?

The Brâhmana said:

Thus addressed, O descendant of Vrishni! that Siddha answered these questions in order. Hear me relate what (he said).

---

[1] This was difficult, as the Siddha possessed extraordinary powers, such as that of concealed movement, &c.

[2] Sic in MSS.

[3] Cf. as to getting rid of nature, Gîtâ, pp. 75–106. As to the body produced from nature, cf. ibid. p. 112, and pp. 317–318 infra.

[4] I. e. the Brahman, says Nîlakantha.

The Siddha said:

When those actions, productive of long life and fame[1], which a man performs here, are entirely exhausted, after his assumption of another body, he performs (actions of an) opposite character, his self being overcome at the exhaustion of life[2]. And his ruin being impending, his understanding goes astray. Not knowing his own constitution[3], and strength, and likewise the (proper) season, the man not being self-controlled, does unseasonably what is injurious to himself. When he attaches himself to numerous very harassing (actions); eats too much[4], or does not eat at all; when he takes bad food, or meat[5], or drinks, or (kinds of food) incompatible with one another, or heavy food in immoderate quantities, or without (previously taken food) being properly digested; or takes too much exercise, or is incontinent; or constantly, through attachment to action, checks the regular course (of the excretions[6]); or takes juicy food[7]; or sleeps by day[8]; or (takes food) not thoroughly prepared; (such a man) himself aggravates the dis-

---

[1] One reading omits 'fame,' as to which cf. Taittirîya-upanishad, p. 129; *Kh*ândogya, pp. 122–227. As to long life, cf. *Kh*ândogya. p. 272; exhausted, i.e. by enjoyment of fruit in another world.

[2] Cf. *S*ârîraka Bhâshya, p. 753 seq., where we have a slightly different view.

[3] Arguna Misra renders the original, sattva, by svabhâva.

[4] Cf. for all this, Gîtâ, pp. 62, 69, 118, which passages, however, are from a slightly different point of view. See also *Kh*ândogya, p. 526.

[5] A various reading here excludes meat. But cf. Âpastamba I, 1, 2, 23; Gautama II, 13.

[6] So says Nîlaka*n*tha.

[7] I.e. which turns to juice in digestion, much juice being a cause of indigestion, say the commentators.

[8] This is doubtful. The sense may be, 'who takes juicy or not thoroughly prepared food by day and night.' But see Âsvalâyana G*ri*hya-sûtra, p. 90; Âpastamba I, 1, 2, 24; Gautama II, 13.

orders (in the body) when the time comes[1]. By aggravating the disorders (in) his own (body), he contracts a disease which ends in death, or he even engages in unreasonable (acts), such as hanging[2] (oneself). From these causes, the living[3] body of that creature then perishes. Learn about that correctly as I am about to state it. Heat being kindled in the body, and being urged by a sharp wind[4], pervades the whole frame, and, verily, checks the (movements of all the) life-winds. Know this truly, that excessively powerful heat, if kindled in the body, bursts open the vital parts—the seats of the soul[5]. Then the soul, full of torments, forthwith falls away from the perishable (body). Know, O best of the twice-born! that (every) creature leaves the body, when the vital parts are burst open, its self being overcome with torments. All beings are constantly distracted with birth and death; and, O chief of the twice-born! are seen abandoning (their) bodies, or entering the womb on the exhaustion of (their previous) actions[6]. Again, a man suffers similar torments, having his joints broken and suffering from

[1] The time of destruction, says Arguna Misra.

[2] Which, say the commentators, leads to death, even without any disease.

[3] So I construe the original, having regard to the question, 'how does the body perish?' The other reading, which is in some respects better, is equivalent to 'the life falls away from the body of that creature.'

[4] This is different, as the commentators point out, from the ordinary life-winds.

[5] The original here is gîva, not âtman, which we have rendered 'self.' This refers rather to the vital principle. As to the seats, cf. Yâgñavalkya Smriti III, 93 seq.

[6] I adopt the reading karmanâm, which I find in one of the MSS. I consulted. I think it probable that that was the reading before the commentators. The other reading is marmanâm.

cold, in consequence of water[1]. As the compact association of the five elements is broken up, the wind in the body, distributed within the five elements[2], between the upward and downward life-winds, being aggravated by cold, and urged by a sharp wind[3], goes upwards[4], abandoning the embodied (self) in consequence of pain. Thus it[5] leaves the body, which appears devoid of breath. Then devoid of warmth, devoid of breath, devoid of beauty, and with consciousness destroyed, the man, being abandoned by the Brahman[6], is said to be dead. (Then) he ceases to perceive (anything) with those very currents[7] with which the supporter of the body[8] perceives objects of sense. In the same way, it is the eternal soul which preserves in the body the life-winds which are produced from food[9]. Whatever (part of the body) is employed in the collection[10] of that, know

[1] Having spoken of heat, he now speaks of the effects of cold. I am not sure if the water here refers to the water of the 'juicy' substances before referred to.

[2] This means, I presume, within the dissolving body. Cf. Maitrî-upanishad, p. 42.

[3] See note 4, last page.

[4] To the head, Arguna Misra.

[5] That is, the wind, I suppose, and then the breath departs from the body, and the man is said to die. 'Devoid of beauty,' further on, means, disfigured in the state of death.

[6] I.e. the mind, Arguna Misra.

[7] The senses. Cf. *S*vetâsvatara, p. 288.

[8] See and cf. p. 262 infra.

[9] This, says Arguna Misra, is in answer to the possible question why this 'sharp wind' does not work with the life-winds. The answer is, that such working requires the presence of the soul, which Arguna Misra says here means 'mind.' As to 'production from food,' cf. *Kh*ândogya, p. 421 seq., and Taittirîya Âra*n*yaka, p. 893.

[10] Collection of that = turning the food into semen, says Arguna Misra, who adds, 'in those vital parts, which are useful for this purpose, the life-wind dwells.'

that to be a vital part, for thus it is seen (laid down) in the Scriptures. Those vital parts being wounded, that (wind) directly comes out therefrom, and entering the bosom of a creature obstructs the heart[1]. Then the possessor of consciousness knows nothing[2]. Having his knowledge enveloped by darkness[3], while the vitals are still enveloped, the soul[4], being without a fixed seat, is shaken about by the wind. And then he heaves a very deep and alarming gasp, and makes the unconscious body quiver as he goes out (of it). That soul, dropping out of the body, is surrounded on both sides by his own actions[5], his own pure and meritorious, as also his sinful (ones). Brâhma*n*as, possessed of knowledge, whose convictions are correctly (formed) from sacred learning, know him by (his) marks as one who has performed meritorious actions or the reverse. As those who have eyes see a glow-worm disappear here and there in darkness, so likewise do those who have eyes of knowledge. Such a soul, the Siddhas see with a divine eye, departing (from the body), or coming to the birth, or entering into a womb[6]. Its three descriptions[7] of seats are here learnt from the Scriptures. This world is the world of actions[8], where

---

[1] Arguna Misra renders this to mean 'mind.'

[2] As the mind is obstructed, says Arguna Misra. The possessor of consciousness = the self, Arguna.

[3] I.e. pain, Arguna Misra.

[4] I.e. mind, Arguna Misra. [5] Cf. B*r*ihadâra*n*yaka, p. 843.

[6] See Aitareya-upanishad, p. 222, and *S*aṅkara's commentary there. The coming to the birth is the coming out of the womb into the world. Cf. also Gîtâ, p. 112.

[7] As stated further on, viz. this world, the next world, and the womb. With this compare *Kh*ândogya, p. 359.

[8] Cf. our Bhart*r*ihari (Bombay series), Notes (Nîtisataka), p. 27.

creatures dwell. All embodied (selfs), having here performed good or evil (actions), obtain (the fruit). It is here they obtain higher or lower enjoyments by their own actions. And it is those whose actions here are evil, who by their actions go to hell. Harassing is that lower place where men are tormented. Freedom from it is very difficult, and the self should be specially protected from it. Learn from me now the seats in which creatures going up [1] dwell, and which I shall describe truly. Hearing this, you will learn the highest knowledge, and decision regarding action [2]. All (the worlds in) the forms of stars, and this lunar sphere [3], and also this solar sphere which shines in the world by its own lustre, know these to be the seats of men who perform meritorious actions. All these, verily, fall down again and again in consequence of the exhaustion of their actions [4]. And there, too, in heaven, there are differences of low, high, and middling [5]. Nor, even there, is there satisfaction, (even) after a sight of most magnificent splendour. Thus have I stated to you these seats distinctly. I will after this (proceed to) state to you the production of the fœtus [6]. And, O twice-born one! hear that attentively from me as I state it.

---

[1] Cf. on this and 'lower place,' Gitâ, p. 109; Sâṅkhya Kârikâ, 44.

[2] The readings here are most unsatisfactory. The meaning of the printed reading adopted above would seem to be, 'decision as to what actions should be performed,' &c.

[3] Cf. Gitâ, p. 81, and Sanatsugâtîya, p. 158.

[4] Cf. Gitâ, p. 84.

[5] Arguna Misra says, 'In heaven = in the next world, low = inferior (?), high = heaven, and middling = the space below the skies (antariksha).' For the three degrees of enjoyment in heaven, see Yogavâsishtha I, 35 seq.

[6] This is the third of the three seats above referred to.

CHAPTER III.

There is no destruction here of actions good or not good[1]. Coming to one body after another they become ripened in their respective ways[2]. As a fruitful (tree) producing fruit may yield much fruit, so does merit performed with a pure mind become expanded[3]. Sin, too, performed with a sinful mind, is similarly (expanded). For the self engages in action, putting forward this mind[4]. And now further, hear how[5] a man, overwhelmed with action, and enveloped in desire and anger[6], enters a womb. Within the womb of a woman, (he) obtains as the result of action a body good or else bad[7], made up of virile semen and blood. Owing to (his) subtlety and imperceptibility, though he obtains a body appertaining to the Brahman, he is not attached anywhere; hence is he the eternal Brahman[8]. That is the seed of all beings; by that

[1] Cf. Maitrî-upanishad, p. 53, and Mu*nd*aka, p. 270. And see generally as to this passage, *S*ârîraka Bhâshya, pp. 751–760.

[2] I.e. they yield their respective fruits; cf. Maitrî, p. 43, and *K*h*â*ndogya, p. 358.

[3] This explains, say the commentators, how even a little merit or sin requires sometimes more than one birth to enjoy and exhaust.

[4] As a king performs sacrifices 'putting forward' a priest, Ar*g*una Mi*s*ra; and cf. Dhammapada, the first two verses.

[5] Ar*g*una Mi*s*ra has tathâ, 'in the same way,' instead of this, and renders it to mean 'putting forward' the mind.

[6] Hence he does not get rid of birth and death.

[7] Good = of gods or men; bad = of the lower species of creatures, Ar*g*una.

[8] He, in the preceding sentences, according to Ar*g*una Mi*s*ra, means the self, through the mind, or 'putting forward' the mind, as said above. In this sentence, he takes 'he' to mean the mind itself; Brahman = the self; and the mind, he says, is called the Brahman, as it, like the self, is the cause of the *K*aitanya, intelligence, in all creatures.

all creatures exist. That soul, entering all the limbs of the fœtus, part by part, and dwelling in the seat of the life-wind[1], supports (them) with the mind[2]. Then the fœtus, becoming possessed of consciousness, moves about its limbs. As liquefied iron being poured out assumes the form of the image[3], such you must know is the entrance of the soul into the fœtus. As fire entering a ball of iron, heats it, such too, you must understand, is the manifestation of the soul in the fœtus. And as a blazing lamp shines in a house, even so does consciousness light up bodies[4]. And whatever action he performs, whether good or bad, everything done in a former body must necessarily be enjoyed (or suffered). Then[5] that is exhausted, and again other (action) is accumulated, so long as the piety which dwells in the practice of concentration of mind for final emancipation[6] has not been learnt. As to that, O best (of men)! I will tell you about that action by which, verily, one going the round of various births, becomes happy. Gifts, penance, life as a Brahma*k*ârin, adherence to prescribed regulations, restraint of the senses[7], and also

[1] I. e. the heart.

[2] Ar*g*una Mi*s*ra says that the soul at the beginning of the sentence means the mind, and mind here means knowledge or intelligence. Cf. p. 238 supra.

[3] In the mould of which, that is to say, it is poured.

[4] Cf. Gîtâ, p. 106. The three similes, says Nîlaka*nth*a, show that the soul pervades the whole body, is yet imperceptible, and also unattached to the body. Ar*g*una Mi*s*ra's explanation is different, but I prefer Nîlaka*nth*a's.

[5] I. e. by the enjoyment or suffering.

[6] I. e. while he does not possess the knowledge which leads to the piety necessary as a preliminary for final emancipation, and which ultimately destroys action. Cf. Gîtâ, p. 62.

[7] I. e. keeping the senses of hearing &c. from all operations

tranquillity, compassion to (all) beings, self-restraint, and absence of cruelty, refraining from the appropriation of the wealth of others, not acting dishonestly even in thought towards (any) being in this world, serving mother and father, honouring deities and guests, honouring preceptors, pity, purity, constant restraint of the organs [1], and causing good to be done; this is said to be the conduct of the good [2]. From this is produced piety, which protects people to eternity. Thus one should look (for it) among the good, for among them it constantly abides. The practice to which the good adhere, points out (what) piety (is) [3]. And among them dwells that (course of) action which constitutes eternal piety. He who acquires that, never comes to an evil end [4]. By this are people held in check from making a slip in the paths of piety [5]. But the devotee who is released [6] is esteemed higher than these. For the deliverance from the course of worldly life of the man who acts piously and well, as he should act, takes place after a long time [7]. Thus a creature always meets with (the effects of) the action performed (in a) previous (life). And that [8] is the sole cause by which he comes here (in a) degraded (form). There is

save those relating to the Brahman. Tranquillity is the same thing as regards the mind.

[1] This I take to mean restraint of the active organs, such as speech, &c. 'Self-restraint' is rendered by Nîlakantha to mean 'concentration of mind.'

[2] Cf. Maitrî, p. 57; Khândogya, p. 136; and Gîtâ, pp. 103, 119.

[3] Cf. Âpastamba I, 1, 1, 2; I, 7, 20, 7; Sakuntalâ, p. 30 (Williams).

[4] Cf. Gîtâ, p. 72.

[5] By this, i.e. by the practice of the good, Arguna Misra.

[6] From delusion, Arguna Misra; emancipated by force of his devotion, Nîlakantha.

[7] Cf. Gîtâ, p. 73; Khândogya, pp. 136, 137. [8] Scil. the action.

in the world a doubt as to what originally was the source from which he became invested with a body. And that I shall now proceed to state. Brahman, the grandfather of all people, having made a body for himself, created the whole of the three worlds, moving and fixed[1]. From that he created the Pradhâna, the material cause of all embodied (selfs), by which all this is pervaded, and which is known in the world as the highest[2]. This is what is called the destructible[3]; but the other[4] is immortal and indestructible. And Pragâpati, who had been first created, created all creatures and (all) the fixed entities, (having) as regards the moving (creation), a pair separately for each[5] (species). Such is the ancient (tradition) heard (by us). And as regards that, the grandsire fixed a limit of time, and (a rule) about migrations among (various) creatures, and about the return[6]. What I say is all correct and proper, like (what may be said by) any talented person who has in

---

[1] I.e. animate and inanimate. 'A body for himself'=undeveloped Âkâsa, Nîlakantha. But see Sânkhya-sâra, p. 19, and Sânkhya Prav. Bhâshya I, 122, and III, 10.

[2] Cf. inter alia Gîtâ, p. 58 and note, and Sânkhya-sâra, p. 11. As to the words at the beginning of this sentence, 'from that,' cf. Taittirîya-upanishad, p. 67, where everything is derived from Âkâsa, mentioned in the last note, and Âkâsa from the Brahman.

[3] Cf. Gîtâ, p. 113, where there are three principles distinguished from each other.

[4] I.e. the self, Arguna Misra.

[5] A pair, i.e. a male and female for each species, such as man, &c., Arguna Misra.

[6] Pragâpati fixed the limit of life for every 'moving' creature, and the rule as to going from one species of body into another, and as to going from one world to another. As to a part of 'the ancient tradition,' the first stanza of the Mundaka-upanishad may be compared.

a former birth perceived the self[1]. He who properly perceives pleasure and pain to be inconstant, the body to be an unholy aggregate[2], and ruin to be connected with action[3], and who remembers that whatever little there is of happiness is all misery[4], he will cross beyond the fearful ocean of worldly life, which is very difficult to cross. He who understands the Pradhâna[5], (though) attacked by birth and death and disease, sees one (principle of) consciousness in all beings possessed of consciousness[6]. Then seeking after the supreme seat, he becomes indifferent to everything[7]. O best (of men)! I will give you accurate instruction concerning it. Learn from me exhaustively, O Brâhma*n*a! the excellent knowledge concerning the eternal imperishable seat, which I am now about to declare.

CHAPTER IV.

He who becoming placid[8], and thinking of nought, may become absorbed in the one receptacle[9], abandoning each previous (element), he will cross beyond

[1] Ar*g*una Mi*s*ra says the strength of the impression in the former birth would give him this knowledge in the subsequent birth.

[2] Cf. Sanatsu*g*âtîya, p. 155.
[3] Cf. inter alia p. 256 infra.

[4] Cf. Gîtâ, p. 79.
[5] Otherwise called Prak*ri*ti, or nature.

[6] Cf. Gîtâ, p. 124.
[7] Cf. Gîtâ, p. 111.

[8] We now begin, as Nîlaka*n*tha points out, the answer to the question put above by Kâ*s*yapa about the emancipation of the self. Placid, Ar*g*una Mi*s*ra renders to mean 'silent, taciturn.' See p. 234 supra.

[9] The path of knowledge, says Ar*g*una Mi*s*ra; the Brahman, says Nîlaka*n*tha. Abandoning each element = absorbing the gross into the subtle elements, and so forth, Nîlaka*n*tha; abandoning each elementary mode of worship till one reaches that of contemplating the absolute Brahman, Ar*g*una Mi*s*ra.

(all) bonds. A man who is a friend of all, who endures all, who is devoted to tranquillity[1], who has subdued his senses, and from whom fear and wrath have departed, and who is self-possessed[2], is released. He who moves among all beings as if they were like himself[3], who is self-controlled, pure, free from vanity[4] and egoism, he is, indeed, released from everything. And he, too, is released who is equable towards both life and death[5], and likewise pleasure and pain, and gain and loss, and (what is) agreeable and odious[6]. He who is not attached to any one, who contemns no one, who is free from the pairs of opposites, and whose self is free from affections[7], he is, indeed, released in every way. He who has no enemy, who has no kinsmen, who has no child, who has abandoned piety, wealth, and lust altogether, and who has no desire, is released. He who is not pious and not impious[8], who casts off (the merit or sin) previously accumulated, whose self is tranquillised by the exhaustion of the primary elements of the body[9], and who is free from the pairs of opposites, is released. One who does no action[10], and who has no desire, looks on this universe as

---

[1] This, in the terminology of the Vedânta, means keeping the mind from everything save 'hearing' &c. about the Brahman.

[2] One who has his mind under his control. But see Gîtâ, p. 63.

[3] Cf. Gîtâ, p. 71.

[4] I.e. the desire to be honoured or respected, Arguna Misra. Cf. Sanatsugâtîya, p. 161.

[5] Who does not care when death comes.

[6] Cf. p. 151 supra.

[7] Cf. Gîtâ for all this, pp. 101, 103, 125, &c.

[8] Cf. Ka*th*a, p. 101.

[9] Nîlaka*nth*a says this means the constituents of the body. Arguna Misra says, 'Prâ*n*a or life-wind,' &c. They are seven. See gloss on *K*'*h*ândogya-upanishad, p. 441, and p. 343 infra.

[10] Because, says Arguna Misra, he has no desire. Nîlaka*nth*a says this means an ascetic, sannyâsin. See p. 257 infra, note 1.

transient, like an A*s*vattha tree[1], always full of birth, death, and old age[2]. Having his understanding always (fixed) upon indifference to worldly objects, searching for his own faults[3], he procures the release of his self from bonds in no long time. Seeing the self void of smell[4], void of taste, void of touch, void of sound, void of belongings, void of colour, and unknowable, he is released. He who sees the enjoyer of the qualities[5], devoid of qualities, devoid of the qualities of the five elements[6], devoid of form, and having no cause, is released. Abandoning by the understanding[7] all fancies bodily and mental[8], he gradually obtains tranquillity[9], like fire devoid of fuel. He who is free from all impressions[10], free from the pairs of opposites, without belongings, and who moves among the collection of organs with penance[11], he is indeed released. Then freed from all impressions, he attains to the eternal

---

[1] Cf. Gîtâ, p. 111, where *S*ankara explains the name to mean 'what will not remain even till to-morrow.'

[2] Cf. Gîtâ, p. 109, and other passages.

[3] Ar*g*una Mi*s*ra has a different reading, which means 'particularly observing the evils of (the three kinds of) misery.'

[4] Cf. Ka*th*a, p. 119; Mu*nd*aka, p. 267; and Mâ*nd*ukya, p. 371.

[5] Cf. Gîtâ, pp. 104, 105, and Ka*th*a, p. 112.

[6] Nîlaka*nth*a says this refers to the gross elements, the next expression to the subtle ones, and being free from these two, he is 'devoid of qualities,' viz. the three qualities. [7] Cf. Gîtâ, p. 65.

[8] I.e. those which cause bodily and mental activity.

[9] Cf. Maitri, p. 178. The original is the famous word 'Nirvâ*n*a.'

[10] Scil. derived from false knowledge, says Ar*g*una Mi*s*ra. Nîlaka*nth*a says all impressions from outside oneself which are destroyed by those produced from concentration of mind, &c. See p. 391 infra.

[11] I.e. all those operations by which the internal man is rendered pure and free from all taints; see below, p. 248, where Nilaka*nth*a renders it as 'the performance of one's duty which is called penance.' But see, too, pp. 74, 119, 166 supra. The meaning seems to be that the

Supreme Brahman, tranquil, unmoving, constant, indestructible[1]. After this I shall explain the science of concentration of mind, than which there is nothing higher, (and which teaches) how devotees concentrating (their minds) perceive the perfect self[2]. I will impart instruction regarding it accurately. Learn from me the paths[3] by which one directing the self within the self perceives the eternal[4] (principle). Restraining the senses, one should fix the mind on the self; and having first performed rigorous penance[5], he should practise concentration of mind for final emancipation. Then the talented Brâhma*n*a, who has practised penance, who is constantly practising concentration of mind, should act on (the precepts of) the science of concentration of mind[6], seeing the self in the self by means of the mind[7]. If such a good man is able to concentrate the self on the self, then he, being habituated to exclusive meditation[8], perceives the self in the self. Being

man in question lets his senses work, but does not permit himself to be in any way identified with their operations. Cf. Gîtâ, p. 64.

[1] Cf. the expressions at Gîtâ, p. 45. 'Unmoving,' which occurs at Îsa, p. 10, is there explained by *S*aṅkara to mean 'always the same.' The same sense is given by Mahîdhara. Weber's *S*atapatha, p. 980.

[2] 'Perfect' would seem to mean here free from all bonds or taints, the absolute.

[3] I.e. sources of knowledge, says Ar*g*una Mi*s*ra.

[4] Cf. as to 'directing the self within the self,' Gîtâ, p. 69. Nîlaka*n*/*h*a says, 'paths, means of mental restraint, the self, mind; in the self, in the body.'

[5] See p. 247, note 11. Nîlaka*n*/*h*a's note there referred to occurs on this passage. See also p. 166, note 1 supra.

[6] It is not easy to say what this science is. Is it Pata*ñg*ali's system that is meant? No details occur to enable one to identify the 'science.' But, probably, no system is alluded to.

[7] See note 4 above.

[8] Nîlaka*n*/*h*a has a very forced explanation of the original word.

self-restrained and self-possessed[1], and always concentrating his mind, and having his senses subjugated, he who has achieved proper concentration of mind[2] sees the self in the self. As a person having seen one in a dream, recognises him (afterwards), saying, 'This is he;' so does one who has achieved proper concentration of mind perceive the self[3]. And as one may show the soft fibres, after extracting them from the Muñga, so does a devotee see the self extracted from the body. The body is called the Muñga; the soft fibres stand[4] for the self. This is the excellent illustration propounded by those who understand concentration of mind. When an embodied (self) properly perceives the self concentrated[5], then there is no ruler over him, since he is the lord of the triple world[6]. He obtains various bodies as he pleases; and casting aside old age and death, he grieves not and exults not. The man who

---

which also occurs further on; he takes the meaning to be, 'he who is habituated to that by which the One is attained, viz. meditation.'

[1] The original is the same as at Gîtâ, p. 63.

[2] That is to say, one who has got the power of concentrating his mind as he pleases; and the words 'always concentrating' &c., just before, would mean 'one who always exercises that power.'

[3] I.e. having perceived the self in the state of concentration, he sees the whole universe to be the self in this state when the concentration has ceased, Nîlakantha. Arguna Misra says, 'having perceived the self at the time of concentration, he recognises it as the same at the time of direct perception,' meaning, apparently, the time of final emancipation.

[4] I.e. the reality, which in this simile forms the substratum of what are called the fibres; the simile is in the Katha-upanishad; see, too, Sanatsugâtîya, p. 176.

[5] I.e. on the supreme self, as above explained.

[6] Cf. Sanatsugâtîya, p. 161; Svetâsvatara, p. 290; and Brihadâranyaka, p. 218; Khândogya, p. 523; Aitareya, p. 26; Kaushîtaki, p. 126.

has acquired concentration of mind, and who is self-restrained, creates for himself even the divinity of the gods[1]; and abandoning the transient body, he attains to the inexhaustible Brahman. When (all) beings are destroyed, he has no fear; when (all) beings are afflicted, he is not afflicted by anything[2]. He whose self is concentrated, who is free from attachment, and of a tranquil mind, is not shaken by the fearful effects of attachment and affection[3], which consist in pain and grief[4]. Weapons do not pierce him[5]; there is no death for him; nothing can be seen anywhere in the world happier than he. Properly concentrating his self, he remains steady to the self; and freed from old age and grief, he sleeps at ease. Leaving this human frame, he assumes bodies at pleasure. But one who is practising concentration should never become despondent[6]. When one who has properly achieved concentration perceives the self in the self, then he forthwith ceases to feel any attachment to Indra himself[7].

[1] I do not quite understand the original. The other reading, dehatvam for devatvam, is not more intelligible. But comparing the two, the meaning seems to be, that the divinity of the gods, i.e. their qualities and powers as gods, are within his reach, if he likes to have them.

[2] Cf. Gîtâ, p. 107.

[3] Affection is the feeling that a thing is one's own; attachment is the feeling of liking one has for a thing acquired with difficulty, Arguna Misra.

[4] Pain appears to be the feeling immediately following on hurt or evil suffered; grief is the constant state of mind which is a later result.

[5] Cf. Yoga-sûtra Bhâshya, p. 208.

[6] Cf. Gîtâ, p. 70. Despondency is the feeling that one has not acquired 'concentration' after much practice, and that therefore the practice should be abandoned.

[7] The other reading here may be rendered, 'Then forthwith Indra himself esteems him highly.'

Now listen how one habituated to exclusive meditation attains concentration. Thinking[1] of a quarter seen before, he should steady his mind within and not out of the city in which he dwells. Remaining within (that) city, he should place his mind both in its external and internal (operations) in that habitation in which he dwells. When, meditating in that habitation, he perceives the perfect one, his mind should not in any way wander outside. Restraining the group of the senses, in a forest[2] free from noises and unpeopled, he should meditate on the perfect one within his body with a mind fixed on one point. He

[1] This is all rather mystical. Nîlakan*th*a takes 'city' to mean 'body,' and 'habitation' to mean the mûlâdhâra, or other similar mystic centre within the body, where, according to the Yoga philosophy, the soul is sometimes to be kept with the life-winds, &c. 'Thinking of a quarter,' &c., he explains to mean 'meditating on the instruction he has received after studying the Upanishads.' I do not understand the passage well. 'City' for 'body' is a familiar use of the word. Cf. Gîtâ, p. 65. The original word for habitation occurs at Aitareya-upanishad, p. 199, where *S*aṅkara explains it to mean 'seat.' Three 'seats' are there mentioned,—the organs of sight, &c.; the mind; and the Âkâ*s*a in the heart. There, too, the body is described as a 'city,' and Anandagiri explains habitation to mean 'seat of amusement or sport.' Here, however, the meaning seems to be that one should work for concentration in the manner indicated, viz. first fix the mind on the city where one dwells, then on the particular part of it oftenest seen before, then one's own habitation, then the various parts of one's body, and finally one's own heart and the Brahman within it. Thus gradually circumscribed in its operations, the mind is better fitted for the final concentration on the Brahman. As to external and internal operations, cf. note 8, p. 247. The perfect one is the Brahman. Cf. Sanatsugâtîya, p. 171. As to âvasatha, which we have rendered by 'habitation,' see also Mâ*nd*ukya, p. 340; B*ri*hadâra*n*yaka, p. 751; and the alternative sense suggested by *S*aṅkara on the Aitareya, loc. cit.

[2] Cf. Maitrî-upanishad, p. 100.

should meditate on his teeth[1], palate, tongue, neck, and throat likewise, and also the heart, and likewise the seat of the heart. That talented pupil, O destroyer of Madhu! having been thus instructed by me, proceeded further to interrogate (me) about the piety (required) for final emancipation, which is difficult to explain. 'How does this food eaten from time to time become digested in the stomach? How does it turn to juice and how also to blood? And how, too, do the flesh, and marrow, and muscles, and bones—which all (form) the bodies for embodied (selfs)—develop in a woman as that (self) develops? How, too, does the strength develop? (And how is it also) about the removal of non-nutritive (substances)[2], and of the excretions, distinctly? How, too, does he breathe inwards or outwards? And what place does the self occupy, dwelling in the self[3]? And how does the soul moving about carry the body? And of what colour and of what description (is it when) he leaves it? O sinless venerable sir! be pleased to state this accurately to me.' Thus questioned by that Brâhma*n*a, O Mâdhava! I replied[4], 'O you of mighty arms! O

[1] Nîlaka*n*/*h*a cites numerous passages from works of the Yoga philosophy in illustration of this. He takes 'heart' to mean the Brahman seated in the heart (cf. *K*/*h*ândogya, p. 528), and 'the seat of the heart' to mean the one hundred and one passages of the heart. The latter expression Arguna Misra seems to render by 'mind.' See also generally on this passage, Maitrî-upanishad, p. 133, and Yoga-sûtra III, 1 and 28 seq., and commentary there.

[2] Literally, 'those which are void of strength.' I adopt Arguna Misra's reading. The other reading literally means 'obstructions.'

[3] The self here means the body, I take it. See p. 248 supra.

[4] The reply does not appear here. Nîlaka*n*/*h*a says that the succeeding chapters contain it. Arguna Misra seems to say that the answer has been already given. The context here is obscure.

restrainer of (your) foes! according to what (I had) heard. As one placing any property in his store-room should fix his mind on the property[1], so placing one's mind in one's body, and (keeping) the passages confined, one should there look for the self and avoid heedlessness[2]. Being thus always assiduous and pleased in the self, he attains in a short time to that Brahman, after perceiving which he understands the Pradhâna[3]. He is not to be grasped by the eye, nor by any of the senses. Only by the mind (used) as a lamp is the great self perceived[4]. He has hands and feet on all sides; he has eyes, heads, and faces on all sides; he has ears on all sides; he stands pervading everything in the world[5]. The soul sees the self[6] come out from the body; and abandoning his body, he perceives the self,—holding it to be the immaculate Brahman,—with, as it were, a mental smile[7]. And then depending upon it thus, he attains final emancipation in me[8].

[1] Nîlaka*n*tha says the original means household effects; Ar*g*una Mi*s*ra says wealth, and adds, the mind is fixed on it from fear of others finding it out.

[2] Cf. Sanatsu*g*âtîya, p. 152. Here, however, the sense is the ordinary one.

[3] I.e. all nature, that from which the universe is developed.

[4] Cf. Ka*th*a, pp. 117–130. See *S*ânti Parvan (Moksha) CCXL, 16.

[5] Cf. Gîtâ, p. 103. The stanza occurs often in the Bhârata. This, says Ar*g*una Mi*s*ra, answers the question 'how the soul carries the body.' The soul can do that as it is all-pervading.

[6] The individual soul, which has acquired true knowledge, perceives the self to be distinct from the body. See p. 249 supra.

[7] I.e. at the false notions which he entertained. Nîlaka*n*tha says, 'smile, i.e. amazement that he should have been deceived by the mirage-like course of worldly life.'

[8] I.e. final emancipation and assimilation with the supreme; 'depending upon it thus' = taking refuge with the Brahman in the way above stated.

This whole mystery I have declared to you, O best of Brâhma*n*as[1]! I will now take my leave, I will go away; and do you (too) go away, O Brâhma*n*a! according to your pleasure.' Thus addressed by me, O K*ri*sh*n*a! that pupil, possessed of great penance, —that Brâhma*n*a of rigid vows,—went away as he pleased.

Vâsudeva said:

Having spoken to me, O son of P*ri*thâ! these good words relating to the piety (required) for final emancipation, that best of Brâhma*n*as disappeared then and there. Have you listened to this, O son of P*ri*thâ! with a mind (fixed) on (this) one point only[2]? For on that occasion, too, sitting in the chariot you heard this same (instruction). It is my belief, O son of P*ri*thâ! that this is not easily understood by a man who is confused, or who has not acquired knowledge with his inmost soul purified[3]. What I have spoken, O chief of the descendants of Bharata! is a great mystery (even) among the gods. And it has never yet been heard by any man in this world, O son of P*ri*thâ! For, O sinless one! there is no other man than you worthy to hear it. Nor is it easily to be understood by (one whose) internal self (is) confused. The world of the gods[4], O son of Kuntî! is filled by those who perform

[1] Arguna Misra says, the only questions among those stated above, which are of use for final emancipation, have been here answered. The others should be looked for elsewhere.

[2] The original words here are identical with those at Gîtâ, p. 139.

[3] I adopt Nîlaka*n*/*h*a's reading here. Arguna Misra reads 'vigagdhena,' which he explains to mean 'one who eats kinds of food incompatible with one another.' A third reading is 'k*ri*taghnena,' ungrateful!

[4] See Gîtâ, p. 84.

actions. And the gods are not pleased with a cessation of the mortal form[1]. For as to that eternal Brahman, O son of P*ri*thâ! that is the highest goal, where one, forsaking the body, reaches immortality and is ever happy. Adopting this doctrine, even those who are of sinful birth, women, Vai*s*yas, and *S*ûdras likewise, attain the supreme goal. What then (need be said of) Brâhma*n*as, O son of P*ri*thâ[2]! or well-read Kshatriyas, who are constantly intent on their own duties, and whose highest goal is the world of the Brahman? This has been stated with reasons; and also the means for its acquisition; and the fruit of its full accomplishment, final emancipation, and determination regarding misery[3]. O chief of the descendants of Bharata! there can be no other happiness beyond this. The mortal, O son of Pâ*nd*u! who, possessed of talents, full of faith, and energetic[4], casts aside as unsubstantial the (whole) substance of this world[5], he forthwith attains the highest goal by these means. This is all that is to be said, there is nothing further than this. Concentration of mind comes to him, O son of P*ri*thâ! who practises concentration of mind constantly throughout six months[6].

---

[1] Cf. B*ri*hadâra*n*yaka, p. 234, where *S*aṅkara quotes the original stanza, but with a reading which means, 'And the gods are not pleased at mortals rising above (them).' That is a better reading.

[2] See Gîtâ, pp. 85, 86, where the words are nearly identical with those in the text.

[3] This is not quite clear. Does 'determination regarding misery,' the original of which is du*h*khasya *k*a vinir*n*aya*h*, mean 'conclusion of all misery?' Comp. Gîtâ, p. 79.

[4] Ar*g*una Mi*s*ra says this means assiduous.

[5] I.e. wealth and so forth, says Nîlaka*nth*a. Cf. 'human wealth' at Sanatsu*g*âtîya, p. 161.

[6] Cf. Maitrî-upanishad, p. 154. The copy of Ar*g*una Mi*s*ra's

CHAPTER V.

On this [1], too, O chief of the descendants of Bharata! they relate this ancient story, (in the form of) a dialogue, which occurred, O son of P*ri*thâ! between a husband and wife. A Brâhma*n*a's wife, seeing the Brâhma*n*a her husband, who had gone through all knowledge and experience [2], seated in seclusion, spoke to him (thus): 'What world, indeed, shall I go to, depending on you as (my) husband, you who live renouncing (all) action, and who are harsh and undiscerning [3]. We have heard that wives attain to the worlds acquired by (their) husbands. What goal, verily, shall I reach, having got you for my husband?' Thus addressed, that man of a tranquil self, spoke to her with a slight smile: 'O beautiful one! O sinless one! I am not offended at these words of yours. Whatever action there is, that can be caught (by the touch) [4], or seen, or heard, that only do the men of action engage in as action. Those who are devoid of knowledge only lodge [5] delusion in themselves by means of action. And freedom from action is not to be attained in this world even for an

---

commentary which I have used, says that the Anugîtâ ends here. But, as we have shown, there is a verse coming further on, which *S*ankarâ*k*ârya cites as from the Anugîtâ. In the printed copies of the Mahâbhârata the next chapter is called the Brâhma*n*agîtâ.

[1] I.e. the questions at p. 252, Nîlaka*n*t*h*a; more probably, perhaps, the 'doctrine' mentioned at p. 254 is what is alluded to.

[2] Cf. Gîtâ, p. 57 and note.

[3] Nîlaka*n*t*h*a says this means 'ignorant that the wife has no other support.' Ar*g*una Mi*s*ra interprets kînâ*s*a to mean 'indigent' instead of 'harsh.'

[4] So Ar*g*una Mi*s*ra. Nîlaka*n*t*h*a's reading and his interpretation of the passage are different.

[5] I follow Ar*g*una Mi*s*ra; the original literally means 'restrain.'

instant[1]. From birth to the destruction of the body, action, good or bad, by act, mind or speech[2], does exist among (all) beings. While the paths[3] (of action), in which the materials are visible, are destroyed by demons[4], I have perceived by means of the self the seat abiding in the self[5]—(the seat) where dwells the Brahman free from the pairs of opposites, and the moon together with the fire[6], upholding (all) beings (as) the mover of the intellectual principle[7]; (the seat) for which[8] Brahman and others concentrating (their minds) worship that indestructible (principle), and for which learned men have their senses restrained, and their selfs tranquil, and (observe) good vows. It is not to be smelt by the nose, and not to be tasted by the tongue. It is not to be touched by the sense of touch, but is to be apprehended by the mind. It cannot be

[1] Cf. Gîtâ, pp. 52, 53; see also, as to freedom from action, Gîtâ, p. 127.

[2] I.e. thought, word, and deed. I have in the text kept to a more literal rendering.

[3] This is Nîlakantha's reading and interpretation. Arguna Misra reads 'actions visible and invisible.'

[4] Cf. inter alia Kumâra-sambhava II, 46.

[5] I.e. says Arguna Misra, the safe place, within the body; and says Nîlakantha, the seat called Avimukta, between the nose and the brows; as to which cf. Gîtâ, p. 67. In the Kenopanishad (p. 220) the word âyatana is used to signify a means to the attainment of the Brahman.

[6] The moon and fire constitute the universe, says Arguna Misra. Cf. Gîtâ, p. 113. Nîlakantha interprets this more mystically as referring to the Idâ and Pingalâ arteries.

[7] So Nîlakantha, but he takes it to stand for 'vâyu' or wind, as a distinct principle. The sense is by no means clear. But the moon being the deity of the mind also may, perhaps, be described as she is here, on that account.

[8] This is Arguna Misra's interpretation of the original locative.

conquered by the eyes, and is entirely beyond the senses of hearing. It is devoid of smell, devoid of taste and touch, devoid of colour and sound, and imperishable[1]. (It is that) from which (this whole) expanse[2] (of the universe) proceeds, and on which it rests. From this the Prâna, Apâna, Samâna, Vyâna, and Udâna also proceed, and into it they enter[3]. Between the Samâna and the Vyâna, the Prâna and the Apâna moved. When that[4] is asleep, the Samâna and Vyâna also are absorbed[5]; and between the Prâna and the Apâna dwells the Udâna pervading (all). Therefore the Prâna and the Apâna do not forsake a sleeping person. That is called the Udâna, as the life-winds are controlled[6] (by it). And therefore those who study the Brahman engage in penance[7] of which I am the goal[8]. In

[1] Cf. note 4, p. 247 supra, and p. 253.

[2] Arguna Misra says this means the five great elements, the eleven organs (active and perceptive, and the mind), the life-wind, and the individual soul.

[3] The Prâna is at the nose, the Apâna at the arms, the Samâna at the navel, the Vyâna pervades the whole body, and the Udâna is at all the joints; cf. Yoga-sûtra III, 38 seq. Nilakantha says this explains how the 'expanse' (meaning, he says, the operations of the creation, &c.) 'proceeds' from the Brahman. See on the life-winds, Brihadâranyaka, p. 667; Khândogya, pp. 42–188; Sânkhyatattvakaumudî, p. 96; Vedânta Paribhâshâ, p. 45; p. 271 infra.

[4] The self, Arguna Misra. Nilakantha says, 'the Prâna accompanied by the Apâna.'

[5] I.e. into the Prâna and Apâna, Arguna Misra.

[6] Nilakantha derives the word thus, utkarshena ânayati.

[7] I.e. the subjugation of the life-winds as indicated at Gîtâ, p. 61.

[8] The meaning of the passage as a whole is not very clear, and the commentators afford but little help. The sense appears to be this: The course of worldly life is due to the operations of the life-winds which are attached to the self and lead to its manifestations as individual souls. Of these, the Samâna and Vyâna are

the interior[1], in the midst of all these (life-winds) which move about in the body and swallow up one another[2], blazes the Vaisvâna fire[3] sevenfold. The nose, and the tongue, and the eye, and the skin, and the ear as the fifth, the mind and the understanding, these are the seven tongues[4] of the blaze of Vaisvânara. That which is to be smelt, that which is to be drunk, that which is to be seen, that which is to be touched, and likewise that which is to be heard, and also that which is to be thought of, and that which is to be understood, those are the seven (kinds of) fuel for me[5]. That which smells, that which eats, that which sees, that which touches, and that which hears as the fifth, that which thinks, and that which understands, these are the seven great officiating priests[6]. And mark this always,

controlled and held under check by the Prâna and Apâna, into which latter the former are absorbed in sleep. The latter two are held in check and controlled by the Udâna, which thus controls all. And the control of this, which is the control of all the five, and which is otherwise called penance, destroys the course of worldly life, and leads to the supreme self.

[1] I.e. within the body. [2] As explained in note 8, p. 258.

[3] This, says Nîlakantha, explains the word 'I' in the sentence preceding. Vaisvânara is a word often used to denote the self. The Vishamaslokî derives it thus, 'that which saves all beings from hell;' see the Prasna-upanishad, pp. 167–188 (where seven tongues are also referred to); Mundaka, p. 292; Khândogya, p. 364; Mândukya, p. 341.

[4] Cf. Taittirîya-âranyaka, p. 802.

[5] I.e. the Vaisvânara. Cf. Taittirîya-âranyaka, p. 803 and gloss.

[6] These I take to be the powers of hearing, &c., which are presided over by the several deities; or, better, perhaps, they may mean the soul distinguished as so many with reference to these several powers; cf. Brihadâranyaka, p. 169; Maitrî, p. 96; Prasna, pp. 214, 215; Kaushîtaki, p. 96; Aitareya, p. 187; Khândogya, p. 616. The latter sense is accepted by Arguna Misra.

O beautiful one! The learned sacrificers throwing (in) due (form) the seven offerings into the seven fires in seven ways, produce them in their wombs[1]: (namely), that which is to be smelt, that which is to be drunk, that which is to be seen, that which is to be touched, and likewise that which is to be heard, that which is to be thought of, and also that which is to be understood. Earth, air, space, water, and light as the fifth, mind and understanding, these seven, indeed, are named wombs. All the qualities which stand[2] as offerings are absorbed in the mouth of the fire[3]; and having dwelt within that dwelling are born in their respective wombs[4]. And in that very (principle), which is the generator of all entities, they remain absorbed during (the time of) deluge. From that[5] is produced smell; from that is produced taste; from that is produced colour; from that touch is produced; from that is produced sound; from that doubt[6] is produced; from that is produced determination. This (is what) they know as the sevenfold production. In this very way was it[7] comprehended by the ancients. Becoming perfected by the perfect sacrifice[8], they were perfectly filled with light.'

---

[1] The next clause explains this; that which is to be smelt is earth, and so on throughout. The men who sacrifice all sensuous objects, get such powers that they can create the objects whenever they like. As to 'in their wombs,' see Yoga Bhâshya, p. 108.

[2] I.e. are so treated in the above allegory.

[3] I.e. the Brahman.

[4] I.e. when the sacrificer wishes, as stated in note 1.

[5] That principle—viz. the Brahman.

[6] This is the operation of the mind, see Gîtâ, p. 57 note.

[7] The Brahman, Arguna Misra. Or it may be the 'sevenfold production.'

[8] The wholesale sacrifice of all sensuous perceptions. The

CHAPTER VI.

The Brâhma*n*a said:

On this, too, they relate this ancient story. Learn now of what description is the institution of the ten sacrificial priests[1]. The ear[2], the skin, the two eyes, the tongue, the nose, the two feet, the two hands, speech, the genital organ, and the anus, these, verily, are ten sacrificial priests, O beautiful one! Sound, touch, colour, and taste, smell, words, action, motion, and the discharge of semen, urine, and excrement, these are the ten oblations. The quarters, wind, sun, moon, earth and fire, and Vish*n*u also, Indra, Pragâpati, and Mitra, these, O beautiful one! are the ten fires[3]. The ten organs are the makers of the offering; the offerings are ten, O beautiful one! Objects of sense, verily, are the fuel; and they are offered up into the ten fires. The mind is the ladle[4]; and the wealth is the pure, highest knowledge[5]. (Thus) we have heard, was the universe duly divided[6]. And the mind, which is the instru-

---

root corresponding with perfect occurs three times in the original, hence the repetition of perfect above.

[1] Cf. Taittirîya-brâhma*n*a, p. 411, and Âra*n*yaka, p. 281.

[2] Cf. B*ri*hadâra*n*yaka, p. 459. The reading in the printed edition of Bombay is defective here.

[3] See p. 337 seq., where all this is more fully explained. And cf. the analogous Buddhistic doctrine stated at Lalita Vistara (Translation by Dr. R. Mitra), p. 11.

[4] See Taittirîya-âra*n*yaka loc. cit., and cf. Gîtâ, p. 61. 'The wealth' probably means the Dakshi*n*â to be given to the priests, which is mentioned at Gîtâ, p. 119.

[5] The 'priests' here being the senses, the knowledge would accrue to them, as to which cf. Gîtâ, p. 108.

[6] See note 3.

ment of knowledge, requires everything knowable[1] (as its offering). The mind is within the body the upholder of the frame, and the knower is the upholder of the body[2]. That[3] upholder of the body is the Gârhapatya fire; from that another is produced, and the mind which is the Âhavanîya; and into this the offering is thrown. Then the lord of speech was produced[4]; that (lord of speech) looks up to the mind. First, verily, are words produced; and the mind runs after them.

---

[1] Each sense can only offer up its own perceptions—the mind offers up all knowledge whatever.

[2] Arguna Misra says this is an implied simile, the mind is an upholder of the body as the 'knower' or self is.

[3] Arguna Misra says this means 'the mind.' I think it better to take it here as the self (see p. 238 supra), to which the 'mind' and the 'other,' mentioned further on, would be subordinate; the 'other' Arguna Misra renders by the 'group of the senses.' The senses are compared to fires at Gîtâ, p. 61. The passage at Taittirîya-âranyaka above cited refers only to the Gârhapatya and Âhavanîya fires. Nîlakantha's text and explanation of this passage are, to my mind, not nearly so satisfactory as Arguna Misra's.

[4] In the Taittirîya-brâhmana and Âranyaka loc. cit., the equivalent of the original word for 'lord of speech' here occurs, viz. Vâkpati for Vâkaspati here; but that is there described as the Hotri priest, and speech itself as the Vedî or altar. The commentator there interprets 'lord of speech' to mean the wind which causes vocal activity, and resides in the throat, palate, &c. As to mind and speech, see also Khândogya, pp. 285–441, and comments of Sankara there. The meaning of this passage, however, is not by any means clear to my mind. The Dasahotri mantras in the Taittirîya are stated to be the mantras of the Ishti, or sacrifice, performed by Pragâpati for creation. It is possible, then, that the meaning here is, that speech which is to be learnt by the pupil, as stated further on—namely, the Vedas—was first produced from that Ishti (cf. Kullûka on Manu I, 21). But to understand that speech, mind is necessary; hence it is said to look up to the mind. The Brâhmana's wife, however, seems to understand speech as ordinary speech, hence her question.

The Brâhma*n*a's wife said:

How did speech come into existence first, and how did the mind come into existence afterwards, seeing that words are uttered (after they have been) thought over by the mind? By means of what experience does intelligence come to the mind, and (though) developed, does not comprehend[1]? What verily obstructs it?

The Brâhma*n*a said:

The Apâna becoming lord changes it into the state of the Apâna in consequence. That is called the movement of the mind, and hence the mind is in need (of it)[2]. But since you ask me a question regarding speech and mind, I will relate to you a dialogue between themselves. Both speech and mind went to the self of all beings[3] and spoke (to him thus), 'Say which of us is superior; destroy our doubts, O lord!' Thereupon the lord positively said to speech, 'Mind (is superior).' But speech thereupon said to him, 'I, verily, yield (you) your desires[4].'

[1] This, again, is to my mind very hard to understand. The original word for 'intelligence' is mati, which at *Kh*ândogya, p. 514, *S*añkara interprets thus: 'intelligence is pondering, application to (literally, respect for) the subject of thought.' The original for 'developed,' Arguna Mi*s*ra renders by 'mixed or assimilated with;' and 'does not comprehend,' he takes to mean 'does not understand—speech or words.' This question appears to be suggested by the last words of the previous speech.

[2] These two sentences are again very obscure. Nîlaka*n*/*h*a, as usual, deserts his original, giving peculiar meanings to the words without producing any authority. Arguna Mi*s*ra is very meagre, and besides the MS. is very incorrect. See p. 264, note 5 infra.

[3] I. e. Pragâpati, says Arguna Mi*s*ra, which seems to be justified by the sequel. Nîlaka*nt*/*h*a takes it to mean the individual self, which doubtless is its meaning elsewhere, e. g. Maitrî, p. 56.

[4] I. e. speech conveys information on all matters, Arguna Mi*s*ra;

The Brâhmana[1] said:

Know, that (in) my (view), there are two minds[2], immovable and also movable. The immovable, verily, is with me; the movable is in your dominion. Whatever mantra, or letter, or tone goes to your dominion, that indeed is the movable mind[3]. To that you are superior. But inasmuch, O beautiful one! as you came personally to speak to me (in the way you did)[4], therefore, O Sarasvatî! you shall never speak after (hard) exhalations[5]. The goddess speech, verily, dwelt always between the Prâna and Apâna[6]. But, O noble one! going with the Apâna

---

as the means of acquiring desired fruit, visible or invisible, is learnt by speech, Nîlakantha. Cf. as to all this, Brihadâranyaka-upanishad, pp. 50 seq. and 261.

[1] I.e. Nîlakantha says, 'the Brâhmana named mind,' alluding apparently to p. 310 infra. But the reading of some of the MSS., viz. Brahman for the Brâhmana, seems preferable, having regard to what follows. Apparently, the Brâhmana's own speech should begin at 'The goddess speech' further on.

[2] Nîlakantha says, immovable = to be understood by the external senses; movable = not perceptible by senses, such as heaven, &c., which is not quite intelligible. Arguna Misra says, the immovable mind is that of the teacher, which is fixed, as it has not to learn or acquire anything, while that of the pupil is movable as acquiring new impressions and knowledge.

[3] I.e. it is the movable mind which takes cognisance of the significations of all mantras (sacred texts), letters, tones, in which, I presume, sacred instruction is conveyed. To this mind, speech is superior, as that mind only works on what speech places before it; but the mind which is 'with' Pragâpati, is superior to speech as it is not dependent on speech like the other.

[4] I.e. proudly, about her being the giver of desires to Brahman.

[5] I.e., says Arguna Misra, the words will not come out with the Prâna life-wind and convey any sense to the hearer, but will be absorbed down into the Apâna life-wind, and not be articulated as speech at all. Cf. Kaushîtaki, p. 41; Katha, p. 184 (with glosses); and Khândogya, p. 42.

[6] I.e., I presume, was dependent on the two life-winds named.

wind[1], though impelled, (in consequence of) being without the Prâna, she ran up to Pragâpati, saying, 'Be pleased[2], O venerable sir!' Then[3] the Prâna appeared again nourishing speech. And therefore speech never speaks after (hard) exhalation. It is always noisy or noiseless. Of those two, the noiseless is superior to the noisy[4] (speech). This excellent (speech), like a cow, yields milk[5], and speaking of the Brahman it always produces the eternal (emancipation). This cow-like speech, O you of a bright smile! is divine, with divine[6] power. Observe the difference of (its) two subtle, flowing (forms)[7].

The Brâhmana's wife said:

What did the goddess of speech say on that occasion in days of old, when, though (she was) impelled with a desire to speak, words could not be uttered?

The Brâhmana said:

The (speech) which is produced in the body by

Cf. p. 353 infra. For this sense of the word 'between,' see p. 258 supra, and Khândogya-upanishad, p. 623.

[1] And not with the Prâna, so as to be articulated. Cf. p. 264.

[2] I. e. to withdraw the 'curse' pronounced, as above stated.

[3] After the curse was withdrawn, says Arguna Misra. Cf. Brihadâranyaka, p. 317.

[4] Since, says Arguna Misra, noiseless speech is the source of all words—Vânmaya. Perhaps we may compare Aitareya-brâhmana (Haug), p. 47.

[5] Viz. Vânmaya; milk, as a source of pleasure.

[6] I. e. enlightening, Arguna Misra. But, perhaps, the translation should be, 'has powers divine and not divine.' As to this, cf. Sânkhya Bhâshya on III, 41, and Sânkhyatattvakaumudî, p. 118, and Wilson's Sânkhya Kârikâ, p. 37 (Sanskrit), and Svetâsvatara, p. 284 (gloss).

[7] Arguna Misra refers to a 'Satapatha text' in praise of the subtle speech. I cannot trace the text. But see Nirukta (Roth), pp. 167–187.

means of the Prâ*n*a [1], and which then goes into the Apâna, and then becoming assimilated with the Udâna leaves the body [2], and with the Vyâna envelopes all the quarters [3], then (finally) dwells in the Samâna [4]. So speech formerly spoke. Hence the mind is distinguished by reason of its being immovable, and the goddess distinguished by reason of her being movable [5].

Chapter VII.

The Brâhma*n*a said:

On this, too, O beautiful one! they relate this ancient story, (which shows) of what description is the institution of the seven sacrificial priests [6]. The

---

[1] Cf. *Kh*ândogya, p. 285, and the passage there quoted by *S*aṅkara as well as Ânandagiri's gloss. And see, too, p. 353 infra.

[2] Viz. the part of it which specially appertains to speech—the throat, &c.

[3] All the nâ*d*îs or passages of the body, Ar*g*una Mi*s*ra.

[4] I. e. at the navel in the form of sound, as the material cause of all words. There and in that condition speech dwells, after going through the body, as above stated. There, adds Ar*g*una Mi*s*ra, devotees are to meditate on speech.

[5] This is not quite clear, but the meaning seems to be, that the merit of the immovable mind consists in its unchangeability, and that of speech in being the cause of variations in the movable mind by conveying new knowledge and new impressions. Cf. on this result, *Kh*ândogya-upanishad, p. 482.

[6] Ar*g*una Mi*s*ra says, the last chapter explained Prâ*n*âyâma, and this explains Pratyâhâra. Prâ*n*âyâma is the restraint of the life-winds, Pratyâhâra that of the senses, according to the Yoga philosophy (see the quotation in the commentary at Yoga-sûtra III, 1, and see also pp. 141–145). Cf. also Gîtâ, p. 61. The Saptahot*ri*-vidhâna as taught in the Taittirîya-brâhma*n*a and Âra*n*yaka is to be found a few pages after the pages referred to for the Da*s*ahot*ri*-vidhâna at p. 261 supra. And the other Vidhânas also are to be found in the same parts of those books.

nose, and the eye, and the tongue, and the skin, and the ear as the fifth, mind and understanding, these are the seven sacrificial priests separately stationed. Dwelling in a minute space, they do not perceive each other. Do you, verily, O beautiful one! learn about these sacrificial priests, (which are) seven according to (their several) natures.

The Brâhmaṇa's wife said:

How (is it) these do not perceive each other, dwelling (as they do) in a minute space? What are their natures, O venerable sir? Tell me this, O lord!

The Brâhmaṇa said:

Not knowing the qualities (of anything) is ignorance (of it). Knowledge of the qualities is knowledge. And these never know the qualities of each other. The tongue, the eye, the ear likewise, the skin, the mind, and the understanding also, do not apprehend smells, the nose apprehends them. The nose, the eye, the ear likewise, the skin, the mind, and the understanding also, do not apprehend tastes, the tongue apprehends them. The nose, the tongue, the ear likewise, the skin, the mind, and the understanding also, do not apprehend colours, the eye apprehends them. The nose, the tongue, and next the eye, the ear, the understanding, the mind likewise, do not apprehend (objects of) touch, the skin apprehends them. The nose, the tongue, and the eye, the skin, the mind, and the understanding also, do not apprehend sounds, the ear apprehends them. The nose, the tongue, and the eye, the skin, the ear, and the understanding also, do not apprehend doubt, the mind apprehends it. The nose, the tongue, and the eye, the skin, the ear, and the mind also, do not apprehend final determination, the understanding apprehends it. On this, too, they relate this ancient story,—a dialogue, O beautiful one! between the senses and the mind.

The mind said:

The nose smells not without me, the tongue does not perceive taste, the eye does not take in colour, the skin does not become aware of any (object of) touch. Without me, the ear does not in any way hear sound. I am the eternal chief among all elements[1]. Without me, the senses never shine, like an empty dwelling, or like fires the flames of which are extinct. Without me, all beings, like fuel half dried and half moist, fail to apprehend qualities or objects, even with the senses exerting themselves[2].

The senses said:

This would be true as you believe, if you, without us, enjoyed the enjoyments (derived from) our objects[3]. If when we are extinct, (there is) pleasure and support of life, and if you enjoy enjoyments, then what you believe is true; or if when we are absorbed[4], and objects are standing, you enjoy objects according to their natures by the mere operation of the mind.

---

[1] Cf. Kaushîtaki-upanishad, p. 93; *Kh*ândogya, p. 297; Maitrî, p. 158; and B*ri*hadâra*n*yaka, p. 284. The passages in the last two works seem to be identical ones.

[2] I. e. in their respective operations.

[3] The implication, of course, is, as Arguna Misra says, that this is not so, as what is not perceived by the senses cannot be the object of the mind's operations,—a proposition which reminds one of the maxim, 'Nihil est in intellectu quod non fuerit in sensu,' apparently without Leibnitz's limitation of it. Cf. Archbishop Thomson's Laws of Thought, p. 52.

[4] As in sleep, &c.

If again you think your power over our objects is constant[1], then take in colours by the nose, take in tastes by the eye, take in smells by the ear, take in (objects of) touch by the tongue, and take in sounds by the skin, and also (objects of)[2] touch by the understanding. For those who are powerful have no rules (to govern them); rules are for the weak. You should accept enjoyments unenjoyed before; you ought not to enjoy what has been tasted[3] (by others). As a pupil goes to a preceptor for Vedic learning, and having acquired Vedic learning from him, performs the directions of the Vedic texts, so you treat as yours[4] objects shown[5] by us, both past and future[6], in sleep and likewise wakefulness. Besides, when creatures of little intelligence are distracted in mind, life is seen to be supported, when our objects[7] perform their functions. And even after having carried on numerous mental operations, and indulged in dreams, a creature, when troubled by desire to enjoy, does run to objects of sense only. One entering upon enjoyments, resulting from mental operations (alone), and not connected with objects

---

[1] I.e. if you can enjoy objects independently of the senses, whenever you choose to perform your operations. This, says Arguna Misra, meets an objection which might be made, that the mind at the time stated does not desire objects.

[2] Sic in original. It comes twice.

[3] Eating what has been tasted by another is a cause of degradation. Cf. *Kh*ândogya, p. 81; Maitrî, p. 103; and p. 363 infra.

[4] You incorrectly attribute to yourself the quality of apprehending them.

[5] I.e. presented before you by us.

[6] This is not quite clear. Arguna Misra has, 'not past, not future;' literally, 'not come, not gone.'

[7] Viz. smell, sound, &c.; not by the mere operations of the mind, but by obtaining the objects, is life supported.

of sense, (which is) like entering a house without a door[1], always meets death, on the exhaustion of the life-winds[2], as a fire which is kindled (is extinguished) on the exhaustion of fuel. Granted, that we have connexions with our (respective) qualities, and granted that we have no perception of each other's qualities; still, without us, you have no perception[3], and so long no happiness can accrue to you.

Chapter VIII.

The Brâhma*n*a said:

On this, too, they relate an ancient story, O beautiful one! (showing) of what description is the institution of the five sacrificial priests. The learned know this to be a great principle, that the Prâ*n*a and the Apâna, and the Udâna, and also the Samâna and the Vyâna, are the five sacrificial priests.

The Brâhma*n*a's wife said:

My former belief was that the sacrificial priests were seven by (their) nature[4]. State how the great principle is that there are verily five sacrificial priests[5].

---

[1] The senses are the doors of the house here, as they are among the doors of the city at Gîtâ, p. 65.

[2] Owing to the want of food, &c. Cf. Maitrî, p. 112, and *Kh*ândogya, p. 422.

[3] Perception of pleasure, says Arguna Misra; but he takes the subsequent clause to mean this, 'and without you no pleasure accrues to us either.' The text is here in an unsatisfactory state.

[4] As stated in the last chapter; some MSS. read 'your' for 'my' at the beginning of the sentence.

[5] Arguna Misra says that in this Pa*ñk*ahot*ri*-vidhâna the five chief Hot*ri*s only are stated for briefly explaining the Prâ*n*âyâma.

The Brâhma*n*a said:

The wind prepared by the Prâ*n*a afterwards becomes the Apâna. The wind prepared in the Apâna then works as the Vyâna. The wind prepared by the Vyâna works as the Udâna. And the wind prepared in the Udâna is produced as Samâna[1]. They formerly went to the grandsire, who was born first, and said to him, 'Tell us which is greatest among us. He shall be the greatest among us[2].'

Brahman said:

He, verily, is the greatest, who being extinct, all the life-winds in the body of living creatures become extinct; and on whose moving about, they again move about. (Now) go where (you) like.

The Prâ*n*a said:

When I am extinct, all the life-winds in the body

---

[1] Ar*g*una Misra says, 'The wind going to the Prâ*n*a, and being obstructed in upward progress by the Prâ*n*a, goes to the Apâna, and then unable to go upwards or downwards, enters the passages or nâ*d*îs of the body and becomes Vyâna. In the same way Udâna, by the collision of the two, produces sound in the throat, and depends on Prâ*n*a and Apâna; so, too, the Samâna dwelling in the navel and kindling the gastric fire is also dependent on those two.' The meaning seems to be that one life-wind is distributed in the different places, and gets different names, as stated, in the order mentioned. See Maitrî, p. 28.

[2] A similar visit on the part of the Prâ*n*as (who, however, are not there the life-winds only, but the Prâ*n*a life-wind and the active organs) to Pra*g*âpati is mentioned at B*r*ihadâra*n*yaka-upanishad, p. 1016, and *Kh*ândogya, p. 297. Cf. also Prasna, p. 178; B*r*ihadâra*n*yaka, p. 317; and Kaushîtaki, p. 63. See also, generally, as to the life-winds and their functions, B*r*ihadâra*n*yaka, p. 280, and *S*a*n*kara's comment there; Yoga-sûtras III, 38, and comment; Cowell's note at Maitrî, p. 247; *S*ânti Parvan (Moksha Dharma), chap. 184, st. 24-25; chap. 185, st. 1 seq.; and p. 258 supra.

of living creatures become extinct; and on my moving about, they again move about. I am the greatest. See I am extinct!

The Brâhma*n*a said:

Then the Prâ*n*a became extinct, and again moved about. Then the Samâna and Udâna also[1], O beautiful one! spoke these words, 'You do not pervade all this here as we do. You are not the greatest among us, O Prâ*n*a, because the Apâna is subject to you[2].' The Prâ*n*a again moved about[3], and the Apâna[4] said to him.

The Apâna said:

When I am extinct, all the life-winds in the body of living creatures become extinct; and on my moving about, they again move about. I am the greatest. See I am extinct!

The Brâhma*n*a said:

Then the Vyâna and the Udâna addressed him who was speaking (thus): 'You are not the greatest, O Apâna! because the Prâ*n*a is subject to you.' Then the Apâna moved about, and the Vyâna spoke to him: 'I am the greatest among (you) all. Hear the reason why. When I am extinct, all the life-winds in the body of living creatures become extinct.

[1] Arguna Misra says, Vyâna and Apâna also by force of the two 'ands' which occur in the original; and so in other places too.

[2] Arguna Misra says on this, 'The Prâ*n*a moves upwards through the help of the Apâna. If it moved downwards, it would be simply absorbed into the Apâna.'

[3] I.e. recommenced its proper operation in its proper place.

[4] And the other life-winds also, Arguna Misra says, the name Prâ*n*a being merely 'indicative,' as the phrase is, of the class to which it belongs.

And on my moving about, they again move about. I am the greatest. See I am extinct!'

The Brâhma*n*a said:

Then the Vyâna became extinct, and again moved about. And the Prâ*n*a and Apâna, and the Udâna, and the Samâna, spoke to him, 'You are not the greatest among us, O Vyâna! because the Samâna[1] is subject to you.' The Vyâna moved about again, and the Samâna spoke again. 'I am the greatest among (you) all. Hear the reason why. When I am extinct, all the life-winds in the body of living creatures become extinct; and on my moving about, they again move about. I am the greatest. See I am extinct!' Then the Samâna moved about, and the Udâna said to him: 'I am the greatest among (you) all. Hear the reason why. When I am extinct, all the life-winds in the body of living creatures become extinct; and on my moving about, they again move about. I am the greatest. See I am extinct!' Then the Udâna became extinct, and again moved about. And the Prâ*n*a and Apâna, and the Samâna, and the Vyâna also, spoke to him: 'O Udâna! you are not the greatest. The Vyâna[2] only is subject to you.'

The Brâhma*n*a said:

Then Brahman, the lord of (all) creatures, said to them who were assembled together: 'You are all greatest, and not greatest[3]. You are all possessed

[1] Because the Samâna helps in the digestion of the food which afterwards goes to the Vyâna for distribution through the nâ*d*îs.

[2] Because the Udâna is able to generate sound after the nâ*d*îs are filled up by the Vyâna.

[3] 'Not greatest' because none of them is independent of the other. 'Greatest' Ar*g*una Mi*s*ra renders by 'superior to objects.'

of one another's qualities[1]. All are greatest in their own spheres, and all support one another. There is one unmoving[2] (life-wind). There are others moving about, (which are) five, owing to (their) specific qualities. My own self is one only[3], (but) accumulated in numerous (forms). Being friendly with one another, and pleasing one another, go away happily. Welfare be to you! Support one another.'

CHAPTER IX.

The Brâhma*n*a said:

On this, too, they relate this ancient story, a dialogue between Nârada and the sage Devamata.

Devamata said:

When a creature is about to be born, what comes into existence first, his Prâ*n*a, or Apâna, or Samâna, or Vyâna, or else Udâna?

Nârada said:

By whichever the creature is produced, that which is other than this first comes to him. And the pairs of the life-winds should be understood, which (move) upwards, or downwards, or transversely.

---

[1] This is not quite clear. I presume it means that each one has the generic qualities which make the others great in their own spheres; but the specific qualities are different.

[2] The one life-wind is supposed here to be generally unmoving, but its distribution among the different parts of the body as specified, for instance, in the commentary on the Yoga-sûtra III, 38, gives it the different names. The expression does not seem to be quite accurate for this, which nevertheless seems to be the true, sense.

[3] Another reading is, 'That one is my own self.' Cf. Maitrî, pp. 28 seq., 105, and B*ri*hadâra*n*yaka, p. 169.

Devamata said:

By which (of the life-winds) is a creature produced? and which (of them) first comes to him? Explain to me also the pairs of the life-winds, which (move) upwards, or downwards, or transversely.

Nârada said:

Pleasure is produced from a mental operation[1], and (it) is also produced from a sound, (it) is also produced from taste, and (it) is also produced from colour, and (it) is also produced from touch, and (it) is also produced from smell. This is the effect[2] of the Udâna; the pleasure is produced from union[3]. From desire the semen is produced; and from the semen is produced menstrual excretion. The semen and the blood are produced by the Samâna and the Vyâna in common[4]. From the combination of the semen and the blood, the Prâ*n*a comes first into operation; and the semen being developed by the Prâ*n*a, the Apâna then comes into operation. The pair Prâ*n*a and Apâna go upwards and downwards, and the Samâna and Vyâna are called the pair (moving) transversely. It is the teaching of the

[1] I.e. desire. 'Sound' = recollection of a woman's voice; 'taste,' scil. of chastity; 'colour' = the beauty of a woman, Arguna Misra. Cf. Âpastamba I, 2, 7, 8, and Lalita Vistara, p. 19.

[2] Literally, 'form,' which Arguna Misra interprets to mean effect, and adds, 'The Udâna causes mental activity, and by mental activity sound &c. are apprehended.'

[3] I.e. of Udâna and mind, Arguna Misra; adding, 'the result is that a creature is produced by the Udâna.'

[4] Or, perhaps, generally, that is to say, the store of them, the specific semen being produced from desire, as before stated. The Samâna's function is the digestion of food, and that of the Vyâna is the distribution of the digested food to the whole body through the nâ*d*is, hence the proposition in the text.

Veda, that the fire verily is all the deities[1], and knowledge (of it) arises among Brâhmanas, being accompanied by intelligence[2]. The smoke of that (fire), which is of excellent glory, (appears) in the shape of (the quality of) darkness; (its) ashes, (the quality of) passion; and (the quality of) goodness is that in connexion with it[3], in which the offering is thrown. Those who understand the sacrifice understand the Samâna and the Vyâna as the principal (offering). The Prâna and Apâna are portions[4] of the offering of clarified butter, and between them is the fire. That is the excellent seat of the Udâna as understood by Brâhmanas[5]. As to that which is distinct from these pairs[6], hear me speak about

[1] Cf. inter alia, Aitareya-brâhmana (Haug's ed.), p. 1.

[2] Arguna Misra says intelligence means 'discussion, or argument.' The connexion of this with what has gone before, according to Arguna Misra, is this, that the author having first stated the five Hotris fully, now explains in what the Prâna and Apâna are to be offered up for acquiring the Prânâyama. The fire he takes to mean the self. Cf. what has been said about Vaisvânara above, p. 259.

[3] That is to say, the flame, I take it. He is drawing out here the figure of the fire.

[4] These are only a subordinate part of the offering, called Âgyabhâga. They are called subordinate, I suppose, as the operations of the Samâna and Vyâna are more practically important for vitality. The fire is the self. The place of the principal offering is between the Âgyabhâgas, as stated by Arguna Misra.

[5] The Udâna is here treated as the life-wind into which the others are to be offered up. See p. 258, and note 8 there.

[6] The next three sentences seem to indicate what is to be destroyed in common with the life-winds. One has to get rid of all notions about day and night, good and evil, existence and non-existence, and then final emancipation is reached. The fire, which is common to all the passages, stands for the self; into that apparently all the ideas of time, and good and evil, and so forth, are to be offered as the life-winds are; and that fire stands in the place of the Udâna, for this purpose, as into the last all the other life-winds

that. Day and night are a pair, between them is the fire. That is the excellent seat of the Udâna as understood by Brâhma*n*as. That which exists and that which does not exist are a pair, between them is the fire. That is the excellent seat of the Udâna as understood by Brâhma*n*as. The two—good and evil—are a pair, between them is the fire. That is the excellent seat of the Udâna as understood by Brâhma*n*as. First[1], the Samâna and Vyâna, their function[2] is performed: then, secondly, the Samâna comes into operation again. Then the Vâmadevya[3] for tranquillity, and tranquillity is the eternal Brahman. This is the excellent seat of the Udâna as understood by Brâhma*n*as.

Chapter X.

On this, too, they relate an ancient story (showing) of what nature is the institution of the *K*âturhotra[4]. The due performance of it in its entirety is now taught. Hear me, O good woman! state this won-

have to be offered. As to that which exists, &c., cf. Gîtâ, p. 103, and p. 370, note 9 infra. As to good and evil and generally, cf. *Kh*ândogya, p. 60; Kaushîtaki, p. 19. They are nothing to one who knows the Brahman. Day and night Ar*g*una Mi*s*ra takes to mean the I*d*â and Piṅgalâ nâ*d*îs, between which is the Sushum*n*â, as they are connected with the sun and moon. But the sense of the whole passage is far from clear.

[1] Ar*g*una Mi*s*ra understands these to be three Savanas.

[2] Of taking into the nâ*d*îs the food digested in the night, this is the morning Savana; the afternoon Savana is the kindling of the gastric fire for digesting new food.

[3] The Vâmadevya is a sûkta beginning 'Kayâ na*s* *k*itrâ' (Rv. IV, 31, 1). The singing of it is the third Savana, Ar*g*una Mi*s*ra. And see Taittirîya-âra*n*yaka, p. 889.

[4] Cf. Aitareya-brâhma*n*a (Haug), pp. 132, 133.

derful mystery. The instrument, the action, the agent, and emancipation[1], these, indeed, O you of a (pure) heart! are the four Hotris by whom this universe is enveloped. Hear also the assignment of causes exhaustively[2]. The nose, and the tongue, and the eye, and the skin, and the ear as the fifth, mind and understanding, these seven should be understood to be the causes of (the knowledge of[3]) qualities. Smell, and taste, and colour, sound, and touch as the fifth, the object of the mental operation and the object of the understanding[4], these seven are causes of action. He who smells, he who eats, he who sees, he who speaks, and he who hears as the fifth, he who thinks, and he who understands, these seven should be understood to be the causes of the agents[5]. These[6], being possessed of qualities[7], enjoy their own qualities, agreeable and disagreeable. And I am here devoid of qualities. Thus these seven are the causes of emancipation[8]. And among the learned who understand (everything), the

[1] Cf. as to the three first, Gîtâ, p. 123. They are the four categories, to one or other of which everything in the world may be referred.

[2] The texts here differ. Arguna Misra's reading he interprets to mean 'the subjugation of these Hotris.' The reading followed in the text seems to some extent to be supported by the sequel. But the passage altogether is not very clear.

[3] So Arguna Misra—through these the knowledge of the qualities of objects of sense is acquired.

[4] The sensations, or perceptions, referred to lead to action.

[5] This seems to mean, that the powers of smelling, &c., when attributed to the self, make him appear as an agent, as an active principle.

[6] I. e. action, agent, and instrument, Arguna Misra.

[7] I. e. the three, goodness, passion, and darkness.

[8] It is these seven from which the self is to be emancipated. 'I' must mean the self, not the Brâhmana who speaks.

qualities[1] which are in the position of the deities, each in its own place, always enjoy the offering according to prescribed rules. To him who is not learned, eating various (kinds of) food, the (feeling of this or that being) mine adheres. And cooking food for himself, he, through the (feeling of this or that being) mine, is ruined[2]. The eating of that which should not be eaten, and drinking of intoxicating drinks also destroys him. He destroys the food, and destroying that food he is destroyed in return. The learned man, being (himself) a ruler, destroying this food again produces it[3]. And not even a trifling obstacle[4] arises to him from that food. Whatever is thought by the mind[5], whatever is spoken by speech, whatever is heard by the ear, whatever is seen by the eye, whatever is touched by the sense of touch, and whatever is smelt by the nose, absorbing all these offerings from all sides, together with those (senses) which with the mind are six[6], my fire[7] of (high) qualifications[8], shines dwelling within the body. My sacrifice of concentration of mind is in progress, the performance of which yields the fire[9] of knowledge;

[1] I. e., I presume, the senses. Cf. Gîtâ, p. 55. The learned do not suppose their self to have aught to do with them. Cf. Gîtâ, p. 64.

[2] Cf. Gîtâ, p. 53; Manu III, 118.

[3] His knowledge gives him this power. He is not 'destroyed' by the food as the other man is. Nîlakan*th*a compares Br*ih*adâra*n*yaka, p. 884. See, too, p. 260, note 1 supra.

[4] I. e. mischief owing to the destruction of life necessary for getting food, says Nîlakan*th*a quoting Br*ih*adâra*n*yaka, p. 913.

[5] This includes the operation of the understanding also. Nîlakan*th*a says this verse explains what the word 'food' means here.

[6] For the phrase cf. Gîtâ, p. 112.

[7] That is to say, my self, Ar*g*una Mi*s*ra. See p. 259, note 3 supra.

[8] As the objects of sense &c. are all absorbed into it.

[9] It is called 'fire,' as it burns up all action. Cf. Gîtâ, p. 62.

the Stotra in which, is the upward life-wind; the *S*astra, the downward life-wind; and which is very beneficial on account of the abandonment of everything[1]; the Brahman priest in which, is the counsellor in all action[2]; the Hot*ri* priest, the self; the Adhvaryu priest, (the self) whose hymn of praise[3] is the offering; the *S*astra of the Pra*s*âst*ri*, truth; and the Dakshi*n*â, final emancipation. On this, too, *Rik* verses are recited by the men who understand Nârâya*n*a[4]—the god Nârâya*n*a to whom they formerly offered animal[5] (offerings). On that Sâman hymns[6] are sung, of which an illustration is stated[7].

---

[1] Arguna Mi*s*ra's commentary is not intelligible here, so I follow Nîlaka*n*th*a*, but diffidently.

[2] I. e. the mind, say the commentators. 'Mantâ' simply is given among the synonyms of Ahańkâra at Sâńkhya-sâra, p. 16.

[3] I. e. the actions performed for knowledge of the truth, Arguna Mi*s*ra.

[4] Nîlaka*n*th*a* refers to a *Rik* 'Tapa âsîd-g*ri*hapati*h*,' and also the famous allegory at the end of the Taittirîya-âra*n*yaka. These are cited, he says, as authorities for this 'sacrifice (consisting of) concentration of mind.'

[5] I. e. the senses, Nîlaka*n*th*a*. Arguna Mi*s*ra compares the whole passage with the Purusha Sûkta, which are the *Rik* verses alluded to, according to him. He refers for further explanations to his own commentary on that sûkta of the Rig-veda.

[6] They sing these hymns, out of the gratification produced by knowledge of the self, says Nîlaka*n*th*a*, and he cites Taittirîya-âra*n*yaka, p. 749. See also Taittirîya-upanishad, p. 138, and *S*ańkara's commentary there.

[7] The readings of our texts here are not very satisfactory. The illustration is stated, says Nîlaka*n*th*a*, whose reading we follow, by the Taittirîyas in the passage referred to in the last note. Arguna Mi*s*ra's reading means 'such as Tâhu *k*âhu,' which would seem to be the words of the Sâman hymn referred to. But his commentary does not show what the words before him were. The whole figure as drawn out in this passage is not quite clear, though the general sense is pretty intelligible. Cf. the allegories at Aitareya-brâhma*n*a, pp. 132, 133, and at the close of the Taittirîya-âra*n*yaka.

O modest one! understand that god Nârâyana, who is the self of everything.

CHAPTER XI.

There is one director[1]; there is no second director. I speak concerning him who abides in the heart. This being, the director, dwells in the heart and directs (all creatures). Impelled by that same (being), I move as I am ordered, like water on a declivity. There is one instructor; there is no second (different) from him. I speak concerning him who abides in the heart. Taught by that instructor, all snakes whatever are ever hated in the world[2]. There is one kinsman; there is no second (different) from him. I speak concerning him who abides in the heart. Taught by him kinsmen are possessed of kinsmen[3], (and) the seven *Ri*shis, O son of P*ri*thâ[4]! shine in heaven[5]. There

---

[1] I.e. the Supreme Being, Arguna Misra. Nîlaka*n*/*h*a connects this with the preceding chapter by saying that this describes Nârâya*n*a, who is there mentioned. See *S*ânti Parvan (Moksha Dharma), chap. 226, st. 8 (Bombay ed.)

[2] The natural feelings of animosity are caused by the Supreme Being within. Such seems to be the meaning. Cf. Gîtâ, pp. 128, 129. I may remark that Arguna Misra seems to interpret the original words, which we have rendered by 'I speak concerning him,' &c., to mean 'I repeat what has been said by,' &c. This does not seem to me to be satisfactory; and it may be added, too, that Arguna Misra's interpretation appears in his gloss not on the first verse, about the 'director,' but only on the second, about the 'instructor.' Hated = full of animosity, Nîlaka*n*/*h*a.

[3] I.e. the feeling of kinsmanship arises from his inspiration.

[4] The poet seems to be nodding here, as this expression cannot form part of the Brâhma*n*a's speech to his wife.

[5] The seven sages are always mentioned together, and may well be spoken of as types of the feeling of kinship.

is one hearer[1]; there is no second (different) from him. I speak concerning him who abides in the heart. Living under that instructor, (according to the proper mode of) living with an instructor, *S*akra[2] acquired immortality in all worlds. There is one enemy; there is no second (different) from him. I speak concerning him who abides in the heart. Taught by that instructor, all snakes whatever are ever hated in the world[3].

On this, too, they relate an ancient story, (about the) instruction of the snakes, and the gods, and sages, by Pra*g*âpati. The gods, and sages, and the snakes, and the demons, approaching Pra*g*âpati, said (to him): 'Tell us the highest good.' To them who were inquiring about the highest good, the venerable one said, 'Om[4], the Brahman, in a single syllable.' Hearing that, they ran away in (various) directions[5]. When they were running for instruction regarding the self, the inclination of the snakes to biting had been already formed. The natural inclination of the demons towards ostentatiousness had been formed. The gods had been engaged in gifts, and the great sages in restraint of the senses. Having had one teacher,

[1] Nîlaka*n*/*h*a takes this to mean pupil, but it is difficult to reconcile that with the rest of the passage. Ar*g*una Mi*s*ra renders it by 'the destroyer of every one's doubts.' For that, it will be necessary to take the word as a form of the causative, and not the simple root *s*ru, to hear. But see, too, p. 283, 'the instructor . . . the hearer.'

[2] Cf. Sanatsu*g*âtîya, p. 152, note 1.

[3] The words here are nearly the same as before; the commentators give no explanation of the repetition. But see p. 281, note 2.

[4] Cf. Gîtâ, p. 79. The full sense is that from the study of this Om the highest good is attained.

[5] I.e. to their own dwellings, believing that they had learnt what they wanted.

and having been instructed with one word, the snakes, the gods, the sages, and the demons, all engaged in different[1] (pursuits). One hears what is said (to one) and apprehends it duly; (but even) to one who inquires and extols highly, there is no other instructor[2]. And by his counsel does action afterwards take place. The instructor, the learner, the hearer, and the enemy, are always within the heart. Acting sinfully in the world, he becomes (a man of) sinful conduct. Acting virtuously in the world he becomes (a man of) virtuous conduct[3]. And he becomes a man of conduct according to his own desire[4], who, owing to his desires, is given up to the pleasures of the senses. But he who, casting aside vows[5] and actions, merely adheres to the Brahman, he moving about in the world identifying himself with the Brahman, becomes a Brahma*k*ârin. To him the Brahman itself is the fuel, the Brahman the fire, the Brahman his origin, the Brahman water, the Brahman the instructor. He is rapt in the

---

[1] The meaning seems to be that the original inclination was not altered by the new instruction received by them. Nîlaka*nth*a seems to understand the passage differently. What has been rendered in the text by 'when they were running for instruction,' he renders by 'when they were practically carrying out the instruction received by them;' but this rendering seems to omit all consideration of the words 'Pûrvameva tu'—already. Though, therefore, there are one or two circumstances in favour of this construction, I have adopted the other. Cf. B*ri*hadâra*n*yaka, p. 964.

[2] The meaning is that the real instructor is within oneself, 'abiding in the heart,' as said before, although instruction may in form be received from one outside, of whom one seeks to learn, and whom one respects (or extols highly, as the text has it), and although such instruction may be well apprehended.

[3] Cf. B*ri*hadâra*n*yaka, pp. 546–853. [4] See Gitâ, p. 117.

[5] I.e. fasts and other like observances.

Brahman[1]. Such is this subtle life as a Brahma*k*ârin understood by the wise. Understanding it they practised it, being instructed by the Kshetra*g*ña[2].

CHAPTER XII.

The Brâhma*n*a said:

I have crossed beyond that very impassable place, in which fancies are the gadflies and mosquitoes[3], in which grief and joy are cold and heat, in which delusion is the blinding darkness, in which avarice is the beasts of prey and reptiles, in which desire and anger are the obstructors, the way to which consists in worldly objects, and is to be crossed by one singly[4]. And I have entered the great forest[5].

The Brâhma*n*a's wife said:

Where is that forest, O very intelligent person! what are the trees (there), and what the rivers, and the hills and mountains; and at what distance is that forest?

---

[1] Cf. Gîtâ, p. 61. The water is that required for the sacrifice. The words 'the Brahman is his origin' are not quite clear, as being not connected with the figure employed. Perhaps it might be taken otherwise thus, 'the Brahman (is) the fire produced from the Brahman,' this last standing for the ara*n*i.

[2] I. e. one who understands the truth, Nîlaka*n*/*h*a; God, Ar*g*una Mi*s*ra. The same sentence winds up two of the following chapters; and at p. 310 K*ri*sh*n*a says the Kshetra*g*ña signifies the supreme self. See Gîtâ, p. 102 seq.

[3] Cf. Lalita Vistara, p. 44.

[4] I. e. not with the help of son, wealth, &c., says Nîlaka*n*/*h*a, as each man's salvation after having got into the course of worldly life depends on himself. Cf. *S*ânti Parvan (Moksha Dharma), chap. 193, st. 32, and Manu IV, 240; obstructor, thief, Ar*g*una Mi*s*ra.

[5] I. e. the Brahman. Nîlaka*n*/*h*a compares a text from the *S*ruti, 'Ki*m* svid vana*m* ka u sa v*ri*ksha âsa;' see Rig-veda X, 31, 7.

The Brâhma*n*a said:

There is nothing else more delightful than that, when there is no distinction from it. There is nothing more afflicting than that, when there is a distinction from it[1]. There is nothing smaller than that, there is nothing larger than that[2]. There is nothing more subtle than that; there is no other happiness equal to that. Entering it, the twice-born do not grieve, and do not exult[3]. They are not afraid of anybody, and nobody is afraid of them. In that forest[4] are seven large trees[5], seven fruits, and seven guests; seven hermitages, seven (forms of) concentration, and seven (forms of) initiation. This is the description of the forest. That forest is filled with trees producing splendid flowers and fruits of five colours[6]. That forest

[1] Cf. *Kh*ândogya, pp. 516, 517.

[2] Cf. Sanatsugâtîya, p. 180 and note there.

[3] Cf. as to all this Gîtâ, p. 101.

[4] This is not the forest spoken of before, but what has been before called the 'impassable place,' but which also at p. 286 is by implication called a forest, viz. the course of worldly life.

[5] Viz. the eye, ear, tongue, skin, and nose, and the mind, and understanding—these are called trees, as being producers of the fruits, namely, the pleasures and pains derived from their several operations; the guests are the powers of each sense personified—they receive the fruits above described; the hermitages are the trees above mentioned, in which the guests take shelter; the seven forms of concentration are the exclusion from the self of the seven functions of the seven senses &c. already referred to; the seven forms of initiation refer to the initiation into the higher life, by repudiating as not one's own the actions of each member out of the group of seven. Cf. as to this *Kh*ândogya, p. 219, and commentary there.

[6] Cf. for these different numbers of colours, Yoga-sûtra II, 19, and commentary, p. 105, and Sâṅkhya-sâra, p. 18. The trees here meant are the Tanmâtras, or subtle elements, and the theory is that the Gandha-tanmâtra, or subtle element of smell, has five qualities, its

is filled with trees producing flowers and fruits of four colours. That forest is filled with trees producing flowers and fruits of three colours, and mixed. That forest is filled with trees producing flowers and fruits of two colours, and of beautiful colours. That forest is filled with trees producing flowers and fruits of one colour, and fragrant. That forest is filled with two large trees producing numerous flowers and fruits of undistinguished colours [1]. There is one fire [2] here, connected with the Brahman [3], and having a good mind [4]. And there is fuel here, (namely) the five senses. The seven (forms of) emancipation from them are the seven (forms of) initiation [5]. The qualities are the fruits, and the guests eat the fruits. There, in various places, the great sages receive hospitality. And when they have been worshipped and have disappeared [6], another forest shines forth, in which intelligence is the tree, and emancipation the fruit, and which possesses shade (in the form of) tran-

own special one, so to say, and the four special ones of the others; the next is taste, the next colour, the next touch, and the last sound; each has one quality less than its predecessor. See Yoga-sûtra, p. 106, and gloss; Sâṅkhya-sûtra I, 62; and Vedânta Paribhâshâ, p. 45.

[1] These are mind and understanding; the fruits and flowers are here of 'undistinguished colours,' as the text expresses it, since they include the colours of all the fruits of all the other five sets of trees; that is to say, the subject-matter of their operations is sound, taste, &c., the subject-matters of all the senses together. 'Undistinguished colours' is, perhaps, more literally 'of colours not clear.' Arguna Misra paraphrases it by 'of variegated colours,' which is no doubt the true ultimate sense.

[2] The self, Nîlakantha. See p. 279, note 7 supra.

[3] I. e., I presume, devoted to the Brahman.

[4] I. e. true knowledge, Arguna Misra.

[5] See note 5, p. 285.

[6] I.e. when the senses having worked, as unconnected with the self, are finally absorbed into it. Cf. Sâṅkhya-kârikâ 49 and Katha, p. 151.

quillity, which depends on knowledge, which has contentment for its water, and which has the Kshetragña within for the sun. The good who attain to that, have no fear afterwards. Its end cannot be perceived upwards or downwards or horizontally[1]. There always dwell seven females there[2], with faces (turned) downwards, full of brilliance, and causes of generation. They absorb[3] all the higher delights of people, as inconstancy (absorbs) everything[4]. In that same[5] (principle) the seven perfect sages, together with their chiefs, the richest[6], abide, and again emerge from the same. Glory, brilliance, and greatness, enlightenment, victory, perfection, and power[7]—these seven rays follow after this same sun. Hills and mountains also are there collected together, and rivers and streams flowing with water produced from the Brahman[8]. And there is the confluence of the rivers in the secluded place[9] for the

---

[1] It extends on all sides, its end cannot be perceived on any side.

[2] These are, according to Arguna Misra, the Mahat, Ahankâra, and five Tanmâtras. Their faces are turned downwards, as they are obstacles in the way upwards, viz. the way of final emancipation; they are brilliant, as they light up the course of worldly life; and hence, too, they are 'causes of generation.' They give birth to the universe.

[3] They conceal the higher delight of final emancipation.

[4] I follow Arguna Misra, but the text is doubtful.

[5] Viz the Brahman.

[6] Cf. *Kh*ândogya, pp. 295–300. The word sages here, as before, means the various organs. See B*ri*hadâra*n*yaka, p. 415.

[7] Glory = renown; brilliance = Brahmic splendour (Brahmategas); perfection = obtaining what is desired; power = not being conquered by others, Arguna Misra. About the sun, see line 3 of text above.

[8] I. e. contentment. See the second line in the text above.

[9] I. e. the space in the heart, the sacrifice being that of 'concentration of mind,' yogayagña,—Nilaka*nth*a. A confluence of

sacrifice, whence those who are contented in their own selfs repair to the divine grandsire himself. Those whose wishes are reduced[1], whose wishes are (fixed) on good vows, whose sins are burnt up by penance, merging the self in the self[2], devote themselves to Brahman. Those people who understand the forest of knowledge[3], praise tranquillity. And aspiring to that forest, they are born so as not to lose courage[4]. Such, indeed, is this holy forest, as understood by Brâhmanas. And understanding it, they act (accordingly), being directed by the Kshetragña.

Chapter XIII.

The Brâhmana said:

I do not smell smells, I perceive no tastes, I see no colour, and I do not touch, nor yet do I hear various sounds, nor even do I entertain any fancies[5]. Nature desires objects which are liked; nature hates all (objects) which are hateful[6]. Desire and hatred are born from nature[7], as the upward and

---

rivers is very sacred—here the meaning intended seems to be the absorption of all desires by contentment into the heart.

[1] Literally, 'lean.' [2] I. e. the body in the soul, Arguna Misra.

[3] Knowledge is Brahman, which is described as a forest here, Arguna Misra.

[4] Cf. Gîtâ, p. 70.

[5] This is the name for the operations of the mind.

[6] The sense is similar to that at Gîtâ, p. 55. The self has nothing to do with these feelings; the qualities deal with the qualities.

[7] Cf. Gîtâ, p. 65. The meaning of nature here, as in the Gîtâ, is in substance the result of all previous action with which the self has been associated, which result, of course, exists connected not with the self, but with the developments of nature, in the form of body,

downward life-winds, after attaining to the bodies of living creatures. Apart from them, and as the constant entity underlying them, I see the individual self in the body. Dwelling in that (self), I am in no wise attached[1] (to anything) through desire or anger, or old age, or death. Not desiring any object of desire, not hating any evil, there is no taint on my natures[2], as there is no (taint) of a drop of water on lotuses[3]. They are inconstant things appertaining to this constant (principle) which looks on various natures. Although actions are performed, the net of enjoyments does not attach itself to it, as the net of the sun's rays does not attach itself to the sky[4]. On this[5], too, they relate an ancient story, (in the shape of) a dialogue between an Adhvaryu priest and an ascetic. Understand that, O glorious one! Seeing an animal being sprinkled[6] at a sacrificial ceremony, an ascetic who was sitting (there) spoke to the Adhvaryu, censuring (the act) as destruction of life. The Adhvaryu

senses, &c. The comparison appears to mean that the feelings of desire &c. are, like the life-winds, unconnected with the self, though associated with it, and are both alike manifestations of nature.

[1] Nîlakantha compares Brihadâranyaka, p. 770. Arguna Misra has a different reading, meaning 'liable (to be subjugated).'

[2] The plural, which is in the original, is unusual. The various aspects of the 'result' stated in p. 288, note 7, being looked at separately, are described as 'natures,' like the leaves of a lotus, which in their ensemble make one lotus.

[3] Lalita Vistara, p. 2, and p. 64 supra.

[4] The figure seems to be somewhat like that at Gîtâ, p. 82, about the atmosphere and space, which latter remains untainted by the former. Looking on various natures, i.e. as distinct from the self.

[5] Viz. the remaining untainted.

[6] I.e. with water, preparatory to its being offered up for the sacrifice.

answered him (saying), this goat will not be destroyed. (This) creature will obtain welfare, since the Vedic text is such. For that part of him which is of the earth will go to the earth; whatever in him is produced from water, that will enter water. His eye (will enter) the sun, (his) ear the quarters, and his life-winds likewise the sky[1]. There is no offence on my part, adhering (as I do) to the scriptures[2].

The Ascetic said:

If you perceive (that) good (will) result upon his life being severed (from him), then the sacrifice is for the goat, what benefit (is it) to you? Let the brother, father, mother, and friend (of the goat) give you their consent[3]; take him (to them) and consult (them), especially as he is dependent. You ought to inquire of those who can give their consent thus. After hearing their consent, (the matter) will be fit for consideration[4]. The life-winds[5], too, of this goat have gone to their sources, and I think only his unmoving body remains. To those who wish to derive enjoyment from the slaughter (of a living creature), the unconscious body being comparable to fuel, that which is called an animal becomes

[1] Cf. B*ri*hadâra*n*yaka, p. 542, and p. 337 below.

[2] Cf. *Kh*ândogya-upanishad, p. 627, and also *S*ârîraka Bhâshya on Sûtra III, 1, 25, p. 774.

[3] I.e. for his slaughter, which is to bring welfare to the goat. Arguna Misra says that this is a sort of reductio ad absurdum, as the sacrifice is in truth not in the interests of the goat at all.

[4] Viz. whether the goat should be killed. Without their consent he ought not to be slaughtered; with their consent, it becomes a matter for consideration, Arguna Misra.

[5] It may also mean the senses, as in the *Kh*ândogya, p. 297.

the fuel[1]. The teaching of the elders[2] is, that refraining from slaughter (of living creatures) is (the duty) among all duties. We maintain that that action should be performed which involves no slaughter. (Our) proposition is no slaughter (of living creatures). If I spoke further, it would be possible to find fault with your proceedings in many ways[3]. Always refraining from the slaughter of all beings is what we approve. We substantiate (this) from what is actually visible[4], we do not rely on what is not visible.

The Adhvaryu said:

You enjoy the earth's quality of fragrance, you drink watery juices, you see the colours of shining bodies, you touch the qualities of the air, you hear the sound produced in space, you think by the mind (on the objects of) mental operations. And all these entities, you believe, have life. You have not (then) abstained from taking life. You are (engaged) in the slaughter (of living creatures)[5]. There is no movement[6] without slaughter (of living creatures). Or what do you think, O twice-born one?

---

[1] This is not very clear, but the meaning seems to be that the slaughter is committed for the enjoyment of the sacrificer; the sacrificer only requires fuel, and the slaughtered animal is then used for that purpose.

[2] Cf. *Kh*ândogya, p. 627, and next note; and Gîtâ, inter alia, p. 114, and p. 348 infra. [3] See Sâṅkhyatattvakaumudî, p. 7.

[4] I.e. a rule expressly laid down. What is not visible means what is not expressly stated, but is to be derived by inference, and so forth (cf. Âpastamba I, 1, 4, 8). The express text is the famous one, 'Na himsyâtsarvâ bhûtâni.' Hi*m*sâ, which is rendered slaughter here, may mean also 'giving pain' generally.

[5] This is the tu quoque argument. The sustentation of life requires some sort of slaughter.

[6] I.e. the support of the body, says Arguna Misra.

The Ascetic said:

The indestructible and the destructible, such is the double manifestation of the self. Of these the indestructible is the existent[1], the manifestation as an individual[2] (entity) is called the destructible[3]. The life-winds, the tongue, the mind, and (the quality of) goodness, together with (the quality of) passion[4], (these make up) the manifestations as individual entities. And to one who is free from these manifestations, who is free from the pairs of opposites, who is devoid of expectations, who is alike to all beings, who is free from (the thought that this or that is) mine, who has subdued his self, and who is released on all hands[5], there is no fear anywhere[6].

The Adhvaryu said:

O best of talented men! one should in this (world)

---

[1] Arguna Misra takes it otherwise, 'the true nature of the Sat, the self.' Nîlakantha renders the original by sadrûpam without further explanation. This indestructible seems to correspond to that mentioned at Gîtâ, p. 113, which should be considered in connection with Gîtâ, pp. 73, 74. The note at the former page is, perhaps, not quite accurately expressed, as the word 'material cause' conveys some inadmissible associations. Perhaps 'underlying principle' might be a nearer approach to the correct idea. The existent will thus be that which really exists, as it is indestructible.

[2] Cf. Gîtâ, p. 77. [3] See Sânti Parvan (Moksha), ch. 240, st. 31.

[4] Arguna Misra says, 'The life-winds here are indicative of the operations of the organs of action (as to which see p. 290, note 5 supra), the tongue of the perceptive senses, the mind of the internal activities, the quality of goodness of all sources of pleasure, and passion of all sources of pain,' the last two apparently covering the external world, the previous ones the human activities, internal and external.

[5] Released scil. from piety or impiety, &c.,—Arguna Misra, who says 'self' in the phrase preceding means mind.

[6] Because, says Arguna Misra, according to the very authority which says there is sin in slaughter, all sin is destroyed by knowledge. Cf. Gîtâ, p. 64.

dwell in company of good men only[1]. For having heard your opinion, my mind is enlightened. O venerable sir! I approach you, in the belief (that you are) the Lord; and I say (to you), O twice-born one! there is no fault (attaching) to me, performing (as I have done) the rites performed by others[2].

The Brâhma*n*a said:

With this explanation, the ascetic thereafter remained silent, and the Adhvaryu also proceeded with the great sacrifice, freed from delusion. Thus Brâhma*n*as understand the very subtle emancipation to be of this nature, and understanding it, they act (accordingly), being directed by the Kshetra*gñ*a.

CHAPTER XIV.

The Brâhma*n*a said:

On this[3], too, they relate an old story, (in the shape of) a dialogue, O you of a pure heart! between Kârtavîrya and the ocean. (There lived once) a king named Ar*g*una[4], a descendant of K*ri*tavîrya, possessed of a thousand arms, who with his bow conquered the (whole) earth up to the ocean. Once

---

[1] Cf. Taittirîya-upanishad, p. 40.

[2] The readings here in the MSS. are not satisfactory. I adopt as the best that which appears to have been before Ar*g*una Misra. The meaning seems to be this:—I have now understood the truth, but I cannot be blamed for having hitherto done that which I saw every one else do. Now I have had the benefit of conversation with a good man, and have become free from my delusion.

[3] Namely, that final emancipation is not to be obtained by action, and that slaughter is sinful.

[4] He is also called a Yogin at Raghuva*m*sa VI, 38. See Mallinâth's commentary there.

on a time, as we have heard, he was walking about near the sea, proud of his strength, and showering hundreds of arrows on the sea. The ocean, saluting him, and with joined hands, said, 'O brave man! do not throw arrows (on me). Say, what shall I do for you? The creatures, who take shelter with me, are being destroyed, O tiger-like king! by the great arrows thrown by you. Give them security, O Lord!'

Arguna said:

If there is anywhere any wielder of the bow equal to me in battle, who might stand against me in the field, name him to me.

The ocean said:

If, O king! you have heard of the great sage Gamadagni, his son is (the) proper (person) to show you due hospitality[1].

Then the king, full of great wrath, went away, and arriving at that hermitage approached Râma only. In company with his kinsmen, he did many (acts) disagreeable to Râma, and caused much trouble to the high-souled Râma. Then the power of Râma, whose power was unbounded, blazed forth, burning the hosts of the enemy, O lotus-eyed one! And then Râma, taking up his axe, hacked away that man of the thousand arms in battle, like a tree of many branches. Seeing him killed and fallen, all (his) kinsmen assembled together, and taking swords and lances, surrounded the descendant of Bhrigu. Râma also taking up a bow, and hurriedly mounting a chariot, shot away volleys of arrows, and blew away the army of the king. Then some of the

[1] I.e. by giving him what he desired—a 'foeman worthy of his steel' to fight with him.

Kshatriyas, often troubled by fear of the son of *G*amadagni, entered mountains and inaccessible places, like antelopes troubled by a lion. And the subjects of those (Kshatriyas) who were not performing their prescribed duties[1] through fear of him, became V*ri*shalas, owing to the disappearance of Brâhma*n*as[2]. Thus the Dravi*d*as, Âbhîras, Pau*nd*ras, together with the *S*âbaras, became V*ri*shalas[3], owing to the abandonment of their duties by Kshatriyas. Then when the heroic (children) of Kshatriya women were destroyed again and again, the Kshatriyas, who were produced by the Brâhma*n*as[4], were also destroyed by the son of *G*amadagni. At the end of the twenty-first slaughter, a bodiless voice from heaven, which was heard by all people, spoke sweetly to Râma, 'O Râma! O Râma! desist (from this slaughter). What good, dear friend, do you perceive, in taking away the lives of these kinsmen of Kshatriyas over and over again?' Then, too, his grandfathers[5], with *Rik*îka as their head, likewise said to the high-souled (Râma), 'Desist, O noble one[6]!' But Râma, not forgiving his father's

---

[1] Viz. the protection of their subjects.

[2] As the kings failed to protect the people, the Brâhma*n*as apparently were nowhere forthcoming.

[3] Cf. Muir, Sanskrit Texts, vol. i, pp. 482 seq., 358, 391; vol. ii, p. 423; *S*ânti Parvan, ch. 65, st. 13; ch. 207, st. 42 (Râgadharma).

[4] As Kshatriyas were required for the protection of the people, the Brâhma*n*as procreated them on Kshatriya women. See Muir, Sanskrit Texts, vol. i, p. 451 seq. And as they were the offspring of these anomalous connexions they are described as 'kinsmen of Kshatriyas.' Cf. *Kh*ândogya, p. 317; B*ri*hadâra*n*yaka, p. 1037 and comments there. As to heroic, see Muir, Sanskrit Texts, vol. iv, p. 302 note.

[5] Cf. Gîtâ, p. 40, note 1.

[6] See as to the whole story, Muir, Sanskrit Texts, vol. i, p. 442.

murder, said to those sages, 'You ought not to keep me back from this.'

The Pitris said:

O best of victors! you ought not to destroy these kinsmen of Kshatriyas. It is not proper for you, being a Brâhmana, to slaughter these kings.

Chapter XV.

The Pitris said:

On this[1], too, they relate an ancient story; hearing that (story), O best of the twice-born! you should act accordingly. There was (once) a royal sage, named Alarka, whose penance was very great, who understood duty, who was veracious, high-souled, and very firm in his vows. Having with his bow conquered this world as far as the ocean,—having performed very difficult deeds[2],—he turned his mind to subtle[3] (subjects). While he was sitting at the foot of a tree, O you of great intelligence! his thoughts, abandoning (those) great deeds, turned to subtle (questions).

Alarka said:

My mind is become (too) strong[4]; that conquest is constant in which the mind is conquered. (Though) surrounded by enemies, I shall direct my arrows elsewhere[5]. As by its unsteadiness, it wishes[6] to

---

[1] The impropriety or sinfulness of slaughter.

[2] Such as the subjugation of enemies and so forth.

[3] The Brahman, says Nîlakantha.

[4] I.e. too strong to be under control.

[5] That is to say, elsewhere than towards the external foes with whom he was waging war.

[6] The text is unsatisfactory here. I adopt Nîlakantha's reading.

make all mortals perform action, I will cast very sharp-edged arrows at the mind.

The mind said:

These arrows, O Alarka! will not penetrate through me at all. They will only pierce your own vital part, and your vital part being pierced, you will die. Look out for other arrows by which you may destroy me.

Hearing that, he then spoke these words after consideration:—

Alarka said:

Smelling very many perfumes, one hankers after them only. Therefore I will cast sharp arrows at the nose.

The nose[1] said:

These arrows, O Alarka! will not penetrate through me at all. They will only pierce your own vital part, and your vital part being pierced, you will die. Look out for other arrows by which you may destroy me.

Hearing that, he then spoke these words after consideration:—

Alarka said:

Enjoying savory tastes, this (tongue) hankers after

---

[1] This and the other corresponding words must be understood to refer not to the physical nose and so forth, but the sense seated there. The nose here, for instance, stands for the sense of smell. Nîlaka*nth*a understands all these words of Alarka as indicating the so-called Ha*th*a-yoga, which, he adds, invariably occasions death. As to the throwing of arrows at the mind, he says, it means, 'I will subdue the mind by the restraint of the excretive organs by means of the Ha*th*a-yoga.' And finally he says, 'A man, having restrained all the senses by means of the Ha*th*a-yoga, merely droops away; becoming deficient in those senses, he does not accomplish his end.'

them only. Therefore I will cast sharp arrows at the tongue.

The tongue said:

These arrows, O Alarka! will not penetrate through me at all. They will only pierce your own vital part, and your vital part being pierced, you will die. Look out for other arrows by which you may destroy me.

Hearing that, he then spoke these words after consideration:—

Alarka said:

Touching various (objects of) touch, the skin hankers after them only. Therefore I will tear off the skin by various feathered arrows.

The skin said:

These arrows, O Alarka! will not penetrate through me at all. They will only pierce your own vital part, and your vital part being pierced, you will die. Look out for other arrows by which you may destroy me.

Hearing that, he then said after consideration:—

Alarka said:

Hearing various sounds, the (ear) hankers after them only. Therefore I (will) cast sharp arrows at the ear.

The ear said:

These arrows, O Alarka! will not penetrate through me at all. They will only pierce your own vital part, and then you will lose (your) life. Look out for other arrows by which you may destroy me.

Hearing that, he then said after consideration:—

Alarka said:

Seeing numerous colours, the eye hankers after them only. Therefore I will destroy the eye with sharp arrows.

The eye said:

These arrows, O Alarka! will not penetrate through me at all. They will only pierce your own vital part, and your vital part being pierced, you will die. Look out for other arrows by which you may destroy me.

Hearing that, he then said after consideration:—

Alarka said:

This (understanding) forms various determinations by its operation. Therefore I will cast sharp arrows at the understanding.

The understanding said:

These arrows, O Alarka! will not penetrate through me at all. They will only pierce your own vital part, and your vital part being pierced, you will die. Look out for other arrows by which you may destroy me.

The Brâhma*n*a[1] said:

Then Alarka even there employed himself in a fearful penance[2] difficult to perform; but he did not obtain any arrows for these seven by his devotions. Then that king deliberated with a mind very intent on one (subject), and after deliberating for a long time, O best of the twice-born! Alarka, the best of talented (men), could not arrive at anything better

[1] Sic in our copies. It should be the Pit*ri*s, seeing that they are relating Alarka's story to Parasurâma.

[2] Meditation, or pondering, according to Nîlaka*n*/*h*a.

than concentration of mind[1]. Then directing his mind to one point[2], he became steady, and applied himself to concentration of mind. And (then) the brave man forthwith destroyed the senses with one arrow; and entering the self by means of concentration of mind, he reached the highest perfection. And the royal sage, amazed, then uttered this verse, 'O! Alas! that we should have engaged in all external (matters); that being possessed of a desire for enjoyments, we should have devoted ourselves before now to sovereignty! I have now subsequently learnt that there is no higher happiness than concentration of mind.' Do you understand this too, O Râma! and do not kill Kshatriyas. Perform a fearful[3] penance, thence you will obtain the highest good. Thus spoken to by (his) grandfathers, the noble son of *G*amadagni engaged himself in fearful penance, and attained that perfection which is difficult to reach.

Chapter XVI.

The Brâhma*n*a said:

There are, verily, three foes in (this) world, and they are stated to be (divided) ninefold, according to qualities. Exultation, pleasure, joy[4], these three

---

[1] I.e. the râga-yoga, says Nilaka*n*t*h*a, which consists in mere control of the mind. Cf. Sâṅkhya-sâra, p. 39.

[2] See Yoga-sûtra, p. 45.

[3] This means difficult, and occasioning many trials to one who performs it.

[4] Nilaka*n*t*h*a says exultation is when one is sure of obtaining what is desired, pleasure when it is obtained, and joy when the thing obtained is enjoyed. Ar*g*una Misra takes a different distinction; but our copy of his commentary is not quite intelligible in

are qualities appertaining to the quality of goodness. Grief, wrath, persistent hatred, these are stated to be qualities appertaining to the quality of passion. Sleep, sloth, and delusion, these three qualities are qualities appertaining to the quality of darkness. Cutting these off by multitudes of arrows[1], a courageous man, free from sloth, having a tranquil self, and senses controlled, is energetic about subjugating others[2]. On this, people who know about ancient times celebrate verses which were sung of old by the king Ambarîsha, who had become tranquil (in mind). When vices[3] were in the ascendant, and good (men) were oppressed, Ambarîsha, of great glory, forceably possessed him-

the beginning. Pleasure he takes to mean 'pride felt in supposing oneself to possess some merit,' and joy that produced when impending danger is averted. As to the next triad, the text is again unsatisfactory. The text printed in the edition which contains Nîlakantha's commentary, is 'desire, anger,' &c. There is nothing about them in the commentary. Arguna Misra's text is the one we have adopted. He says, 'grief, pain caused by loss of what is desired; anger, the pain caused by the counteraction of one's attempts to injure another; persistent hatred, the pain caused by believing another to be doing harm to oneself.' Persistent hatred is Nîlakantha's interpretation. I think his interpretation is preferable. The two triads seem to be based on one principle of gradation. The distinctive marks of the three qualities are pleasure, pain, and delusion respectively, and those characterise the three triads stated in the text. See Sânti Parvan (Moksha), chap. 194, st. 27 seq.

[1] Tranquillity and so forth, Nîlakantha; practising yoga or concentration of mind, Arguna Misra.

[2] I.e. external, says Arguna Misra; external foes of one's own emancipation is, I presume, what is meant.

[3] Arguna Misra says, 'his own and those of others.' Nîlakantha takes good to mean not men, but tranquillity, &c. The next sentence seems rather to militate against this view, which in itself is not a well-founded one.

self of the kingdom[1]. He (then) restraining his own vices, and honouring good men, attained high perfection, and sang these verses: 'I have conquered most vices; destroyed all foes; but there is one, the greatest, vice which should be destroyed and which I have not destroyed—that (vice), being impelled by which, a creature does not attain freedom from desire, and being troubled by desire, understands (nothing) while running into ditches[2]; (that vice), being impelled by which, a man even does what ought not to be done. That avarice—cut (it) off, cut (it) off with sharp swords. For from avarice[3] is born desire; then anxiety comes into existence; and he who desires, mostly acquires qualities appertaining to the quality of passion. Obtaining those, he mostly acquires qualities appertaining to the quality of darkness[4]. When the bodily frame is destroyed, he, owing to these qualities, is born again and again, and engages in action. And at the expiration of life, again with his body dismembered and scattered about, he meets death, and again birth. Therefore, properly perceiving this, and restraining avarice by courage, one should wish for sovereignty in the self. This is sovereignty[5]; there is no other sovereignty here. The self properly understood is itself the sovereign.' Such were

[1] For the good of the people, says Arguna Misra.

[2] I.e. base actions, Nîlakantha.

[3] Avarice, according to Arguna Misra, is the belief that one has not got that which one has, and desire is the wish for more and more. Avarice, seems, however, to be the general frame of mind, always wishing for something, never being contented, and desire is the wish for a specific object.

[4] Which are sources of delusion. Cf. a similar doctrine at Âpastamba II, 5, 140.

[5] Nîlakantha compares Taittirîya, p. 26.

the verses sung with regard to the great sovereignty, by the glorious Ambarîsha, who destroyed the one (chief vice), avarice.

CHAPTER XVII.

The Brâhma*n*a said:

On this[1], too, they relate this ancient story (in the shape of) a dialogue, O you of a pure heart! between a Brâhma*n*a and *G*anaka. King *G*anaka, by way of punishment, said to a Brâhma*n*a who had fallen into some offence: 'You should not live within my dominions.' Thus spoken to, the Brâhma*n*a then replied to that best of kings: 'Tell me, O king! how far (extend) the dominions which are subject to you. I wish, O Lord! to live in the dominions of another king, and, O master of the earth! I wish to do your bidding according to the *S*âstras.' Thus spoken to by that glorious Brâhma*n*a, the king then heaved frequent and warm sighs, and said nothing in reply. While that king of unbounded power was seated, engaged in meditation, a delusion suddenly came upon him, as the planet[2] upon the sun. Then when the delusion had gone off, the king recovered himself, and after a short while spoke these words to the Brâhma*n*a.

*G*anaka said:

Though this country, which is the kingdom of my father and grandfather, is subject (to me), I cannot

---

[1] On getting rid of the notion that this, that, and the other thing is one's own,—Ar*g*una Mi*s*ra. Nîlaka*n*/*h*a agrees, and adds also on the subject of cutting off avarice.

[2] That is to say, Râhu.

find my domain[1], searching through the (whole) earth. When I did not find it on the earth, I looked for Mithilâ; when I did not find it in Mithilâ, I looked for my own offspring. When I did not find it among them, then came the delusion on me. Then on the expiration of the delusion, intelligence again came to me. Now I think that there is no domain (of mine), or that everything is my domain. Even this self is not mine, or the whole earth is mine. And as mine, so (is it) that of others too, I believe, O best of the twice-born! Live (here, therefore) while you desire, and enjoy while you live[2].

The Brâhma*n*a said:

Tell me, what belief you have resorted to, by which, though this country, which is the kingdom of your father and grandfather, is subject to you, you have got rid of (the notion that this or that is) mine. What conviction have you adopted, by which verily you consider your whole domain as not (your) domain, or all as your domain?

*G*anaka said:

I understand (all) conditions here, in all affairs, to be terminable[3], hence I could not find anything that should be (called) mine[4]. (Considering) whose this

[1] Meaning, apparently, that over which he and no one else has power. He contracts his vision gradually, and finds nothing at all which he can call his own to the exclusion of others. He explains, further on, how he arrives at the alternative conviction stated towards the close of this speech. In the B*ri*hadâra*n*yaka (p. 916) he is said to have offered his kingdom to Yâg*ñ*avalkya and himself as his slave, after learning the Brahma-vidyâ. See too Muir, Sanskrit Texts, vol. iv, p. 426 seq.

[2] See *S*ânti Parvan (Moksha) I, 13.

[3] Conditions of indigence or affluence, Nilaka*nth*a. Arguna Misra's reading is different.

[4] There is a familiar verse, ascribed to *G*anaka, which says, 'If

was, (I thought of) the Vedic text about anybody's property, (hence) I could not find by my intelligence anything that should be (called) mine [1]. Resorting to this conviction, I have got rid of (the notion that this or that is) mine. Now hear the conviction, holding which, my domain (appears to me to be) everywhere [2]. I do not desire for myself even smells existing in the nose [3]. Therefore the earth [4] being conquered is always subject to me. I do not desire for myself tastes even dwelling in the mouth. Therefore water being conquered is always subject to me. I do not desire for myself the colour (or) light appertaining to the eye. Therefore light being conquered is always subject to me. I do not desire for myself the (feelings of touch) which exist in the skin. Therefore air being conquered is always

Mithilâ is on fire, nothing of mine is burnt (in it).' The verse occurs in the Mahâbhârata, *S*ânti Parvan (Moksha Dharma), chap. 178, st. 2, and also chap. 276, st. 4. See too Muir, Sanskrit Texts, vol. i, p. 429.

[1] This is not clear. I have followed Nîlaka*nth*a's text. Ar*g*una Mi*s*ra's is in the earlier part more intelligible, 'Whose is this to-day, whose to-morrow?' But I cannot find that there is any Vedic text to this effect. Nîlaka*nth*a cites on his text Î*s*opanishad, p. 5. The meaning here seems to be, 'When I considered as to whom the things I saw in my thoughts belonged to, I remembered the Vedic text that one should not wish to obtain another's property, and so, thinking about the matter with that caution, I could not make out that there was anything which I could call my own.'

[2] This is the alternative conclusion he has come to.

[3] The sense of smell enjoys the smell, my self has nothing to do with it. Cf. Gîtâ, p. 55, also Maitrî, pp. 112, 113.

[4] Whenever there is any smell, it is supposed that particles of earth are there; so the meaning here is 'all things having the quality of smell are subject to me,' and so throughout. The objects of sense are all used for the purposes of the prescribed actions, the benefits of which accrue to gods, &c. Cf. Gîtâ, pp. 53, 54, and see also pp. 84, 85.

subject to me. I do not desire for myself sounds even though existing in the ear. Therefore sounds being conquered are always subject to me. I do not desire for myself the mind always within me. Therefore the mind being conquered is always subject to me. All these actions of mine are, verily, for this purpose, (namely) for the gods, the Pit*ri*s, the Bhûtas, together with guests. Then the Brâhma*n*a, smiling, again said to *G*anaka: 'Know me to be Dharma, come here to-day to learn (something) about you[1]. You are the one person to turn this wheel, the nave of which is the Brahman[2], the spoke the understanding, and which does not turn back[3], and which is checked by the quality of goodness as its circumference[4].'

CHAPTER XVIII.

The Brâhma*n*a said:

O modest one! I do not move about in this world in the way which, according to your own understanding, you have guessed. I[5] am a Brâhma*n*a, I am

---

[1] I.e. to put him to the test. Such examinations are often referred to in our later literature.

[2] I.e. Veda, says Ar*g*una Misra.

[3] I.e. says Ar*g*una Misra, which leads to the seat from which there is no return. Cf. Gitâ, p. 112.

[4] The wheel is the yoga, says Ar*g*una Misra. The expression is noteworthy, as being that used of Buddha's teaching. See on that Davids' Buddhism, p. 45.

[5] The man who has achieved final emancipation has got that, in which the benefits to be derived from the course of life of a Brâhma*n*a, &c., are included (see p. 191 supra). Hence, says he, the

emancipated, I am a forester, and I likewise perform the duties of a householder, observing vows. I am not such, O beautiful one! as you see me with the eye. I pervade every single thing that is in this world. Whatever creatures there are in the world, movable or not moving, know me to be the destroyer of them as fire is of wood[1]. Sovereignty over the whole world, and even over heaven; that, or else this knowledge; (of these two) knowledge is my only wealth[2]. This[3] is the path of the Brâhma*n*as, by which those who understand that[4] proceed, to households, or residence in forests, or, dwelling with preceptors, or among mendicants[5]. With numerous unconfused symbols only one knowledge is approached. And those who, adhering to various symbols and Â*s*ramas, have their understanding full of tranquillity[6], go to the single entity as rivers to the ocean. This path is traversed by the understanding, not by the body[7]. Actions have a beginning and an end, and the body is tied down by action. Hence, O beautiful one! you

doubt, on which your question is based as to what world you will go to by being joined to me, is wrong. See p. 256 supra.

[1] He is speaking here on the footing of the essential identity of everything. Cf. Gîtâ, p. 62.

[2] The expression here is clumsy; the meaning is that he prefers knowledge to sovereignty, if the alternative is offered him.

[3] Viz. knowledge.

[4] I.e. the Brahman.

[5] These are the four orders or Â*s*ramas.

[6] The knowledge to be acquired, by whatever symbols the attempt to acquire it is made, is but this, that all is one; and that is acquired certainly when tranquillity has been achieved.

[7] I.e. by realising the identity of everything, not by the actions performed with the body, which, as he goes on to show, are perishable, and cannot lead to any lasting result.

(need) have no fear occasioned by the other world. With your heart intent upon the real entity, you will certainly come into my self.

Chapter XIX.

The Brâhma*n*a's wife said:

This is not possible to be understood by one whose self[1] is frivolous, or by one whose self is not refined; and my intelligence is very frivolous, and narrow, and confused. Tell me the means by which this knowledge is acquired. I (wish to) learn from you the source from which that knowledge proceeds.

The Brâhma*n*a said:

Know that he who devotes himself to the Brahman is the (lower) Ara*n*i, the instructor is the upper Ara*n*i. Penance and sacred learning cause the attrition[2], and from that the fire of knowledge is produced.

The Brâhma*n*a's wife said:

As to this symbol of the Brahman which is denominated the Kshetra*gñ*a, where, indeed, is (to be found) a description of it, by which it[3] is capable of being comprehended?

---

[1] I.e. mind, Ar*g*una Mi*s*ra.

[2] Scil. of the Ara*n*is (i.e. the wood used for kindling fire); the sense is, that the pupil who has penance and Vedic learning goes to a teacher for knowledge. See *S*vetâ*s*vatara, pp. 307, 308.

[3] I.e. the Brahman, says Ar*g*una Mi*s*ra, of which the Kshetra*gñ*a is only a symbol. For a definition of Kshetra*gñ*a, see *S*ânti Parvan (Moksha), chap. 187, st. 23.

The Brâhma*n*a said:

He is without symbols[1], and also without qualities; nothing exists that is a cause of him. I will only state the means by which he can be comprehended or not. A good means is found, namely, action[2] and knowledge, by which that[3] (entity), which has the symbols (useful) for knowledge[4] attributed to it through ignorance, is perceived as by bees[5]. In the (rules for) final emancipation, it is not laid down, that a certain thing should be done, and a certain thing should not[6]. But the knowledge of the things beneficial to the self is produced in one who sees and hears[7]. One should adopt as many of these things, (which are) means of direct perception, as may here be practicable—unperceived, and those whose form is perceived[8], in hundreds and in thousands, all of various descriptions. Then one comes near to that beyond which nothing exists.

The Deity said:

Then the mind of the Brâhma*n*a's wife, after the

---

[1] See Sanatsugâtîya, p. 160.

[2] Viz. that which is required as a preliminary to the acquisition of knowledge, and hence is necessary for final emancipation.

[3] The Brahman.

[4] I. e. symbols which are to convey a knowledge of the Brahman.

[5] I. e. in a way not perfect; as bees hovering above a flower get the fragrance of it without grasping the flower itself, so these means give one an imperfect knowledge of the Brahman to be afterwards perfected by constant meditation upon it (nididhyâsa).

[6] As it is in the prior portion of the Vedas, as to sacrifices, &c.

[7] Sees, i. e. by contemplation; hears, i. e. from a teacher, Arguna Misra.

[8] This seems to mean such things as hearing, reading, &c., which would be 'perceived' scil. by the senses; and all intellectual operations which would be 'unperceived.'

destruction of the Kshetragña[1], turned to that which is beyond (all) Kshetragñas by means of a knowledge of the Kshetra[2].

Arguna said:

Where, indeed, O Krishna! is that Brâhmana's wife, and where is that chief of Brâhmanas, by both of whom this perfection was attained? Tell me about them both, O undegraded one!

The Deity said:

Know my mind to be the Brâhmana, and know my understanding to be the Brâhmana's wife. And he, O Dhanañgaya! who has been spoken of as the Kshetragña, is I myself[3].

CHAPTER XX.

Arguna said:

Be pleased to explain to me the Brahman which is the highest object of knowledge; for by your favour my mind is much interested in (these) subtle[4] (subjects).

Vâsudeva said:

On this, too, they relate an ancient story (in the shape of) a dialogue, connected with final emancipation, between a preceptor and a pupil. A talented

---

[1] I.e. after the identification of the individual self with the universal self, when the individual ceases to be perceived as such. Cf. Sânti Parvan (Moksha), chap. 187, st. 23.

[2] That beyond Kshetragñas = the absolute supreme self. Cf. Gîtâ, p. 106.

[3] The substance of this speech, says Arguna Misra, is that the mind and understanding devoted to the supreme lead to final emancipation.

[4] See p. 296 supra. The last chapter closes what in some of the MSS. is called the Brahma Gîtâ, or Brâhmana Gîtâ contained in the Anugîtâ Parvan. See further as to this our Introduction, where the point is further dwelt on.

pupil, O terror of your foes! asked a Brâhma*n*a preceptor of rigid vows, (when he was) seated, something about the highest good. 'I' (he said), 'whose goal is the highest good, am come to you (who are) venerable; I pray of you with (bowed) head, O Brâhma*n*a! that you should explain to me what I ask.' The preceptor, O son of P*ri*thâ! said to the pupil who spoke thus: 'I will explain to you everything, O twice-born one! on which you verily have any doubt.' Thus addressed by the preceptor, O best of the Kauravas! he who was devoted to the preceptor, put (his) questions with joined hands. Listen to that, O you of great intelligence!

The pupil said:

Whence am I[1], and whence are you? Explain that which is the highest truth. From what were the movable and immovable entities born? By what do entities live, and what is the limit of their life? What is truth, what penance, O Brâhma*n*a? What are called the qualities by the good? And what paths are happy? What is pleasure, and what sin? These questions of mine, O venerable Brâhma*n*a sage! O you of excellent vows! do you be pleased to explain[2] correctly, truly, and accurately. There is none else here who can explain these questions. Speak, O best of those who understand piety! I feel the highest curiosity (in this matter). You are celebrated in the worlds as skilled in topics connected with the piety (required for) final emancipation. And there exists none else but you who can destroy all

[1] Compare the questions at the beginning of the *S*vetâ*s*vatara-upanishad.

[2] A similar expression to that in the Sanatsu*g*âtîya, p. 149, and elsewhere.

doubts. And we[1], likewise, are afraid of worldly life, and also desirous of final emancipation.

Vâsudeva said:

That talented preceptor, who preserved (all) vows, O son of Prithâ! O chief of the family of the Kauravas! O restrainer of foes! duly explained all those questions to that pupil, who had approached him (for instruction), who put (his) questions properly, who was possessed of (the necessary) qualifications, who was tranquil, who conducted himself in an agreeable manner, who was like (his) shadow[2], and who was a self-restrained ascetic and a Brahmakârin.

The preceptor said:

All this, which is connected with the knowledge of the Vedas[3] and involves a consideration of the real entity, and which is cultivated by the chief sages, was declared by Brahman. We consider knowledge only as the highest thing; and renunciation[4] as the best penance. And he who understands determinately the true object of knowledge which is impregnable[5]—the self abiding in all entities—and who can move about anywhere[6], is esteemed highest. The learned man who perceives the abiding together[7],

---

[1] It is not easy to account for the change here from the singular to the plural.

[2] I.e. always attended on the preceptor. Cf. generally, Mundaka, p. 283.

[3] The question was not quite from his own imagination, says Nilakantha. Arguna Misra has a different reading, which he interprets to mean 'that on which the Vedas are all at one.'

[4] Of the fruit of action, Arguna Misra.

[5] I.e. not such as to require modification by any other knowledge, as knowledge of the world does.

[6] Nilakantha compares Khândogya, pp. 523-553.

[7] I.e. of Kit and Gada, says Nilakantha; of Brahman and its manifestations, as alluded to, inter alia, at pp. 105, 106, 191 supra.

and the severance also, and likewise unity and variety[1], is released from misery. He who does not desire anything, and has no egoism about anything, becomes eligible for assimilation with the Brahman, even while dwelling in this world[2]. He who knows the truth about the qualities of nature, who understands the creation of all entities, who is devoid of (the thought that this or that is) mine, and who is devoid of egoism, is emancipated; there is no doubt of that. Accurately understanding the great (tree) of which the unperceived[3] is the sprout from the seed, which consists of the understanding as its trunk, the branches of which are the great egoism, in the holes of which are the sprouts, namely, the senses, of which the great elements are the flower-bunches[4], the gross elements the smaller boughs, which is always possessed of leaves, always possessed of flowers, and from which pleasant fruits are always produced, on which all entities subsist, which is eternal, and the seed of which is the Brahman; and cutting it with that excellent sword—knowledge—one attains immortality, and casts off birth and death[5]. I will state to you to-day, O highly

[1] I.e. that variety is only in this world, but that the unity of everything is the true proposition. Cf. inter alia Gîtâ, p. 104.

[2] Cf. B*ri*hadâra*n*yaka, p. 858, and Gîtâ, p. 65.

[3] I.e. the Prak*ri*ti of the Sâṅkhyas.

[4] The great elements are the five tanmâtras of earth, water, fire, air, and space, which afterwards produce what we have called the gross elements in the text, namely, the earth &c. which we perceive.

[5] The tree typifies worldly life. Cf. pp. 111–189 supra. The leaves and flowers, Ar*g*una Mi*s*ra says, stand for volition and action; and Nilaka*nt*ha seems to agree. The tree is called eternal, as worldly life is supposed to have had no beginning. Cf. Sârîraka Bhâshya, p. 494. 'sprout from the seed,' this rendering is necessitated by Brahman being described as the seed. Cf. Mu*nd*aka, p. 288; *S*vetâ*s*vatara, p. 362; Ka*th*a, pp. 143, 144.

talented one! the true conclusion[1] about the past, the present, the future, and so forth, and piety, desire, and wealth[2], which is understood by the multitudes of Siddhas, which belongs to olden times, and is eternal, which ought to be apprehended, and understanding which talented men have here attained perfection. Formerly[3], the sages, Brihaspati, Bharadvâga, Gautama, and likewise Bhârgava, Vasishtha, and also Kâsyapa, and Visvâmitra, and Atri also, desiring knowledge, met each other, after having travelled over all paths[4], and becoming wearied of their own actions. And those twice-born (sages), giving the lead to the old sage Âṅgirasa, saw Brahman, from whom (all) sin has departed, in Brahman's mansion. Having saluted that high-souled one who was sitting at ease, the great sages, full of humility, asked him this momentous (question) concerning the highest good: 'How should one perform good action? how is one released from sin? what paths are happy for us? what is truth and what vice? By what action are the two paths southern and northern obtained[5]? (and what is) destruction[6] and emancipation, the birth and death of entities?' What the grandsire said conformably to the scriptures[7],

[1] I. e. the means of arriving at it, Arguna Misra.

[2] The triad, the acquisition of which worldly men aspire to.

[3] He explains how the doctrine belongs to olden times.

[4] I. e. paths of action, Nîlakantha. See Sanatsugâtîya, p. 165.

[5] Namely, the Pitriyâna and Devayâna (Arguna Misra), as to which see Khândogya, p. 341, Kaushîtaki, p. 13, and Brihadâranyaka, p. 1034.

[6] Nîlakantha seems to interpret this to mean the temporary and final dissolutions of the worlds, on which see, inter alia, Vedânta Paribhâshâ, p. 48.

[7] So Nîlakantha. May it not be 'according to the received tradition?'

when thus spoken to by the sages, I will state to you. Listen (to that) O pupil!

Brahman said:

From the truth were the entities movable and immovable produced. They live by penance[1]. Understand that, O you of excellent vows! By their own action they remain transcending their own source[2]. For the truth joined with the qualities is invariably of five varieties. The Brahman[3] is the truth; penance is the truth; Pragâpati also is truth; the entities are born from the truth; the universe consisting of (all) creatures is the truth. Therefore Brâhmanas whose final goal is always concentration of mind, from whom anger and vexation have departed, and who are invariably devoting themselves to piety, are full of the truth. I will speak about those (Brâhmanas) who are restrained by one another[4], who are possessed of knowledge, who are the establishers of the bridge of piety, and who are the constant creators of the people[5]. I will speak of the four (branches of) knowledge, and likewise of the castes, and of the four orders, distinctly. The wise always speak of piety as one, (but) having

[1] I.e. by action, Nilakantha. Cf. Mundaka, p. 280, and see p. 166 supra, note 1.

[2] I.e. they remain apart from the Brahman, being engaged in action. This answers some of the questions put by the pupil to the preceptor. As to 'the truth,' see p. 162, note 2 supra.

[3] I.e. Îsvara, or god; penance=piety; Pragâpati=the individual soul, Nîlakantha. Brahman='that' (but how is 'that' 'joined with qualities?'); Pragâpati=Brahman, Arguna Misra. They agree about penance and entities (which they take to mean the gross elements) and creatures. Brahman and Pragâpati=Virâg and Hiranyagarbha(?), p. 186 supra. Cf. Sânti Parvan (Moksha), chap. 190, st. 1.

[4] I.e. who commit no breach of piety through fear of one another, Nîlakantha.

[5] Cf. Gîtâ, p. 86.

four quarters. I will speak to you, O twice-born ones! of the happy path, which is productive of pleasure, and which has been invariably travelled over by talented men in old days for (obtaining) assimilation with the Brahman. Learn, O noble ones! from me, now speaking exhaustively, of that highest path which is difficult to understand, and of the highest seat. The first step is said to be the order of Brahma*k*ârins; the second is that of householders: next after that is that of foresters; and next after that too, the highest step must be understood to be that relating to the Adhyâtma[1]. Light[2], space, sun, air, Indra, Pra*g*âpati, one sees not these, while one does not attain to the Adhyâtma[3]. I will subsequently state the means to that, which you should understand. The order of foresters, (the order) of the sages who dwell in forests and live on fruits, roots and air, is prescribed for the three twice-born (castes). The order of householders is prescribed for all castes. The talented ones speak of piety as having faith for its characteristic. Thus have I described to you the paths leading to the gods[4], which are occupied by good and talented men by means of their actions, and which are bridges of piety. He who, rigid in his vows, takes up any one of these modes of piety separately, always comes in time to perceive the production and dissolution of

[1] That is to say, that of the ascetic, who specially devotes himself to the acquisition of knowledge about the relation of the supreme and individual self (Adhyâtma).

[2] The deity presiding over the bright fortnight, says Ar*g*una Misra. The words space and sun and air must be similarly interpreted.

[3] Nilaka*n*/*h*a says 'one sees these only while one has not had a perception of the self.' He takes light &c. to mean the 'universe.'

[4] I.e. the means of reaching the Devayâna path (mentioned at p. 314, note 5), Nilaka*nth*a. Cf. also Mu*nd*aka, p. 312.

(all) entities[1]. Now I shall state with accuracy and with reasons, all the elements which abide in parts in all objects. The great self[2], the unperceived[3] likewise, and likewise also egoism, the ten senses and the one[4] (sense), and the five great elements, and the specific characteristics of the five elements[5], such is the eternal creation. The number of the elements is celebrated as being twenty-four plus one. And the talented man who understands the production and dissolution of (all) elements, he, of all beings, never comes by delusion. He who accurately understands the elements, the whole of the qualities[6], and also all the deities[7], casting aside sin, and getting rid of (all) bonds, attains to all the spotless worlds.

CHAPTER XXI.

Brahman said:

That unperceived (principle), all-pervading, everlasting, and immutable, which is in a state of equilibrium[8], should be understood (to become) the city of nine portals, consisting of three qualities, and five

---

[1] Namely, how they are all manifestations of the Brahman, and are all dissolved in it. Cf. inter alia Gîtâ, pp. 74, 92.

[2] See the Ka*th*opanishad, p. 149. See also p. 332 infra.

[3] See p. 313, note 3 supra.

[4] I. e. the mind. Cf. Gîtâ, p. 102. [5] Viz. smell, sound, &c.

[6] Tranquillity, self-restraint, &c., Arguna Misra. Are they not rather the three qualities? As to 'twenty-four plus one' above, see p. 368.

[7] Does this mean the senses, as at Gîtâ, p. 123? An accurate understanding of the things noted requires a knowledge of their relation to the supreme, which is the means of final emancipation. And see p. 337 infra.

[8] See Gîtâ, p. 107, and Sâṅkhya-sâra, p. 11, and note 2, p. 331 infra.

constituent principles[1], encircled by the eleven[2], consisting of mind[3] as the distinguishing power, and of the understanding as ruler, this is (an aggregate made up of) eleven[4]. The three currents[5] which are within this (city) support (it)[6] again and again, and those three channels run on, being constituted by the three qualities. Darkness, passion, and goodness, these are called the three qualities, which are all coupled with one another, and likewise serve one another, which depend on one another, and attend on one another, and are joined to one another[7]. And the five constituent principles

[1] The five gross elements of which the body is composed (cf. Mahâbhârata, *S*ânti Parvan, Moksha Dharma, chap. 183, st. 1 seq.) are developments of the unperceived principle, the Prak*ri*ti. Cf. Gîtâ, p. 112, where the words 'which remain (absorbed) in nature' have been inadvertently omitted after 'with the mind as the sixth.' As to the nine portals cf. Gîtâ, p. 65.

[2] The five active organs, the five perceptive senses, and the mind.

[3] This Ar*g*una Mi*s*ra takes to mean 'egoism.' Nîlaka*nth*a takes the usual meaning, and adds, objects are produced from mental operations; 'distinguishing,' that is, manifesting as distinct entities.

[4] The eleven are, according to Ar*g*una Mi*s*ra, the three qualities, the five gross elements, the group of organs and senses as one, egoism, and understanding.

[5] Viz. the nâ*d*îs, I*d*â, Piṅgalâ, and Sushum*n*â, Ar*g*una Mi*s*ra, who adds that they are respectively of the quality of darkness, passion, and goodness.

[6] The three nâ*d*îs, says Ar*g*una Mi*s*ra, support the life-winds. Nîlaka*nth*a takes the three currents to be the threefold inclination of the mind, viz. towards a pure piety, towards injuring other living creatures, and towards that mixed piety which requires the destruction of life for its performance. Nîlaka*nth*a also has a different reading from Ar*g*una Mi*s*ra, which means 'are replenished' instead of 'support.' And the three channels are, according to Nîlaka*nth*a, the Sa*m*skâras, or effects of previous actions of piety or impiety.

[7] Coupled = always existing in association with one another; serving = being necessary to the operations of one another; depending = supporting one another like three staves, says Nîlaka*nth*a;

(are made up of) the three qualities. Goodness is the match of darkness, and passion is the match of goodness; and goodness is also the match of passion, and darkness the match of goodness. Where darkness is restrained, passion there prevails. Where passion is restrained, goodness there prevails[1]. Darkness should be understood to consist in obscurity. It has three qualities[2], and is called delusion. Its characteristic is also impiety, and it is constant in sinful actions. This is the nature of darkness; it also appears combined (with others). Passion is said to consist in activity, and is the cause of successive[3] (acts). When it prevails, its characteristic, among all beings, appears to be production[4]. Light, lightness[5], faith, such is stated to be the nature of goodness (prevailing) among all beings, as accepted by good men. The true nature of their characteristics, in aggregation and separation, will now be stated together with the reasons; learn those accurately. Delusion, ignorance,

---

upholding, says Arguna Misra, as the total absence of one would lead to the absence of the others also; attending=becoming subordinate to whichever of them is dominant for the time being; joined=so as to become one organic whole. Cf. as to all this, Yoga-sûtra II, 18, and commentary, p. 101; Sânkhya-kârikâ, Kârikâ 12, with Vâkaspati Misra's comments on it.

[1] Cf. Gitâ, p. 108, and the quotation in the Sânkhyatattvakaumudî, p. 64.

[2] I.e. characteristics, viz. obscurity (which seems to stand for ignorance), delusion (which is false knowledge), and impiety (doing that which is known to be sinful and wrong).

[3] The original means, according to Nilakantha, wrong, unlawful conduct. As to all this cf. Sânti Parvan (Moksha), chap. 194, st. 29.

[4] I.e. apparently perpetually doing something. Cf. Gitâ, p. 108.

[5] Cf. as to this, and generally also, Sânkhya-kârikâ 13, and commentary of Vâkaspati Misra (p. 64). The blazing upwards of fire is said to illustrate the lightness of the quality of goodness which belongs to fire.

want of liberality, indecision about actions [1], sleep, haughtiness [2], fear, avarice, grief, finding fault with good acts, want of memory [3], immaturity (of intellect), nihilism [4], violation of (the rules of) conduct, want of discrimination [3], blindness, behaviour of the lowest [5] quality, pride of performance without (actual) performance, pride of knowledge without (actual) knowledge, unfriendliness, evil disposition, want of faith, deluded convictions, want of straightforwardness, want of knowledge [6], sinful action, want of knowledge (of the subtle principle), stolidity [7], lassitude, want of self-restraint, going into inferior ways; all these qualities, O Brâhma*n*as! are celebrated as being dark. And whatever other states of mind, connected with delusion, are found in various places in this world, all these are dark qualities. Constant talk in disparagement of gods, Brâhma*n*as and Vedas, want of liberality, vanity, delusion [8], anger, want of forgiveness likewise, and also animosity

[1] According to Gîtâ, p. 108, doing nothing—stolid laziness—is a mark of darkness. Cf. generally on this passage Gîtâ, pp. 107, 118, 124 seq.; Maitrî, p. 49.

[2] The same word as at Gîtâ, pp. 116, 125 (headstrong in the latter passage should have been haughty). Cf. as to the word, *Kh*ândogya, p. 383.

[3] Cf. Gîtâ, p. 51.

[4] The opposite of the belief mentioned at Gîtâ, p. 126.

[5] The same word as at Gîtâ, p. 109. But the commentators render it here by hi*m*sra, i.e. destructive.

[6] I am not sure about the original word here, and the word next but one after this. The latter Arguna Misra renders by sûkshmatattvâvedanam, which I have translated above in the text. The former seems to mean general unintelligence.

[7] Heaviness and dulness, induced by indolence, &c., Nîlaka*nth*a. Lassitude is drooping from despondency. Going into inferior ways, Arguna Misra says, means falling into the inferior castes; Nîlaka*nth*a says it means love for base actions.

[8] Not being cognisant of one's own shortcomings, Arguna Misra.

towards people, this is considered to be dark conduct. Whatever vain[1] actions (there are), and whatever vain gifts, and vain eating, that is considered to be dark conduct. Reviling, and want of forgiveness, animosity, vanity, want of faith also, this is considered to be dark conduct. And whatever such people there are in this world, doers of sinful acts, who break through (all) regulations, they are all held to be dark. I will state the wombs appointed for these (men) of sinful actions. They go to the hell, (namely) the brute (species), to be born in the lower hell[2]; (or become) the immovable entities[3], animals, beasts of burden, demons, and serpents, and worms, insects, birds, and also creatures born from eggs, and all quadrupeds, and idiots, deaf and dumb men, and whatever others are attacked by diseases generated by sin[4]. These dark, evil-conducted men, who are sunk in darkness, who bear the marks of their own actions, the current of whose (thoughts) is downwards[5], sink into darkness. I will now proceed to state their improvement and ascent; how, becoming men of meritorious actions, they attain to the worlds of those who perform good acts[6]. Resorting to a contrary[7] (course of life), and growing old in (good) actions[8], they exert

[1] Cf. Gîtâ, p. 83. [2] Cf. Gîtâ, p. 116.

[3] Such as trees and so forth, which are also forms of life.

[4] This is alluded to in some Smritis too. And cf. *Kh*ândogya, p. 358, and the quotation in the commentary on Sânkhya-sûtra V, 122.

[5] Such, says Nîlaka*nth*a, as to fit them for the nether world. See Tattvakaumudî, p. 113. As to marks, cf. p. 239 supra.

[6] Cf. Gîtâ, p. 130.

[7] I.e. contrary to that already described as dark.

[8] Nîlaka*nth*a renders this to mean 'destroyed for Agnihotra and such ceremonies,' like the goat referred to above at p. 290.

themselves, and through the ceremonies (performed for them) by benevolent Brâhma*n*as devoted to their own duties, they go upwards to the same world (as the Brâhma*n*as)—the heaven of the gods. Such is the Vedic text. Resorting to a contrary[1] (course of life), and growing old in their own duties, they become men in this world whose nature is to return[2]. Coming to a sinful womb, as *K*â*nd*âlas[3], or deaf, or lisping men, they attain to higher and higher castes in order; going beyond the *S*ûdra womb, and (beyond) whatever other dark qualities there are which abide in the quality of darkness[4] in the current (of this world). Attachment to objects of desire is laid down to be the great delusion. There, sages and saints and gods become deluded, wishing for pleasure. Darkness[5], delusion, the great delusion, the great obscurity called anger, and death the blinding obscurity; anger is called the great obscurity. I have now duly described to you, O Brâhma*n*as! this quality of darkness, in full and accurately with reference to

[1] See note 7 on last page. The sequence of ideas seems not to be properly brought out here. In the course of transmigration after their course of conduct is altered they become men, and then proceed to heaven. This seems the real sense here.

[2] To return to life and death, and so on, until they fit themselves for final emancipation. Cf. Âpastamba II, 5, 11, 10–11.

[3] Cf. *Kh*ândogya, p. 359.

[4] This is not very clear, and the commentators give but little help. The meaning probably is, that they gradually, in course of improvement, cross beyond the *S*ûdra caste, and all those qualities or tempers of mind, and so forth, which have been stated to appertain to the quality of darkness.

[5] Cf. Sâṅkhya-kârikâ, pp. 47, 48, and Vâ*k*aspati's comment. There these are identified with the 'afflictions' of the Yoga-*s*âstra—ignorance, self-consciousness, affection, aversion, persistent attachment, and they are five divisions of false knowledge, or the quality of darkness, as it is here called. See, too, *S*vetâ*s*vatara (comm.), p. 284.

its nature, and also its qualities, and also its source. Who, indeed, understands this properly; who, indeed, perceives this properly? The definition of the essence of darkness is, that one sees the real in what is unreal. The qualities of darkness have been described to you in many ways. And darkness in its higher and lower[1] (forms) has been accurately stated. The man who always understands these qualities gets rid of all dark qualities.

CHAPTER XXII.

Brahman said:

O best (of men)! I will explain to you accurately the quality of passion. Learn, O noble ones! the action of the quality of passion. Injuring (others), beauty[2], toil, pleasure and pain, cold and heat, power[2], war, peace, argument, repining[3], endurance, strength, valour, frenzy, wrath, exercise and quarrel too, vindictiveness, desire, backbiting, battle, the thought (that this or that is) mine, preservation[4], slaughter, bonds, affliction, buying and selling, touching[5] other people's weak points, by cutting, breaking, piercing; fierceness and cruelty, vilifying, pointing out others' weaknesses, thinking of (this) world, harbouring evil thoughts, animosity, abuse,

---

[1] Generally and specifically, says Arguna Misra.

[2] Arguna Misra says these mean pride of beauty and pride of power respectively. Cf. as to this list generally, Maitrî, pp. 50, 51.

[3] Cf. Sanatsugâtîya, p. 168.

[4] I presume this means solicitude for preserving what one has got. Cf. Gîtâ, p. 48.

[5] Literally, piercing. 'Cutting, breaking piercing,' further on, seems to indicate the greater or less offensiveness of the operation of 'touching others' weak points.'

uttering falsehoods, bad[1] gifts, doubt, boasting, censure, praise, laudation[2], prowess, defiance, attendance (on another), obedience[3], service, harbouring desire, management[4], policy, heedlessness, contumely, belongings[5], and the various decorations which prevail in this world, for men, for women, for living creatures, for articles, and for houses, vexation, and also want of faith, vows and regulations[6], and actions with expectations, and the various acts of public charity[7], the ceremony of Svâhâ, the ceremony of Svadhâ, the ceremony of Vashat[8], salutation, both officiating at sacrifices and imparting instruction, and also sacrificing and study, gifts and acceptance of gifts, expiations, auspicious rites, the wish 'this may be mine and that may be mine,' affection generated by the qualities[9], treachery and likewise deception, disrespect and respect, theft, slaughter, disgust, vexing (oneself), wakefulness, ostentation, haughtiness, and attachment also, devotion, pleasure and delight, gambling, common scandal, association with women,

[1] I. e. to undeserving persons, Arguna Misra. Probably it includes the other defects also pointed out at Gîtâ, p. 120. As to doubt, see Gîtâ, p. 63.

[2] The one is attributing merits which do not exist, the other is merely parading merits which do exist.

[3] Arguna Misra takes this literally to mean 'wish to hear.'

[4] Cleverness in worldly affairs, Nîlakantha.

[5] Cf. Gîtâ, passim, and see also Yoga-sûtras II, 30, and commentary (pp. 127–129, Calc. ed.)

[6] Fasts and other observances for special benefits.

[7] E. g. digging tanks and wells, &c.

[8] Vashat and Svâhâ indicate offerings to gods, Svadhâ to the manes. See Brihadâranyaka, p. 982, and Mândukya (Gaudapâda Kârikâ), p. 443, and commentaries there.

[9] I presume this means attachment to the operations of the qualities. Cf. Gîtâ, p. 48. As to the wish just before, see Gîtâ, pp. 115, 116.

devotion to dancing, and instrumental or vocal music, all these qualities, O Brâhmaṇas! are described as passionate. The men who meditate on past, present, and future entities in this world[1], who are always devoted to the triad—piety, wealth, and lust also[2]—who acting under (the impulse of) desires exult on the success of all their desires, these men, who are enveloped by passion, have (their) currents downwards[3]. Born again and again in this world, they rejoice[4], and wish for the fruit appertaining to the life after death[5] and that appertaining to this world also. They give and receive, and make Tarpaṇa[6], and also sacrifice. The qualities of passion have been described to you in many ways, and the action of the quality has also been stated accurately. The man who always understands these qualities, gets rid of all passionate qualities.

CHAPTER XXIII.

Brahman said:

Now I shall proceed to describe the third—the best—quality, beneficial to all creatures, and unblamable, the duty of the good. Joy[7], pleasure, nobility, enlightenment and happiness also, absence of stinginess, absence of fear, contentment, faith, forgiveness, courage, harmlessness, equability, truth, straightforwardness, absence of wrath, absence of calumnia-

---

[1] I. e. who are always thinking of what they have done and what they have to do, and so forth. Cf. Gîtâ, pp. 115, 116.

[2] And not that which is higher than these, viz. final emancipation.

[3] See p. 321 and note 5 there.

[4] Cf. inter alia, Gîtâ, p. 48.

[5] Viz. heaven. Cf. Gîtâ, p. 48.

[6] I.e. offerings to the manes.

[7] Cf. p. 300 supra, and Sânti Parvan (Moksha), chap. 194, st. 34; chap. 219, st. 36. For nobility, Arguna Misra has manifestation of joy.

tion, purity, dexterity, valour. He who possesses the piety of concentration of mind, (holding) knowledge to be vain[1], (good) conduct vain, service vain, and labour vain, he attains the highest in the next world. Devoid of (the notion that this or that is) mine, devoid of egoism, devoid of expectations, equable everywhere, not full of desires, (to be) such is the eternal duty of the good. Confidence, modesty[2], forgiveness, liberality, purity, freedom from laziness, absence of cruelty, freedom from delusion, compassion to (all) creatures, absence of backbiting, joy, contentment, joviality, humility, good behaviour, purity in all action for (acquiring) tranquillity[3], righteous feelings, emancipation[4], indifference[5], life as a Brahma*k*ârin, abandonment on all hands, freedom from (the notion that this or that is) mine, freedom from expectations[6], unbroken piety[7], (holding that) gifts (are) vain, sacrifices vain, learning vain, vows vain, receipt of gifts vain, piety vain, penance vain. Those talented Brâhma*n*as in this world, whose conduct is of this description, who adhere to the quality of goodness, abiding in the seat of the Brahman[8], perceive (everything) aright. Getting rid of all

[1] Such is Nîlaka*n*t*h*a's reading, and he takes knowledge to mean mere knowledge derived from books, &c. Ar*g*una Mi*s*ra has a different reading for vain, which he interprets to mean 'wish for fruit.'

[2] See Sanatsu*g*âtîya, p. 162.

[3] I. e. pure and straightforward conduct in the performance of whatever is done for attaining final emancipation.

[4] Of other people from sorrow, Ar*g*una Mi*s*ra.

[5] The state of being unconcerned, udâsîna, Nîlaka*n*t*h*a.

[6] Cf. Gîtâ, p. 60, inter alia.

[7] Ar*g*una Mi*s*ra understands the original here to mean 'not being under the control of another.'

[8] I. e. the source of the Vedas, according to Nîlaka*n*t*h*a. The supreme is called Brahmayoni, the original word here, at *S*vetâ-

sins, and free from grief, those talented men reach heaven, and create (various) bodies [1]. The power of governing, self-restraint, minuteness [2], these those high-souled ones make (for themselves) by (the operations of their own) minds like the gods dwelling in heaven. They are said to have their currents upwards [3], and to be gods, and of the quality of goodness [4]; and having gone to heaven they verily change in various ways, by means of nature [5]. They obtain and divide [6] whatever they desire. Thus, O chiefs of the twice-born! have I described to you the conduct of the quality of goodness. Understanding this according to rule, one obtains whatever one desires. The qualities

svatara, p. 354, where Brahman is rendered to mean Prakriti by Sankara. See Sanatsugâtîya, p. 186, note 6, and Taittirîya-âranyaka, p. 894. As to the probable sense here, see p. 339, note 2 infra.

[1] I. e. for themselves. Cf. p. 345 infra; Yoga-sûtras, p. 227; and Brihadâranyaka, p. 849.

[2] These include, according to Nîlakantha, the other qualities of the same class unnamed here, for which see Yoga-sûtra III, 44 (p. 207). The power of governing, i. e. producing, destroying, or combining worldly objects as one pleases; self-restraint, i. e. in the presence of tempting objects; minuteness = power of becoming as minute as one pleases. The other qualities are lightness, largeness, and heaviness; power of attracting everything so as to be near oneself (e. g. touching the moon with the finger), power of obtaining one's wish.

[3] Cf. p. 321 supra and note 5. Arguna Misra, and Nîlakantha also, here render it by 'those who go upwards.' As to which, see Gîtâ, p. 109.

[4] Cf. for this sense, which is given by Arguna Misra, Sânkhya-sâra, p. 19.

[5] Nîlakantha says this means that they change their minds for purposes of enjoyment by means of the impression of previous enjoyments. The changes, however, seem to be those above referred to—minuteness, &c., and the acquisition of other bodies. As to nature, cf. Gîtâ, pp. 58 and 112, with the correction made at p. 318 supra.

[6] This is not quite clear. Does it mean distribute among themselves or others?

of goodness have been specifically described, and the operation of the qualities has been accurately stated. The man who always understands these qualities, enjoys the qualities[1], but is not attached to the qualities.

Chapter XXIV.

Brahman said:

The qualities cannot be explained altogether distinctly (from one another). Passion, goodness, and darkness likewise are seen mixed up (with one another). They are attached to one another, they feed on one another. They all depend on one another, and likewise follow one another[2]. There is no doubt of this, that as long[3] as there is goodness so long darkness exists. And as long as goodness and darkness, so long is passion said (to exist) here. They perform their journey together, in union, and moving about collectively. For they act with cause or without cause[4], moving in a body. Of all these acting with one another, but differing in development, the increase and diminution will now be stated. Where darkness is increased, abiding[5] in the lower entities, there passion should be understood to be little, and goodness likewise to be less. Where

[1] Cf. Gîtâ inter alia, p. 104. [2] Cf. p. 318 supra.

[3] So Arguna Misra. Nîlakan*th*a says on this, 'However much goodness may be increased, it is still held in check by darkness, and thus there is the continual relation of that which checks and that which is checked between the three qualities; hence they are alike. So also passion being increased, holds goodness and darkness in check. The sense seems to be that the qualities dominate all in this world and exist together though varying in strength' (Gîtâ, p. 73).

[4] I. e. spontaneously, Arguna Misra. Cf. *S*ânti Parvan (Moksha), chap. 194, st. 35.

[5] It is in the lower species that darkness is predominant.

passion is developed, abiding in those of the middle current[1], there darkness should be understood to be little, and goodness likewise to be less. And where goodness is developed, abiding in those of the upward current[2], there darkness should be understood to be little, and passion likewise to be less[3]. Goodness is the cause of the modifications in the senses, and the enlightener[4]. For there is no other higher duty laid down than goodness. Those who adhere to (the ways of) goodness go up; the passionate remain in the middle; the men of the quality of darkness, being connected with the lowest quality, go down[5]. The three qualities abide in the three castes thus: darkness in the *S*ûdra, passion in the Kshatriya, and the highest, goodness, in the Brâhma*n*a[6]. Even from afar[7], darkness, goodness, and passion also, are seen to have been together and moving about collectively. We have never heard of them (as existing) separately. Seeing the sun rising, evil-doers are alarmed, and travellers, suffering trouble from the heat, feel the warmth. The sun is goodness developed, evil-doers likewise are darkness, and the heat to the travellers is said to be a property of

[1] I.e. the human species, Arguna Misra. Cf. Gîtâ, p. 109.

[2] See Gîtâ, p. 109, also p. 327 supra. In his Sâṅkhyatattva-kaumudî, Vâ*k*aspati Misra applies the epithet to Yogins (see p. 13 of Târânâth's edition, and the editor's note there).

[3] Cf. Gîtâ, p. 108.

[4] Cf. Gîtâ, p. 108. The modifications of the senses constituting perception by them is an operation of the quality of goodness. This seems to be the meaning of the text; as to this, cf. Tattva-kaumudî, p. 14 (Târânâth's edition).

[5] See Gîtâ, p. 109; the words are nearly identical.

[6] Cf. *S*ânti Parvan (Moksha), chap. 188, st. 15. The Vaisya is omitted here.

[7] I.e. Arguna Misra says, even after much observation.

passion[1]. The light in the sun is goodness; the heat is the quality of passion; and its eclipse on the Parvan[2] days must be understood to be of the quality of darkness. So in all shining bodies, there exist three qualities. And they act by turns in the several places in several ways. Among immovable entities, darkness is in the form of their belonging to the lower species; the qualities of passion are variable; and the oleaginous property is of the quality of goodness[3]. The day should be understood to be threefold, the night is stated to be threefold, and likewise months, half-months, years, seasons, and the conjunctions[4]. Threefold are the gifts given[5], threefold the sacrifices performed, threefold are the

[1] This illustrates the existence of the qualities as one body. Even the enlightening sun, which embodies the quality of goodness, produces effects which belong to the other qualities. The fear and sorrow which evil-doers, that is thieves, feel, is an effect of the rising of the sun, which appertains to the quality of darkness, and the heat as being the cause of vexation and consequent delusion to travellers, appertains to the quality of passion.

[2] I. e. the days of the moon's conjunction or opposition.

[3] I understand this to mean that in the 'immovable entities' the three qualities co-exist; the birth in the lower species is an effect of darkness; the variable qualities, viz. the heat, &c., as Arguna Misra says, are the properties of passion; and the oleaginous properties among them appertain to goodness, as, says Arguna Misra, they are sources of pleasure (cf. Gîtâ, p. 118). Nilaka*ntha* says, 'Immovable entities being very unintelligent, darkness is very much developed among them,' but this last, as an interpretation of tiryagbhâvagata, appears to me to be alike unwarranted and inappropriate here.

[4] Does this mean the period about the close of one and beginning of another yuga or age? That is the only sense ejusdem generis with the words preceding it that I can think of; yet the jump from years to yuga-sandhis is a long one.

[5] Cf. Gîtâ, p. 120. With reference to some, at least, of the things enumerated here, the division would be rather fanciful.

worlds, threefold the gods, threefold the (departments of) knowledge, and threefold the path[1]. The past, the present, and the future; piety, wealth, and lust; the Prâna, the Apâna, and the Udâna; these are the three qualities. And whatever there is in this world, all that is (made of) these three qualities[2]. The three qualities—goodness, passion, and darkness also—are always acting unperceived. The creation of the qualities is eternal. Darkness, unperceived, holy[3], constant, unborn, womb, eternal, nature, change[4], destruction, Pradhâna, production and absorption, not developed, not small, unshaking, immovable, immutable, existent and also non-existent[5]—all these, the unperceived, (consisting) of the three qualities, is said to be. These names should be learnt by men who ponder on matters relating to the self. He who understands correctly all the names of the unperceived, and the qualities, and its pure operations, he, freed from the body, understanding the truth about (all) distinctions, and being free from all misery, is released from all qualities.

---

[1] See these three mentioned at *Khândogya*, pp. 340–359. As to departments of knowledge, cf. Gîtâ, p. 84; Arguna Misra reads, 'threefold the Vedas.'

[2] The universe is all developed from the Prakriti, which is merely the three 'qualities in equilibrium.' Cf. Sânkhya-sûtra I, 61.

[3] Because it gives final emancipation to one who discriminates it from Purusha, Arguna Misra. Cf. Sânkhya-sûtra II, 1 seq., and Sânkhya-kârikâ, p. 56 seq., and commentary. For another list of names of Prakriti, see *Svetâsvatara* (comm.), p. 283.

[4] Nature is not a development from anything, and hence is called avikriti in Sânkhya-kârikâ 3; but 'change' here probably means the whole aggregate of Vikritis, 'changes' or developments, which make up Prakriti; or by a different derivation it may, perhaps, also mean that from which all development or change takes place.

[5] See Sânkhya-sûtra V, 52–56; and also I, 26, and commentary here. The Vedântins speak of Mâyâ—which answers to what the

CHAPTER XXV.

Brahman said:

From the unperceived was first produced the great self[1], of great intelligence, the source of all qualities[2]; it is said to be the first creation. That great self is signified by these synonymous terms—the great self, intelligence, Vish*n*u[3], *G*ish*n*u, *S*ambhu, the valiant, the understanding, means of knowledge, means of perception, and likewise cognition, courage, memory. Knowing that (great self), a learned Brâhma*n*a comes not by delusion. It has hands and feet on all sides[4], it has eyes, heads, and faces on all sides; it stands pervading everything in the world[5]. The being of great power is stationed in the heart of all. Minuteness[6], lightness, (the power of) obtaining (everything) (are his); he is the governor, the light, inexhaustible. Now people who comprehend the understanding, and who are always possessed of a good heart, who practise meditation, who are constant at concentration of mind, who are true to their promises, and whose senses are subdued, who are possessed of knowledge, who are not avaricious, who have subdued wrath, whose minds are clear, who are talented, who are devoid of (the thought that this or that is) mine, who are devoid of egoism,

---

Sâṅkhyas call Prak*r*iti (see *S*vetâ*s*vatara, p. 340, and Sâṅkhya-sûtra I, 69, and commentary there)—as 'sattvâsattvâbhyâmanirvâ*k*ya.'

[1] I. e. the understanding, on which see Sâṅkhya-sûtra I, 61–64. It is called being (Purusha) further on, as it dwells in the body (Puri).

[2] I. e. of the effects of all qualities (namely, the universe; cf. Gitâ, p. 48), Nîlaka*n*t*h*a.

[3] I. e. all-pervading, Arguna Mi*s*ra. On the whole passage, see Sâṅkhya-sâra, pp. 15, 16, and note 3 on page 333 infra.

[4] As, says Arguna Mi*s*ra, it is the source of all activity.

[5] The words are identical with those at Gîtâ, p. 103.

[6] See p. 327 supra.

these being emancipated, attain greatness[1]. And the talented man who understands that high and holy goal, the great self[2], he among all people comes not by delusion. The self-existent Vishnu is the Lord in the primary creations[3]. And he who thus knows the lord lying in the cave[4], the transcendent, ancient being, of universal form, and golden[5], the highest goal of those possessed of understanding, that talented man, abides transcending the understanding[6].

CHAPTER XXVI.

Brahman said:

That Mahat which was first produced, is (afterwards) called egoism; when it is born as (the feeling itself)[7] I, that is said to be the second creation. That egoism is stated to be the source of all entities[8],

---

[1] I.e., says Arguna Misra, the world of the understanding. Does this mean the world of Hiranyagarbha? The understanding is said to be the 'subtle body' of Hiranyagarbha (Vedânta Paribhâshâ, p. 46). Probably the reference spiritually interpreted is to the state in which egoism and all its products are non-existent.

[2] Literally, 'the high and holy passage to the great self.'

[3] The Mahat first manifests itself as Vishnu before it manifests itself as Brahman or Siva (Sânkhya-sâra, p. 16), hence he is said to be the Lord in the primary creation. It may be added, that in the Sânkhya-sâra where this passage is quoted the original word rendered 'cognition' above (khyâti) does not occur, but in lieu of it occurs Brahman. The sentence 'And the talented man' &c. is also wanting there.

[4] I.e. the understanding. See Sankara on Svetâsvatara, p. 329; Katha, p. 100.

[5] Source of enlightenment, Arguna Misra. Cf. Mundaka, pp. 303–308 (gloss).

[6] I.e. attaching himself to the Purusha, as the never-changing reality, and rising above Prakriti and its manifestations.

[7] I.e. when the Mahat develops into the feeling of self-consciousness—I—then it assumes the name of egoism.

[8] See on this Sânkhya-sâra, Hall's Introd. p. 31, note.

that from which the changes take place[1]; it is full of light, the supporter of consciousness; it is that from which the people are produced, the Pragâpati. It is a deity, the producer of the deities, and of the mind; it is the creator of the three worlds. That which feels[2] thus—'I am all this'—is called (by) that (name). That eternal world is for those sages who are contented with knowledge relating to the self, who have pondered on the self, and who are perfected by sacred study and sacrifice. By[3] consciousness of self one enjoys the qualities; and thus that source of all entities, the producer of the entities, creates (them): and as that from which the changes take place, it causes all this to move; and by its own light, it likewise charms the world.

---

[1] So Arguna Misra. Nîlakantha says it means 'born from the change, or development, viz. Mahat.' The Sânkhya-sâra, p. 17, however, shows it means 'appertaining to the quality of goodness.' See also Sânkhya-kârikâ 25, and commentary there, which is of great help here. The sense is this: Egoism is of three descriptions; it appertains to the quality of goodness, and as such is the creator of the deities and mind, the deities being those presiding over the ten senses (cf. Sânkhya-sâra, p. 17); it is full of light, or appertains to the quality of passion (cf. ibid.), and as such imparts to the other two qualities their virtue of activity (cf. Sânkhya-kârikâ commentary, p. 91, Târânâth's ed.); it is also of the quality of darkness, and as such the producer of the triple world (see ibid.). See Sânkhya-sûtra II, 17, 18, and comment, where a view somewhat different in one or two details is stated.

[2] Sânkhya-sâra, p. 16; Sânkhya-kârikâ 24, p. 89 (Târânâth's ed.).

[3] Arguna Misra says that the words Ahankâra &c. are here explained; qualities here means objects, as at Gîtâ, p. 55. The meaning of the first clause is, that the feeling that the objects are for oneself, and therefore enjoying them, gives the name of Ahankâra to the principle in question; its creation of all the elements gives it the name of Bhûtâdi. It is called Vaikârika, as the cause of the various activities and developments going on. The last clause seems to be an explanation of the epithet Taigasa, also applied to egoism.

CHAPTER XXVII.

Brahman said:

From egoism, verily, were the five great elements born—earth, air, space, water, and light as the fifth. In these five great elements, in the operations of (perceiving) sound, touch, colour, taste, and smell, creatures are deluded [1]. When, at the termination of the destruction of the great elements, the final dissolution approaches, O talented one! a great danger for all living beings arises [2]. Every entity is dissolved into that from which it is produced. They are born one from the other, and are dissolved in the reverse order [3]. Then when every entity, movable or immovable, has been dissolved, the talented men who possess a (good) memory [4] are not dissolved at all. Sound, touch, and likewise colour, taste, and smell as the fifth; the operations (connected with these) have causes [5], and are inconstant, and their name is delusion. Caused by the production of avarice [6], not different from one another [7], and insignificant [8], connected with flesh and blood, and depending upon one another,

---

[1] The contact of the objects of sense with the senses is the source of delusion.

[2] Cf. Gîtâ, p. 107, and note 1 there.

[3] Cf. Sânkhya-sûtra I, 121, and p. 387 infra.

[4] I.e. knowledge of the truth, Arguna Misra.

[5] Hence, as they have a beginning, they also must have an end, and hence they are inconstant.

[6] This and following epithets expand the idea of inconstancy.

[7] Being all in substance connected with the Prakriti, the material world, so to say.

[8] Containing no reality, Nîlakantha.

excluded from the self[1], these are helpless and powerless. The Prâ*n*a and the Apâna, the Udâna, the Samâna, and the Vyâna, these five winds also are joined to the inner self[2], and together with speech, mind, and understanding make the eight constituents of the universe[3]. He whose skin, nose, ear, eye, tongue, and speech are restrained, and whose mind is pure, and understanding unswerving[4], and whose mind is never burnt by these eight fires[5], he attains to that holy Brahman than which nothing greater exists. And the eleven organs, which are stated as having been produced from egoism—these, O twice-born ones! I will describe specifically. The ear, the skin, the two eyes, the tongue, the nose also as the fifth, the two feet, the organ of excretion, and the organ of generation, the two hands, and speech as the tenth; such is the group of organs, the mind is the eleventh. This group one should subdue first, then the Brahman shines (before him). Five (of these) are called the organs of perception, and five the

---

[1] Nîlaka*nt*h*a apparently takes the original here to mean of gross nature, not subtle, such as anything connected with the self would be. They are helpless and powerless without support from other principles, and mainly the self.

[2] He here states what is more closely connected with the self, and, as Nîlaka*nt*h*a puts it, accompanies the self till final emancipation. The inner self Nîlaka*nt*h*a takes to mean the self associated with egoism or self-consciousness.

[3] Nîlaka*nt*h*a cites certain texts to show that the perceptive senses work only through the mind, and that the objects of the senses are produced from the senses, and hence the universe, he says, is constituted of the eight enumerated above.

[4] I. e. from the truth.

[5] I. e. vexed by the operations of any of these.

organs of action. The five beginning with the ear are truly said to be connected with knowledge. And all the rest are without distinction connected with action. The mind should be understood to be among both[1], and the understanding is the twelfth. Thus have been stated the eleven organs in order. Understanding these[2], learned men think they have accomplished (everything). I will now proceed to state all the various organs. Space[3] is the first entity; as connected with the self it is called the ear; likewise as connected with objects (it is) sound; and the presiding deity there is the quarters. The second entity is air; it is known as the skin as connected with the self; as connected with objects (it is) the object of touch; and the presiding deity there is lightning. The third (entity) is said to be light; as connected with the self it is called the eye; next as connected with objects (it is) colour; and the presiding deity there is the sun. The fourth (entity) should be understood to be water; as connected with the self it is called the tongue; as connected with objects it is taste; and the presiding deity there is Soma. The fifth entity is earth; as connected with the self it is the nose; as connected with objects likewise it is smell; and the presiding deity there is the wind. Thus are the five entities stated to be divided among the three[4]. I will now proceed to state all the various organs.

---

[1] Cf. Sânkhya-kârikâ 27; Sânkhya-sâra, p. 17.

[2] Cf. Ka*th*a, p. 148.

[3] Cf. Lalita Vistara (translated by Dr. R. Mitra), p. 11.

[4] The above sentences show the entities in the three different aspects mentioned, which correspond to each other; the ear is the sense, that which is connected with the self; sound is the object of that sense, as connected with the external world; and the

As connected with the self, the feet are mentioned by Brâhma*n*as, who perceive the truth; as connected with objects it is motion; the presiding deity there is Vish*n*u. The Apâna wind, the motion of which is downward, as connected with the self, is called the organ of excretion; as connected with objects it is excretion [1]; and the presiding deity there is Mitra. As connected with the self the generative organ is mentioned, the producer of all beings; as connected with objects it is the semen; and the presiding deity there is Pra*g*âpati. Men who understand the Adhyâtma speak of the two hands as connected with the self; as connected with objects it is actions; and the presiding deity there is Indra. Then first, as connected with the self, is speech which relates to all the gods; as connected with objects it is what is spoken; and the presiding deity there is fire. As connected with the self they mention the mind, which follows after the five entities [2]; as connected with objects it is the mental operation; the presiding deity there is the moon. Likewise (there is) egoism, the cause of the whole course of worldly life, as connected with the self; as connected with objects, self-consciousness; the presiding deity there is Rudra. As connected with the self, they mention the understanding impelling the six senses [3];

quarters, Dik, are the deities presiding over the senses; as to this cf. Sâṅkhya-sâra, p. 17, and Vedânta Paribhâshâ, p. 45, which show some discrepancies. The distinctions of Adhyâtma &c. are to be found in the Upanishads; cf. inter alia, *Kh*ândogya, p. 227, and cf. Gîtâ, p. 77.

[1] As to the original word, cf. inter alia, *S*vetâ*s*vatara, pp. 197–202.

[2] This probably means the five senses which can perceive only when associated with the mind. See p. 268 supra.

[3] The understanding is called the charioteer at Ka*th*a, p. 111.

as connected with objects that which is to be understood; and the presiding deity there is Brahman. There are three seats for all entities—a fourth is not possible—land, water, and space. And the (mode of) birth is fourfold. Those born from eggs, those born from germs, those born from perspiration, and those born from wombs—such is the fourfold (mode of) birth of the group of living beings[1]. Now there are the inferior beings and likewise those moving in the air. Those should be understood to be born from eggs, as also all reptiles. Insects are said to be born from perspiration; and worms of the like description. This is said to be the second (mode of) birth, and inferior. Those beings, however, which are born after the lapse of some time, bursting through the earth, are said to be born from germs, O best of the twice-born! Beings of two feet or more than two feet, and those which move crookedly, are the beings born from wombs. Understand about them also, O best of men! The eternal seat (where) the Brahman[2] (is to be attained) should be understood to be twofold—penance[3] and meritorious action. Such is the doctrine of the learned. Action should be understood to be of various[4]

[1] Cf. *Kh*ândogya, pp. 404–406, and glosses; Aitareya, p. 243; Vedânta Paribhâshâ, p. 47; Sâṅkhya-sûtra V, 111; Manu I, 43; Max Müller's note at p. 94 of his *Kh*ândogya in this series.

[2] So Nîlaka*nth*a, but he also adds that this means birth as a Brâhma*n*a, which seems to be quite wrong. Ar*g*una Misra's 'means of acquiring Brahman' is right. See p. 369 infra.

[3] I. e., I presume, 'knowledge.' *S*aṅkara has so interpreted the word at Mu*nd*aka, p. 270, and Ka*th*a, p. 127, and elsewhere; and see Sanatsu*g*âtîya, p. 166 supra.

[4] Another reading is 'of two kinds.' But I prefer this, as three kinds are mentioned further on.

descriptions, (namely) sacrifice, gift at a sacrifice, and sacred study[1], for (every one) who is born[2]. Such is the teaching of the ancients. He who duly understands this, becomes possessed of concentration of mind, O chief of the twice-born! and know, too, that he is released from all sins. Space[3] is the first entity; as connected with the (individual) self it is called the ear; as connected with objects likewise it is called sound; and the presiding deity there is the quarters. The second entity is air; as connected with the (individual) self it is called the skin; as connected with objects it is the object of touch; and the presiding deity there is the lightning. The third is called light; as connected with the (individual) self it is laid down to be the eye; next as connected with objects it is colour; the presiding deity there is the sun. The fourth should be understood to be water; as connected with the (individual) self it is stated to be the tongue; as connected with objects it should be understood to be taste; the presiding deity there is Soma. The fifth element is earth; as connected with the (individual) self it is called the nose; as connected with objects likewise it is called smell; the presiding deity there is Vâyu. Thus have I

[1] Cf. as to this *Kh*ândogya, p. 136, which justifies our rendering, though the commentator Ar*g*una Mi*s*ra seems to understand the passage differently.

[2] Ar*g*una Mi*s*ra seems to understand this to mean 'twice-born.'

[3] This is a repetition of what occurs at p. 337, and apparently is spurious. But two of the MSS., both those containing commentaries, contain the passage twice. One of the other MSS. omits the passage where it occurs before, and has it here. I think that the passage is in its place before, and probably interpolated here.

accurately described to you the creation[1] as connected with the (individual) self. A knowledge of this, O ye who understand piety! is here obtained by those who possess knowledge. One should place all these together,. (viz.) the senses, the objects of the senses, and the five great elements, and hold them by the mind[2]. When everything is absorbed into the mind, the pleasures of (worldly) life[3] are not esteemed. The learned (men) whose understandings are possessed of knowledge esteem the pleasure derived from that[4]. Now[5] I shall proceed to describe that discarding of all entities by (means) gentle and hard[6], which produces attachment to subtle[7] (topics), and is sanctifying. The (mode of) conduct in which qualities are not (treated as) qualities[8], which is free from attachment, in which one lives alone[9], which is uninterrupted[10], and which is full of the Brahman[11], is called happiness (dwelling) in one aggregate[12].

---

[1] I am not quite sure that this is a correct rendering. But I can think of none better, and the commentators afford no help.

[2] Nîlaka*nth*a says, 'Thinking that the great elements are not distinct from the senses, one should hold them absorbed in the mind.' Arguna Mirra says, 'In the mind as their seat they should be placed,' as being not distinct from the mind, I presume. Cf. Ka*th*a, p. 148.

[3] Literally, 'birth.'

[4] From knowledge, I presume. The commentators afford no help.

[5] Arguna Mirra's text appears to commence a new chapter here.

[6] Such as meditation or upâsana, and prâ*n*âyama or restraint of life-winds respectively, Arguna Mirra.

[7] Cf. p. 310 supra.

[8] I. e. bravery, learning, &c. are treated as not being merits, as they cause pride, &c., Nîlaka*nth*a.

[9] I. e. in solitude, Nîlaka*nth*a; devoting oneself to the self only, Arguna Mirra. Cf. also p. 284 supra, note 4.

[10] Or, says Nîlaka*nth*a, free from any belief in distinctions.

[11] Another reading would mean 'which exists among Brâhma*n*as.'

[12] I. e. all collected together, I presume.

The learned man who absorbs objects of desire from all sides, as a tortoise (draws in) his limbs [1], and who is devoid of passion, and released from everything [2], is ever happy. Restraining objects of desire within the self [3], he becomes fit for assimilation with the Brahman [4], having his cravings destroyed, and being concentrated in mind, and friendly and affectionate [5] to all beings. The fire of the Adhyâtma [6] is kindled in a sage by his abandoning the country [7], and by the restraint of all the senses which hanker after objects of sense. As fire kindled with fuel shines forth with a great blaze, so the great self [8] shines forth through the restraint of the senses. When one with a tranquil self perceives all entities in one's own heart, then being self-illumined [9], one attains to that which is subtler than (the most) subtle (thing) [10], and than which there is nothing higher. It is settled, that the body in which the colour [11] is fire, the flowing [12]

[1] Cf. Gîtâ, pp. 50, 51, and *S*ânti Parvan (Moksha Dharma) I, 51, where the phrase is precisely the same as here.

[2] I. e. from all bonds, I suppose. See p. 292 supra.

[3] Cf. Gîtâ, p. 51. [4] Cf. Gîtâ, p. 110. [5] Cf. Gîtâ, p. 68.

[6] I. e. experience, Nîlaka*n*t*h*a. It means direct perception of the relations between the supreme and individual self. Cf. Gîtâ, p. 111.

[7] As opposed to forests. See Sanatsu*g*âtîya, p. 159, note 9.

[8] This must mean here the supreme self, apparently.

[9] I. e. being devoted to the self only, Ar*g*una Mi*s*ra. The ordinary meaning of the word, however, is one who has direct experience or perception without the aid of senses, &c. Cf. B*r*ihadâra*n*yaka, p. 765, and *S*ârîraka Bhâshya, pp. 648, 784, &c.

[10] Nîlaka*n*t*h*a says, 'The supreme Brahman which is subtler than the Brahman within the lotus-like heart.'

[11] I. e. that which perceives colour, viz. the sense, Ar*g*una Mi*s*ra. This applies to the analogous words coming further on.

[12] I. e. taste, says Ar*g*una Mi*s*ra, which seems to be more correct than Nîlaka*n*t*h*a's blood and such other liquid elements of the body.

(element) water, and the feeling of touch is air, the hideous holder of the mud[1] is earth, and likewise the sound is space; which is pervaded by disease and sorrow; which is surrounded by the five currents[2]; which is made up of the five elements; which has nine passages[3] and two deities[4]; which is full of passion; unfit to be seen[5]; made up of three qualities and of three constituent elements[6]; pleased with contacts[7]; and full of delusion[8]; —this same (body), which is difficult to move in this mortal world, and which rests on the real (entity)[9], is the very wheel of time which rotates in this world[10]. It is a great ocean, fearful and unfathomable, and is named[11] delusion. The world, together with the immortals, should cast it aside, curtail it,

[1] I. e. the flesh, bone, and so forth, Nîlakantha; the mucus in the nose, Arguna Misra.

[2] I. e. the senses. Cf. p. 238 supra, note 7.

[3] Cf. Gîtâ, p. 65. [4] See Sanatsugâtîya, p. 187 supra.

[5] As being unholy, Nîlakantha; as the bodies of Kândâlas &c. when seen are productive of sin, Arguna Misra. See p. 155 supra.

[6] Viz. vâta, pitta, sleshma, or wind, bile, and phlegm. The dhâtus are sometimes spoken of as seven. See Yoga-sûtras, p. 192; Taitt. Âr. p. 874, commentary, and p. 246 supra. See, too, however, Svetâsvatara, commentary, p. 287.

[7] Which is delighted only by contact with food and so forth, not otherwise, Nîlakantha.

[8] I. e. cause of delusion. The original word for 'it is settled' at the beginning of this sentence is otherwise rendered by Arguna Misra. He takes it to mean 'in this light (namely, as above stated) should one contemplate the body.' The other rendering is Nîlakantha's.

[9] I. e. the self, Arguna Misra; the understanding, Nîlakantha; difficult to move = difficult to adjust if attacked by disease, &c., Nîlakantha.

[10] It is owing to this body that the self becomes limited by time, Arguna Misra. Nîlakantha's gloss I do not follow. Cf. p. 187 supra, and p. 355 infra.

[11] I. e. characterised by delusion, Arguna Misra.

and restrain it[1]. Desire, wrath, fear, avarice, treachery, and falsehood also, (all these), which are difficult to get rid of, the good do get rid of by restraint of the senses[2]. And he who in this world has vanquished the three qualities and the five constituent elements[3], obtains the highest[4]—the infinite—seat in heaven. Crossing the river of which the five senses are the lofty banks, the agitation of mind[5] the mighty waters, and delusion the reservoir[6], one should vanquish both desire and wrath. Freed from all sins, he then perceives that highest (principle), concentrating the mind within the mind[7], and seeing the self within the self[8]. Understanding everything, he sees the self with the self in all entities as one[9], and also as various,

[1] I am not sure about the meaning here. Arguna Misra says, (reading visriget, 'send forth,' for vikshipet, 'cast aside,') 'send forth at the creation, curtail at the dissolution, and restrain at the final emancipation.' The commentary reads rodhayet, which we have adopted above. The text in the same copy, however, is bodhayet. Arguna Misra adds, as far as I can make out from an incorrect copy: 'as in this life everything is accomplished by these actions' (namely, I suppose, the casting aside, &c.). Nîlaka*nt*ha says, 'This same thing is the cause of creation, destruction, and knowledge,' reading bodhayet.

[2] Cf. Gîtâ, p. 57.

[3] I.e. the five great elements, as stated in Williams' Dictionary, citing Yâ*gñ*avalkya III, 145. See *S*ânti Parvan (Moksha), chap. 182, st. 16; chap. 184, st. 1.

[4] I.e. the seat of the Brahman, Nîlaka*nt*ha.

[5] See Gîtâ, p. 66, where the word is the same, viz. vega.

[6] From which, namely, the river issues. Cf. for the whole figure, *S*ânti Parvan (Moksha), chap. 251, st. 12.

[7] The mind = the lotus-like heart, Nîlaka*nt*ha. Cf. Gîtâ, p. 79. Concentrating = withdrawing from external objects, &c.

[8] I.e. in the body, Nîlaka*nt*ha. See p. 248.

[9] Cf. Gîtâ, p. 83, and note 4 there. Nîlaka*nt*ha says, 'as one, i.e.

changing from time to time[1]. He can always perceive (numerous) bodies like a hundred lights from one light. He verily is Vishnu, and Mitra, and Varuna, Agni, and Pragâpati. He is the supporter, and the creator. He is the lord whose faces are in all directions[2]. (In him) the great self—the heart of all beings—is resplendent. Him, all companies of Brâhmanas, and also gods, and demons, and Yakshas, and Pisâkas, and Pitris, and birds, and the bands of Rakshases, and the bands of Bhûtas[3], and also all the great sages, ever extol.

CHAPTER XXVIII.

Brahman said:

Among men the royal Kshatriya is the middle[4] quality; among vehicles the elephant[5], and among denizens of the forest the lion; among all sacrificial animals the sheep, and among the dwellers in holes the snake; among cattle also the bull, and among

---

by direct perception of the unity of the individual and supreme, and as various, i. e. in the all-comprehending form.'

[1] I. e. creating or acting, Arguna Misra. I think it probable that it was meant to go with the preceding words. See Gîtâ, p. 83 note; but, for this, 'changing' must be in the accusative. It is in the nominative. As the original stands, and on Arguna Misra's interpretation, the sense seems to be that when he is about to engage in the work of creation, he can obtain as many bodies as he likes. Nîlakantha compares *Khândogya*, p. 526. And see pp. 249, 327 supra. Can always perceive = invariably obtains when he wishes.

[2] Cf. Gîtâ, pp. 83, 93, and note 1 there.

[3] Cf. Gîtâ, pp. 85, 118.

[4] I. e. passion—that quality is dominant in the Kshatriya, Nîlakantha. See p. 329 supra.

[5] Commenting on Gîtâ V, 18 (p. 65) Sankara calls the elephant atyantatâmasa, belonging entirely to the quality of darkness.

females a male[1]. The Nyagrodha, the *G*ambu, the Pippala, and likewise the *S*âlmali, the *S*in*s*apâ, and the Meshas*ri*ṅga, and likewise the bamboo and willow[2]; these are the princes among trees in this world, there is no doubt of that. The Himavat, the Pâriyâtra, the Sahya, the Vindhya, the Trikû*t*avat, the *S*veta, the Nîla, the Bhâsa, and the Kosh*th*avat mountain, the Mahendra, the Guruskandha, and likewise the Mâlyavat mountain, these are the princes among mountains[3]. Likewise the Maruts are (the princes) among the Ga*n*as; the sun is the prince among the planets, and the moon[4] among the Nakshatras; Yama is the prince among the Pit*ri*s, and the ocean among rivers; Varu*n*a is the king of the waters, and Indra is said to be (the king) of the Maruts. Arka is the king of hot (bodies), and Indu is said to be (the king) of shining bodies. Fire is ever the lord of the elements[5], and B*ri*haspati of Brâhma*n*as; Soma is the lord of herbs, Vish*n*u is the chief among the strong; Tvash*t*r*i* is the prince

---

[1] As to the constructions here, cf. generally Gîtâ, p. 88, and see the remarks of Râmânu*g*a and *S*ridhara on Gîtâ X, 21. The meaning here is, of course, the male is ruler over females.

[2] I do not know what distinction is intended between these two. Generally kî*k*aka is used for the hollow bamboo, which whistles when the wind blows through it.

[3] Some of these mountains are mentioned in Pata*ñg*ali. See Introduction.

[4] This list may be compared with that at Gîtâ, chapter X. Sometimes the same object occurs more than once with reference to more than one class; thus the moon occurs as lord of Nakshatras, of shining bodies, and of herbs—unless Soma there stands for the Soma plant. See Gîtâ, p. 113. Ar*g*una Misra says expressly that the moon occurs more than once as the correlatives, the classes with reference to which she is mentioned, are different. In such cases I have kept the original names untranslated; Arka = sun; Indu = moon.

[5] Cf. Ka*th*a, p. 83.

of the Rudras, and *S*iva is the ruler of (all) creatures; likewise, sacrifice of (all) initiatory ceremonies[1], and Maghavat[2] likewise of the gods; the north among the quarters, and among all vipras the powerful king Soma[3]; Kubera (is lord) of all jewels, Purandara of (all) deities. Such is the highest creation among all entities. Pra*g*âpati (is lord) of all peoples; and of all entities whatever I, who am full of the Brahman, and great, (am lord). There is no higher being than myself or Vish*n*u. The great Vish*n*u full of the Brahman is the king of kings over all. Understand him to be the ruler, the creator, the uncreated Hari. For he is the ruler of men, Kinnaras, and Yakshas; of Gandharvas, snakes, and Rakshases; of gods, demons, and Nâgas. Among all those who are followed by (men) full of desires, (the chief) is[4] the great goddess Mâhe*s*varî, who has beautiful eyes. She is called Pârvatî. Know the goddess Umâ[5] to be the best and (most) holy of (all) females. Among women who are (a source[6] of) happiness, likewise, the brilliant[7] Apsarases (are chief). Kings desire

[1] This must mean, I presume, that the sacrifice is higher than the initiation, as male than female, see p. 346, note 1.

[2] This is another repetition. Indra has been mentioned before, and Purandara is mentioned further on.

[3] As to king Soma, see inter alia B*r*ihadâra*n*yaka, p. 237; *Kh*ândogya, p. 342, where *S*aṅkara explains 'king' by adding 'of Brâhma*n*as.' Vipras = Brâhma*n*as.

[4] I. e. Mâhe*s*varî is the most beautiful of womankind.

[5] It is well known that Umâ, Pârvatî, Mâhe*s*varî are names of the consort of the third member of the Hindu Trinity; see Kena, p. 13, and *S*aṅkara's comment there. See, too, Muir, Sanskrit Texts, vol. iv, p. 421, and Taittirîya-âra*n*yaka, p. 839.

[6] The idea of 'source' is supplied by Ar*g*una Mi*s*ra.

[7] Literally, 'rich.' Ar*g*una Mi*s*ra paraphrases it by '*G*yotishmatî.' Nîlaka*n*t*h*a's explanation here is not quite clear.

piety; and Brâhma*n*as are the bridges[1] of piety. Therefore a king should always endeavour to protect the twice-born[2]. Those kings in whose dominions good men lie low, lose all their qualifications[3], and go into wrong paths after death. But those high-souled kings in whose dominions good men are protected, rejoice in this world, and attain the infinite (seat) after death. Understand this, O chiefs of the twice-born! I shall now proceed to state the invariable characteristics of piety. Non-destruction is the highest piety[4], and destruction is of the nature of impiety. Enlightenment[5] is the characteristic of gods; action[6] the characteristic of men; sound is the characteristic of space; (the sensation of) touch is the characteristic of air; colour is the characteristic of light; taste is the characteristic of water; the characteristic of earth, the supporter of all beings, is smell; words are the characteristic of speech[7] refined into vowels and consonants; the characteristic of mind is thought. Likewise as to what is described here as understanding, a deter-

---

[1] I. e. instrumental in piety, or guides to piety. Cf. *S*vetâ*s*vatara, p. 370; Mu*nd*aka, p. 297.

[2] So literally, doubtless Brâhma*n*as only are intended here.

[3] I. e., I presume, they lose all their merits, their good points are destroyed by this dereliction of duty.

[4] Cf. p. 291 supra. Arguna Mi*s*ra begins a fresh chapter with 'I shall now,' &c.

[5] Knowledge of the truth, Arguna Mi*s*ra.

[6] I. e. action performed for the purpose of obtaining the fruit of it. The next five items refer to the five elements and their characteristic properties. Nîlaka*nt*ha's explanation, that all these are merely parallels not stated for their own relevancy here, but as illustrations, seems to be the only available one.

[7] I. e. the learning of other people, Nîlaka*nt*ha. The meaning seems to be that we know speech only in its manifestation in the form of words.

mination is here formed by (that) understanding about objects which have been thought over by the mind[1]. And there is no doubt of this that determination is the characteristic of the understanding. The characteristic of mind is meditation[2]; and the characteristic of a good man is (living) unperceived[3]. The characteristic of devotion is action[4]; and knowledge the characteristic of renunciation. Therefore a man of understanding should practise renunciation, giving prominence to knowledge[5]. The renouncer possessed of knowledge attains the highest goal. And crossing beyond darkness, and transcending death and old age, he repairs to that which has no second[6]. Thus have I duly spoken to you concerning the characteristic of piety. I will now proceed to explain properly the comprehension[7] of the qualities. As to the smell of the earth, verily, that is comprehended by the nose; and the wind[8] likewise residing in the nose is appointed[9] to the knowledge of smell. Taste[10],

---

[1] The text here is rather unsatisfactory; I have adopted that which I find in the copy containing Arguna Misra's commentary.

[2] Frequent pondering on matters learnt from Sâstras or common life, Nîlakantha. Why mind comes twice the commentators do not explain.

[3] Does this refer to what is said at Sanatsugâtîya, p. 159?

[4] Devotion means here, as in the Gîtâ, action without desire of fruits. For action the word here is the same as at Gîtâ, p. 115, note 2.

[5] Cf. Gîtâ, p. 52, note 7.

[6] This is Arguna Misra's interpretation, and appears to me to be correct. Nîlakantha's is different, but seems to omit all account of abhyeti, 'repairs.'

[7] Arguna Misra's interpretation seems to be different, but our copy is not quite intelligible.

[8] See p. 337 supra. The wind is the presiding deity of the nasal organ.

[9] I. e. that is its function. Arguna Misra says, 'it is pondered on,' which is not clear.

[10] Cf. Gitâ, p. 74, as to taste and water.

the essence of water, is always comprehended by the tongue. And the moon likewise, who resides in the tongue, is appointed to the knowledge of taste. The quality of light is colour, and that is comprehended by the eye; and the sun residing in the eye is appointed always to the knowledge of colour. The (sensation of) touch, belonging to the air, is perceived by the skin, and the wind[1] residing in the skin is always appointed to the knowledge of (the objects) of touch. The quality of space is sound, and that is comprehended by the ear. And all the quarters residing in the ear are celebrated as (being appointed) to the knowledge of sound. Thought is the quality of mind, and that is comprehended by the understanding. The supporter of consciousness[2] residing in the heart is appointed to the knowledge of mind[3]. The understanding (is comprehended in the form of) determination, and the Mahat[4] of knowledge. To (this) positive comprehension, the unperceived[5] (is appointed), there is no doubt of that. The Kshetrag*ñ*a, which is in its essence devoid of qualities and eternal, is not to be comprehended by any

[1] This cannot be the presiding deity here, though one expects such deity to be mentioned; see p. 337 supra.

[2] The text of more than one of the lines here is rather doubtful; we follow Nîlaka*n*t*h*a, who takes this to mean the *g*îva, the individual soul. Cf. p. 239, note 2 supra.

[3] I. e. thought, as Nîlaka*n*t*h*a points out.

[4] Mahat is properly the same as buddhi, understanding, but as it is here mentioned separately, I suppose, it signifies Ahaṅkâra. Nîlaka*n*t*h*a takes its operation, here called knowledge, to mean 'the feeling I am,' which agrees with our interpretation, for which some support is also to be derived from p. 333 supra.

[5] I here follow Ar*g*una Misra, though somewhat diffidently. The knowledge 'this is I,' and the knowledge 'this is so and so and nothing else' is presided over by the unperceived—the Prak*ri*ti.

symbols. Therefore the characteristic of the Kshetragña, which is void of symbols[1], is purely knowledge. The unperceived is stated to be the Kshetra[2] in which the qualities are produced and absorbed. And I always see, know, and hear it, (though) concealed. The Purusha knows it, therefore is he called Kshetragña[3]. And the Kshetragña likewise perceives all the operations of the qualities[4]. The qualities created again and again, do not know themselves[5], being non-intelligent, to be created and tied down to a beginning, middle, and end[6]. Only the Kshetragña attains, no one (else) attains, to the truth, which is great, transcendent, and beyond the qualities and the entities (produced)[7] from the qualities. Hence a man who understands piety, abandoning qualities, and the creation[8], in this world, and transcending the qualities, and having his sins destroyed, then enters into the Kshetragña. One who is free from the pairs of opposites, free from the ceremony of salutations, and

---

[1] See Sanatsugâtîya, p. 146. See also p. 309 supra.

[2] See Gîtâ, p. 102 seq. [3] I. e. he who knows the Kshetra.

[4] Enlightenment, activity, and delusion, Nîlakantha.

[5] I. e. do not know the self, Nîlakantha; better, I think, 'the qualities do not know themselves, only the Kshetragña knows them.' Cf. Sânti Parvan (Moksha Dharma), chap. 194, st. 41.

[6] I. e. production, existence, and destruction, Nîlakantha. This must, however, mean their manifestation, continuance, and dissolution in any particular form. For the prakriti, which is made up of the three qualities, is beginningless. Cf. Gîtâ, p. 104.

[7] I. e. the actual physical manifestations, as we may say, of the qualities.

[8] The original, sattva, Nîlakantha renders by buddhi, and qualities by visible objects. In the familiar Sânkhya phrase sattvapurushânyatâpratyaya sattva means creation, or what is other than purusha (cf. Sânkhyatattvakaumudî, pp. 9–144). That is the meaning here. See too p. 371 infra, and Sânti Parvan (Moksha Dharma), chap. 194, st. 38 seq. and comments there.

from the svâhâ ceremony[1], who is unmoving, and homeless[2], is the Kshetragña, he is the Supreme Lord.

CHAPTER XXIX.

Brahman said:

I will state truly all about that which has a beginning, middle, and end[3], and about the means for its comprehension, together with names and characteristics[4]. It is stated that day was first and then night; that months have the bright[5] first, the Nakshatras Sravana[6] as the first (among them), and the seasons the winter as the first (among them). The earth is the source[7] of smells, water of tastes, the light (of) the sun is the source of colours, the wind is stated to be the source of (the feelings of) touch; likewise space is the source of sound. These are the qualities of the elements. Now I shall proceed to state the highest and first of all entities. The sun is

[1] See p. 324 supra.

[2] See Gîtâ, p. 101. Unmoving probably means 'not perturbed by the qualities' (Gîtâ, p. 110), or perhaps the same thing as 'of steady mind' at Gîtâ, p. 101. The sense is pretty much the same in both places.

[3] Which has birth &c., Nîlakantha, i.e. all the creation, I presume.

[4] The names, that is to say, of the various elements, and their qualities.

[5] This must mean fortnights.

[6] This is specified, says Arguna Misra, as the six months of the northern solstice are caused by the sun being at this Nakshatra. As to those six months, cf. Gîtâ, p. 81. For the same reason, Arguna Misra adds, the winter season is mentioned as the best.

[7] The word âdi, literally beginning, is used in the whole of this passage in different senses; it means the source, it means the best, and it means the first in order.

the first among shining bodies[1]; fire is said to be the first of the elements[2]; Sâvitrî[3] of all branches of learning; Pragâpati of deities; the syllable Om of all the Vedas; and the Prâ*n*a life-wind, of all words[4]; whatever is prescribed in this world, all that is called Sâvitrî[5]. The Gâyatrî is the first among metres; among (sacrificial) animals, the goat[6] is mentioned (as the first). Cows are the first among quadrupeds, and the twice-born among men[7]. The *S*yena is first among birds; among sacrifices, the offering (into the fire) is the best; and among all reptiles, O best of the twice-born! the snake[8] is the highest. Of all ages the K*ri*ta is the first, there is no doubt of that. Among all precious things, gold (is the first), and among vegetable (products) likewise the barley seed[9]. Among all things to be eaten or swallowed food is the highest; and of

[1] This should be compared with the enumeration at p. 345 supra, and that in the Gîtâ there referred to.

[2] Cf. p. 346 supra. Nîlaka*n*/*h*a takes fire to mean the gastric fire, and bhûta, rendered by us elements, to mean the species of beings born from eggs and wombs.

[3] The famous verse 'Tat savitur,' &c. See inter alia B*ri*hadâra*n*yaka, p. 999; Âpastamba I, 1, 1, 9; Manu II, 77 seq., 104–170.

[4] See pp. 264, 265 supra.

[5] Here he turns back to the Sâvitrî, 'looking back in the manner of the lion,' says Nîlaka*n*/*h*a, and for purposes of upâsanâ. He does not give up the thread of his discourse entirely, but simply interjects this little clause. Nîlaka*n*/*h*a adds, Sâvitrî here includes every mode of worship prescribed for Brâhma*n*as, &c., and even for Mle*kkh*as. Cf. note 3, and Gautama (Bühler's ed.), p. 174 note.

[6] Cf. *Kh*ândogya, p. 109, and *S*aṅkara's commentary. Arguna Mi*s*ra compares this text, Tasmâdesha eteshâm pa*s*unâm *s*resh/*h*a-tamoga*h*. Where it occurs I know not.

[7] Cf. *S*ânti Parvan (Râgadharma), chap. 11, st. 11.

[8] I.e. Vâsuki, Nîlaka*n*/*h*a. More probably it refers to the species.

[9] As it is used in various ceremonies.

all liquid substances which are to be drunk, water is the best. And among all immovable entities, without distinction, the Plaksha, the ever holy field of Brahman [1], is stated to be the first. I, too, (am the first) among all the patriarchs [2], there is no doubt of that. And the unthinkable, self-existent Vishnu is stated to be my own self. Of all mountains, the great Meru is stated to be the first-born. And among all quarters and sub-quarters, likewise, the eastern quarter [3] is the first. Likewise the Gangâ going in three paths is stated to be the first-born among rivers. And likewise of all wells and reservoirs of water, the ocean is the first-born. And of all gods, Dânavas, Bhûtas, Pisâkas, snakes, and Rakshases, and of men, Kinnaras, and Yakshas, Îsvara [4] is the lord. The great Vishnu, who is full of the Brahman, and than whom there is no higher being in these three worlds, is the source of all the universe. Of all orders [5], that of householders (is the first), there is no doubt of that. The unperceived is the source of the worlds; and the same is also the end of everything. Days end with (the sun's) setting [6]; the night ends with (the sun's) rising; the end of pleasure is ever grief;

[1] I.e. the Creator; his field means, I presume, his special seat.

[2] Beings from whom all creatures were born. See inter alia Sânti Parvan (Moksha Dharma), chap. 208, st. 5; Manu I, 34.

[3] At p. 347 the north is mentioned. Arguna Misra has 'ûrdhva,' or upward here, and yet 'north' before. Is the north the best as the seat of the higher world mentioned at Sânti Parvan (Moksha Dharma), chap. 192, st. 8 seq.?

[4] I.e. Rudra, says Nilakantha.

[5] Viz. Brahmakârin, householder, forester, and Samnyâsin. Cf. Sânti Parvan (Moksha), ch. 191, st. 10; Manu VI, 89; Gautama, p. 190.

[6] These stanzas also occur in the Sânti Parvan, chap. 27, st. 31 seq. (Râgadharma). A part of them appears to be quoted in Sânkhya-sûtra V, 80. And the commentator Vigñâna Bhikshu introduces it with the expression 'iti srûyate.' But it is not a Vedic text.

the end of grief ever pleasure. All accumulations end in exhaustion; all ascents end in falls; all associations end in dissociations; and life ends in death. All action ends in destruction; death is certain for whatever is born[1]; (everything) movable or immovable in this world is ever transient. Sacrifice, gift, penance, study, observances, and regulations, all this ends in destruction[2]. There is no end for knowledge. Therefore one whose self is tranquil, whose senses are subjugated, who is devoid of (the idea that this or that is) mine, who is devoid of egoism, is released from all sins by pure knowledge.

CHAPTER XXX.

Brahman said:

The wheel of life[3] moves on; a wheel of which the spoke is the understanding, of which the pole[4] is the mind, of which the bonds are the group of the senses, of which the outer rim[5] is the five great elements, of which the environment is home[6]; which

[1] Cf. Gîtâ, p. 45.

[2] All this is action, the fruit of which is perishable; the fruit of knowledge, on the other hand, is everlasting.

[3] Literally, time; it seems, however, to stand for the vicissitudes of worldly life. Cf. *S*vetâ*s*vatara, p. 283. The body is called 'wheel of time' at p. 53 supra, but Arguna Mi*s*ra there says 'it is the wheel which causes the rotation of the wheel of time.'

[4] The cause of its being large in dimensions, Arguna Mi*s*ra; the supporting pillar, Nîlaka*n*t*h*a. I prefer the former, and take the sense to be that worldly life is co-extensive with the operations or 'fancies' of the mind.

[5] What is outside the elements, the physical manifestations of Prak*ri*ti, is beyond the domain of worldly life.

[6] The possession of 'home' is equivalent to a dwelling in the midst of worldly life. Hence the idea of homelessness at inter alia Gîtâ, pp. 101–103.

abounds in old age and grief, which moves in the midst of disease and misfortune, which rotates in[1] space and time; the noise of which is trouble and toil, the rotations[2] of which (constitute) day and night; which is encircled with cold and heat; of which pleasure and pain are the joints, and hunger and thirst the nails fixed into it, of which sunshine and shade are the ruts; which staggers in the opening or closing of an eyelid, which is enveloped in the fearful waters of delusion, which is ever revolving and void of consciousness[3], which is measured by months and half months, is ever-changing[4], which moves through (all) the worlds[5]; the mud[6] for which is penance and regulations, the mover of which is the force of the quality of passion[7]; which is lit up[8] by the great egoism, which is sustained by the qualities; the fastenings in which are vexations[9];

---

[1] This means, I presume, that worldly life is conditioned, so to say, by space and time. See p. 343 supra.

[2] I.e. the cause of the rotation, Nîlakantha.

[3] I.e. unintelligent.

[4] Now takes the form of a man, now of an animal, and then of some other thing, Nîlakantha. I think, however, that the meaning is, that it is not alike to all; different persons are in different states in this world.

[5] Arguna Misra says this means that it is the cause of the movements in all the worlds. That is the sense I extract from his words, which are not quite clear, lokânâm samkarane hetus. The rendering in the text follows Nîlakantha.

[6] I.e., I presume, that which retards the revolutions of the 'wheel.' Instead of 'penance,' Nîlakantha's reading is 'the quality of darkness.'

[7] Cf. Sânkhya-kârikâ, p. 13, and Vâkaspati's commentary thereon.

[8] 'Animated,' Nîlakantha. Egoism is the cause of the world, and of all knowledge of it. Cf. Sânkhya-kârikâ, p. 24.

[9] The text here is unsatisfactory. I follow Nîlakantha, who says 'vexations=those arising from not obtaining what is desired.'

which revolves in the midst of grief and destruction [1], which is full of actions and instruments of action [2], which is large, and which is extended by means of attachments [3], which is rendered unsteady by avarice and desire [4], which is produced by ignorance of various (matters) [5], which is attended upon by fear and delusion, and which is the cause of the delusion of all beings, which moves towards joy and pleasure [6], which has desire and wrath as its appurtenances, which is made up of (the entities) beginning with the Mahat and ending with the gross elements [7], which is unchecked, the imperishable source (of all) [8], the speed of which is like that of the mind, and which is (never) fatigued. This wheel of life, which is associated with the pairs of opposites, and which is devoid of consciousness, all the world, together with the immortals, should cast away, abridge, and check [9]. That man, among all creatures, who always

---

[1] Revolves in the midst of, = lives upon, is fed by, Nîlakan*th*a.

[2] I.e. the organs of action, I presume.

[3] The more attachments one has, the more one is tied down to worldly life, and the more comprehensive such life becomes.

[4] Avarice is coveting another's wealth when one has one's own; desire is the wish for that which one has not.

[5] Nîlakan*th*a reads 'vi*k*itra,' which he renders to mean diversified, as being made up of the three qualities, ignorance there being the same thing as Prak*ri*ti, which is probably a better sense altogether than that obtainable from Ar*g*una Mi*s*ra's reading.

[6] Which moves by attachment to external pleasures, &c., Nîlakan*th*a. See p. 300 supra.

[7] I.e. all the world developed from Prak*ri*ti—a common phrase.

[8] This is Nîlakan*th*a's forced meaning. But the text here is doubtful. Perhaps the sense is 'in which production and dissolution are going on unchecked.'

[9] See p. 344 note. For the last word, the variant here is sthâpayet, make steady or stop.

accurately understands the movement and stoppage[1] of the wheel of life is never deluded. (That) sage, released from all impressions[2], transcending all pairs of opposites, and released from all sins, attains the highest goal. The householder, and the Brahma*k*ârin, the forester, and also the beggar[3], all these four orders are stated to have the order of householder for their basis. Whatever system of rules[4] is prescribed in this world, to follow it is good; this has been celebrated from ancient times[5]. He who has been first refined by ceremonies[6], and who has duly observed vows, being (born) in a caste of (high) qualifications[7], and who understands the Vedas, should return[8] (from his preceptor's house). Always devoted to his own wife, behaving like[9] good men, with his senses restrained, and full of faith, one should perform the five sacrifices[10] in this world. The sage who eats what remains after (offerings) to deities[11] and guests, who is devoted to Vedic rites, who duly performs sacrifices and

---

[1] I.e. the causes of the revolution and stoppage, Nîlaka*nth*a.

[2] Impressions of previous actions, delusions, &c. And see p. 247 supra.

[3] I.e. the Samnyâsin. [4] *S*âstra. Cf. Gîtâ, p. 117.

[5] 'Such is the eternal fame,' literally.

[6] I.e. on whom the Vedic rites or Sa*m*skâras are duly performed. And see Gîtâ, p. 122.

[7] I.e. one of the three higher castes.

[8] The original is the technical word for the return of a Brahma*k*ârin after finishing his studies. He is describing the 'householder.'

[9] I.e. following the rule of conduct sanctioned by the good.

[10] Vide Williams' Dictionary, s.v. mahâyag*ñ*a; Âsvalâyana G*ri*hya III, 1, 3; Manu II, 69; IV, 21.

[11] Cf. Gîtâ, p. 62; a guest must always be fed, and unless he is satisfied the host must not eat. Cf. *S*ânti Parvan (Moksha), chap. 192, st. 15; Manu III, 106; Âpastamba II, 3, 7, 3.

gifts according to his means, who is not thoughtlessly active[1] with the hand or foot, who is not thoughtlessly active with the eye, and who is not thoughtlessly active with his speech or any of his limbs, to such a one the (word) good applies. One should always have the sacred thread and a clean cloth, and be of pure vows, and self-restrained, and should always associate with good men, making gifts, and with one's external organs restrained; one should restrain one's lust and hunger[2], should be kind, should behave like the good, and keep a bamboo stick and a water-pot filled with water[3]. One should learn and teach, should likewise perform sacrifices and officiate at others' sacrifices, and should give and receive gifts,—(thus) one should adopt the sixfold mode of life[4]. Know that three (of these) duties are the means of livelihood for Brâhmaṇas, the two teaching and officiating at sacrifices, and also receiving untainted gifts[5]. And as to the other remaining three duties, gift, study, and sacrifice, they are pious[6] duties. With regard to those three duties, the sage who understands piety, who is self-restrained, kind, possessed of forgiveness, and equable to all creatures, should avoid heedlessness[7]. The

[1] The same word as at Gîtâ, p. 114, there rendered 'vain activity.'

[2] Cf. Âpastamba II, 1, 1, 2 seq.

[3] Cf. Manu IV, 36; Âpastamba II, 1, 1, 15.

[4] These are the well-known six duties of Brâhmaṇas as specified by Manu and others. See the discussion of this point in the Introduction.

[5] Another reading is 'gifts from an untainted (source).'

[6] What is the exact meaning of this here? I suppose the meaning is that the performance of them is a pure performance of duty; the others are duties the performance of which supplies one's own wants, and is therefore interested. Cf. Gautama X, 1 and 2.

[7] I.e. omission or mistake in performance.

Brâhmana householder, who is of rigid vows, who is thus devoted, discharging all these duties as much as is in his power, conquers heaven.

Chapter XXXI.

Brahman said:

Thus[1] duly studying to the best of his power, in the way above[2] stated, and likewise living as a Brahmakârin, one who is devoted to his own duty and learned, who is a sage with all his senses restrained, who applies himself to what is agreeable and beneficial to the preceptor, who is pure[3], and constant in veracity and piety, should, with the permission of the preceptor, take food without decrying it[4], should eat (the leavings) of sacrificial offerings, and alms, and should stand, sit, and take exercise[5] (duly), should sacrifice twice to the fire after becoming clean and with a concentrated (mind), and should always bear a staff of the Bilva or Palâsa[6] (wood). The clothing of the twice-born (man) should be of linen, or of cotton, or also a deerskin, or a cloth entirely (dyed with) reddish colour. There should also be a girdle of muñga; he should have matted hair, and likewise always (carry) water (with him), and have his sacred thread, be engaged in sacred

[1] Arguna Misra says, 'Having described first the order of householder, as that is the chief, he now describes that of Brahmakârin.' Cf. Âpastamba II, 9, 21, 1, and note.

[2] Where? This is obscure.

[3] Both internally and externally, I presume.

[4] Cf. Taittirîya, p. 129; Sânti Parvan (Moksha), chap. 192, st. 6.

[5] Cf. Gîtâ, p. 69. Arguna Misra says, 'Having exercise by means of standing and sitting; the meaning is not sleeping except at the proper time.'

[6] Cf. Manu II, 41 seq.

study, and free from avarice, and of rigid observances. (Such) a Brahma*k*ârin, always making offerings likewise of pure water to satisfy the deities, being restrained in mind[1], is esteemed. One who is thus devoted[2], who is concentrated in mind, and continent[3], conquers heaven, and reaching the highest seat, does not return to birth. Refined by means of all ceremonies, and likewise living as a Brahma*k*ârin[4], a sage who has renounced[5] (all) should go out of towns and dwell in forests[6]. Wearing a skin or the bark of a tree, he should bathe (every) morning and evening, and always living within the forest, should not enter a town again. He should honour guests, and should also give them shelter at (the proper) time, living on fruits and leaves, and roots and *S*yâmâka grain. He should without sloth feed on water, air, and all forest-products down to grass as they come, in order[7], in accordance with the (regulations[8] at his) initiation. He should honour a guest who comes, by (giving him) water accompanied with roots, fruits, and leaves. And he should always without sloth give alms out of whatever he has for food. He should also eat always after the deities and guests[9]

[1] Or it may be, 'being self-restrained and with (all his) heart.' The constructions in the original vary greatly, and so they do in the translation.

[2] Applying himself to his duties.

[3] Cf. Maitrî, p. 18, and comment there.

[4] Cf. Manu VI, 1 seq.

[5] I.e. who is a mendicant ascetic.

[6] Cf. p. 173 supra, note 9. Here he gives a description of the third order of forester, as to which compare generally Manu VI.

[7] First the jungle-products, then air, &c., Ar*g*una Misra. The sense seems to be that the restrictions should become gradually harder. Cf. Manu VI, 24–31; Âpastamba II, 9, 22, 2 seq.; II, 9, 23, 2.

[8] I.e. whatever restriction he put on himself when entering upon the particular mode of life.

[9] Supra, p. 358, and cf. Taittirîya, p. 38.

(are satisfied) and with his speech restrained, having a mind free from envy[1], eating little, and depending on the deities. Restraining the external senses, kind, full of forgiveness, preserving his hair and moustache, performing sacrifices, addicted to sacred study, and devoted to veracity and piety, pure in body[2], always dexterous[3], always in forests, and concentrated in mind,—a forester whose senses are subdued and who is thus devoted[4] conquers the worlds.

A householder, or a Brahma*k*ârin, or again a forester, who wishes to apply himself to final emancipation should adopt the best (line of) conduct[5]. Offering safety to all beings, the sage should become free from all action[6], and be agreeable to all beings, kind, and restrained in all his senses. He should make a fire[7] and feed on the alms (obtained) without asking[8] and without trouble[9], and which have come spontaneously[10], in a place free from smoke and where people have already[11] eaten. One who

[1] I.e. of others for obtaining more, and so forth. Ar*g*una Mi*s*ra's reading is different, and he renders it to mean, 'one by whom the rule of life as a Brahma*k*ârin has not been violated.'

[2] Ar*g*una Mi*s*ra's reading, 'one who has cast away (all attachment to) the body.' Compare as to hair and moustache, Manu VI, 6 seq.

[3] See Gîtâ, p. 127. Here the meaning is probably assiduous in the performance of duties, vows, and so forth.

[4] I.e. applies himself to his duties.

[5] Ar*g*una Mi*s*ra says this means ânandâ*s*ramam, but there must be some bad copying here. I take the word as it stands to mean something like the 'godlike endowments' at Gîtâ, p. 114.

[6] See Gîtâ, pp. 54, 127. The meaning here is probably that of action without egoism. See Gîtâ, p. 55.

[7] I.e. Ar*g*una Mi*s*ra says, 'not at night.' The readings are unsatisfactory. I read k*ri*tvâ vahnim, but diffidently. Is the allusion to the rule at Âpastamba II, 9, 21, 10? Cf. Gautama III, 27.

[8] Cf. Kaushîtaki, p. 32. [9] I.e. to the giver. Cf. Gîtâ, p. 120.

[10] See Gîtâ, p. 10. [11] Cf. Manu VI, 56; Gautama III, 15.

understands final emancipation should seek to obtain alms after the cleaning[1] of the vessels (used for cooking), and should not rejoice if he obtains, and should not be dejected if he does not obtain (alms). Nor should he beg for too much alms[2], seeking merely to sustain life. Eating only a little, he should go about for alms with a concentrated mind, looking out for the (proper) time. He should not wish for earnings in common with another, nor should he eat when honoured; for an ascetic should be averse from all earnings (accompanied) with honour[3]. When eating, he should not taste any articles of food which have been eaten by others[4], or which are pungent, astringent, or bitter, and likewise no sweet juices. He should eat just enough for his livelihood—for the support of life. One who understands final emancipation should seek for a livelihood without obstructing (other) creatures; and when he goes about for alms, he should not go following after another[5]. He should not parade (his) piety, he should move about in a secluded place, free from passion. He should resort for shelter to an empty house, or a forest, or the foot of a tree, or a river likewise, or the cavern of a mountain. In summer, (he should pass) but a single night[6] in a town; and in the rains, he may dwell in one place. He should move about the

[1] I.e., I presume, in order to avoid interfering with others' comforts. And see last note.

[2] See Manu VI, 55. As to proper time further on, see last note.

[3] Cf. Sanatsugâtîya, pp. 145–147; 'without respect' at Gîtâ, p. 120, means probably with disrespect, otherwise that passage and this would be somewhat inconsistent. See too Manu II, 162.

[4] Cf. Manu II, 56; Gîtâ, p. 118; and p. 269 supra.

[5] As that other may get nothing if they go together, Arguna Misra. Cf. Manu VI, 51.

[6] Cf. Gautama III, 21.

world like a worm [1], his path being pointed out by the sun, and he should walk with circumspection over the earth out of compassion to all beings [2]. He should not make any accumulations; and should eschew dwelling with friends [3]. And the man who understands final emancipation should verily do all acts which he has to do, always with clean water. A man should always bathe in clean water. And with his senses restrained, he should devote himself to these eight observances [4],—harmlessness, life as a Brahma*k*ârin, veracity, and also straightforwardness, freedom from anger, freedom from (the habit of) carping, restraint of the external organs, and habitual freedom from (the habit of) backbiting. He should always practise a sinless (mode of) conduct, not deceptive and not crooked; and free from attachment should always make one who comes (as a guest) take a morsel of food. He should eat just enough for livelihood—for the support of life. And he should eat (only) what has been obtained with piety [5], and should not follow his own (mere) desire [6]. He should not accept anything at all other than food and clothing. And he should accept as much as he eats and no more. He should not receive from others, nor should he ever give to others [7].

---

[1] I.e. not very fast, Ar*g*una Mi*s*ra; 'the path being pointed out by the sun'=not at night, for fear of destroying worms, &c.

[2] This seems to be very like the practice of the *G*ainas of the present day. And cf. Manu VI, 69.

[3] Cf. Gîtâ, pp. 68–103.

[4] Cf. Gîtâ, p. 114, and cf. also Sanatsu*g*âtîya, p. 153.

[5] That is to say, obtained without violation of any binding obligation, or rule of the *S*âstras.

[6] Cf. Gîtâ, p. 117.

[7] This is not very clear, and Ar*g*una Mi*s*ra's comments are not intelligible. The sense seems to be this, 'He should not take more than is wanted, nor should he keep any accumulations from which to give to others, but should at once share with others all that is earned.'

But owing to the helplessness of people, a wise man should always share (with others). He should not appropriate another's riches, and should not take (anything) unasked. Nor, verily, after enjoying any object should one become afterwards attached to it. One who has anything to do[1] should take earth, water, pebbles likewise, and leaves, flowers, and fruits which are not secured[2] (by anybody), as they come[3]. One should not live by the occupation of an artisan[4], nor should one wish for gold. One should not hate, should not teach[5], and should be void of (all) belongings[6]. One should eat what is consecrated by faith[7], and should avoid (all) controversies, should act without a purpose[8], should be free from attachment, and without fixed appointments with people[9]. One should not perform, or cause to be performed, any action involving expectation of fruit, or involving any destruction of life, or the assemblage of people[10]. Rejecting all things,

[1] Arguna Misra says that this means if he wants them for any particular purpose he should take the earth, &c.

[2] I.e. apparently, taken possession of and preserved as one's own by anybody.

[3] Arguna Misra renders this by 'which lead to action.' Is it not rather the 'spontaneous earnings' at Gîtâ, p. 60?

[4] Cf. Manu III, 64; Âpastamba I, 6, 18, 18; Gautama XVII, 7.

[5] I.e. teach one who does not ask to be instructed. Cf. Manu II, 110.

[6] Cf. Gîtâ, p. 60; the original word, however, is not the same.

[7] See p. 360, note 3 supra; Manu II, 54-55; Gautama IX, 59. 'Controversies;' the original is nimitta, and the interpretation is what appears to be Arguna Misra's. It may also mean 'omens.' That this is the true sense appears from Manu VI, 50.

[8] Cf. Gîtâ, p. 48.

[9] Arguna Misra says, 'e.g. I shall come to you to-morrow for alms,' &c. Cf. Âpastamba I, 6, 19, 12.

[10] The words are the same as at Gîtâ, p. 54, 'keeping people (to

and being equable to all beings, moving and unmoving, one should become an ascetic with small belongings. One should not perturb any other (person), nor should one be perturbed by any other (person[1]). He who is trusted by all beings is said to be the foremost among those who understand final emancipation. One should not think of what is not come[2], nor reflect on that which is past; one should disregard the present, being concentrated (in mind) and indifferent to time[3]. He should not defile[4] anything by the eye, or the mind, or by speech, nor should he do anything wrong openly or in secret. One who draws in the senses from all sides as a tortoise (draws in) his limbs[5], and in whom the senses, mind, and understanding are absorbed[6], who is free from desires, who understands all truth, who is free from the pairs of opposites, and from the ceremony of svâhâ, and who is free from salutations[7], and who is free from (the thought that this or that is) mine, who is free from egoism, who is free from anxiety for new acquisitions or protection of old acquisitions, and self-controlled[8], who is free from

their duties),' but the sense seems to be different. The commentators say nothing on this.

[1] Cf. Gîtâ, p. 101.

[2] I.e. one should not look to the future with any aspirations or expectations, and should not look back on the past with grief. Arguna Misra. See too p. 170, note 9 supra.

[3] I am not sure if this is a correct interpretation. But it does not seem likely that the other possible sense—literally 'expecting time'—can be intended here.

[4] This is obscure. Is the sense this, that one should not observe, or think, or speak badly or of the bad side of things?

[5] Cf. p. 342 supra, note 1.

[6] Cf. Ka*th*a, p. 151.

[7] See p. 352 supra, note 1.

[8] Cf. Gîtâ, p. 48, where the original words are the same.

expectations, who is free from attachments to any entity, and who is dependent on none[1], who is attached to the self, and who understands the truth, is emancipated, there is no doubt of that. Those who perceive the self, which is without hands, foot, or back, without a head, without a stomach, which is free from the operations of the qualities[2], absolute, untainted, and stable, devoid of smell, devoid of taste or touch, devoid of colour, and also devoid of sound, which is to be understood[3], which is unattached, and which is also devoid of flesh, which is free from anxiety[4], imperishable, divine, and though dwelling in a house[5], always dwelling in all entities, they never die[6]. There the understanding reaches not, nor the senses, nor the deities, nor Vedas, sacrifices, nor worlds[7], nor penance, nor valour[8]; the attainment to it of those who are possessed of knowledge is stated to be without comprehension of symbols[9]. Therefore the learned man who knows (the) property of being void of symbols[10], being devoted to pious conduct, and

---

[1] Cf. Gîtâ, p. 60.

[2] These are effects of Prakriti by which the Purusha is unaffected.

[3] Literally, 'pursued.'

[4] This is obscure. Arguna Misra's text is niskityam. Does that mean 'which should be accurately understood?' The rendering in the text of Nîlakantha's reading may mean that the Brahman has no such thoughts (kintâ) as are referred to at Gîtâ, p. 115.

[5] Does this mean the body?

[6] I.e. are free from birth and death. Cf. Âpastamba I, 8, 22, 4.

[7] This, again, is not quite clear. Probably the explanation is to be found in the passage at Gîtâ, p. 79.

[8] Nîlakantha's reading is 'observances or vows.'

[9] I.e. 'not to be acquired by inference,' Arguna Misra, p. 351 supra.

[10] See p. 309 supra; 'who is without symbols, and knows piety,' according to Arguna Misra's reading.

resorting to concealed[1] piety should adopt the mode of life (necessary) for experience[2]. Though undeluded, he should act in the manner of the deluded[3], not finding fault with piety[4]. He should perform piety, behaving so that others would always disrespect him[5], and should not find fault with the ways of the good[6]. That sage is said to be the best who has adopted this (line of) conduct. The senses, and the objects of the senses, and the five great elements, and mind, understanding, egoism, the unperceived, and the Purusha likewise[7], by an accurate determination about the truth, after understanding all these, one attains heaven[8], being released from all bonds. One who knows the truth, understanding these same (entities) at the time of the termination (of his life), should meditate, exclusively pondering on one point[9]; and then, depending on none[10], he gets emancipation. Freed from all attachments, like the atmosphere dwelling in space[11], with his accumulations[12] exhausted, and free from distress[13], he attains to the highest seat.

---

[1] See p. 159 supra, note 7, and cf. Manu III, 109, which is the text referred to in note 5 there.

[2] I.e. direct perception of the Brahman. See Gîtâ, p. 57, note 5.

[3] See p. 160 supra, note 8, and cf. also Manu II, 110.

[4] Arguna Misra compares Gîtâ, p. 55, about 'shaking convictions.'

[5] Cf. pp. 159-161 supra.

[6] This means, I presume, the good devoted to action and not to knowledge only.

[7] These are the famous elements of the Sâṅkhyas; see Sûtra I, 61.

[8] Cf. p. 159 and note 2.

[9] Cf. p. 300 supra.

[10] Cf. Gîtâ, p. 60.

[11] Cf. Gîtâ, p. 82, note 3.

[12] Of actions previously performed. See p. 246 supra.

[13] Cf. Gîtâ, p. 101, where, however, the original word is different.

CHAPTER XXXII.

Brahman said:

The ancients who perceived the established (truth) call renunciation[1] penance; and the Brâhmaṇas dwelling in the seat of the Brahman[2] understand knowledge to be concerned with the Brahman[2]. The highest Brahman is very far off[3], and (the attainment of it) depends on Vedic knowledge[4]; it is free from the pairs of opposites, devoid of qualities[5], everlasting, of unthinkable qualities, and supreme. The men of talent, who are pure[6], and whose minds are refined, transcending passion, and being untainted, perceive that supreme (principle) by means of knowledge and penance. Those who are constantly devoted to renunciation[7], and understand the Brahman and wish for the supreme, go to the happy path by penance. Penance[8] is said to be a light; (correct) conduct is the means to piety; knowledge verily should be understood to be the highest, and renunciation the best penance. He who understands determinately the self which is unperturbed, which abides in all entities, and which is the essential

[1] Abandoning of fruit, Arguna Misra. Cf. Gîtâ, p. 121.

[2] Cf. p. 339 supra, note 4, dwelling in=adhering to.

[3] See Gîtâ, p. 104.

[4] Cf. Sanatsugâtîya, p. 158 seq.

[5] Viz. the three famous ones.

[6] Pure, refined, and untainted are not easily distinguished. Probably 'pure' refers to external cleanliness; 'untainted' to freedom from sin and such taints; and 'refined' to freedom from error.

[7] I.e. who have no 'belongings,' Arguna Misra.

[8] Action without desire, Arguna Misra, who adds that it is called a light, as it leads to knowledge. See too p. 166, and p. 247, note 11, and p. 340 supra.

element in knowledge, he is laid down[1] (as being able) to move everywhere. The learned man who perceives, association and dissociation, and likewise unity and diversity[2], is released from misery. He who desires nothing, and despises nothing[3], becomes eligible, even dwelling in this world, for assimilation with the Brahman[4]. He who knows the truth about the qualities of Pradhâna[5], and understands the Pradhâna of all entities[6], who is free from (the thought that this or that is) mine, and free from egoism[7], is emancipated, there is no doubt of that. One who is free from the pairs of opposites, free from the (ceremonies of) salutation, free from (the ceremony of) svadhâ[8], attains to that everlasting (principle) which is free from the pairs of opposites, and devoid of qualities, by tranquillity only. Abandoning all action, whether agreeable or disagreeable, developed from the qualities[9], and abandoning both truth and falsehood[10], a creature is emancipated, there is no doubt of that. The great tree of Brahman[11] is

[1] 'Laid down' is literally 'wished.'

[2] I presume this means the real fact underlying the appearances of association and so forth, namely, that there is but one reality, and all appearances of difference &c. are unreal. Cf. Gîtâ, p. 124. See also p. 313 supra, note 1, and p. 374 infra.

[3] Cf. Gîtâ, p. 65, and see Ka*th*a, p. 155. [4] Cf. Gîtâ, p. 65.

[5] The qualities, viz. the three, of Pradhâna, i.e. constituting Prak*ri*ti, or nature. [6] See Gîtâ, p. 106, and note 3 there.

[7] For this whole expression, which occurs so frequently, cf. Maitrî, p. 44, and comment there.

[8] See p. 324 supra, note 8. [9] Cf. Gîtâ, p. 48; *S*vetâsvatara, p. 360.

[10] I. e., I presume, what is real and unreal in a worldly view,—the great truth is not to be 'abandoned.' Cf. Taittirîya, pp. 97–99; p. 191 supra; *S*ânti Parvan (Moksha), chap. 174, st. 53; Âpastamba II, 9, 21, 13.

[11] I. e., says Arguna Misra, the tree of worldly life produced from the Brahman. Compare chapter XII supra.

eternal; a tree which is produced from the unperceived as the seed, which consists of the understanding as its trunk, whose collection of boughs is the great egoism, the sprouts within which are the senses, the great branches of which are the great elements, and the side branches the objects of sense, which is always possessed of leaves, always possessed of flowers, in which agreeable and disagreeable fruits are always produced, and which is fed upon by all creatures. Cutting and piercing this (tree)[1] with the sword of knowledge of the truth, and abandoning the bonds in the shape of attachment, which cause birth, death, and old age[2], a wise man who is free from (the thought that this or that is) mine, and who is devoid of egoism, is emancipated, there is no doubt of that. There are these two birds[3], (which are) unchanging, and which should also be known to be unintelligent[4]. But as to that other who is above them, he is called intelligent. (When) the inner self, devoid of knowledge of nature[5], and (as it were) non-intelligent[6], understands that which is

[1] Cf. Gîtâ, p. 111; and Mu*nd*aka, p. 307, and commentary there.

[2] So I render the original, though the sense at first sight appears to be 'which are caused by birth,' &c.

[3] Viz. the understanding and egoism, which dwell in the 'tree,' Ar*g*una Mi*s*ra. Nîlaka*nth*a says, 'the great and the individual self.'

[4] Cf. Sâṅkhya-kârikâ 11, and comment of Vâ*k*aspati Mi*s*ra. The self is not unintelligent; and as the birds are so described, they must stand for some manifestation of Prak*ri*ti, which understanding and egoism are. Otherwise 'bird' does stand for 'self.' See p. 189 supra.

[5] The original word here is sattva, on which see p. 351 supra. Ar*g*una Mi*s*ra renders it here by Prak*ri*ti.

[6] So Nîlaka*nth*a; 'the only intelligent principle,'—Ar*g*una Mi*s*ra. On Nîlaka*nth*a's interpretation 'inner self' must be the same thing as Bhûtâtman at Maitrî, p. 41.

beyond nature, then understanding the Kshetra [1], and with an understanding comprehending all, and transcending the qualities [2] he is released from all sins.

CHAPTER XXXIII.

Brahman said:

Some (think of) the Brahman as a tree; some (think of) the Brahman as a great forest; and some (think of) the Brahman as unperceived; and some as transcendent and without misery [3]; and they [4] think all this to be produced from and absorbed into the unperceived. He who even for (the space of) a (single) exhalation, at the time of the termination (of life [5]) becomes equable [6], attaining to the self, becomes fit for immortality. Restraining the self in the self [7], even for (the space of) a wink, he repairs to the inexhaustible acquisition [8] of those who have knowledge, through the tranquillity of the self [9]. And restraining the life-winds again and

---

[1] See p. 351 supra. [2] See Gîtâ, p. 109.

[3] As to the first two clauses comp. pp. 284–371 supra; the last two are said by Arguna Misra to represent the Sânkhya and Yoga doctrines respectively.

[4] I presume this means all teachers. But Nîlakantha takes it to mean the Sânkhyas, and he takes the preceding words as indicating two views based on Sruti texts, viz. the first, that the world is a development of the Brahman, and the other that the Brahman does not undergo any development or change. Anâmaya he takes to mean changeless, and Brahmamaya he takes to mean developed from the Brahman.

[5] Cf. Gîtâ, pp. 77, 78.

[6] One who sees the supreme as the only real entity, Arguna Misra. Nilakantha takes it to mean one who identifies himself with everything. See Gîtâ, p. 65, and note 4 there.

[7] See p. 344 supra. [8] I.e. the goal to be acquired.

[9] 'Tranquillity'—the original may also be rendered by 'favour,'

again by control of the life-winds[1], of ten or twelve[2] (modes), (he repairs to) that which is beyond the twenty-four[3]. Thus having first a tranquil self, he obtains whatever he desires. When the quality of goodness predominates in the unperceived[4], that fits one for immortality. The men of knowledge extol nothing else beyond goodness. By inference[5] we understand the (attainment of the) being to depend on goodness. It is not possible otherwise[6] to attain that being, O best of the twice-born! Forgiveness, courage, harmlessness, equability, truth, straightforwardness, knowledge, abandonment[7], and also renunciation are laid down as (constituting) con-

as to which cf. p. 234 supra, but further on the phrase 'having a tranquil self' occurs, where the latter sense is not quite suitable. See Gîtâ, p. 51, and Yoga-sûtra I, 33.

[1] I.e. the specific modes which are mentioned of control of life-winds, e.g. at Gîtâ, p. 61, or Yoga-sûtra II, 49 seq.

[2] Nîlaka*n*/*h*a proposes two interpretations of this. He says the ten are the eight mentioned in Yoga-sûtra II, 29, and in addition tarka and vairâgya (as to which see Yoga-sûtra I, 15 and 17). To make up the twelve he substitutes for the last two the four named at Yoga-sûtra I, 33. He also suggests that 'ten or twelve' may mean twenty-two, which he makes up thus. The five modes of yama (Yoga-sûtra II, 30), five of niyama (ibid. 32), the remaining six in Yoga-sûtra II, 29, the four in Yoga-sûtra I, 33, and tarka and vairâgya as before.

[3] The twenty-four are the elements according to the Sâṅkhya system. See Sâṅkhya-sâra, p. 11, and p. 368 supra. That which is beyond them is Purusha.

[4] The unperceived, it should be noted, is made up of the three qualities; the predominance of goodness indicates enlightenment or knowledge. Cf. Gîtâ, p. 108.

[5] The middle term in the inference being, says Arguna Misra, the enlightening effect of the quality in question.

[6] Cf. p. 167 supra.

[7] The original is tyâga, which Arguna Misra renders by 'abandonment of all belongings;' renunciation, scil. of fruit. Cf. Gîtâ, p. 121, and p. 114.

duct of the quality of goodness. By this very inference the wise verily believe in the Being and nature as one, there is no doubt of that. Some learned men who are devoted to knowledge, assert the unity of the Kshetra*gñ*a and nature [1]. But that is not correct. That they are always distinct (from one another) is also (said) without (due) consideration [2]. Distinction and also association [3] should be accurately understood. Unity and diversity [4] are likewise laid down. Such is the doctrine of the learned. Between the gnat and the udumbara [5] there is observed unity and diversity also. As a fish is in water distinct (from it), such is their relation; (such is) the relation of the drops of water with the leaf of the lotus.

The preceptor said:

Then those Brâhma*n*as, who were the best of sages, having again felt doubts, interrogated the grandsire of the people who spoke to them thus.

---

[1] Here, says Nîlaka*n*/*h*a, the author indicates an objection to the proposition stated just before. But the passage is not clear.

[2] This, says Nîlaka*n*/*h*a, is a reply to the Sâṅkhyas, who hold the two to be distinct. Nîlaka*n*/*h*a adds, that if the two are distinct, nature will, conceivably, adhere even to an emancipated creature; and if they are one, then the being or self would be really engaging in action and so forth, and that activity being really a property of the self, could not be destroyed save by the destruction of the self. Hence that view is also wrong.

[3] Like that of sea and wave, Nîlaka*n*/*h*a.

[4] Unity of Brahman and diversity of manifestation of nature, Ar*g*una Mi*s*ra, who adds—by reason of the association they are spoken of as one, by reason of the unity and diversity they are distinct. The next sentence contains three parallel cases.

[5] Cf. as to all this, Sânti Parvan, chap. 194, st. 38 seq. (Moksha Dharma); chap. 249, st. 20 seq.; chap. 285, st. 33 seq.

CHAPTER XXXIV.

The sages said:

Which (form of) piety is deemed to be the most worthy of being performed? We observe the various modes of piety to be as it were contradictory. Some say (it [1] remains) after the body (is destroyed); some say that is not so. Some (say) everything [2] is doubtful; and others that there is no doubt. Some say the permanent (principle) is impermanent, and others, too, that it exists, and (others) that it exists not [3]. Some (say it is) of one form or twofold, and others (that it is) mixed [4]. Some Brâhmaṇas, too, who know the Brahman and perceive the truth, believe it to be one; others distinct; and others again (that it is) manifold [5]. Some say both time and space (exist) [6], and others that that is not so. Some have matted hair and skins; and some (are) clean-shaven and without covering. Some people are for bathing; some for the omission [7] of bathing. Some are for taking food; others are intent on fasting. Some people extol action, and

---

[1] I.e. the piety, Arguna Misra; the self, Nîlakaṇṭha.

[2] I.e. such as piety, &c., Arguna Misra.

[3] I follow Arguna Misra, who says 'permanent' means soul, &c. The correct expression would seem to be 'that which is called permanent by others is impermanent.'

[4] This is the view of those who hold the theory of Pariṇâma, or development, says Arguna Misra.

[5] 'To be one'=knowledge to be all of one description, 'distinct'=knowledge having various entities for its distinct objects (this is the view of the holders of the Vigñânavâda, says Arguna Misra); manifold=that the selfs are numberless. The words here are nearly identical with those at Gîtâ, p. 83, see note 4 there.

[6] I.e. help in action, Arguna Misra.

[7] See Âpastamba I, 1, 1, 2 (comment).

others tranquillity. Some extol final emancipation; some various kinds of enjoyments; some wish for riches, and others indigence. Some (say) means[1] should be resorted to; others that that is not so. Some are devoted to harmlessness, and some given up to destruction; some are for merit and glory: and others say that is not so. Some are devoted to goodness; some are in the midst of doubts; some are for pleasure, and some for pain[2]. Some people (say) meditation[3], other Brâhma*n*as (say) sacrifice, and others, gifts; but others extol penance, and other persons sacred study; some knowledge, and renunciation[4]; and those who ponder on the elements[5], nature[6]. Some extol everything, and others nothing[7].

---

[1] I.e. for the acquisition of anything desirable, Arguna Misra, who adds, 'by those who wish for piety.' Nîlaka*nth*a says means= 'meditation and so forth;' as to 'that is not so' he cites what he calls a *S*ruti, which is however one of the Kârikâs of Gau*d*apâda on the Mâ*nd*ukya; see p. 432.

[2] This, too, is not quite clear, but Nîlaka*nth*a says, 'meditation should be practised for release from pain, and for acquisition of pleasure;' 'and others say not so, it should be done without desire.'

[3] That is to say, they hold that meditation should be practised.

[4] Arguna Misra seems to take this to mean 'renunciation of knowledge,' i.e. a blank, and says this was the view of the Mâdhyamikas,—I suppose the Mâdhyamika Bauddhas.

[5] I.e. the *K*ârvâkas, Arguna Misra.

[6] *S*vetâsvatara, p. 276, and *S*aṅkara's commentary there.

[7] Were there optimists and pessimists at the time of the Anugîtâ in India? This verse, however, does not occur in some MSS. Nîlaka*nth*a's note on this passage may be of some interest. He says, 'Some hold that the self exists after the body is lost; others, that is the Lokâyatas or *K*ârvâkas, hold the contrary. Everything doubtful is the view of the Syâdvâdins; nothing doubtful that of the Tairthikas, the great teachers (I presume, about their own respective doctrines). Everything impermanent, Târkikas; permanent, Mîmâ*m*sakas; nothing exists, the *S*ûnyavâdins; something exists, but only momentarily,

And, O best of the gods! piety being thus confused and abounding in contradictions, we are deluded, and come to no determination. People are acting, (saying) this is good, this is good. And he who is attached to a certain (form of) piety, always esteems that. Here (therefore) our understanding breaks down, and our mind is distracted. We wish, O best (of beings)! to be informed of what is good. Be pleased now to proceed to state what is (so) mysterious, and what is the cause of the connexion between the Kshetra*gñ*a and nature. Thus addressed by those Brâhma*n*as, the venerable, holy, and talented creator of worlds told them accurately (what they asked).

Saugatas; knowledge is one, but the ego and non-ego are two different principles, the Yogâ*k*âras; mixed, U*d*ulomas; one, is the view of the worshippers of the Brahman as possessed of qualities; distinct, other Mîmâ*m*sakas, who hold that the special actions are the cause (of everything, is meant, I presume); manifold = the atomists; time and space = astrologers. Those who "say that is not so," that is to say, that what we see has no real existence at all, are the V*ri*ddhas, ancient philosophers; omission to bathe = the condition of Naish*th*ika Brahma*k*ârins; bathing = householder's condition; "means should be resorted to, that is not so," those who are against all meditation, &c., according to the *S*ruti text, which Nîlaka*nth*a quotes; "merit and glory, that is not so," some say there is no merit as the Lokâyatas or *K*ârvâkas; "knowledge, renunciation," the former is to be gained only by means of the latter; "ponder on elements" = who are intent on the investigation of the true nature of things; nature = abundance of resources, by which alone knowledge is produced, not by mere renunciation.' It will be understood, that this commentary assumes a different syntactical construction of the original in some places from that adopted in our translation.

CHAPTER XXXV.

Brahman said:

Well then, I will declare to you what you ask of me, O best (of men)! Learn what a preceptor told a pupil who went to him. Hearing it all, deliberate on it properly. Non-destruction of all creatures, that is deemed to be the greatest duty[1]. This is the highest seat[2], free from vexation and holy in character. The ancients who perceived the established (truth) call knowledge the highest happiness. Therefore by pure knowledge one is released from all sins. And those who are constantly engaged in destruction, and who are infidels[3] in their conduct, and who entertain avarice and delusion, go verily to hell. Those who without sloth perform actions with expectations, rejoice in this world, being born again and again. But those wise and talented men, who perform actions with faith, free from any connexion with expectations, perceive correctly[4]. Now I will proceed to state how the association and dissociation of Kshetra*gñ*a and nature (take place). Learn that, O best (of men)! The relation here is said to be that between the object and subject[5]. The subject

[1] See p. 291 supra, and note 3 there.

[2] So literally; the sense is—that which one is to aim at.

[3] The original is nâstika, the contrary of that 'âstikya,' which at Gîtâ, p. 126, we have rendered by 'belief (in a future world),' following *S*rîdhara. Râmânuga, whose commentary came to hand too late for any other than a very occasional use in the translation of the Gîtâ, renders it by 'belief in the truth of the teaching of the Vedas.'

[4] I. e. learn the truth.

[5] I use the terms subject and object here in the philosophical sense explained by Sir W. Hamilton, viz. the thinking agent and the object of thought respectively. And cf. also the passage referred to in note 3 on p. 379 infra.

is always the being, and nature is stated to be the object. It has been explained in the above mode, as (having the relation) of the gnat and the udumbara[1]. Nature which is non-intelligent knows nothing, though it is the object of enjoyment[2]. Who enjoys and what is enjoyed[3] is learnt from the *S*âstras. Nature is said always to abound in the pairs of opposites, and to be constituted of the qualities; the Kshetra*gñ*a is free from the pairs of opposites, devoid of parts, and in essence free from the qualities. He abides in everything alike[4], and is connected with (all) knowledge[5]; and he always enjoys nature as a lotus-leaf (enjoys) water. Even brought into contact with all qualities, a learned man remains untainted[6]. There is no doubt that the being is unattached just like the unsteady drop of water placed upon a lotus-leaf[7]. It is established that nature is the property[8] of the being. And the relation of the two is like that of matter and the maker[9]. As one goes into (a) dark (place) taking a light (with him), so those who wish for the supreme go with the light of nature[10]. While there is oil

[1] P. 374 supra. The relation is one of close connexion, coupled with some identity of nature (because, says Nîlaka*n*t*h*a, an entirely extraneous thing could not get into the inside of the fruit, and the gnat's body therefore must have come from the fruit itself), but still the elements are distinct.

[2] See p. 371 supra, note 4.

[3] Cf. Maitrî, p. 108.

[4] Cf. Gîtâ, pp. 105, 106.

[5] Knowledge of the Kshetra*gñ*a forms part of all real knowledge. Ar*g*una Mi*s*ra's reading and interpretation are different. He says, 'As he is seen coming to light everywhere alike, so,' &c.

[6] Cf. Gîtâ, pp. 55–110.

[7] Again the common simile.

[8] The original is dravya, rendered 'matter' in the next sentence. Ar*g*una Mi*s*ra paraphrases it by 'upakarana,' paraphernalia.

[9] So the original, the sense is not clear. But see *S*vetâ*s*vatara, p. 368.

[10] Knowledge, which, says Nîlaka*n*t*h*a, is a manifestation of nature. Ar*g*una Mi*s*ra says the knowledge of the truth which the

and wick[1], the light shines; but the flame is extinguished when the oil and wick are exhausted. Thus nature is perceived[2]; the being is laid down (as being) unperceived. Understand this, O Brâhma*n*as! Well now, I will tell you something more. One who has a bad understanding does not acquire knowledge even with a thousand (admonitions). And one who is possessed of knowledge enhances (his) happiness even with a fourth share[3]. Thus should one understand the accomplishment of piety by (apt) means. For the talented man who knows (these) means, attains supreme happiness[4]. As a man travelling along some way without provisions for the journey, travels with great discomfort, and may even be destroyed on the way, so should one understand, that by action[5] the fruit is or is not produced. For a man to see within (his) self[6] what is agreeable and what is disagreeable to him is good. And as one who is devoid of a perception of the truth rashly travels on foot by a long way unseen before[7], while (another) goes by the same

self acquires is by means of nature. Cf. Sâṅkhya-kârikâ 56, and comment.

[1] So Nîlaka*nth*a. Ar*g*una Mi*s*ra does not take gu*n*a here to mean 'wick.'

[2] I. e., I presume, in its manifestations; it is perceived for some time and then vanishes. Cf. Sâṅkhya-kârikâ 59-61; the Purusha is not 'perceived' in this sense. [3] Viz. of admonition, Ar*g*una Mi*s*ra.

[4] Cf. Gîtâ, p. 70, where the same phrase occurs.

[5] The fruit of this is uncertain; knowledge which is in one's self is the thing to be worked for.

[6] I. e. the mind, Nîlaka*nth*a. The meaning is, he should not care for external pleasure and pain. Cf. Gîtâ, inter alia, p. 50.

[7] This seems to be so left imperfect in the original. The construction seems to be this: the progress of the latter is as great as that of one who drives in a chariot as compared with that of one who goes on foot with much suffering. Cf. the construction on next page.

way in a carriage[1] drawn by horses, and going swiftly, such is the progress of the men of understanding. Having climbed up a mountain one should not look at the surface of the earth[2]. One sees a man travelling in a chariot, and void of intelligence, afflicted by reason of the chariot. As far as there is a carriage-path, he goes in the carriage; where the carriage-path stops, a learned man goes on abandoning the carriage. So travels the talented man, who understands the procedure respecting (knowledge of the) truth and devotion[3], and who knows about the qualities, comprehending the gradations[4] one above the other. As one who without a boat dives into the ocean with his arms only, through delusion, undoubtedly wishes for destruction; while a wise man likewise knowing distinctions[5], and having a boat with good oars, goes in the water without fatigue, and soon crosses the reservoir, and having crossed (it) goes to the other shore, throwing

[1] I.e. the *S*âstras, says Nîlaka*nth*a. Cf. Gîtâ, p. 117.

[2] When one has arrived at knowledge,—the highest seat, says Nîlaka*nth*a,—one need not perform the dictates of the *S*âstras, which are only preliminary to the acquisition of knowledge. Cf. Gîtâ, pp. 48, 73. Cf. as to this figure of the chariot and the next one about the boat, B*ri*hadâra*n*yaka, p. 695.

[3] I adopt Arguna's rendering of the original here, viz. Yoga. The meaning, on that rendering, is the same as it is in the Gîtâ.

[4] According to Arguna Mi*s*ra, action with desire, action without desire, and lastly, knowledge. According to Nîlaka*nth*a, action laid down in the *S*âstras, then Yoga, and then the condition of Ha*m*sa, Paramaha*m*sa, &c.

[5] Literally, one knowing divisions. I presume the meaning is distinctions between various things as to which suits which, and so forth. The boat, says Nîlaka*nth*a, is a preceptor, and even a preceptor is not to be sought for after a man has achieved Yoga; hence the text proceeds to speak further on of casting aside the boat. Wishes for destruction = is sure to meet destruction.

aside the boat, and devoid of (the thought that this or that is) mine. This has been already explained by the parallel of the carriage and pedestrian. One who has come by delusion through affection, adheres to that like a fisherman to his boat, being overcome by (the thought that this or that is) mine. It is not possible to move on land after embarking in a boat. And likewise one cannot move in water after entering a carriage. Thus there are various actions in regard to different objects[1]. And as action is performed in this world, so does it result to them[2]. That which sages by their understanding meditate upon, which is void of any smell whatever, void of taste, and void of colour, touch, or sound, that is called the Pradhâna[3]. Now that Pradhâna is unperceived; a development of the unperceived is the Mahat; and a development of the Pradhâna (when it is) become Mahat is egoism. From egoism is produced the development, namely, the great elements; and of the elements respectively, objects of sense are verily stated to be the development[4]. The unperceived is of the nature of seed[5], and also productive in its essence. And we have heard

[1] I. e. appertaining to the various orders of householders, &c., Nîlaka*nt*ha. But I am not aware of any authority for this sense of vishaya.

[2] I. e. those who perform them.

[3] Nîlaka*nt*ha says, 'Having stated above the means of knowledge, he now states the proper object of knowledge.'

[4] See p. 332 supra. The original for development is gu*n*a, literally quality.

[5] The meaning of this passage seems to be identical with that of Sânkhya-kârikâ 3. Productive (Prasavâtmakam) is probably to be explained as Prasavadharmi is at Sânkhya-kârikâ 11 (see commentary of Vâ*k*aspati, pp. 59, 60), viz. always undergoing development. The great elements are of course the tanmâtras.

that the great self is of the nature of seed and a product. Egoism is of the nature of seed and a product also again and again. And the five great elements are verily of the nature of seed and products. The objects of the five elements are of the nature of seed[1], but they do not yield products. Learn about their properties. Now space has one quality, air is said to have two qualities; it is said that light has three qualities; and water, too, is of four qualities; and earth, abounding with movables and immovables, the divine source of all entities, full of examples of agreeable and disagreeable (things), should be understood to be of five qualities[2]. Sound, touch, colour likewise, taste, and smell as the fifth—these, O best of the twice-born! should be understood to be the five qualities of earth. Smell always belongs to the earth[3]; and smell is stated to be (of) numerous descriptions. I will state at length the numerous qualities of smell[4]. Smell is agreeable or disagreeable, sweet, sour, and bitter likewise, diffusive and compact also, soft, and rough, and clear also[5]—thus should

---

[1] This is not clear, unless 'product' above means productive, and seed means a product, it being a product of the aṅkura or sprout. Nîlakaṇṭha says, 'seed=cause; product=effect. The unperceived is an effect, and so the contrary doctrine of the Sâṅkhya is here shown to be wrong. The objects are causes, as their enjoyment causes an impression.'

[2] See pp. 285, 286 supra.

[3] That is to say, smell is the special property of the earth only, the other qualities are common to it with the other elements. The word in the original is guṇa or quality everywhere.

[4] See *S*ânti Parvan (Moksha Dharma), chap. 184, st. 27.

[5] Bitter, Nîlakaṇṭha exemplifies by the smell of the chili, apparently interpreting kaṭvi, as it may be interpreted, to mean sharp; diffusive=overcoming all other smells, like Asafoetida; compact=made up of many smells. Nîlakaṇṭha adds, that soft is like that of

smell, which belongs to the earth, be understood to be of ten descriptions. Sound, touch, and colour likewise, and taste, are stated to be the qualities of water. I will now give (some) information about taste. Taste is stated to be of numerous descriptions. Sweet[1], sour, bitter, sharp, astringent, and saltish likewise—thus are the forms of taste, which is a development of water, said to be of six descriptions. Sound, touch, and likewise colour; thus is light said to have three qualities. The quality of light is colour, and colour is stated to be of numerous descriptions. White, black, red likewise, green, yellow, and grey likewise, short, long, narrow[2], broad, square, and circular—thus is the colour of light said to be of twelve forms. It should be understood[3] by aged Brâhma*n*as, who speak the truth, and are conversant with piety. Sound and touch also should be understood; air is said to have (these) two qualities. And touch is the quality of air, and touch is stated to be of numerous descriptions. Rough, cold and hot likewise, tender and clear also, hard, glutinous, smooth, slippery, hurtful, and soft[4] —thus the quality of air is properly said by Brâhma*n*as who have reached perfection, who are conversant with piety and perceive the truth, to be of twelve descriptions. Now space has one quality.

liquid ghee, rough of the oil of mustard, and clear as of cooked rice. The *S*ânti Parvan passage omits 'sour.' [1] Cf. Gîtâ, p. 118.

[2] Literally, lean and fat. These are rather unusual qualities to attribute to colour. The *S*ânti Parvan passage gives more.

[3] Sic. Does it mean 'it is understood?' Cf. Pâ*n*ini III, 3, 113.

[4] Tender = like the touch of a son, &c.; clear = like that of an excellent cloth, Nilaka*n*/*h*a; glutinous = like that of oil; smooth = like that of a gem; slippery = not really smooth, but appearing to be such, like that of saliva (?), Arguna Mis*r*a. The enumeration of these in the *S*ânti Parvan loc. cit. is again different.

and that is stated to be sound only. I will speak at length of the numerous qualities of sound. Shadga, *Ri*shabha, together with Gândhâra, Madhyama, and likewise Pa*ñk*ama, and beyond these should be understood to be Nishâda and Dhaivata likewise[1]; agreeable and disagreeable sound also, compact, and of (many) ingredients[2]. Thus sound, which is produced in space, should be understood to be of ten descriptions. Space is the highest element[3], egoism is above that; above egoism is understanding, and above that understanding is the self[4]; above that is the unperceived, and above the unperceived is the being. One who knows which is superior and inferior among entities, and who knows the proper procedure in all actions, and who identifies himself with every being[5], repairs to the imperishable self.

CHAPTER XXXVI.

Brahman said:

Since the mind is ruler of these five elements, in (the matter of) absorbing or bringing (them) forth[6],

[1] This is the Hindu Gamut.

[2] These are not in the *S*ânti Parvan; of many ingredients = collection of sounds, Ar*g*una Mi*s*ra.

[3] Being all-pervading, Ar*g*una Mi*s*ra. Cf. its position at Taittirîya, p. 67.

[4] Cf. Ka*th*a, pp. 114, 115, 149, and *S*aṅkarâ*k*ârya's commentary there, for an explanation of the whole passage. And see Sâṅkhyasâra, p. 16, as to what are here called self and understanding.

[5] Cf. Gîtâ, p. 64, where the words are identical.

[6] The elements are perceived or are not perceived by the senses under the direction of the mind; absorbing = destroying; bringing forth = producing, Nîlaka*nth*a. See p. 268 supra, and *S*ânti Parvan (Moksha), chap. 240, st. 12.

the mind itself is the individual self[1]. The mind always presides over the great elements. The understanding proclaims its power[2], and it is called the Kshetra*gñ*a. The mind yokes the senses as a charioteer (yokes) good horses. The senses, the mind, and the understanding are always joined to the Kshetra*gñ*a[3]. That individual self, mounting the chariot to which big horses[4] are yoked, and in which the understanding is the drag[5], drives about on all sides. The great chariot which is pervaded by the Brahman[6], has the group of the senses yoked (to it), has the mind for a charioteer, and the understanding for a drag. That learned and talented person verily, who always understands thus the chariot pervaded by the Brahman, comes not by delusion in the midst of all entities[7]. This forest of the Brahman[8] begins with the unperceived, and ends with the gross objects[9]:

[1] The word is the same as at Maitrî, p. 41, the comment on which should be seen.

[2] I.e. the mind's power is to be perceived by itself, Nîlaka*n*/*th*a. The meaning seems to be that the understanding can only operate on what the mind places before it.

[3] The passage at Ka*th*a, p. 111 seq., and *S*ankara's commentary there, throw light on this, though the figure is not drawn out in the same way in both places. For a definition of Kshetra*gñ*a, see *S*ânti Parvan (Moksha), chap. 187, st. 23.

[4] I.e. the senses.

[5] I.e. that which holds the horses in check. Nîlaka*nth*a seems to render it by 'whip,' but that is not correct, I think.

[6] So Ar*g*una Misra. Nilaka*nth*a says, 'The senses, &c., when they turn towards the outer world make the self drive about as an individual self; when turned inwards they show him that he is the Brahman.' Nîlaka*nth*a thus likens this to the Ka*th*a passage. See also p. 187 and notes there.

[7] Or it may mean, among all men.

[8] See p. 164 supra, note 2; and p. 285, note 4.

[9] That is to say, it includes all Sa*m*sâra, all the elements recognised by the Sânkhya philosophy, save the Being or Purusha.

and includes movables and immovables, receives light from the radiance of the sun and moon, is adorned with planets and nakshatras, and is decked on all sides with nets of rivers and mountains, and always beautified likewise by various (descriptions of) waters; it is (the means of) subsistence for all entities[1], and it is the goal of all living creatures. In this the Kshetra*g*ña always moves about. Whatever entities (there are) in this world, movable or immovable, they are the very first[2] to be dissolved; and next the developments produced from the elements[3]; and (after) these developments, all the elements. Such is the upward gradation[4] among entities. Gods, men, Gandharvas, Pi*s*âkas, Asuras, Râkshasas, all have been created by nature[5], not by actions, nor by a cause. These Brâhma*n*as[6], the creators of the world, are born here again and again. And what-

[1] Cf. p. 371 supra.

[2] Another reading means 'they are dissolved in the waters.' As to the order, cf. Vedânta Paribhâshâ, p. 48, and p. 335 supra.

[3] I take these to mean the gross elements of which things movable and immovable may be said to be made, if one may use a non-idealist phrase in the Sâṅkhya philosophy. Then the elements next spoken of are the subtle ones or tanmâtras. Cf. the references in note 2. As to developments, see p. 382, note 4.

[4] Viz. gross object, gross element, subtle element.

[5] The original is svabhâva, which Ar*g*una Mi*s*ra renders by Prak*ri*ti. 'Actions' both Nîlaka*n*/*h*a and Ar*g*una Mi*s*ra take to mean sacrifices, &c., and 'cause' the former interprets by Brahman; the latter by tanmâtras or subtle elements, and adds, 'the sense is—not by sacrifice or tanmâtras only.' Nîlaka*n*/*h*a says, 'The gods, &c., are produced by nature, as the gods, &c., seen in a dream.' The meaning seems to be that there are energies in nature which evolve these forms of being. Cf. also Gîtâ, p. 65.

[6] I presume this means that the patriarchs (Marî*k*i and others, says Nîlaka*n*/*h*a) are also born again and again—that is to say, in different kalpas, I suppose—by nature only.

ever is produced from them[1] is dissolved in due time in those very five great elements, like billows in the ocean. The great elements are in every way (beyond) the elements that make up the world[2]. And he who is released, even from those five elements, goes to the highest goal. The Lord Pragâpati created all this by the mind[3] only. And in the same manner[4] the sages attained the godhead[5] by means of penance[6]. And in like manner, those who have achieved perfection, who have acquired concentration by a course of penance, and who likewise feed on fruits and roots, perceive the triple world[7] here by penance. Medicines, and herbs, and the various sciences are all acquired[8] by means of penance alone. For all acquisition[9] has penance for its root. Whatever is difficult to obtain[10], difficult to

---

[1] I think this must mean the elements, though it might at first sight be referred to the Brâhma*n*as.

[2] I.e. the gross elements, I take it; the others are the tanmâtras.

[3] I.e. the meditation which constitutes true knowledge, Arguna Misra. But see Gîtâ, p. 87, note 1, and Sâṅkhya-sûtra.

[4] I.e. by the mind, as to which cf. Taittirîya, p. 89; Ka*th*a, p. 164. Arguna Misra says, 'This apparent deviation from the ordinary modes of cause and effect is not altogether without parallel, so he adds this to show that.'

[5] Literally, 'the gods,' but the meaning seems to be that given in the text, as Arguna Misra says.

[6] This is only the concentration of mind and senses on one object, Nîlaka*nth*a. See p. 166, note 1 supra.

[7] See p. 174 supra.

[8] Literally, 'are accomplished,' which seems to mean that they are acquired so as to be practically at one's command when required.

[9] The original word is derived from the same root as the subject of the last note.

[10] Difficult to obtain = the seat of Indra, &c.; to learn = Vedas, &c.; to vanquish = fire, &c.; to pass through = a great deluge, &c.,

learn, difficult to vanquish, and difficult to pass through; all that can be accomplished by penance, for penance is difficult to overcome. One who drinks spirituous liquors, one who kills a Brâhmana, one who steals, one who destroys an embryo, one who violates the bed of his preceptor[1], is released from that sin only by penance well performed. (Those) men, Pitris, gods, (sacrificial) animals[2], beasts and birds, and all other creatures movable or immovable, (who are) constantly devoted to penance, always reach perfection by penance. And in like manner the noble(-minded) gods went to heaven[3]. Those who without sloth perform actions with expectations, and being full of egoism, they go near Pragâpati[4]. Those high-souled ones who are devoid of (the thought that this or that is) mine, and devoid of egoism, by means of a pure concentration (of mind) on contemplation, obtain the great and highest world. Those who best understand the self, attaining concentration (of mind) on contemplation[5], and having their minds always tranquil, enter into the unperceived accumulation of happiness[6]. Those

---

Nîlakantha. Arguna Misra seems to interpret the last word, where his reading is doubtful, to mean 'difficult to do.'

[1] Cf. Khândogya, p. 361. Except the destruction of the embryo (see Taitt. Âran. p. 870, but at Brihadâranyaka, p. 795, Kaushîtaki, p. 77, and Âpastamba I, 6, 19, 16, the commentators render Bhrûna by 'learned Brâhmana'), the rest are the great sins. But note that stealing gold, not theft generally, is mentioned as a great sin.

[2] Or, perhaps, cattle. The original is pasu.

[3] See p. 160 supra, and cf. p. 178.

[4] I.e. Kasyapa, as gods, &c. This seems to be Arguna Misra's interpretation. This condition is inferior to that described in the following sentence.

[5] See p. 162, note 1.

[6] Nîlakantha's rendering is 'that by which (worldly) happiness is

who are free from (all thought that this or that is) mine, and who are free from egoism, attaining concentration (of mind) on contemplation[1], enter the highest world of the great, which is the unperceived. Born from that same unperceived[2] (principle), again acquiring knowledge, and getting rid of the (qualities of) passion and darkness, and resorting to the pure (quality of) goodness, a man gets rid of all sins, and abandons everything as fruitless. He should be understood to be the Kshetragña. He who understands him understands the Vedas[3]. Withdrawing from the mind the objects[4] of mental operations, a sage should sit down self-restrained. (He) necessarily (becomes) that on which his mind[5] (is fixed). This is the eternal mystery. That which begins with the unperceived and ends with the gross objects[6] is stated to be of the nature of ignorance[7]. But (you should) learn that whose nature is devoid

heightened.' He compares Br*i*hadâra*n*yaka, p. 816. See also Taittirîya, p. 112.

[1] See Gîtâ, p. 128, note 1, where dhyâna and yoga are taken separately. Here the compound is in the singular. Nîlaka*n*/*h*a's reading is different.

[2] The sense here is not quite clear. It seems, however, to be this. The acquisitions mentioned in the preceding sentence take the acquirers to some temporary world from which they afterwards return; but when they get rid of the qualities, they get final emancipation. As to the unperceived, cf. inter alia Gîtâ, p. 112, note 2.

[3] Cf. Gîtâ, p. 111, and note 2 there. That seems to approach the question from the opposite point of view.

[4] So Arguna Misra. At Gîtâ XVI, 16, *k*itta means the operation itself. That also will do here.

[5] Cf. Gîtâ, p. 78; Maitrî, p. 178; Prasna, p. 194; and the quotations at Sânkhya-sâra, p. 3.

[6] This phrase has occurred before; it means all the developments which make up worldly life. See Sânkhya-sâra, p. 5.

[7] See p. 371 supra.

of qualities. Two syllables[1] are death; three syllables the eternal Brahman. Mine is death, and not mine is the eternal[2]. Some men of dull understandings extol action. But as to the high-souled ancients they do not extol action[3]. By action a creature is born with a body and made up of the sixteen[4]. Knowledge brings forth[5] the being, and that is acceptable and constitutes immortality. Therefore those who are far-sighted have no attachment to actions. This being is stated to be full of knowledge, not full of action[6]. The self-restrained man who thus understands the immortal, changeless, incomprehensible, and ever indestructible and unattached (principle), he dies not[7]. He who thus understands the self to which there is nothing prior, which is uncreated, changeless, unmoving[8], which is incomprehensible (even) to those who feed on nectar, he certainly becomes immortal[7] and not to be restrained[9], in consequence of these means[10].

---

[1] See *S*ânti Parvan (Râ*g*adharma) XIII, 4. Cf. Maitrî, p. 180. This means the two and three syllables of 'mama' and 'na mama,' mine and not mine. Cf. B*ri*hadâra*n*yaka, p. 970, and *Kh*ândogya, p. 118, and p. 548, for a similar conceit.

[2] Final emancipation follows on abandoning the idea of 'mine;' bondage on harbouring it. [3] See Mu*nd*aka, p. 279.

[4] The eleven organs and the five great elements which go to form the body. See Sânkhya-kârikâ 3, and comment thereon; *S*ânti Parvan, chap. 210, st. 32 seq.; chap. 242, st. 7 seq.; Pra*s*na, p. 230.

[5] I.e. shows. [6] Cf. Gîtâ, p. 118; *S*ânti Parvan, ch. 242, st. 15.

[7] See p. 367 supra, note 6; and cf. Ka*th*a, pp. 155, 156.

[8] I.e. which remains unconcerned, cf. Î*s*a, p. 10. Apûrvam (to which there is nothing prior), Ar*g*una Mi*s*ra renders by 'not familiarly known,' and Nîlaka*n*t*h*a by 'not understood by any other means of knowledge.' See also B*ri*hadâra*n*yaka, p. 502, and *S*ankara on that.

[9] This is not very clear, but I suppose the meaning to be the same as that of 'unconquerable' at p. 161, and see p. 231.

[10] I.e. the means mentioned further on, says Nîlaka*n*t*h*a.

Expelling all impressions[1], and restraining the self in the self[2], he understands that holy Brahman, than which nothing greater exists. And when the understanding is clear, he attains tranquillity[3]. And the nature of tranquillity is as when one sees a dream[4]. This[5] is the goal of those emancipated ones who are intent on knowledge. And they see all the movements[6] which are produced by development. This is the goal of those who are indifferent (to the world). This is the eternal piety. This is what is acquired by men of knowledge. This is the uncensured (mode of) conduct. This goal can be reached by one who is alike to all beings[7], who is without attachment, who is without expectations.

[1] Impressions from external causes. Cf. inter alia Sâṅkhya-sûtra III, 83; see, too, pp, 247–358 supra and notes there.

[2] I.e. restraining the mind in the lotus-like heart, Nîlakaṇṭha. Cf. as to this, pp. 248, 372 inter alia.

[3] Cf. Gîtâ, p. 51. See also Maitrî-upanishad, p. 176, and Muṇḍaka, p. 314.

[4] Arguna Misra says, 'The nature of tranquillity is this, that in that state you perceive everything to be unreal like what is seen in a dream.' Nîlakaṇṭha says, 'The nature of tranquillity is this, that in that state the self abides without attachment to the body, and any external objects, but working within itself as in a dream.' But see on this Kaṭha, p. 147.

[5] Viz. tranquillity, Nîlakaṇṭha.

[6] I.e., says Nîlakaṇṭha, they see all worldly objects past and future. Arguna Misra, 'They see the actions performed for some wealth and so forth.' I am not satisfied with either meaning. Arguna Misra's is besides based on a reading different from that adopted in the text, namely, Parimâṇagâh, instead of Pariṇâmagâh. I think 'pariṇâma' is the development which, according to the Sâṅkhya philosophy, produces the universe, and the movements are the actions which that development—namely, here the activity of egoism and its products—occasions. Cf. as to some extent supporting this, Sâṅkhya-sâra, p. 16.

[7] See inter alia Gîtâ, pp. 68–70.

and who looks alike on everything[1]. I have now declared everything to you, O best of Brâhma*n*a sages! Act thus forthwith; then you will acquire perfection.

The preceptor said:

Thus instructed by the preceptor Brahman, those high-souled sages acted accordingly, and then attained to the worlds[2]. Do you, too, O noble person, of pure self! duly act according to the words of Brahman which I have stated. Then will you attain perfection.

Vâsudeva said:

That pupil thus instructed in the highest piety by the preceptor, did everything (accordingly), O son of Kuntî! and then attained final emancipation. And the pupil, having done all he should have done, attained to that seat, O supporter of the family of the Kauravas! going to which one grieves not[3].

Arguna said:

Who, indeed, was that Brâhma*n*a, O K*ri*sh*n*a! and who the pupil, O *G*anârdana! If this verily is fit to be heard by me, O Lord! then tell it me.

Vâsudeva said:

I[4] am the preceptor, O you of mighty arms! and

[1] See inter alia Gîtâ, pp. 68–70.

[2] I. e., I presume, Bhûr and the rest. But see also *Kh*ândogya, pp. 272, 541, 620, and B*ri*hadâra*n*yaka, pp. 302, 608.

[3] See p. 285 supra, and cf. inter alia *Kh*ândogya, p. 550.

[4] I. e. I, the Kshetra*g*ña, am the preceptor, and the mind is that which has to be taught. This shows that one's instructor must be oneself, Nîlaka*n*tha. Arguna Misra says, 'I am the preceptor, the mind is the pupil. The meaning of this is that anybody who has not acquired knowledge is treated here as a pupil; there is no other special pupil intended.' Cf. also p. 310 supra.

know the mind to be my pupil. And, O Dhanañgaya! I have related this mystery to you out of love for you. If you have love for me, O supporter of the family of the Kauravas! then having heard this (instruction) relating to the self, always duly act[1] (according to it). Then when this piety is duly practised, you will attain the absolute final emancipation, getting rid of all sins. It was this same thing I stated to you before[2] when the time for battle had come, O you of mighty arms! Therefore fix your mind on this. And now[3], O chief of the descendants of Bharata! it is long since I saw the lord my father. I wish to see him, with your consent, O Phâlguna[4]!

Vaisampâyana said:

When Krishna spoke these words, Dhanañgaya replied (saying), 'O Krishna! let us verily go to-day to the city of Gagasa[5]. Be pleased, O you who understand piety! to see there king Yudhishthira, who is of a devout heart, and after taking leave of him to go to your own city.'

---

[1] Nilakantha interprets the words without supplying anything, thus 'be devoted to yama niyama,' &c. Yama &c. are the eight requisites for Yoga or concentration of mind as taught by Patañgali.

[2] That is to say, in the Gîtâ.

[3] Here he takes up the thread of the story. In the first chapter it was hinted that Krishna was anxious to go to Dvârakâ.

[4] This is a name of Arguna.

[5] I. e. Hastinâpur, the capital of the Pândavas. They were, when the dialogue was held, at Indraprastha. See p. 229 supra.

INDEX
OF PRINCIPAL MATTERS.

In this Index, Roman and Italic letters, long and short vowels have been classed together.

SANSKRIT INDEX.

B. = Bhagavadgîtâ; S. = Sanatsu*g*âtîya; A. = Anugîtâ.

N.B. Only in *some* cases have references been given to *all* the passages in which a certain word occurs. In most cases, only the passages in which words are used in noteworthy senses are referred to.

TRANSLITERATION OF ORIENTAL ALPHABETS ADOPTED FOR THE TRANSLATIONS OF THE SACRED BOOKS OF THE EAST.

CONSONANTS.	MISSIONARY ALPHABET. I Class.	II Class.	III Class.	Sanskrit.	Zend.	Pehlevi.	Persian.	Arabic.	Hebrew.	Chinese.
Gutturales.										
1 Tenuis	k	...	...	क	[illegible]	[illegible]	ك	ك	כּ	k
2 „ aspirata	kh	...	...	ख	[illegible]	[illegible]	...	...	כ	kh
3 Media	g	...	...	ग	[illegible]	[illegible]	گ	...	גּ	...
4 „ aspirata	gh	...	...	घ	[illegible]	[illegible]	...	...	ג	...
5 Gutturo-labialis	q	...	...	...	...	...	ق	ق	ק	...
6 Nasalis	ṅ (ng)	...	...	ङ	{[illegible] (ng), [illegible] (N)}	...	...	...	...	...
7 Spiritus asper	h	...	...	ह	[illegible] ([illegible] *hv*)	[illegible]	ه	ه	ה	h, hs
8 „ lenis	'	...	...	...	...	...	ا	ا	א	...
9 „ asper faucalis	'h	...	...	...	...	...	ح	ح	ח	...
10 „ lenis faucalis	'h	...	...	...	...	...	ع	ع	ע	...
11 „ asper fricatus	...	*'h*	...	...	...	...	خ	خ	ח	...
12 „ lenis fricatus	...	*'h*	...	...	...	...	...	...	...	...
Gutturales modificatae (palatales, &c.)										
13 Tenuis	...	*k*	...	च	[illegible]	[illegible]	چ	...	...	*k*
14 „ aspirata	...	*kh*	...	छ	...	...	...	...	...	*kh*
15 Media	...	*g*	...	ज	[illegible]	[illegible]	ج	ج	...	...
16 „ aspirata	...	*gh*	...	झ	...	...	غ	غ	...	...
17 „ Nasalis	...	*ñ*	...	ञ	...	...	...	...	...	...

CONSONANTS (continued).	Missionary Alphabet. I Class.	II Class.	III Class.	Sanskrit.	Zend.	Pehlevi.	Persian.	Arabic.	Hebrew.	Chinese.
18 Semivocalis	y	...	....	य	[illegible]; [illegible] init.	[illegible]	ي	ي	י	y
19 Spiritus asper	...	(ẏ)	....	...	....	...	...	...	...	...
20 „ lenis	...	(ẏ)	....	...	....	...	...	...	...	...
21 „ asper assibilatus	...	*ś*	....	श	[illegible]	[illegible]	ش	ش	...	...
22 „ lenis assibilatus	...	*ź*	....	...	[illegible]	[illegible]	ژ	...	...	*ź*
Dentales.										
23 Tenuis	t	...	....	त	[illegible]	[illegible]	ت	ت	תּ	t
24 „ aspirata	th	...	....	थ	[illegible]	...	...	...	ת	th
25 „ assibilata	...	...	TH	...	....	...	ث	ث	...	...
26 Media	d	...	....	द	[illegible]	[illegible]	د	د	דּ	...
27 „ aspirata	dh	...	....	ध	[illegible]	...	...	...	ד	...
28 „ assibilata	...	...	DH	...	....	...	ذ	ذ	...	...
29 Nasalis	n	...	....	न	[illegible]	[illegible]	ن	ن	נ	n
30 Semivocalis	l	...	....	ल	....	[illegible]	ل	ل	ל	l
31 „ mollis 1	...	*l*	....	ळ	....	...	...	...	...	...
32 „ mollis 2	...	...	L	...	....	...	...	...	...	...
33 Spiritus asper 1	s	...	....	स	[illegible]	[illegible]	س (ث)	س	שׂ	s
34 „ asper 2	...	...	s (ʃ)	...	....	...	...	...	ס	...
35 „ lenis	z	...	....	...	[illegible]	[illegible]	ز (ذ)	ز	ז	z
36 „ asperrimus 1	...	...	z ([illegible])	...	....	...	ص	ص	צ	[illegible]
37 „ asperrimus 2	...	...	[illegible]	...	....	...	ض	...	...	...

Dentales modificatae (linguales, &c.)										
38 Tenuis	...	*t*	....	ट	....	...	ط	ط	ט	...
39 " aspirata	...	*th*	....	ठ	....	...	ظ	ظ	...	...
40 Media	...	*d*	....	ड	[illegible]	[illegible]	...	...	...	...
41 " aspirata	...	*dh*	....	ढ	....	...	...	ض	...	...
42 Nasalis	...	*n*	....	ण	[illegible]	...	...	...	...	...
43 Semivocalis	r	...	....	र	[illegible]	[illegible]	ر	ر	ר	...
44 " fricata	...	*r*	....	...	....	...	...	...	...	r
45 " diacritica	...	...	R	...	....	...	...	...	...	...
46 Spiritus asper	sh	...	....	ष	[illegible]	[illegible]	...	...	...	sh
47 " lenis	zh	...	....	...	....	...	...	...	...	...
Labiales.										
48 Tenuis	p	...	....	प	[illegible]	[illegible]	پ	...	פ	p
49 " aspirata	ph	...	....	फ	....	...	...	...	פ	ph
50 Media	b	...	....	ब	[illegible]	[illegible]	ب	ب	ב	...
51 " aspirata	bh	...	....	भ	....	...	...	...	ב	...
52 Tenuissima	...	*p*	....	...	....	...	...	...	...	...
53 Nasalis	m	...	....	म	[illegible]	[illegible]	م	م	מ	m
54 Semivocalis	w	...	....	...	[illegible]	...	...	...	...	w
55 " aspirata	hw	...	....	...	....	...	...	...	...	...
56 Spiritus asper	f	...	....	...	[illegible]	[illegible]	ف	ف	...	f
57 " lenis	v	...	....	व	[illegible]	[illegible]	و	و	ו	...
58 Anusvâra	...	*m*	....	अं	[illegible]	...	...	...	...	...
59 Visarga	...	*h*	....	अः	....	...	...	...	...	...

VOWELS.	Missionary Alphabet. I Class.	II Class.	III Class.	Sanskrit.	Zend.	Pehlevi.	Persian.	Arabic.	Hebrew.	Chinese.
1 Neutralis	0	...	....	...	....	...	...	...	ְ	ǎ
2 Laryngo-palatalis	ĕ	...	....	...	....	...	...	...	...	...
3 „ labialis	ŏ	...	....	...	....	𐭥 fin.	...	...	...	...
4 Gutturalis brevis	a	...	....	अ	𐬀	𐭠 init.	ـَ	ـَ	ַ	a
5 „ longa	â	(*a*)	....	आ	𐬁	𐭠	ـَا	ـَا	ָ	â
6 Palatalis brevis	i	...	....	इ	𐬌	...	ـِ	ـِ	ִ	i
7 „ longa	î	(*i*)	....	ई	𐬍	𐭩	ـِي	ـِي	ִי	î
8 Dentalis brevis	*li*	...	....	ऌ	....	...	...	...	...	...
9 „ longa	*lî*	...	....	ॡ	....	...	...	...	...	...
10 Lingualis brevis	*ri*	...	....	ऋ	....	...	...	...	...	...
11 „ longa	*rî*	...	....	ॠ	....	...	...	...	...	...
12 Labialis brevis	u	...	....	उ	𐬎	...	ـُ	ـُ	ֻ	u
13 „ longa	û	(*u*)	....	ऊ	𐬏	𐭥	ـُو	ـُو	וּ	û
14 Gutturo-palatalis brevis	e	...	....	...	𐬈(e) 𐬉(e)	...	...	...	ֶ	e
15 „ longa	ê (ai)	(*e*)	....	ए	[illegible], [illegible]	𐭩	...	...	ֵ	ê
16 Diphthongus gutturo-palatalis	âi	(*ai*)	....	ऐ	....	...	ـَيْ	ـَيْ	...	âi
17 „ „	ei (ĕi)	...	....	...	....	...	...	...	...	ei, êi
18 „ „	oi (ŏu)	...	....	...	....	...	...	...	...	...
19 Gutturo-labialis brevis	o	...	....	...	𐬊	...	...	...	ָ	o
20 „ longa	ô (au)	(*o*)	....	ओ	𐬋	𐭥	...	...	וֹ	...
21 Diphthongus gutturo-labialis	âu	(*au*)	....	औ	𐬃𐬎 (*au*)	...	ـَوْ	ـَوْ	...	âu
22 „ „	eu (ĕu)	...	....	...	....	...	...	...	...	...
23 „ „	ou (ŏu)	...	....	...	....	...	...	...	...	...
24 Gutturalis fracta	ǎ	...	....	...	....	...	...	...	...	...
25 Palatalis fracta	ǐ	...	....	...	....	...	...	...	...	...
26 Labialis fracta	ŭ	...	....	...	....	...	...	...	...	ü

SACRED BOOKS OF THE EAST

TRANSLATED BY VARIOUS ORIENTAL SCHOLARS

AND EDITED BY

THE RIGHT HON. F. MAX MÜLLER.

This Series is published with the sanction and co-operation of the Secretary of State for India in Council.

REPORT presented to the ACADÉMIE DES INSCRIPTIONS, May 11, 1883, by M. ERNEST RENAN.

'M. Renan présente trois nouveaux volumes de la grande collection des "Livres sacrés de l'Orient" (Sacred Books of the East), que dirige à Oxford, avec une si vaste érudition et une critique si sûre, le savant associé de l'Académie des Inscriptions, M. Max Müller. . . . La première série de ce beau recueil, composée de 24 volumes, est presque achevée. M. Max Müller se propose d'en publier une seconde, dont l'intérêt historique et religieux ne sera pas moindre. M. Max Müller a su se procurer la collaboration des savans les plus éminens d'Europe et d'Asie. L'Université d'Oxford, que cette grande publication honore au plus haut degré, doit tenir à continuer dans les plus larges proportions une œuvre aussi philosophiquement conçue que savamment exécutée.'

EXTRACT from the QUARTERLY REVIEW.

'We rejoice to notice that a second series of these translations has been announced and has actually begun to appear. The stones, at least, out of which a stately edifice may hereafter arise, are here being brought together. Prof. Max Müller has deserved well of scientific history. Not a few minds owe to his enticing words their first attraction to this branch of study. But no work of his, not even the great edition of the Rig-Veda, can compare in importance or in usefulness with this English translation of the Sacred Books of the East, which has been devised by his foresight, successfully brought so far by his persuasive and organising power, and will, we trust, by the assistance of the distinguished scholars he has gathered round him, be carried in due time to a happy completion.'

Professor E. HARDY, Inaugural Lecture in the University of Freiburg, 1887.

'Die allgemeine vergleichende Religionswissenschaft datirt von jenem grossartigen, in seiner Art einzig dastehenden Unternehmen, zu welchem auf Anregung Max Müllers im Jahre 1874 auf dem internationalen Orientalistencongress in London der Grundstein gelegt worden war, die Übersetzung der heiligen Bücher des Ostens' (*the Sacred Books of the East*).

The Hon. ALBERT S. G. CANNING, 'Words on Existing Religions.'

'The recent publication of the "Sacred Books of the East" in English is surely a great event in the annals of theological literature.'

OXFORD

AT THE CLARENDON PRESS

LONDON: HENRY FROWDE

OXFORD UNIVERSITY PRESS WAREHOUSE, AMEN CORNER, E.C.

A IOXXI

FIRST SERIES.

VOL. I. The Upanishads.

Translated by F. MAX MÜLLER. Part I. The *Kh*ândogya-upanishad, The Talavakâra-upanishad, The Aitareya-âra*n*yaka, The Kaushîtaki-brâhma*n*a-upanishad, and The Vâgasaneyi-sa*m*hitâ-upanishad. *Second Edition.* 8vo, cloth, 10*s.* 6*d.*

The Upanishads contain the philosophy of the Veda. They have become the foundation of the later Vedânta doctrines, and indirectly of Buddhism. Schopenhauer, speaking of the Upanishads, says: 'In the whole world there is no study so beneficial and so elevating as that of the Upanishads. It has been the solace of my life, it will be the solace of my death.'

[See also Vol. XV.]

VOL. II. The Sacred Laws of the Âryas,

As taught in the Schools of Âpastamba, Gautama, Vâsish*th*a, and Baudhâyana. Translated by GEORG BÜHLER. Part I. Âpastamba and Gautama. *Second Edition.* 8vo, cloth, 10*s.* 6*d.*

The Sacred Laws of the Âryas contain the original treatises on which the Laws of Manu and other lawgivers were founded.

[See also Vol. XIV.]

VOL. III. The Sacred Books of China.

The Texts of Confucianism. Translated by JAMES LEGGE. Part I. The Shû King, The Religious Portions of the Shih King, and The Hsiâo King. *Second Edition.* 8vo, cloth, 12*s.* 6*d.*

Confucius was a collector of ancient traditions, not the founder of a new religion. As he lived in the sixth and fifth centuries B.C. his works are of unique interest for the study of Ethology.

[See also Vols. XVI, XXVII, XXVIII, XXXIX, and XL.]

VOL. IV. The Zend-Avesta.

Translated by JAMES DARMESTETER. Part I. The Vendîdâd. *Second Edition.* 8vo, cloth, 14*s.*

The Zend-Avesta contains the relics of what was the religion of

Cyrus, Darius, and Xerxes. It forms to the present day the sacred book of the Parsis, the so-called fire-worshippers.

[See also Vols. XXIII and XXXI.]

VOL. V. Pahlavi Texts.

Translated by E. W. WEST. Part I. The Bundahis, Bahman Yast, and Shâyast lâ-shâyast. 8vo, cloth, 12*s*. 6*d*.

The Pahlavi Texts comprise the theological literature of the revival of Zoroaster's religion, beginning with the Sassanian dynasty. They are important for a study of Gnosticism.

[See also Vols. XVIII, XXIV, XXXVII, and XLVII.]

VOLS. VI AND IX. The Qur'ân.

Parts I and II. Translated by E. H. PALMER. *Second Edition.* 8vo, cloth, 21*s*.

This translation, carried out according to his own peculiar views of the origin of the Qur'ân, was the last great work of E. H. Palmer, before he was murdered in Egypt.

VOL. VII. The Institutes of Vishnu.

Translated by JULIUS JOLLY. 8vo, cloth, 10*s*. 6*d*.

A collection of legal aphorisms, closely connected with one of the oldest Vedic schools, the Kathas, *but considerably added to in later time. Of importance for a critical study of the Laws of Manu.*

VOL. VIII. The Bhagavadgîtâ, with The Sanatsugâtîya, and The Anugîtâ.

Translated by KÂSHINÂTH TRIMBAK TELANG. *Second Edition.* 8vo, cloth, 10*s*. 6*d*.

The earliest philosophical and religious poem of India. It has been paraphrased in Arnold's 'Song Celestial.'

VOL. X. The Dhammapada,

Translated from Pâli by F. MAX MÜLLER; and

The Sutta-Nipâta,

Translated from Pâli by V. FAUSBÖLL; being Canonical Books of the Buddhists. *Second Edition.* 8vo, cloth, 10*s*. 6*d*.

The Dhammapada contains the quintessence of Buddhist morality. The Sutta-Nipâta gives the authentic teaching of Buddha on some of the fundamental principles of religion.

VOL. XI. Buddhist Suttas.

Translated from Pâli by T. W. RHYS DAVIDS. 1. The Mahâparinibbâna Suttanta; 2. The Dhamma-*k*akka-ppavattana Sutta. 3. The Tevigga Suttanta; 4. The Âkankheyya Sutta; 5. The *K*etokhila Sutta; 6. The Mahâ-sudassana Suttanta; 7. The Sabbâsava Sutta. 8vo, cloth, 10*s*. 6*d*.

A collection of the most important religious, moral, and philosophical discourses taken from the sacred canon of the Buddhists.

VOL. XII. The *S*atapatha-Brâhma*n*a, according to the Text of the Mâdhyandina School.

Translated by JULIUS EGGELING. Part I. Books I and II. 8vo, cloth, 12*s*. 6*d*.

A minute account of the sacrificial ceremonies of the Vedic age. It contains the earliest account of the Deluge in India.

[See also Vols. XXVI, XLI, XLIII, and XLIV.]

VOL. XIII. Vinaya Texts.

Translated from the Pâli by T. W. RHYS DAVIDS and HERMANN OLDENBERG. Part I. The Pâtimokkha. The Mahâvagga, I–IV. 8vo, cloth, 10*s*. 6*d*.

The Vinaya Texts give for the first time a translation of the moral code of the Buddhist religion as settled in the third century B.C.

[See also Vols. XVII and XX.]

VOL. XIV. The Sacred Laws of the Âryas,

As taught in the Schools of Âpastamba, Gautama, Vâsish*th*a, and Baudhâyana. Translated by GEORG BÜHLER. Part II. Vâsish*th*a and Baudhâyana. 8vo, cloth, 10*s*. 6*d*.

VOL. XV. The Upanishads.

Translated by F. MAX MÜLLER. Part II. The Ka*th*a-upanishad, The Mu*nd*aka-upanishad, The Taittirîyaka-upanishad, The B*ri*hadâra*n*yaka-upanishad, The *S*vetâsvatara-upanishad, The Pras*n*a-upanishad, and The Maitrâya*n*a-brâhma*n*a-upanishad. *Second Edition.* 8vo, cloth, 10*s*. 6*d*.

VOL. XVI. The Sacred Books of China.

The Texts of Confucianism. Translated by JAMES LEGGE. Part II. The Yî King. 8vo, cloth, 10*s*. 6*d*.

[See also Vols. XXVII, XXVIII.]

VOL. XVII. Vinaya Texts.

Translated from the Pâli by T. W. RHYS DAVIDS and HERMANN OLDENBERG. Part II. The Mahâvagga, V–X. The *K*ullavagga, I–III. 8vo, cloth, 10*s*. 6*d*.

VOL. XVIII. Pahlavi Texts.

Translated by E. W. WEST. Part II. The Dâdistân-î Dînîk and The Epistles of Mânûskîhar. 8vo, cloth, 12*s*. 6*d*.

VOL. XIX. The Fo-sho-hing-tsan-king.

A Life of Buddha by Asvaghosha Bodhisattva, translated from Sanskrit into Chinese by Dharmaraksha, A.D. 420, and from Chinese into English by SAMUEL BEAL. 8vo, cloth, 10*s*. 6*d*.

This life of Buddha was translated from Sanskrit into Chinese, A.D. 420. It contains many legends, some of which show a certain similarity to the Evangelium infantiae, &c.

VOL. XX. Vinaya Texts.

Translated from the Pâli by T. W. RHYS DAVIDS and HERMANN OLDENBERG. Part III. The *K*ullavagga, IV–XII. 8vo, cloth, 10*s*. 6*d*.

VOL. XXI. The Saddharma-pu*nd*arîka; or, The Lotus of the True Law.

Translated by H. KERN. 8vo, cloth, 12*s*. 6*d*.

'The Lotus of the True Law,' a canonical book of the Northern Buddhists, translated from Sanskrit. There is a Chinese translation of this book which was finished as early as the year 286 A.D.

VOL. XXII. *G*aina-Sûtras.

Translated from Prâkrit by HERMANN JACOBI. Part I. The Â*k*ârâṅga-Sûtra and The Kalpa-Sûtra. 8vo, cloth, 10*s*. 6*d*.

The religion of the Gainas was founded by a contemporary of Buddha. It still counts numerous adherents in India, while there are no Buddhists left in India proper.

[See Vol. XLV.]

VOL. XXIII. The Zend-Avesta.

Translated by JAMES DARMESTETER. Part II. The Sîrôzahs, Yasts, and Nyâyis. 8vo, cloth, 10*s*. 6*d*.

VOL. XXIV. Pahlavi Texts.

Translated by E. W. WEST. Part III. Dînâ-î Maînôg-Khira*d*, Sikand-gûmânîk Vigâr, and Sad Dar. 8vo, cloth, 10*s*. 6*d*.

SECOND SERIES.

VOL. XXV. Manu.

Translated by GEORG BÜHLER. 8vo, cloth, 21s.

This translation is founded on that of Sir William Jones, which has been carefully revised and corrected with the help of seven native Commentaries. An Appendix contains all the quotations from Manu which are found in the Hindu Law-books, translated for the use of the Law Courts in India. Another Appendix gives a synopsis of parallel passages from the six Dharma-sûtras, the other Smritis, the Upanishads, the Mahâbhârata, &c.

VOL. XXVI. The Satapatha-Brâhmana.

Translated by JULIUS EGGELING. Part II. Books III and IV. 8vo, cloth, 12s. 6d.

VOLS. XXVII AND XXVIII. The Sacred Books of China.

The Texts of Confucianism. Translated by JAMES LEGGE. Parts III and IV. The Lî Kî, or Collection of Treatises on the Rules of Propriety, or Ceremonial Usages. 8vo, cloth, 25s.

VOL. XXIX. The Grihya-Sûtras, Rules of Vedic Domestic Ceremonies.

Part I. Sânkhâyana, Âsvalâyana, Pâraskara, Khâdira. Translated by HERMANN OLDENBERG. 8vo, cloth, 12s. 6d.

VOL. XXX. The Grihya-Sûtras, Rules of Vedic Domestic Ceremonies.

Part II. Gobhila, Hiranyakesin, Âpastamba. Translated by HERMANN OLDENBERG. Âpastamba, Yagña-paribhâshâ-sûtras. Translated by F. MAX MÜLLER. 8vo, cloth, 12s. 6d.

These rules of Domestic Ceremonies describe the home life of the ancient Âryas with a completeness and accuracy unmatched in any other literature. Some of these rules have been incorporated in the ancient Law-books.

VOL. XXXI. The Zend-Avesta.

Part III. The Yasna, Visparad, Âfrînagân, Gâhs, and Miscellaneous Fragments. Translated by L. H. MILLS. 8vo, cloth, 12s. 6d.

VOL. XXXII. Vedic Hymns.

Translated by F. MAX MÜLLER. Part I. 8vo, cloth, 18s. 6d.

[See also Vol. XLVI.]

VOL. XXXIII. The Minor Law-books.

Translated by JULIUS JOLLY. Part I. Nârada, Brihaspati. 8vo, cloth, 10s. 6d.

VOL. XXXIV. The Vedânta-Sûtras, with the Commentary by *S*aṅkarâ*k*ârya. Part I.
Translated by G. THIBAUT. 8vo, cloth, 12*s*. 6*d*.
[See also Vols. XXXVIII and XLVIII.]

VOLS. XXXV AND XXXVI. The Questions of King Milinda.
Translated from the Pâli by T. W. RHYS DAVIDS. Part I. 8vo, cloth, 10*s*. 6*d*. Part II. 8vo, cloth, 12*s*. 6*d*.

VOL. XXXVII. Pahlavi Texts.
Translated by E. W. WEST. Part IV. The Contents of the Nasks, as stated in the Eighth and Ninth Books of the Dînka*r*d. 15*s*.

VOL. XXXVIII. The Vedânta-Sûtras. Part II. 8vo, cloth, with full Index to both Parts, 12*s*. 6*d*.

VOLS. XXXIX AND XL. The Sacred Books of China. The Texts of Tâoism. Translated by JAMES LEGGE. 8vo, cloth, 21*s*.

VOL. XLI. The *S*atapatha-Brâhma*n*a. Part III.
Translated by JULIUS EGGELING. 8vo, cloth, 12*s*. 6*d*.

VOL. XLII. Hymns of the Atharva-veda.
Translated by M. BLOOMFIELD. 8vo, cloth, 21*s*.

VOL. XLIII. The *S*atapatha-Brâhma*n*a.
Translated by JULIUS EGGELING. Part IV. Books VIII, IX, and X. 12*s*. 6*d*.

VOL. XLIV. The *S*atapatha-Brâhma*n*a.
Translated by JULIUS EGGELING. Part V. Books XI, XII, XIII, and XIV. 18*s*. 6*d*.

VOL. XLV. The *G*aina-Sûtras.
Translated from Prak*ri*t, by HERMANN JACOBI. Part II. The Uttarâdhyayana Sûtra, The Sûtrak*ri*tâṅga Sûtra. 8vo, cloth, 12*s*. 6*d*.

VOL. XLVI. Vedic Hymns. Part II. 8vo, cloth, 14*s*.

VOL. XLVII. Pahlavi Texts.
Translated by E. W. WEST. Part V. Marvels of Zoroastrianism. 8*s*. 6*d*.

VOL. XLVIII. The Vedânta-Sûtras, Part III, with Râmânu*g*a's *S*rîbhâshya.
Translated by G. THIBAUT. 8vo, cloth, 25*s*.

VOL. XLIX. Buddhist Mahâyâna Texts. Buddha*k*arita, translated by E. B. COWELL. Sukhâvatî-vyûha, Va*g*ra*kkh*edikâ, &c., translated by F. MAX MÜLLER. Amitâyur-Dhyâna-Sûtra, translated by J. TAKAKUSU. 8vo, cloth, 12*s*. 6*d*.

ANECDOTA OXONIENSIA.

ARYAN SERIES.

Buddhist Texts from Japan. I. Vagrakkhedikâ; *The Diamond-Cutter.*

Edited by F. MAX MÜLLER, M.A. Small 4to, 3*s.* 6*d.*

One of the most famous metaphysical treatises of the Mahâyâna Buddhists.

Buddhist Texts from Japan. II. Sukhâvatî-Vyûha: *Description of Sukhâvatî, the Land of Bliss.*

Edited by F. MAX MÜLLER, M.A., and BUNYIU NANJIO. With two Appendices: (1) Text and Translation of Sanghavarman's Chinese Version of the Poetical Portions of the Sukhâvatî-Vyûha; (2) Sanskrit Text of the Smaller Sukhâvatî-Vyûha. Small 4to, 7*s.* 6*d.*

The *editio princeps* of the Sacred Book of one of the largest and most influential sects of Buddhism, numbering more than ten millions of followers in Japan alone.

Buddhist Texts from Japan. III. *The Ancient Palm-Leaves containing the* Pragñâ-Pâramitâ-Hridaya-Sûtra *and the* Ushnîsha-Vigaya-Dhâranî.

Edited by F. MAX MÜLLER, M.A., and BUNYIU NANJIO, M.A. With an Appendix by G. BÜHLER, C.I.E. With many Plates. Small 4to, 10*s.*

Contains facsimiles of the oldest Sanskrit MS. at present known.

Dharma-Samgraha, *an Ancient Collection of Buddhist Technical Terms.*

Prepared for publication by KENJIU KASAWARA, a Buddhist Priest from Japan, and, after his death, edited by F. MAX MÜLLER and H. WENZEL. Small 4to, 7*s.* 6*d.*

Kâtyâyana's Sarvânukramanî of the *Ri*gveda.

With Extracts from Shadgurusishya's Commentary entitled Vedârthadîpikâ. Edited by A. A. MACDONELL, M.A., Ph.D. 16*s.*

The Buddha-*K*arita of Asvaghosha.

Edited, from three MSS., by E. B. COWELL, M.A. 12*s.* 6*d.*

The Mantrapāṭha, or the Prayer Book of the Āpastambins.

Edited, together with the Commentary of Haradatta, and translated by M. WINTERNITZ, Ph.D. *First Part.* Introduction, Sanskrit Text, Varietas Lectionis, and Appendices. Small quarto, 10*s.* 6*d.*

OXFORD
AT THE CLARENDON PRESS
LONDON: HENRY FROWDE
OXFORD UNIVERSITY PRESS WAREHOUSE, AMEN CORNER, E.C.